BASIC

BASIC

Bijan Mashaw
California State University, Hayward

MAYFIELD PUBLISHING COMPANY
Palo Alto and London

To my only son, Arsheeya

Sponsoring editor: Raleigh S. Wilson, Jr.
Manuscript editor: Antonio Padial
Managing editor: Pat Herbst
Art director: Nancy Sears
Designer (interior and cover): Gary A. Head
Cover art: Prism (watercolor, 1966), painted by Jürgen Peters
Technical artist: Kelly Solís-Navarro
Production: Mary Forkner and Darlene Bledsoe, Publication Alternatives
Compositor: Graphic Typesetting Service
Printer and binder: George Banta Company

Copyright © 1985 by Bijan Mashaw

First edition

All rights reserved. No portion of this book may be reproduced in any form or by any means without written permission of the publisher.

Library of Congress Catalog Card Number: 84–062032
International Standard Book Number: 0–87484–692–7

Manufactured in the United States of America
10 9 8 7 6 5 4 3 2 1

Mayfield Publishing Company
285 Hamilton Avenue
Palo Alto, California 94301

Disclaimer of Liabilities: Care has been exercised to ensure the accuracy of this book. This text, however, is meant to be used only as an instructional tool. Neither the author nor the publisher is liable for any damage incurred directly or indirectly through the use of this book.

Contents

Preface xiii

Chapter 1

Basics of Programming 1

Organization of the Text 3

Overview of a Computer System 4

Computer Components 5 · Types of Computers 9 · Types of Software 11

Programs and Languages 12

Writing Programs 13

Some Simple Programs 13 · Arithmetic Operators 16 · Priorities of Arithmetic Operations 20 · Variables 23 · The LET Statement 30 · Writing Better Programs 30

Running a Program 32

System Commands 33 · Microcomputer Commands: LLIST/LPRINT 35 · BASIC Immediate Mode 35

Exercises 37

Summary 39

Review Questions/Self-Test 40

Chapter 2
Input and Output 43
Constants in BASIC 46
Numeric Constants 46 · String Constants 46
Output 47
The PRINT Statement 47 · Separators in PRINT Statements 49
Input 56
The READ-DATA Statements 57 · The RESTORE Statement 63 · The INPUT Statement 63
Some Programming Techniques 65
Looping 65 · String Variables 69 · Generating Sequence Numbers 73 · Accumulating Data: Finding the Total 74 · A Complete Program 76 · An Interactive Program 78 · A Game Program 80
Program Spacing 82
Output Spacing 82 · Spaces in the Program 84
Exercises 87
Summary 91
Review Questions/Self-Test 93

Chapter 3
Program Development and Structured Programming 95
Compilation 97
Compiler 98 · Interpreter 98 · Versions of BASIC 100 · BASIC Statements 101
Error Detection 101
Syntax Errors 101 · Execution Errors 103 · Logical Errors 103 · How to Debug a Program 104
Program Planning 107
Algorithms 107 · Programming Tools 109 · Programming Cycle 118
Writing Structured Programs 121

Sequence Structure 121 · Selection Structure 122 · Iteration Structure 123

How to Write a Structured Program 123

Structured Design 123 · Readability 126 · Reliability 129 · Documentation 129

A Case—Printing a Report 130

Step 1: The Problem 130 · Step 2: Input-Output Design 131 · Step 3: Process Design 132 · Step 4: Coding 134 · Step 5: Running, Testing, and Debugging 136 · Step 6: Documentation 140

Exercises 140

Summary 143

Review Questions/Self-Test 144

Chapter 4

Decision Making, Comparing, Branching 145

The IF Statement 147

Problems Using the IF Statement 153

Finding the Largest Number 153 · Terminating a Loop 157

Programming Style and Structured IF Block 161

GOTO Style 162 · GOTO-Less Style 163 · Structured Style 164

Structured Programming 167

Compound IF Statement: Logical Operators 173

Conditional Branching 176

Games 180

Menu in a Program 181

A Case—Generating a Report 182

Step 1: The Problem 183 · Step 2: Input-Output Design 183 · Step 3: Process Design 185 · Step 4: Coding 188 · Step 5: Execution, Testing, and Debugging 189 · Step 6: Documentation 192

Exercises 194

Summary 200

Review Questions/Self-Test 202

Chapter 5
Looping 205

The `FOR-NEXT` Loop 207

The General Form of the `FOR-NEXT` Loop 210 · Loop Flowcharting 212 · Rules of a `FOR-NEXT` Loop 214

Nested Loop 225

The `WHILE` Loop 231

Writing Better Programs 232

Exercises 233

Summary 240

Review Questions/Self-Test 240

Chapter 6
Editing, Data Type, and Strings 243

Output Editing 245

`PRINT USING` Statement 246 · The Format 247 · Printing Strings with `PRINT USING` 247 · Editing Symbols 251

Data Form 257

Numeric Data 257 · Character Data 263

Control Design 274

Exercises 275

Summary 281

Review Questions/Self-Test 282

Chapter 7
One-Dimensional Arrays 285

Array Techniques 287

Subscripted Variables 290 · The Dimension Statement 291 · Reason for Arrays: An Example 294 · Arithmetic Expressions with Arrays 296 · Array Input-Output 299 · Printing Values on One Line 302 · Mirror Printing 302 · Summary of Important Points About Arrays 302

Some Examples of Arrays and Programming Techniques 304

Exercises 312

Summary 321

Review Questions/Self-Test 322

Chapter 8
Two-Dimensional Arrays 325

Array Techniques 327
Dimension Statement 328 · Arithmetic Expressions with Two-Dimensional Arrays 330 · Two-Dimensional Array Input-Output 332 · Summary of Important Points 336

Examples of Two-Dimensional Arrays and Programming Techniques 336

Matrix Operations 346
MAT Statement 346 · Matrix Input-Output 346 · Matrix Manipulation 347 · Matrix Initialization 348

Exercises 350

Summary 358

Review Questions/Self-Test 359

Chapter 9
Subprograms 361

Subroutines 363
Internal Subroutines 364 · External Subroutines 368

Functions 370
Library Functions 370 · User-Defined Functions 373 · Summary of the Rules for Using Functions 377

Importance of Modular Programming 380

Exercises 385

Summary 393

Review Questions/Self-Test 394

Chapter 10
Problem Solving, Programming Techniques, and Some Applications 397

Data Processing 399
Sorting 400 · Searching 404 · Merging 407

Statistics 409
Median 409 · Summation Notation 410 · Regression Analysis 411

Graphing Techniques 413
Plotting a Function 413 · Graphing a Histogram 415

Simulation 418
Random Numbers 418 · Generating Random Numbers 419 · Monte Carlo Simulation 421

Games 428

Management Information and Decision Support Systems 432

Exercises 434

Summary 451

Review Questions/Self-Test 452

Chapter 11
File Processing 455

File Processing—Section I 457
What is a File? 457 · Storage Media 459 · File Organization 461

Sequential File Processing 461
General Steps 461 · Creating a File 462 · Forms of the Statements 463 · Accessing a File 467

File Processing—Section II 469
Control Break Reports 469 · Sorting 472 · Merging 474 · File Maintenance 476

Random-File Processing 483
General Steps 483 · Forms of the Statements 488 Multirecords 490 · Random Accessing by an ID 493

Exercises 495

Summary 504

Review Questions/Self-Test 504

Chapter 12
Program Efficiency 509

Efficiency Factors 511

Interpreter Optimization 512 · Sparing Use of Arrays 513 · Efficient Algorithms 514 · Human Resources 517

Structured Approach 518

Structured Design 518 · Readability 519 · Documentation and Reliability 524

Appendix A
Reserved Words for Selected Systems 525

MicroSoft BASIC Reserved Words (IBM-PC, DEC Rainbow, and Others) 525

BASIC-PLUS Reserved Words 526

Radio Shack TRS-80 LEVEL II Reserved Words 527

APPLESOFT Reserved Words 528

Appendix B
Some BASIC Syntaxes for Selected Systems 529

Appendix C
True BASIC 533

Appendix D
Basic Keywords Summary 535

Index 537

Preface

Since I began programming in the early seventies, I have often wondered whether there could be a better and more efficient way to teach and learn programming. To try to find a better way, I studied factors that seem to increase the efficiency of learning a skill-oriented subject such as programming. The following factors are important:

1. Students learn better with a model. The model can be a figure or an example.
2. Students should practice what is being taught.
3. The instructor should emphasize problem solving, program design, and development, rather than the syntax of the language.
4. The building-block approach (using progressively difficult examples) helps students understand the process of programming.

Through years of teaching and working with students, I have found these conditions invaluable to the learning process. This book synthesizes my discoveries about the most effective ways to teach programming.

The Unique Approach of This Text

This book combines problem-solving methodology with BASIC programming language, a popular and powerful language used with many computer systems. I have tried to present carefully designed, concrete, and meaningful examples and avoid unimaginative ones. Style has been emphasized, as well as the importance of practicing programming and full-fledged program writing at an early stage in the learning process.

The method of presentation is inductive; each example has been designed to introduce programming concepts and practices. After spending a few minutes on an example, students should be able to understand and apply the concepts, rather than merely copy them. The examples and problems are intended to encourage students to create their own applications.

This unique and innovative approach was designed specifically for readers who have had no previous programming instruction. Readers are taught to write programs from the beginning. Other features of the text include:

- Many problems and solutions to enhance the students' self-confidence and inspire new questions
- Special emphasis on program planning, problem-solving and programming techniques, structured programming, and the modular approach
- Abundant exercises and a variety of applications to challenge the students to practice what they have learned

Organization

Each section of the text starts with an example, followed by several points to illustrate the learning objective for that example. These examples are designed to help students understand the program logic, structure, and the problem-solving techniques to be used. Solved problems are presented next to reinforce the learning process and point out novice programmers' common mistakes. Finally, numerous exercises at the end of each chapter, arranged from simple to complex, allow students to practice applying the concepts they have just learned.

No knowledge of mathematics beyond basic algebra or data processing is required or assumed (except in Chapter 10, which discusses applications in several subject areas). Straightforward language is used throughout the text. Concepts are introduced gradually to make learning easier. These concepts include language syntax, problem-solving techniques, structured programming concepts, planning, the modular approach, good programming practices, and the decomposition of a complex problem into a hierarchy of simpler problems.

Topics Covered

The chapter sequence is designed to be flexible; most chapters are independent of the others. Chapter 2 covers the core material. Other chapters can be reordered to meet the needs of a specific course or presentation. For example, Section One of Chapter 11 (on file processing) can be covered right after Chapter 2. Chapter 6, which presents topics such as output editing (PRINT-USING), is not a prerequisite for any other chapter. A brief summary of the prerequisites for each chapter is shown on the next page.

Chapter	Topics	Prerequisite chapter(s)
1	Simple programs	—
2	Basics of output, input, and processing	—
3	Interpreter's job, program planning	2
4	IF statements, programming styles	2
5	Looping techniques	2, 4
6	Output editing, data types, and strings	2, 4, 5
7	One-dimensional arrays	2, 4, 5
8	Two-dimensional arrays and matrices	2, 4, 5, 7
9	Subroutines and functions	2*
10	Applications	2, 4, 5, 7, 8, 9
11	File processing (Section I) File processing (Section II)	2 2, 4, 5, 9
12	Program efficiency and structured programming	2, 3, 4, 5, 7, 9

*A few examples use the FOR-NEXT loop.

Version of BASIC

This text is not written for any specific version of BASIC, because the emphasis is on the basic techniques of programming and problem solving, rather than a specific syntax version. The text emphasizes the existence of a variety of versions, and students are expected to convert a program written in one version of BASIC to another.

All programs in the text have been tested with MBASIC and are portable to any machine, although some might require slight modification. For example, a variable's symbolic name in a program can be longer than one character, but these names were deliberately chosen so that, if all characters after the first are dropped, the program will still run with any version of BASIC. This is explained from the start; nevertheless, the programs are presented as educational vehicles and are not canned.

Alternative Ways of Using the Text

This text covers some rather broad topics, but it remains flexible enough to be used in various ways. The book can be readily used as a text for a three-hour course on BASIC. Chapters 1–5 and selected chapters can be used to present a one-hour introduction to programming. The book could also serve as a supplementary text for a data processing course. It is also structured to be used as a self-guided text suitable for large classes or for individuals interested in learning BASIC.

ACKNOWLEDGMENTS

I would like to express my appreciation to the many individuals who encouraged me in this project. Special thanks to Jerry Weinberg for his encouragement; to Raleigh Wilson, the acquiring editor, for providing motivation; and to Tammy Lord for her patience with the word processor.

Contributions and suggestions were received from many sources. Reviewers are crucial to the development of a successful text, and I have benefited from the advice of these superb colleagues:

James J. Ball, Indiana State University
Murray Berkowitz, University of Texas, Arlington
R. Wayne Headrick, Texas A & M University
Terry Helford, Chaffey Community College
Phillip Mackey, Delaware Technical and Community College
W. Leon Pearce, Drake University
Paul W. Ross, Millersville University
Leonard C. Schwab, California State University, Hayward
Francis J. Svilich, Fresno City College
Charles J. Wertz, State University of New York, College at Buffalo

Bijan Mashaw

BASIC

Basics of Programming

1

In This Chapter:

Organization of the Text

Overview of a Computer System
Computer Components
Types of Computers
Types of Software

Programs and Languages

Writing Programs
Some Simple Programs
Arithmetic Operators
Priorities of Arithmetic Operations
Variables
The LET Statement
Writing Better Programs

Running a Program
System Commands
Microcomputer Commands:
  LLIST/LPRINT
BASIC Immediate Mode

Exercises

Summary

Review Questions/Self-Test

Basics of Programming

You may not realize it, but computers affect your everyday life greatly. When you use a credit card, pay bills, or use your checking account, you use the services of computers indirectly, although you are not involved in programming. You may even be using computers directly, without knowing programming, by employing "ready-to-use" programs. Nevertheless, you might like to learn computer programming for several reasons:

- Because computers are an ever-increasing part of modern life, people need some knowledge about the way computers operate.
- The increasing use of computers has prompted an increasing demand for computer education.
- Learning to get computers to do your work has obvious advantages.
- Programming is fun—writing a computer program and getting the computer to do what you want it to do is enjoyable, challenging, and rewarding.

Programming is easy to learn. This book gives you a sound introduction to the subject. You don't need to be mathematically minded. In fact, knowledge of mathematics beyond basic algebra is not required in most parts of this book. But you should be able to think logically, because programming is a step-by-step, logical process. When you can follow the logic and the pattern of a program, you can say, "I am beginning to learn programming." When you can create the logic and pattern of your own program, you have accomplished the most difficult phase of the work.

ORGANIZATION OF THE TEXT

In this book, you will study examples to learn to program in the language BASIC. Each section includes several examples. The section "Notes," after an example, explains the learning objectives of that example. It is important that you understand the notes. Also, each section contains several problems, which are followed immediately by solutions. It is vital that you understand each of the solved problems fully. Don't look at the answers to a problem until you have thought about the problem and have an answer ready.

Understanding the material in the text is not enough. To learn programming skills, you need to practice the concepts discussed in the text. The exercises in each chapter are designed to help you do this. You should complete some of the exercises before proceeding to the next chapter. Furthermore, you should run several programs on the computer, because programming, like any other skill, is not learned until it is practiced.

Each chapter has the following divisions:

1. *Examples*, which state a *problem*, outline a *solution plan*, list a *program* that solves the problem, and give *notes* that summarize the learning objectives.
2. *Solved problems*, which allow students to learn inductively.
3. *Exercises*, which reinforce learning.
4. *Summary*, which outlines the main concepts in the chapter.
5. *Review questions* comprising a *self-test*, which lets you test your understanding of the material covered in the chapter. The answers are given at the end of the test.

If, like most students, you are learning a programming language for the first time, read each section carefully to understand the material thoroughly. You will benefit most from the text by taking time with each chapter rather than just scanning it. Chapter 1 is divided into the following sections:

1. An overview of a computer system
2. Computer programs and languages
3. Writing simple programs
4. Running a program

OVERVIEW OF A COMPUTER SYSTEM

Knowledge of the internal construction of computers is not a requirement for using BASIC. However, some understanding of a computer's operation and components is helpful to all programmers. This section surveys the components of a computer system, classifies computers by type, and introduces you to several kinds of programs and languages. After reading this section, you will know the meaning of the terms central processing unit (CPU), input-output device, auxiliary storage device, storage medium, large-scale computer, microcomputer, hardware, and software.

Computer Components

A computer is an electronic machine in some ways like a calculator. Both can process information; they accept, store, and manipulate data. Like a calculator, a computer is a "dumb machine"—it needs explicit instructions or programs before it can do anything. The difference between a computer and a calculator is that a computer processes data extremely fast and can store many more instructions and data.

A computer system can accept, process, and output information automatically by means of programs. The programs are called *software*, and the components that accept, process, and output information are called *hardware*. Four basic hardware components in a computer system carry out these functions (see Figures 1.1, 1.2, and 1.3):

1. Input devices
2. Output devices
3. Central processing unit (CPU)
4. Auxiliary storage devices

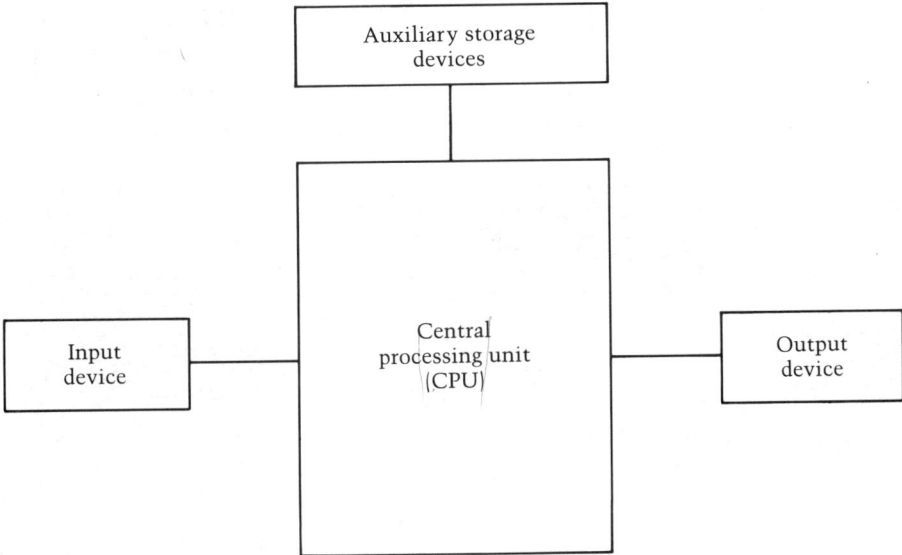

Figure 1.1 Basic components of a computer system

6 *Basics of Programming*

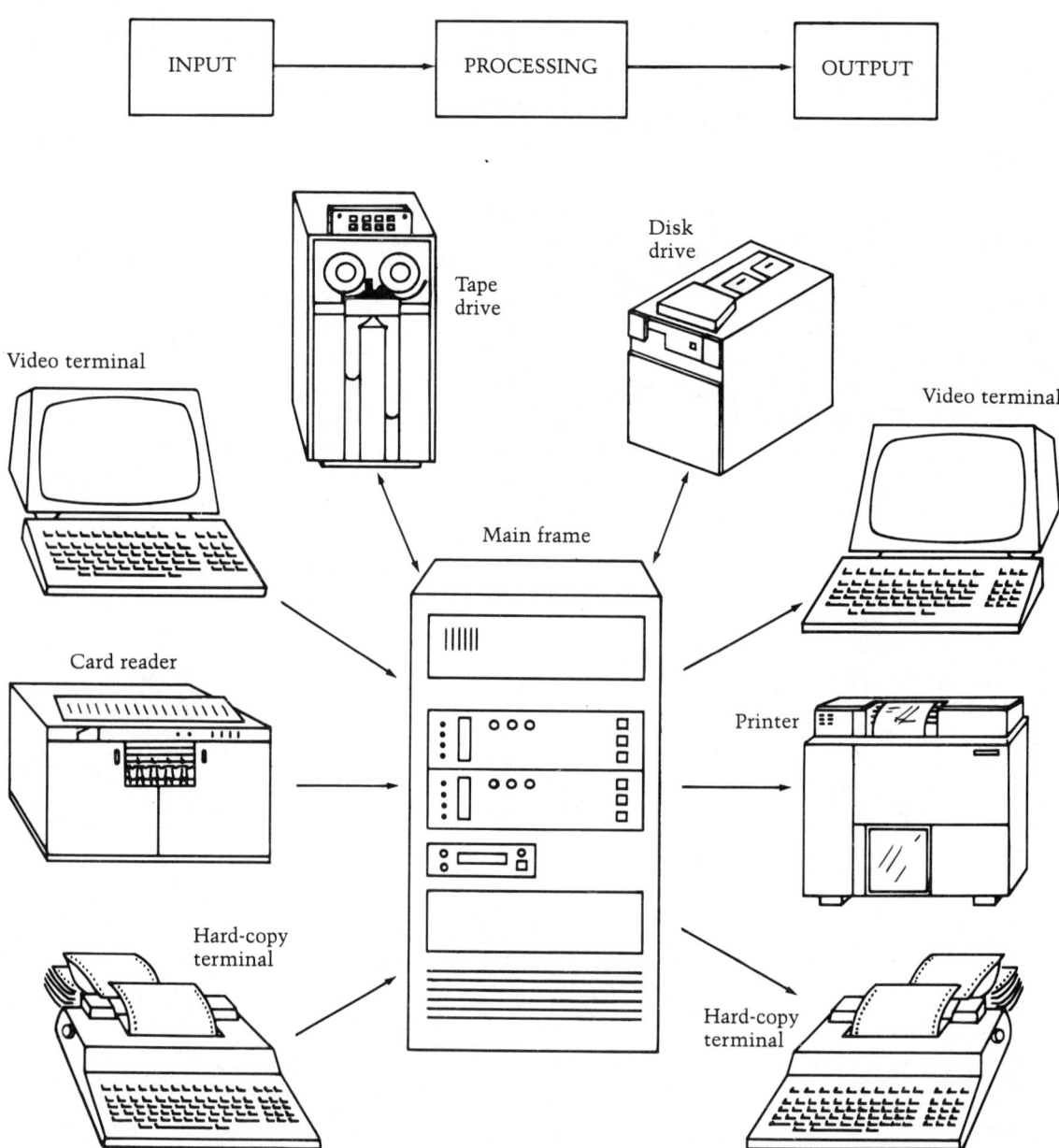

Figure 1.2 A large-scale computer system

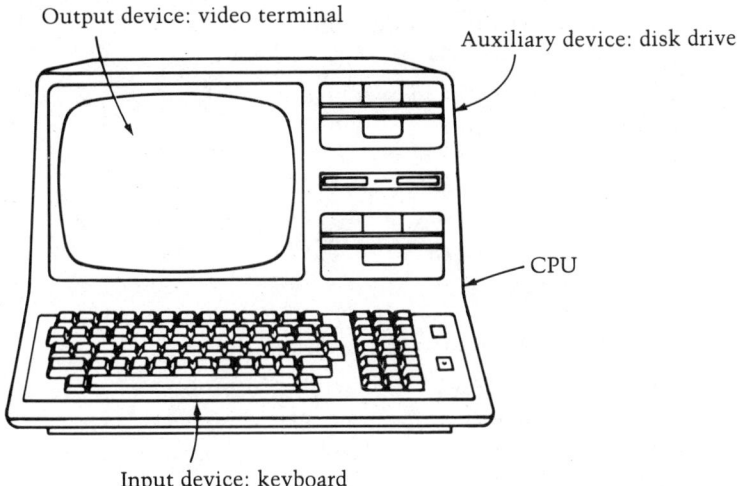

Figure 1.3 A microcomputer system

Instructions (the program) and data are entered into the computer through an input device. The information is processed by the CPU, and finally information is presented through an output device. The information can also be placed in an auxiliary storage for later processing.

Input Devices

Input devices allow humans to communicate with computers. Typical input devices include the following:

1. *Video terminals* look like TV monitors attached to typewriter keyboards. You input data on the keyboard. Information appears on the screen as you type it. Video terminals are also referred to as CRT (cathode ray tubes).
2. *Card readers,* the most common input devices in the 1970s, read information from a deck of punch cards. These cards are punched on a keypunch machine, which also has a keyboard similar to that of a typewriter.
3. *Hard-copy terminals* (printing terminals) look and operate like typewriters. When you use this type of terminal, the typed information is printed on paper as you type it rather than displayed on a screen.
4. Special input devices of various kinds:
   - *Optical character readers (OCRs)* read test score sheets or other specially marked paper.

8 *Basics of Programming*

- *Magnetic character readers* read data, such as account numbers of checks, printed in magnetic ink.
- *Point-of-sale (POS) terminals* are electronic cash registers; they are input devices that also work as cash registers.

Output Devices

Output devices provide the user with desired information. These are some common output devices:

1. *Printers* are used to print information, especially reports, rapidly.
2. *Video terminals* display information on a monitor. Used for output as well as input, they are quickly becoming the most widely used I/O devices. They are also called CRTs.
3. *Hard-copy terminals* provide hard copy (printed copy) of processed information. A hard-copy terminal is normally a slow printer that serves as an input device as well as an output device.

Central Processing Unit

After the user feeds information into the computer, the central processing unit processes the information. The CPU has three basic parts: (1) the main memory, (2) the arithmetic-logic unit (ALU), and (3) the control system (see Figure 1.4).

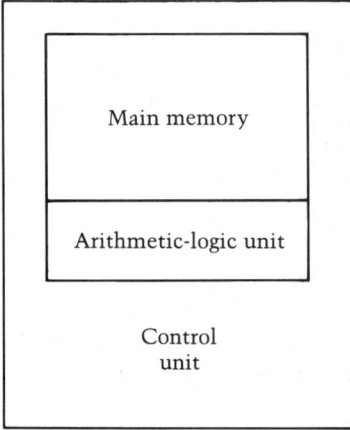

Figure 1.4 The CPU

Generally, the *main memory* first stores the instructions and data. Each piece of information is stored in a cell—a unit of memory. Each unit of memory has an "address," and a program can retrieve the information in any cell by knowing its address.

The *arithmetic-logic unit* (ALU) performs all arithmetic operations, such as addition and subtraction. It also performs logical operations, such as comparing two quantities to determine which is greater.

The *control system* controls the entire computer system. It controls the input-output devices, the operation of the arithmetic-logic unit, and data transfer to and from the main storage section.

A *microprocessor* is a small CPU that has all three components—memory, ALU, and control system—though on a smaller scale. Its main memory, in particular, is very limited.

Auxiliary Storage Devices

Auxiliary devices store information on a storage medium for later processing. These devices are used for both input and output. Typical auxiliary devices include the following:

1. *Tape drives* store information to and retrieve it from a tape.
2. *Disk drives* store information to and retrieve it from a magnetic disk.

The most common types of storage media are tapes, disks, and diskettes (see Figure 1.5).

1. *Tapes* come in a variety of sizes to meet the needs of various computers. Microcomputers often use cassette tapes, and larger computers use tape reels.
2. *Disks* of several kinds are available. Larger computers use a disk pack, which resembles a stack of phonograph records in a clear plastic cover. Data are stored on the surface of each disk.
3. *Diskettes* (also called floppy disks) are single disks made of flexible plastic. The popular sizes are 5¼ and 8 inches in diameter. The diskette rotates inside its black, square jacket. The diskette is a common storage medium for microcomputers.

Types of Computers

Computer systems are commonly classified by how much information they can store and process. Three types of computer systems can be classified on this basis.

10 Basics of Programming

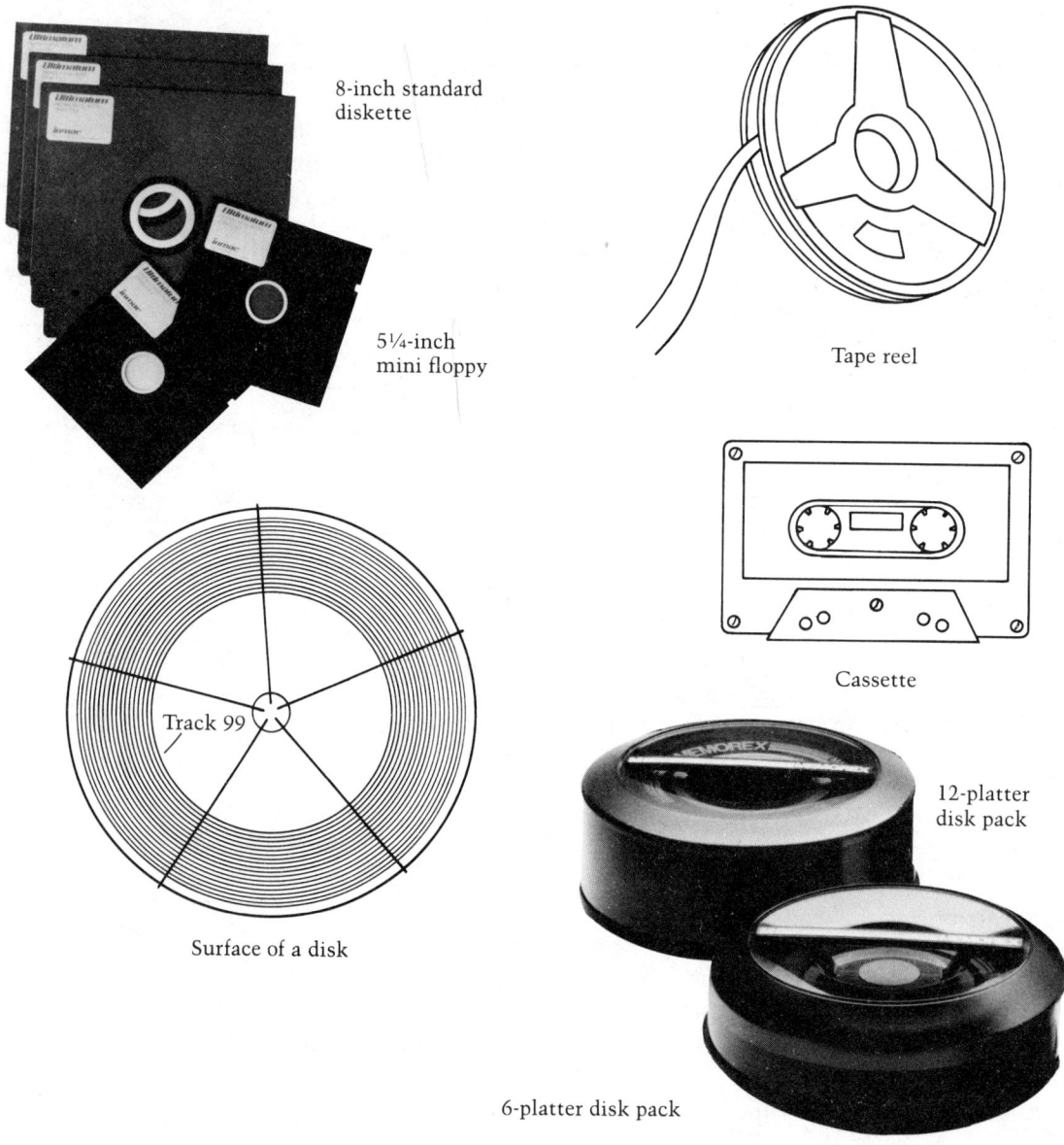

Figure 1.5 Examples of storage media

1. *Large-scale computer systems* are normally used by large organizations. The input-output (I/O) units for large-scale computers are separate from the CPU. A large-scale computer system may have many input or output devices. For example, a typical system may have more than 100 video monitors in different offices, plus other I/O devices. A large computer system is also called a main frame.
2. *Minicomputers* are used by smaller organizations. A variety of minicomputers are available. Of course, minicomputers are less expensive and less powerful than main frames; however, they generally can support a mid-sized organization. Minis also have several input-output devices.
3. *Microcomputers* are small computers often used in homes, businesses, and educational institutions. Microcomputers are becoming popular due to their low cost, high performance, and ease of use. The I/O devices are mounted on the top of the CPU in some microcomputer systems.

Types of Software

Programs that cause automatic processing are referred to as software. The hardware accepts, processes, and outputs the information through software. Various types of software serve different purposes.

Application Programs

Application programs have specific applications. A payroll program and a program that calculates interest are examples.

Operating Systems

Operating systems are complex programs that control the flow of information in computers—input, processing, and output of other programs. The operating system acts as a supervisor for all the activities of the system. It also serves as a middleman between different components of the system. The operating system is also called the supervisor, the control program, the management, the executive system, or the control program monitor (CPM).

Interpreters

Interpreters or compilers are programs that translate human-oriented computer languages, such as BASIC, into the code that the machine understands. For example, the BASIC interpreter translates the instruction

```
100 PRINT A, B
```

into a code the computer can interpret and carry out.

PROGRAMS AND LANGUAGES

People are impressed by the computer's problem-solving ability, yet computers do not really solve problems—people do. A programmer expresses the solution procedure as a series of instructions called a program.

A computer program is a series of instructions that enables the computer to perform a task. These instructions must be specific, detailed, logical, sequential, and clearly phrased. You must tell a computer what to do in complete and precise detail. It is not enough to tell a computer to "solve this problem." A program can, however, instruct a computer to perform a specific function. Generally, a computer can be instructed to:

1. Accept data
2. Store the data in its memory
3. Do arithmetic operations such as addition, subtraction, multiplication, and division, or character manipulation such as putting letters together.
4. Print stored data

All of these functions can be accomplished by a program.

Program instructions are conveyed to the computer through a computer language. A computer language is a combination of predetermined symbols, terms, words, rules, and functions used as a medium of communication. A computer language is a way of conveying these instructions to the computer and translating the results. A part of learning a language is learning the words, rules, and phrases of that language; but more importantly, one must learn the logic and techniques of solving a problem. You will have the opportunity to learn and practice all of these in this text.

Many computer languages are available—BASIC, FORTRAN, COBOL and PL/I, are examples. Each has its own vocabulary and grammar. BASIC, an acronym for "Beginners All-purpose Symbolic Instruction Code," is one of the most widely used languages. Throughout this text, you will learn

BASIC, a language developed in the early 1960s. Because its grammar resembles English grammar, BASIC is easy to use yet flexible enough to solve a variety of problems.

WRITING PROGRAMS

The basic concepts of programming, the foundation, are explained in the following sections. These concepts, though simple, are very important.

Some Simple Programs

You will start with a very simple BASIC program. Pay careful attention to the fact that a program should have three parts:

1. The problem
2. The solution plan
3. The BASIC program that accomplishes the task

Example 1.1

Problem: Find the floor area of a room 15.5 feet long and 9.5 feet wide.

Solution Plan: Call the length of the room L, the width W, and the area A. You can find the area through four steps:

1. Assign values to L and W.
2. Compute the area with the formula A = L × X
3. Print the area.
4. End the program.

Program:
```
1  L=15.5
2  W=9.5
3  A=L*W
4  PRINT A
5  END
```

The output will be

```
147.25
```

Notes:

1. To solve a problem, you must devise a solution plan.
2. Each instruction is on one line.
3. Each instruction begins with a number, which is called the line number.
4. Variables are assigned names, such as W, L, and A.
5. The * in A = L*W is the multiplication symbol.
6. Computation is done on the right side of the =, and the result is assigned to the variable A on the left side.
7. L and W are defined before A is calculated. That is, the value of L and W must be known before A can be calculated.
8. The PRINT statement prints the result.
9. Blank spaces before or after a number, a word, or a symbol have no effect on the program.
10. The statement END is used to end the program.

So far, you have learned that a program is a detailed set of instructions. Here is another simple example:

■ *Example 1.2*

Problem: Calculate the sum and the average of numbers 72.50, 96.10, and 84.90. Print the data on one line, and the average and the sum on the next line.

Solution Plan:

1. Assign the names S and G to the sum and average, respectively, and assign data to variables A, B, and C.

2. Compute:
   S = A + B + C
   G = S divided by 3
3. Print the data.
4. Print the result.

Program:

```
10 A = 72.50
20 B = 96.10
30 C = 84.90
40 S = A + B + C
50 G = S/3
60 PRINT A, B, C
70 PRINT S, G
80 END
```

The output will be

```
72.5            96.1            84.9
253.5           84.5
```

Notes:

1. The line numbers do not have to be in the order 1, 2, 3, ..., but they must be in increasing order.
2. More than one operation (calculation) can be performed in a program; in this case, finding the sum and the average.
3. The slash is the division symbol.
4. More than one variable is printed by each PRINT statement. The first prints A, B, and C, and the second S and G. The variables are separated by a comma in the PRINT statement.
5. In this example, PRINT statement causes the data to be printed at the beginning of a new line.

As you saw in the previous examples, each line in BASIC starts with a number. A line number can be up to five digits. The line numbers need not be sequential (that is, 1, 2, 3, . . .), but they are carried out in increasing order, and each must be unique.

These are the rules for statement numbers in BASIC programs:

1. In BASIC, each program line must start with a number.
2. Each line must be a positive integer, without the plus sign, less than five digits.
3. The computer performs the lines in a program in increasing order, starting with the lowest-numbered line.

It is good programming practice to leave gaps between line numbers so you can add new lines at a later time, if necessary. For example, if your first line is 10, make the second 20, and so on.

Arithmetic Operators

The following operators signal arithmetic operations:

```
^   Exponentiation. Example: Z = X^2  (for X²)
*   Multiplication. Example: P = R*Q
/   Division. Example: A = B/C  (for B ÷ C)
+   Addition. Example: X = Y + Z
-   Subtraction. Example: W = V - X
```

In some systems, ** can also be used for exponentiation.

The following rules apply to the use of arithmetic operators in BASIC programs:

1. Pairs of parentheses can be used freely to group variables.
2. A space before or after an operator is allowed.
3. Two successive operators may not appear next to each other. For example, X + * 3 is not legal.

The expressions below are shown in both ordinary notation and in BASIC.

```
      Ordinary Notation                  BASIC
X = A + B + C - D - H            X = A + B + C - D - H
W = 2X + A·B                     W = 2*X + A*B
    A1 + A2 + A3
A = ─────────────                A = (A1 + A2 + A3)/(3*X + B)
       3X + B
```

Ordinary Notation	BASIC
$Z = (A - B)^2 + \dfrac{3A}{B}$	Z = (A - B)^2 + 3*A/B
$Y = X^3$	Y = X*X*X or Y = X^3
$X = \sqrt{A}$ (is the same as $X = A^{1/2}$ or $X = A^{.5}$)	X = A^.5 or X = A^(1/2)

■ Solved Problems

1.1 Are the following programs correct?

a. 1 X = 9.6
    2 Y = X^2
    3 END
    4 PRINT Y

NO, PRINT Y should preceed end statement

b. 100 A = 3.5
    200 C = A + B
    300 B = 92.1
    400 PRINT C
    500 END

no, not in proper order

c. 50 A = 3.5
    150 B = 92.1
    200 A + B = C
    300 PRINT C
    400 END

no, should read C = A + B

d. 20 A = 3.5
    30 B = 92.1
    10 C = A + B
    40 PRINT C
    50 END

no, Line numbers out of order

e. 10 A = 6.956
    20 PRNT A
    30 END

no, print command misspelled

f. X = 5.0
    Y = 6.0
    Z = X + Y
    PRINT Z
    END

no, no line numbers used

Answers:

   a. No, the END statement should be last.
   b. No, A and B should be defined before C is calculated.
   c. No, computation should be done on the right side of the =.
   d. No, the logical sequence is right, but the statement numbers are not in increasing order.
   e. No, the word PRINT must be spelled correctly.
   f. No, each line of instruction must have a line number.

1.2 Write the following expressions in BASIC.

   a. $d = 2(a + b)(a - b)$ $d = 2*(a+b)*(a-b)$
   b. $Y = 2(5b + 3c)$ $Y = 2*(5*b + 3*c)$
   c. $Y = \dfrac{a \cdot b \cdot c}{X}$ $y = (a*b*c)/x$
   d. $Y = X^4$ $y = X\wedge 4$

Answers:

   a. 10 D = 2*(A + B)*(A - B)
   b. 10 Y = 2*(5*B + 3*C)
   c. 5   Y = A*B*C/X
   d. 25 Y = X^4 or Y = X*X*X*X

Exercises

1.1 Correct the following programs:

   a. 10   C = 56.1
       20   D = C*A - 2.5   20 A = 1000.5
       30   A = 1000.5   30 D = C*A - 2.5
       40   PRINT A
       50   END

   b. 5   PRINT B   5 A = 1296.5
       10   B = A*A   10 B = A*A
       15   A = 1296.5   15 PRINT B
       20   END

   c. X = 3296.50   10 X = 3296.5
       Y = 56.20   20 Y = 56.2
       X + Y = Z   30 Z = X+Y
       PRINT Z   40 PRINT Z
       END   50 END

d. P = 32.9
    Q = 1932.0
    R = (P + Q) - P
    PRINT R

    10 P = 32.9
    20 Q = 1932.0
    30 R = (P+Q) - P
    40 PRINT R
    50 END

e. 5   E = 5.0
    50   F = E*G
    500 G = 9.1

f. 10 S = (A*B + C) - D
    20 PRINT S

You have learned how to start a program and how mathematical expressions should be written in a program. You also have learned how to express the solution plan in statements the computer can understand. Let's look at one more simple example.

Example 1.3

Problem:

Find the average of four numbers: 89.5, 95.8, 81.2, and 98.9. Print the data and the average.

Solution Plan:

Start the program.
Name the variables.
Assign values to the variable names.
Calculate the average by adding all the variables and then dividing by 4.
Print the data and the average.
End the program.

Program:

    100 A = 89.5
    200 B = 95.8
    300 C = 81.2
    400 D = 98.9
    500 X = (A + B + C + D)/4
    600 PRINT A, B, C, D, X
    700 END

The output will be

```
89.5        95.8        81.2        98.9        91.35
```

Notes:

1. You must know how to calculate the average. You cannot ask the computer to "find the average." In other words, you must know how to go about solving the problem before you begin programming.
2. Parentheses are essential in line 500. If parentheses were not used, only D would be divided by 4.
3. The PRINT statement prints variables A, B, C, D, and X on one line.
4. If the END statement is omitted, most computers assume the last line is the end of the program. Some systems, however, print error messages when the END statement is omitted. It is good programming practice always to end a program with the END statement.
5. The start of the program is the lowest-numbered line.

Priorities of Arithmetic Operations

The computer scans an expression from left to right and performs exponentiation first, then multiplication or division, and finally addition or subtraction. Thus, a mathematical expression is evaluated in the following priority:

1. ^   Exponentiation

2. *, /   Multiplication and division

3. +, −   Addition and subtraction

If two operations have the same priority, the leftmost one is performed first. For example, the expression

```
A + X / Y * 2 + 3 * X ^ 2
```

is evaluated in the following order:

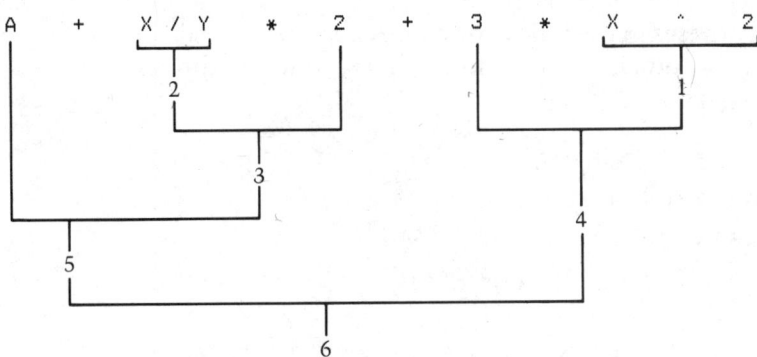

Parentheses, however, overrule these priorities. Mathematical expressions inside parentheses have first priority. If there is more than one pair of parentheses, the innermost pair is evaluated first. For example, the expression

    (5*X + 3*(5 + 3*X))/B^2

is evaluated as follows:

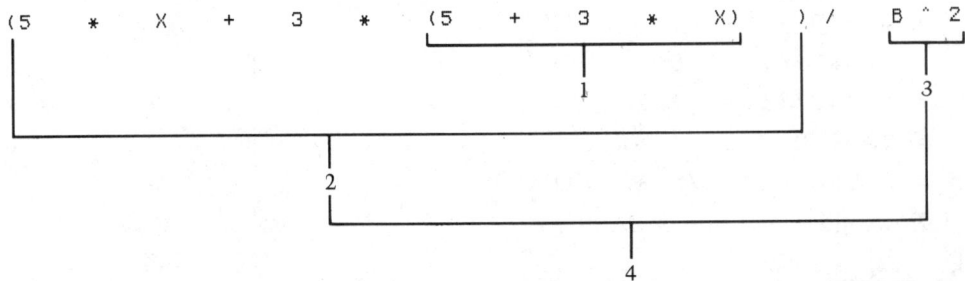

Often, parentheses must be used to make the computer perform the operations in the desired order. It is advisable to use an extra pair of parentheses to ensure the arithmetic is done in the desired order. More importantly, extra spaces and parentheses make expressions easy to read. If you will be using many formulas in your programs, look at the following solved problems; otherwise, skip that section.

Solved Problems

These problems may be skipped without loss of continuity.

1.3 Can any of the parentheses in the following expressions be deleted without changing the order of operations? If so, rewrite the expression.

```
a. 100  P = (A + B - C) + D
b.  10  Y = ((A*B)/C) + D
c.  50  X = (A*B)*(C)^D
d. 200  Y = (8*X) + 13 - (5*(Y^3))
e. 500  Z = ((A + B) + (X - Y) + A/(X + Y))
f.  99  X = ((A/D)*(C*B)/A) + B + (-C)
g.  60  Q = ((X*Y)*Z)/(B*A)) + 2
h.  55  R = ((A + B + C)/(3*X))
i.  85  Z = ((A/B)*C) + (A*C)/B) + (A/(B*C))
```

Answers:

```
a. 100  P = A + B - C + D
b.  10  Y = A*B/C + D
c.  50  X = A*B*C^D
d. 200  Y = 8*X + 13 - 5*Y^3
e. 500  Z = A + B + X - Y + A/(X + Y)
f.  99  X = A/D*C*B/A + B + (-C)
g.  60  Q = X*Y*Z/(B*A) + 2
h.  55  R = (A + B + C)/(3*X)
i.  85  Z = A/B*C + A*C/B + A/(B*C)
```

1.4 Write the following expressions in BASIC.

a. $Y = \dfrac{(3X^5 + 2)^3 + 15(Z + 2)(3P - 7)}{(5X^2 - 3)^3}$

b. $A = 6Q^2 + \dfrac{9X^2 + 3}{2X + 1} - \dfrac{10P - 3X}{12X + 1}$

c. $B = \dfrac{\dfrac{A + 3}{B} + Y}{A - 2 - \dfrac{Y}{A}}$

Answers:

a. 10   `Y = ((3*X^5 + 2)^3 + 15*(Z + 2)*(3*P - 7))/(5*X^2 - 3)^3`

b. 5 A `= 6*Q^2 + (9*X^2 + 3)/(2*X + 1) - (10*P - 3*X)/(12*X + 1)`

c. 80   `B = ((A + 3)/B + Y)/(A - 2 - Y/A)`

Exercises

1.2 Write the following expressions in BASIC.

a. $A = \dfrac{1}{X} + \dfrac{1}{Y}$

b. $B = \dfrac{1}{X + Y}$

c. $X = (A \cdot B) + (C \cdot D)$

d. $P = 2.5R + 3.14R^2 + 6.28$

e. $Q = A^5 + (5A)^3$

1.3 Translate these BASIC expressions into ordinary mathematical notation.

a. 10   `X = B**3 + A`

b. 20   `R = A + B + C/D`

c. 100 `Q = X**3/(A + B + C + 4.5*X)`

Variables

As you have noticed, assigning names to variables is an important step in program planning. There are several reasons for doing this. The most important is that data are stored in the memory of a computer. To use a memory location, you need to name that memory cell. Once you choose a name for a memory cell, you can store data in it, update and change the data, or erase the contents of the cell. The name of the memory cell is called a variable because the content of the cell can vary. Thus, a *variable* refers to a storage location in the memory of the computer. The value of the variable is the value currently stored in that location (see Figure 1.6).

Variables are essential in programs because all data manipulations are done through variables. Actual numbers can also be used in a program.

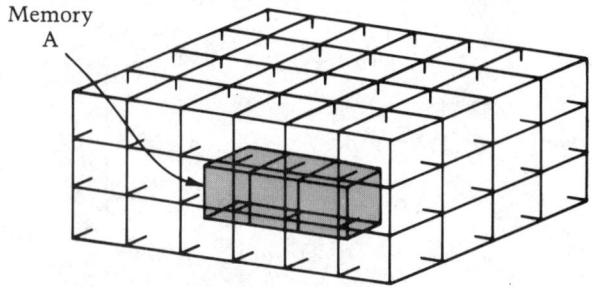

Figure 1.6 A variable in the main memory

The actual numbers are called *constants*. For example, in the statement

Y = 5*X + 2

5 and 2 are constants, X and Y are variables.

You will learn several ways to store a value in a memory cell. One way is to use an assignment statement. For example, X = 3.5 places 3.5 into memory cell called X. Thus, an *assignment statement* assigns a value to a variable. Notice that the = sign in the assignment statement serves the purpose of assigning a value to the variable. Therefore, the equals sign may or may not have the same meaning as in algebra. *In BASIC, the equals sign tells the computer to place the value on the right into the memory cell named on the left.*

The following examples show how the contents of a memory cell (a variable) can be assigned a value, copied, renewed, changed, or erased at any time in a program:

Example 1.4

Problem: What values will the computer print when you run the following program?

Program:

```
10   X = 2.1
20   Y = X
30   X = 6.5
40   X = X + 5.2
50   PRINT X , Y
60   END
```

The printed values are

```
11.7                    2.1
```

Notes:

1. The assignment statement in line 10 assigns 2.1 to X.
2. The assignment statement in line 20 copies X into Y, thus the value of Y is also 2.1.
3. The assignment statement in line 30 changes the value of X to 6.5.
4. The assignment statement in line 40 calculates the new value of X (on the left) as the previous value (6.5) plus 5.2.
5. When a new value is placed in the memory cell, the previous one is erased.

Variables allow flexible programs, which state solutions to problems in general terms rather than in specific terms. For example, A = L * W can be used to calculate any area, no matter what the data are.

Sometimes we use the same variable to accumulate the data. The following simple example shows the technique:

Example 1.5

Problem: What number will the following program print?

Program:
```
50   S = 2.1
100  S = S + 5.2
150  PRINT S
200  END
```

The output will be

```
7.3
```

Note: In the statement S = S + 5.2, the value of S on the right side of the equation is 2.1, and the new value of S, on the left side, is calculated as 7.3. Notice that this equation does not have the meaning it would have in algebra.

This method of assigning a new value to a variable is a common programming technique. The usefulness of the technique will become apparent when you learn more about programming in the following sections.

Variable Names

BASIC allows variables to be named in a variety of ways. In all BASIC systems, <u>a variable name may consist of one letter or one letter and one numeral, but the letter must always precede the numeral</u>. The following are legal variable names:

```
A1    B1    C2
X9    Z5    E8
B     C3    I
```

"Special" characters such as + or *, cannot be used in a symbolic name. Some illegal names are:

VOLTAGE1	<u>More than two characters may be illegal.</u> *except in true basic*
A+1	The + is illegal.
X*Y	The * is illegal.
1X	The first character must be a letter.
A10	More than two characters may be illegal.

Unfortunately, rules about symbolic names cannot be generalized to all versions of BASIC. If you follow the rules above, however, your variables will work with all versions. Some systems accept variable names with more than two characters; other systems accept more than two characters, but only the first two are significant. Refer to the BASIC manual of your computer system to learn the rules governing variable names. (See also Appendix B.) If a system accepts more than one character, it is good programming practice to choose descriptive variable names. For example, the following variable names are descriptive:

| AREA | WAGE | PAY | SPEED | CAR | } as in true basic
|------|------|------|-------|--------|
| ZIP | VOLUME | CITY | FIRST | STREET |

In this text, we use variable names with more than one character to make the programs easy to read. If the computer system you are using does not accept the name when you run one of the examples in the text, drop the characters after the first letter. The names are chosen so that the programs will work if you omit all characters after the first one. The following program uses descriptive variable names. The program is similar to the one in Example 1.1

```
100   SIDE = 14
200   WIDTH = 9.5
300   AREA = SIDE*WIDTH
400   PRINT SIDE, WIDTH, AREA
500   END
```

Again, choosing appropriate symbolic names for variables is very important. It is always advisable to pick a descriptive name for a variable if possible. For example, it is better to designate the area of a room as AREA rather than X. The value of this practice will be apparent later when your programs become long and complicated.

Reserved Words

In BASIC, some words have special meaning for the system. For instance, PRINT tells the system "print the information listed." These are called *reserved words* and cannot be used as variable names. Some examples of reserved words are PRINT, TAB, FOR, RUN, OPEN, NAME, and LEN. The name LEN was not used in the example above because it is reserved. You will learn many reserved words throughout the text. Appendix A presents some of the reserved words for selected systems.

Solved Problems

1.5 Assume a system accepts only one letter or one letter and one numeral as variable names. Which of the following names are legal?

✓ a. P2   ✓ b. C   ✓ c. Q6
✓ d. J1   ✗ e. R10 ✗ f. SI
✗ g. P-Q   ✗ h. PRINT ✗ i. 1N

28 *Basics of Programming*

Answers:

The first four symbols are legal, but the last five are not.

1.6 Identify the errors, if any, in each of the following statements.
   a. X = A + B + C + D + E + F
   b. Y9 + (X1 + X2)/(X3 + X4)
   c. A = B*C/2.5
   d. 2X + 3Y = 3(X + Y)
   e. X = Y^.5
   f. A + B = C
   g. G1 = 3.5 + (A + B + C)^3
   h. S = S + N
   i. A**(I + 2) + O
   j. J = 2*I*J^N
   k. F = ((X + Y) + Z)^2

Answers:
   a. The line number is missing.
   b. The = sign and line number are missing.
   c. The line number is missing.
   d. More than one variable cannot be used on the left of an assignment statement. The line number is also missing.
   e. The line number is missing.
   f. More than one variable cannot be used on the left of an assignment statement. The line number is also missing.
   g. The line number is missing.
   h. The line number is missing.
   i. The = sign and the line number are missing.
   j. The line number is missing.
   k. The line number is missing.

1.7 What values do the following programs print?
   a.
   ```
   100   A = 2.5
   200   B = 11.5
   300   PRINT A, B
   400   C = A + B
   500   PRINT C
   600   END
   ```

b.
```
 90    W = 0
100    W = W + 2.1
200    PRINT W
300    END
```

c.
```
15    X = 5.5
25    X = X + 3.4
35    Y = 2*X
45    PRINT Y
55    END
```

d.
```
100    A = 1.2
200    B = A + 2.1
300    B = 2*B
400    PRINT B
500    END
```

e.
```
10    S = 0
20    I = 1
30    S = S + 1      S = 1
40    J = I + 2      J = 3
50    S = S + J      S = 4
60    PRINT I, J, S
70    END
```

f.
```
20    X = 5.93
30    Y = 3.07
40    AVG = (X + Y)/2.0
50    PRINT X, Y, AVG
60    END
```

Answers:

a. Line 300 prints 2.5 and 11.5, and line 500 prints 14.

b. 2.1

c. 17.8

d. 6.6

e. 1   3   4

f. 5.93   3.07   4.5

The LET Statement

The LET statement is used to assign a value to a variable. The general form of the LET statement is:

```
line no. LET V = e
```

or simply

```
line no. V = e
```

where V is a variable name, and e is an expression. The expression, e, can be a constant, another variable name, a mathematical expression, or a combination of these. The statement is the same assignment statement used in the programs in this chapter, but without the word LET. The following are all assignment statements:

```
400   LET A = B - C - 2
20    LET X = 5.5
300   LET P = 3*X + 5*Y - 2
40    Q = 6*A - 2
130   J = J+1
500   S1 = S1 + A
```

The word LET is optional in assignment statements. It is a matter of convenience whether or not you use the word LET at the beginning of the statement.

Writing Better Programs

To write a program, you need to:

1. Understand the problem to be solved
2. Develop a solution plan
3. Use BASIC statements that carry out the solution

In programming terminology, the solution plan, written in simple English, is called *pseudocode*. Pseudocode is detailed, step-by-step instructions in a narrative form. Developing the solution plan, the pseudocode, is more important than writing the program. Of course, a good solution plan makes the program easy to write. Spend ample time planning before you start writing BASIC statements.

A good program not only gets the job done but also is easy to follow and understand. Write your programs so that anyone reading them can understand what is going on. Readable programs are easy to modify if necessary. To make a program readable, choose an easy-to-follow solution procedure, use descriptive variable names (if allowed), and use blank spaces where appropriate.

Making notes about critical points in a program also enhances the readability of any program. This is done by using the REM statement.

REM Statement

The word REM at the beginning of a line stands for *remark*. The programmer can write any comment after the word REM. The comment will appear in the program listing exactly as it is typed. The following is an example:

Example 1.6 Using REM statements in a program

```
10   REM   *************** PROGRAM: EXAMPLE ********************
20   REM   THIS PROGRAM CALCULATES THE SPEED OF A MOVING OBJECT,
30   REM   THE DISTANCE TRAVELED AND TIME ARE GIVEN.
40   REM
50   REM   ************************************************************
60   REM   * VARIABLE DICTIONARY:                                      *
70   REM   *       X = THE DISTANCE, IN MILES                          *
80   REM   *       T = THE TIME, IN HOURS                              *
90   REM   *       S = SPEED, IN  MILES PER HOUR                       *
100  REM   ************************************************************
110  REM
120  X = 456.5
130  T = 3.5
140  S = X/T
150  PRINT X,  T,  S
999  END
```

A remark line may be placed anywhere before the END statement. The computer does not execute remark lines. They are treated as comments only, not instructions. Remarks appear in the listing of the program, but not on the output.

It is good programming practice to document a program with several remark statements. Normally, several remarks appear at the beginning of a program. They may include the name of the programmer, the date, a summary of the purpose of the program, the solution procedures, and a description of the variables. Remark lines are also used throughout the program to explain variables, the intention of an unclear statement, or other critical points. These comments are very useful to the programmer, as well as to anyone reviewing the program at a later time. Some versions of BASIC permit an exclamation mark (!) instead of REM.

Solved Problems

1.8 Are there errors in the following statements?
  a. `10 COMMENT THIS IS A READ STATEMENT`
  b. `REM THIS IS VARIABLE X`
     `20  X = P*Q`
  c. `100REMTHIS IS TO CALCULATE Y`
     `200 Y = 3*X`
  d. `10   THIS IS A COMMENT`
     `20   PRINT X`
  e. `90   X = 56.5`
     `100 REM PRINT X`
  f. `100 REM THIS PROGRAM CALCULATES THE`
     `200 AVERAGES OF TWO TEST SCORES FOR`
     `300 SEVERAL STUDENTS`
  g. `10   ! THIS IS THE BEGINNING OF THE LOOP`

Answers:
  a. `REM` must be used at the beginning of the line instead of `COMMENT`.
  b. The comment line must have a line number.
  c. Line 100 is correct, but spaces should be used before and after `REM` for readability.
  d. A comment line must start with `REM`.
  e. Line 100 is correct, but notice that the line is a comment line and causes nothing to be printed.
  f. Line 100 is correct, but lines 200 and 300 must start with `REM`.
  g. This is correct if the system allows substituting ! for `REM`.

RUNNING A PROGRAM

Normally a BASIC program is run "on line." That is, the program is typed directly into the computer, one line at a time, through a terminal. The starting procedure varies with the type of computer you use. Some microcomputers are ready as soon as you turn on a switch. Others require you to type the word BASIC after you turn on the switch.

To use larger computers, you need an account number and a password. You must connect the terminal to the computer and "log in." Both of these

Figure 1.7 A typical terminal keyboard (courtesy of IBM)

procedures are done through a series of system commands. After the initial sign-in process, you call up the BASIC interpreter by typing BASIC. The program then can be typed line by line.

The terminal keyboard is like a typewriter keyboard, and you key in the information much as you operate a typewriter (Figure 1.7). However, after you type a line, you must press the ENTER key, called the RETURN key on some keyboards. Pressing this key causes the line just typed to be transmitted to the computer.

System Commands

Certain words cause the system to carry out a specific task immediately. Those words are called *system commands*.

NEW

Before typing a program, you should type NEW. This command tells the system that a new program is to be created. You can accompany this command with a program name, such as NEW ANAME. If you don't type a name after the NEW command, some systems will ask you to enter a program name.

SAVE

Another useful command is SAVE. Use this command to store a newly created or revised program on a storage media.

OLD (LOAD)

If at a later time you type OLD ANAME, the saved program ANAME will be recalled. Some systems use LOAD instead of OLD.

RUN

The system command that tells the computer to execute a program is RUN. RUN causes the program just typed in or recalled by the OLD command to be performed.

LIST

LIST is a very useful command. This command causes the lines of the program just typed or recalled to be displayed. Again, remember that the user must press the ENTER key after typing a command.

RESAVE

Often, a program needs to be corrected or modified. If you wish to correct a line, you need retype only that line. Even if you retype the line at the bottom of the program, the computer places the line in correct line-number order. To add a new line, you need to type the line, with the appropriate line number, at the bottom of the program. Again, the computer places the line in the appropriate order. To delete a line, type only the number of the line you wish to delete and then press the RETURN key.

If you change a program that has already been saved, replace the old program with the corrected one. The command for this purpose can be SAVE, REPLACE, or RESAVE, depending on the system.

BYE

Finally, after you finish the terminal session, use the BYE command to sign off.

System commands do not need line numbers. The most common system commands, which are almost universal among different systems, are summarized below:

NEW	Creates a new program
OLD	Retrieves a saved program (LOAD, in some systems)

RUN	Runs a BASIC program
LIST	Lists a BASIC program
SAVE	Saves a BASIC program
REPLACE	Replaces a saved program after corrections are made (SAVE or RESAVE in some systems)
HELLO	Allows user to log in or start work (in a larger computer)
BYE	Allows user to sign off (in a larger computer)

Figure 1.8 demonstrates a typical run session. (Some of the statements in Figure 1.8 are explained in Chapter 2.)

Microcomputer Commands: LLIST/LPRINT

An important command of special interest to microcomputer users is LLIST. In most (but not all) microcomputers, LLIST (instead of LIST) will cause the computer to send the listing to the printer rather than the monitor, and the program will be printed.

If you wish to print a value with the printer rather than on the monitor, some microcomputers require you to use LPRINT instead of PRINT. For example, the program

```
10 X = 5.5
20 LPRINT X
30 END
```

will cause 5.5 to be printed on hard copy.

Basic Immediate Mode

So far, every BASIC statement you have seen has had a line number. In other words, those statements have been part of a program. This is called *program mode*. Sometimes it is useful to type statements without line numbers. This is called *immediate mode*. Most BASIC systems allow immediate mode.

A statement typed in immediate mode is carried out at once. For example, if you type PRINT 5*3 and press the ENTER key, 15 will be printed immediately. The immediate mode can even be used to print the value of variables. Suppose you have just run this program:

```
10 A = 25.5
20 Y = 31.3
30 PRINT A, Y
40 END
```

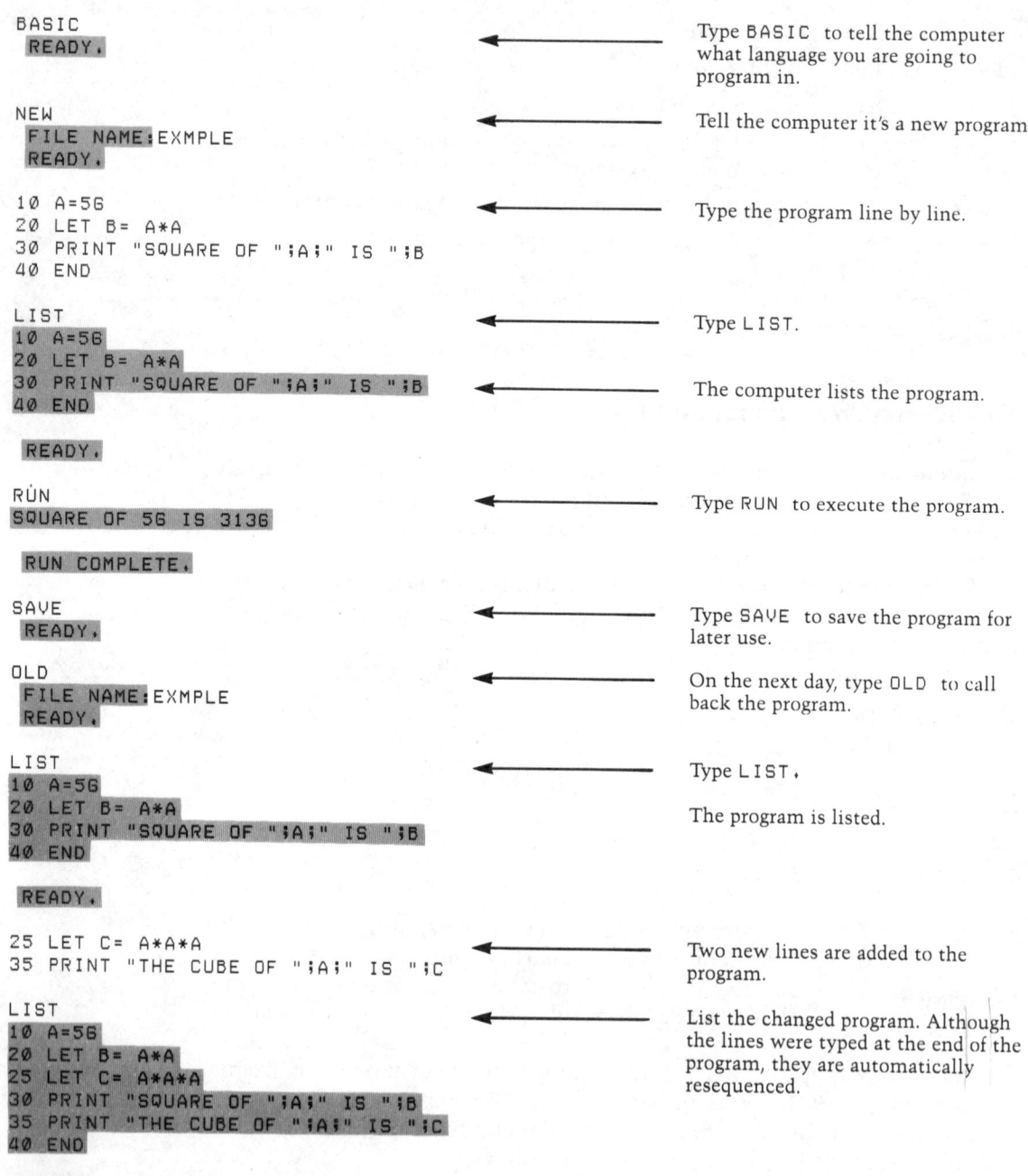

Figure 1.8 A typical run session. Note that the shaded areas are printed by the computer.

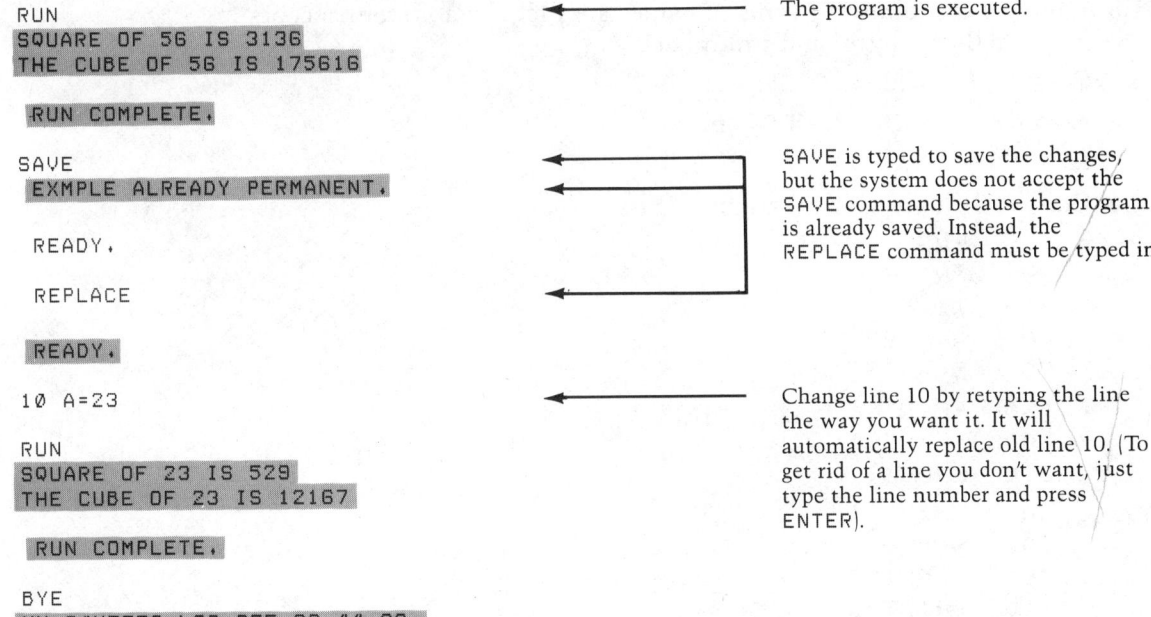

Figure 1.8 *Continued*

If you type PRINT A and press the ENTER key, the value 31.3 will be displayed. The following is another example (note that there are no line numbers):

```
N = 5
M = N*N
PRINT M
```

As soon as you enter the last line, the computer prints 25. Of course, these lines will be lost after execution.

You can use the terminal in immediate mode as a calculator for quick calculations. As you will see in Chapter 3, you can also use immediate mode to find errors in a program.

EXERCISES

1.4 Convert the following into BASIC expressions:

    a. $\dfrac{(A+B)^2 + C}{2} = X$
    b. $(2X + 3Y)^2 + \dfrac{(5X+Y)^2 + X^2}{2} = Z$

    c. $A = \dfrac{A + A^2 + (-4AB)}{2A}$
    d. $(1/2)(5X \cdot Y \cdot Z^2 + X) = W$

1.5 Which of the following variable names are illegal if a system accepts no more than a letter and a number?

    a. X   **b.** W1   **c.** S5   **d.** SOL
    e. L8   **f.** K99   **g.** F9   **h.** AA
    i. M1   **j.** 1X   **k.** A5   **l.** 5A

1.6 Correct the following programs:

    a.
```
10   END
20   PRINT X
30   X = A + B
40   A = 53.1
50   B = 23.1
```

    b.
```
100   PRINT Y
200   Y = 5.1
300   END
```

    c.
```
50    V = 2.1
70    W = V + X
90    X = 1.3
110   PRINT X, V, X
130   END
```

    d.
```
AVRG = C + D/2.0
C = 5.1
D = 2.3
PRINT C, D, AVRG
END
```

    e.
```
FIRST NUMBER = 1.0
SECOND NUMBER = 2.3
AVERAGE = (FIRST NUMBER + SECOND NUMBER)/2.0
PRINT AVERAGE
END
```

    f.
```
1   HRS = 40
2   RATE = 8.75
3   PAY = HOURS*WAGE
4   PRINT HRS, RATE, PAY
5   END
```

1.7 What do the following programs print after execution?

    a.
```
100   A = 2.5
200   B = 2*A
300   PRINT B
400   END
```

```
b. 50    Y = 2.1
   100   X = 5.5
   150   Y = Y + X
   200   PRINT Y
   250   END
c. 50    J = 2
   150   I = 3
   200   S = I + J
   250   M = I * J
   300   N = M * S
   350   N = N + 1
   400   PRINT J, I, N, M, S
   450   END
```

1.8 Suppose the width of a room is 19.5, the length is 25.6, and the height is 12.5. Write a program that prints the width, length, height, and volume of the room. (The volume equals width × length × height.)

1.9 The temperature is 75° Fahrenheit. Write a program to calculate and print the temperature in degrees Celsius. Fahrenheit can be changed to Celsius with the formula $C = [100(F - 32)]/180$.

1.10 Suppose $X = 15$, and $Y = 3.5$. Write a program that calculates Q from the following formulas and then prints X, Y, R, and S on one line and Q on the next.

$$R = 5X^2 + 3Y$$

$$S = \frac{9R^3 + 2X}{5R^2 + 2}$$

$$Q = 2S^2 + 3$$

SUMMARY

You have learned:

1. The computer accepts data through an input device, processes data through the CPU, and delivers the information through an output device. The data can be stored on a storage medium, such as a disk, for later processing. The equipment is called hardware.
2. A computer program is a detailed set of instructions that directs the computer to do a specific task. The programs are called software.
3. A computer language uses predetermined words, terms, and rules to convey instructions to the computer.

4. Fundamental computer operations are accepting data, doing data manipulation, storing data, and printing data.
5. BASIC is an acronym for "Beginners All-purpose Symbolic Instruction Code."
6. A variable represents a quantity that can be changed in a program.
7. When you name a variable, the computer reserves memory space under that name.
8. A variable name can have one letter, or one letter and one numeral. Some systems accept more than two characters as a symbolic name, but the first character must always be a letter.
9. A variable must be defined before it is used.
10. The BASIC mathematical operators are ^, *, /, +, and -. These operators, together with variables, and constants, make up mathematical expressions. Parentheses are often necessary to make expressions unambiguous.
11. Some BASIC words are:

    PRINT   Prints values of variables
    END   Ends a program; the last line in a program
    REM   Prints a comment in the program

12. A BASIC program is normally keyed directly into a computer through a terminal. Some system commands that are carried out immediately are NEW, OLD (or LOAD), RUN, LIST, and SAVE.
13. Statements in a BASIC program start with line numbers. If a statement without a line number is typed in, the computer carries out the instruction immediately. This is called immediate mode.

REVIEW QUESTIONS/SELF-TEST

1.1 Explain briefly:
   a. What is a computer program?
   b. What is a computer language?
   c. What does the term BASIC stand for?

1.2 Write the following mathematical expressions in BASIC:
   a. $B = X^a - P(3X + Y)$
   b. $B = \dfrac{X + Y + Z}{X + 2Y} + 3Z$

c. $B = X \cdot Y \cdot Z + A - 3X^4$

1.3 Which of the following are legal variable names for the BASIC system you are familiar with?

    a. XMAS   b. C10   c. B-A
    d. F9   e. Q-5   f. AV
    g. AAA3   h. A*1   i. 1X
    j. END   k. LIST   l. SAVE

1.4 Which of the following BASIC expressions are correct?

    a. (A + B)/2.0 = G
    b. B + 2 = X
    c. E = (3X + 5Y)(2X - 1)
    d. Q = A^Q*B^X
    e. all of the above

1.5 Correct the following programs. Assume a name cannot be longer than two characters.

```
a. 10   A = 89.5
        AVG = (A + S)/2
        S = 99.3
   50   PRINT A, S, AVG
        END

b. 10   JOHN = 269
   20   KAY = 596
   30   ION = JOHN + KAY
        END
        PRINT ION

c. 10   SCORE1 = 92.5
   20   SCORE2 = 78.2
   30   CALCULATE AVERAGE
   40   PRINT AVERAGE
   50   END
```

1.6 What does the following program cause the computer to print?

```
10   X = 5.2
20   Y = 6.1
30   X = X + Y
40   Y = 3.1
50   X = X + Y
60   PRINT X, Y
70   END
```

1.7 Write a program that calculates the average of two scores, then prints the scores on one line and the average on the next line. Score 1 is 92.5, and score 2 is 89.5.

Answers:

1.2 a. B = X^A - P*(3*X + Y)
   b. B = (X + Y + Z)/(X + 2*Y) + 3*Z
   c. B = X*Y*Z + A - 3*X^4

1.3 The answer depends on the computer system being used. However, most systems accept only letters and digits (in BASIC-PLUS, a period is legal), and the first character must be a letter. Therefore, c, e, h, and i are not correct at all. Also, j, k, and l are not correct because they are reserved words.

1.4 The only correct expression is d.

1.5 a.
```
10   A = 89.5
20   S = 99.3
30   X = (A + S)/2
40   PRINT A, S, X
50   END
```
   b.
```
10   J = 269
20   K = 596
30   I = J + K
40   PRINT I
50   END
```
   c.
```
10   S1 = 92.5
20   S2 = 78.2
30   A = (S1 + S2)/2
40   PRINT A
50   END
```
   Note that the procedure for calculating the average must be given in BASIC.

1.6 It prints: 14.4   3.1

1.7
```
10   S1 = 92.5
20   S2 = 89.5
30   X = (S1 + S2)/2.0
40   PRINT S1, S2
50   PRINT X
60   END
```

Input and Output

2

In This Chapter:

Constants in BASIC
Numeric Constants
String Constants

Output
The PRINT Statement
Separators in PRINT Statements

Input
The READ-DATA Statements
The RESTORE Statement
The INPUT Statement

Some Programming Techniques
Looping
String Variables
Generating Sequence Numbers
Accumulating Data: Finding the Total
A Complete Program
An Interactive Program
A Game Program

Program Spacing
Output Spacing
Spaces in the Program

Exercises

Summary

Review Questions/Self-Test

2

Input and Output

Generally, a program requires three basic processing steps: input of data, manipulation or processing, and output of information.

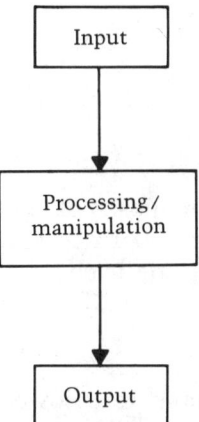

Later in this chapter, the principles of input and output are discussed, beginning with output because output—what we see on the screen or the printout—is the most immediate, visible effect of programming. After those sections, a section devoted to programming techniques explores some elementary processing techniques. The last section explores spacing in the program and in the output. To understand how input, output, and processing work, however, you must begin by understanding an important concept of programming—the constant.

CONSTANTS IN BASIC

The BASIC language is designed to manipulate numeric and character data. In Chapter 1, you learned that a variable is the name of a location in memory. Variables allow you to write flexible programs. However, actual values, as well as variables, can also be used in a program.

Constants are values that do not change. For example, in the statement

```
100    Y = 3*X + 2
```

X and Y are variables; 3 and 2 are constants.

There are two types of constants in BASIC: numeric constants and string constants.

Numeric Constants

A numeric constant is an unchanging, positive or negative, numeric value. The following are examples of numeric constants:

```
       5              +56.0
       3.14           -900
    1000              +1001.1
62389.23              -3289
```

Numeric constants can be composed of digits, a plus or minus sign at the beginning, and a decimal point, if necessary. Other characters, such as commas, cannot be used in numeric constants. If a constant does not have a sign, it is assumed to be positive. The following are examples of *invalid* numeric constants:

56,000	The comma is not allowed.
$62000	The dollar sign is not allowed.
52000+	The trailing sign cannot be used.
32000.00CR	The CR is not allowed.

String Constants

A string constant is a string of characters enclosed in quotation marks. Any digit or character, such as $, ., -, or a blank can be included in the string. The following are examples of string constants:

```
"MY NAME IS:"
"HOW ARE YOU?"
"VAR1="
"4811 E. MICHIGAN ST., MT. PLEASANT, MICHIGAN"
```

OUTPUT

In BASIC, the PRINT statement is the programming tool for output. The PRINT statement is very important because it is the only way that the computer can deliver the information it processes. The PRINT statement allows you to print the values of the variables and expressions, such as PRINT A + B. You can also print a constant, for instance, PRINT 37.

The PRINT Statement

The PRINT statement causes values to be printed. This statement has the following form:

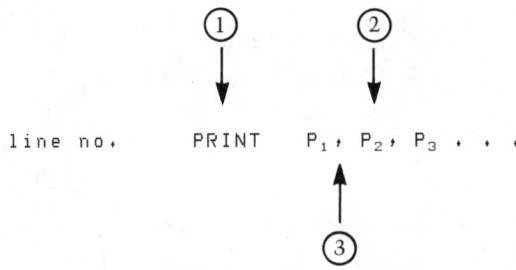

The PRINT statement has three main components:

1. The word PRINT, which must be spelled correctly.
2. The values to be printed, which may be variables (PRINT X), constants (PRINT 3 or PRINT "HI"), arithmetic expressions (PRINT 2*X-7), or a combination of those. Example:

    ```
    10  PRINT X, 2*Y, 5, "HI, MY NAME IS JOE."
    ```
3. The separator, which may be either a comma or a semicolon. (In some systems, a space is also allowed as a separator.) A separator is needed if one statement is to print several values.

The following are some examples:

Example 2.1

Program Segment:

```
10   X = 5.9
20   PRINT "THE VALUE OF X IS", X
```

The output will be

```
THE VALUE OF X IS           5.9
```

Example 2.2

Program Segment:

```
10   A = 5627.5
20   B = 32
30   PRINT A, "WAS A, B IS =", B, "SUM =", A + B
```

The output will be

```
5627.5        WAS A, B IS =32      SUM = 5659.5
```

Example 2.3

Program Segment:

```
10   P = 2.5
20   PRINT "P =", P, "Q =", 2*P, "R =", P^2
```

The output will be

```
P =          2.5         Q =         5         R =          6.25
```

The term PRINT is always needed to print values. When used by itself in a program line, such as 10 PRINT, the PRINT statement generates a blank line. When used with a value, the statement causes that value to be printed. When used with values and separators, the statement prints the values but spaces them in a predesignated way. Some systems allow using a symbol such as ? instead of the word PRINT.

Separators in PRINT Statements

The spacing of the printed information in the previous examples is due to commas used in the PRINT statements. There are two separators, the comma and the semicolon, and each has a different effect.

Comma

A comma in a PRINT statement has the effect of spacing the output at fixed intervals. Normally, the paper (or screen) is divided into horizontal zones; each zone occupies about 15 print positions. When items in a PRINT statement are separated by commas, each item is printed at the beginning of a zone (see Figure 2.1). For example, the number 64, if printed in this

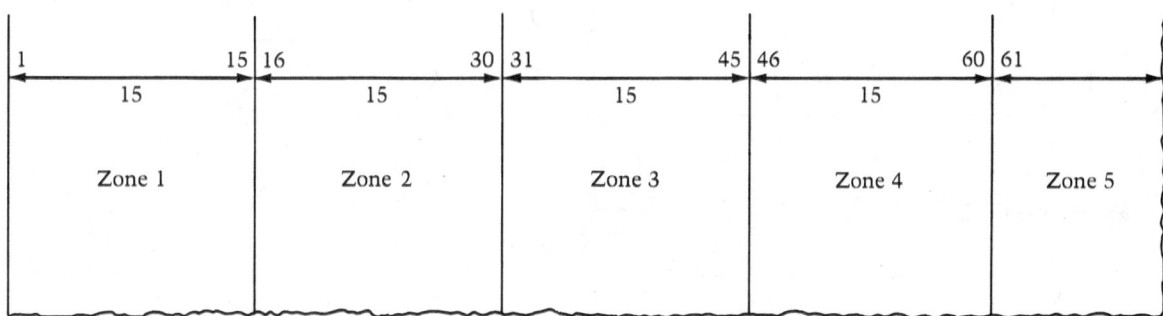

Figure 2.1 Print zones in the output

manner, will occupy a zone of 15 positions, with 1 blank to its left for the sign and 12 blanks to its right. If an item (such as a character constant) takes up more than 14 print positions but less than 29, it will occupy two zones; if a character constant takes up more than 29 print positions but less than 44, it will occupy three zones; and so on. The following rules are also important in using a comma:

1. Two consecutive commas cause a blank zone.
2. If a PRINT statement ends with a comma, then the first item in the next PRINT statement will be printed in the next available zone, if possible.
3. If the paper or screen is not sufficiently wide to contain all the values, the printer automatically starts printing on a new line.
4. The exact length of a zone depends on the system being used. (See Appendix B for the exact length of a zone for selected systems.)

The following are some examples:

Example 2.4

Program:

```
10   X = 3.1
20   PRINT X, X
30   END
```

The output will be

```
3.1             3.1
```

Example 2.5

Program Segment:

```
10   P = 5
20   PRINT "P =", P,
30   PRINT "2P:", 2*P
```

The output will be

```
|<----15----->|<----15----->|<----15----->|<----15----->|
```

```
P =             5          2P:          10
```

Example 2.6

Program:

```
10   X = 5.2
20   S = X^2
30   PRINT "THE VALUE OF X IS =", X, "ITS SQUARE =", S
40   END
```

The output will be

```
|<--------30-------->|<---15--->|<---15--->|<---15--->|
```

```
THE VALUE OF X IS =   5.2          ITS SQUARE= 27.04
```

Example 2.7

Program Segment:

```
10   E1 = 69.5
20   E2 = 93.8
30   E3 = 75.354
40   S = E1 + E2 + E3
50   PRINT "E1 =", E1, "E2 =", E2, "E3 =", E3, "SUM =", S
```

The output will be

```
|<----15----->|<----15----->|<----15----->|<----15----->|
```

```
E1 =          69.5        E2 =          93.8
E3 =          75.354      SUM =         238.654
```

Input and Output

Semicolon

A semicolon can also be used as a separator in a PRINT statement. However, the effect of a semicolon is to compress the printed values. A semicolon puts one "trailing" blank after numeric constants, and no blank after string constants. Thus, a semicolon will automatically place a blank between the values of numeric variables. (In most systems, two blanks appear between numeric values because a space is reserved for the sign of the second value.)

■ *Example 2.8*

Program:

```
10   A = 1.5
20   B = -2.6
30   C = 3.9
40   PRINT A; B; C
50   END
```

The output will be

```
1.5 -2.6  3.9
```

■ *Example 2.9*

Program Segment:

```
50   PRINT "ABC"; "DEF"
```

The output will be

```
ABCDEF
```

■ **Example 2.10**

Program:

```
100   X = 10.2
200   Y = -22.5
300   PRINT "THE VALUE OF X ="; X; "THE VALUE OF Y IS"; Y
400   END
```

The output will be

```
THE VALUE OF X = 10.2 THE VALUE OF Y IS-22.5
```

Note: There is one trailing space after the value of X (10.2), but no trailing spaces after the strings of characters.

You can think of the comma or semicolon in a PRINT statement as controlling the position of the cursor on the screen: the *print position*. A comma causes the cursor to move to the beginning of a new zone. If both semicolons and commas are used in a PRINT statement, then the spacing of the output depends on the number of print positions occupied by the printed items. If, because of semicolons, all the previous information takes up less than one zone, then a comma moves the cursor to a new zone, where the new item is printed. If all the previous information takes up more than one zone but less than two zones, then a comma moves the cursor to the beginning of a third zone, and so on. The following program is an example:

■ **Example 2.11**

Program:

```
100  X = 10.2
200  PRINT "THE VALUE OF X IS ="; X, X
300  END
```

The output will be

```
!<-----------30------------>!
```

```
THE VALUE OF X IS = 10.2     10.2
```

Note: The second 10.2 in the output appears in the third zone because the previous information occupies two zones.

■ **Solved Problems**

2.1 Write short programs that print each of the following:

 a. Your name
 b. The statement THIS IS THE FIRST LINE OF THE PROGRAM.
 c. The question WHAT IS THE VALUE OF VARIABLE A?
 d. The statement THE VALUE OF VARIABLE X IS = immediately followed by the value of variable X (assume X = 5).
 e. The statement THIS IS THE END OF THE REPORT, then two blank lines, then the statement CALL BACK.
 f. The statement TYPE YOUR NAME, ID, AND PASS-WORD.
 g. The statement WELCOME TO THE WORLD OF PROGRAMMING, then a blank line, and then the question WHAT IS YOUR SOCIAL SECURITY NUMBER?

Answers:

 a. 10   PRINT "JACK NEWCOMER"
 b. 10   PRINT "THIS IS THE FIRST LINE OF THE PROGRAM."
 c. 50   PRINT "WHAT IS THE VALUE OF VARIABLE A?"

d. 90   X = 5
   100 PRINT "THE VALUE OF VARIABLE X IS = "; X
e. 10   PRINT "THIS IS THE END OF THE REPORT."
   20   PRINT
   30   PRINT
   40   PRINT "CALL BACK."
   50   END
f. 100 PRINT "TYPE YOUR NAME, ID, AND PASSWORD."
g. 100 PRINT "WELCOME TO THE WORLD OF PROGRAMMING."
   110 PRINT
   120 PRINT "WHAT IS YOUR SOCIAL SECURITY NUMBER?"
   130 END

2.2 Show how the output of the following programs will look. (Make sure to have an answer ready before you look at the answers given.)

a. 10   P = -156.2
   20   Q = 36.5
   30   PRINT "P AND Q ARE ="; P, Q
   40   PRINT
   50   PRINT "P AND Q ARE ="; P; Q
   60   END
b. 10   X = 10
   20   Y = 20
   30   Z = 30
   40   PRINT X; Y; Z
   50   PRINT X, Y, Z
   60   PRINT X; Y, Z
   70   PRINT X, Y; Z
   80   PRINT X,
   90   PRINT Y,
   100 PRINT Z
   110 PRINT
   120 PRINT X;
   130 PRINT Y;
   140 PRINT Z;
   150 END
c. 90   A = 50
   100 PRINT "THE VALUE", "OF A IS", A
   200 PRINT "THE VALUE"; "OF A IS"; A
   300 END

```
d. 10    P = .5
   20    Q = 10
   30    PRINT "RATE", "QUANTITY", "TOTAL"
   40    PRINT P, Q, P*Q
   50    PRINT P; Q; P*Q
   60    END
e. 20    PRINT "THIS IS";" THE BEGIN";"NING OF THE PROGRAM"
   30    PRINT "EMPLOYEE NUMBER"; 6328
   40    END
```

Answers:

```
a. P AND Q ARE = 156.2          36.5
   (one blank line)
   P AND Q ARE = 156.2   36.5
b. 10   20   30
   10             20            30
   10   20       30
   10             20   30
   10             20            30
   (one blank line)
   10   20   30
c. THE VALUE        OF A IS     50
   THE VALUEOF A IS 50
d. RATE             QUANTITY    TOTAL
    .5              10          5
    .5    10    5
e. THIS IS THE BEGINNING OF THE PROGRAM
   EMPLOYEE NUMBER 6328
```

Note that the PRINT statement can be used not only with a numeric variable, but also with a numeric constant (6328).

INPUT

In the program examples in the previous sections, the data were given by assignment statements. In many cases, however, the data are introduced by READ or INPUT statements. The READ statement reads data values already in the program. The INPUT statement is used to accept data that a user types on a terminal. These two statements are explained below.

The READ-DATA Statements

The READ statement causes values to be read for the variables from DATA statements. A READ statement is always accompanied by a DATA statement. The following example shows how this technique is used:

Example 2.12

Problem: Find the average of three exam marks. The marks are 85.6, 78.5, and 90.3.

Solution Plan:

1. Read the values of the variables from the DATA statement.
2. Calculate the average.
3. Print the average.
4. Give these data: 85.6, 78.5, 90.3.
5. End the program.

Program:

```
10   READ A, B, C
20   G = (A + B + C)/3
30   PRINT G
40   DATA 85.6, 78.5, 90.3
50   END
```

The printout will be

```
84.8
```

Notes:

1. The READ statement is followed by the names of the variables to be read.
2. The READ statement tells the computer to read the data in the DATA statement. It reads the first number for A, the second number for B, and the third number for C. Then the average is calculated and printed.

3. In this program, READ A, B, C serves the same purpose as three assignment statements: A = 85.6, B = 78.5, and C = 90.3.

The READ statement places values into the memory cells listed—A, B, and C, in this case. The values are read from the DATA statement.

Data given in the DATA statements are called input data. The difference between input data and data given in assignment statements is input data's greater flexibility of use. Using input data, which are always furnished by either READ statements or INPUT statements, discussed later, is preferable to using assignment statements because input data let you use different sets of data in one program. For this reason, you can use one program many times rather than having to write new programs with new assignment statements.

The following solved problems will help you understand the READ statement:

■ Solved Problems

2.3 Correct the following programs:

```
a. 10    A1 = 201.50
   20    A2 = 6321.1
   30    READ A1, A2
   40    C = (A1 + A2)/2
   50    PRINT C
   60    DATA 201.50, 6321.1
   70    END
b. 10    READ J, K
   20    M = J + K
   30    PRINT M
   40    DATA J = 96, K = 36
   50    END
c. 10    READ W1, W2, A
   20    A = W1 + W2
   30    PRINT A
   40    DATA 12, 18
   50    END
d. 10    PRINT A, B
   20    READ A, B
   30    X = A + B
   40    PRINT X
   50    DATA 632.0, 938.65
   60    END
```

e. 10   3.9 6.2 1.2
    20   Y = U + V + W
    30   READ U, V, W
    40   PRINT U, V, W, Y
    50   END

Answers:

a. The data should be given by either the assignment statements in lines 10 and 20 or by the READ statement, but not by both. READ A1, A2 performs the same function as A1 = 201.50 and A2 = 6321.1. The program should be:

```
10    READ A1, A2
20    C = (A1 + A2)/2
30    PRINT C
40    DATA 201.50, 6321.1
50    END
```

b. The DATA statement should not contain variable names or an equals sign, but only data.

c. The READ statement should not contain A because its value is to be calculated.

d. Line 10 PRINT A, B should either be omitted or placed after the READ statement. Remember that a variable must be defined before it can be used in a calculation or printed.

e. Line 10 is missing the word DATA, and line 20 must be placed after the READ statement. The correct program is:

```
10    READ U, V, W
20    Y = U + V + W
30    PRINT U, V, W, Y
40    DATA 3.9, 6.2, 1.2
50    END
```

A program may have more than one READ or DATA statement. The following program is an example:

Example 2.13

Problem: Write a program that reads the values of A, B, and C from the first READ statement and the values of D, E, and F from the second READ statement. Calculate the sum of the values, then print the data and the sum.

Program:

```
10    READ A, B, C
20    READ D, E, F
30    S = A + B + C + D + E + F
40    PRINT A; B; C; D; E; F; S
50    DATA 15, 22, 18, 59
60    DATA 98, 75
70    END
```

The printout will be

```
15   22   18   59   98   75   287
```

Notes:

1. A program may have more than one DATA statement.
2. The one-to-one correspondence between the variables and values in this example are as follows:

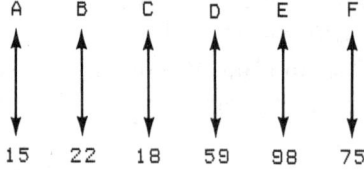

3. The READ statement reads the values of variables sequentially. A value is not read twice.

Generally, the READ-DATA statements are used in pairs. They have the following form:

line no.   READ V1, V2, V3, . . .
   ⋮
line no.   DATA v1, v2, v3, . . .

The following rules also apply to READ-DATA statements:

1. Each variable in a READ statement must have a corresponding value in a DATA statement.
2. Values in the DATA statement are separated by commas.
3. The values in all DATA statements are placed in a data pool and are ordered sequentially as they appear in consecutive DATA statements. A variable receives a value according to the order in which the variable appears in a READ statement. A value is not assigned twice.
4. If there are more values in DATA statements than there are variables in READ statements, the computer ignores the extra values. But if there are fewer values than variables, the computer prints an error message after all the values are exhausted.
5. Any number of DATA statements may appear anywhere in the program, as long as they appear before the END statement. Placing a DATA statement before a READ statement, for example, does not change the logic of value assignment. It is good programming practice, though, to place all DATA statements near the beginning or near the end of a program to make the program readable.

The following solved problems illustrate these points:

Solved Problems

2.4 Find the errors in the following DATA statements:
   a. 100   DATA 5   6.5   10   9
   b. 200   DATA 56; 92; 32
   c. 300   DATA 92, 5.5, 6.2, 92, 38,
   d. 400   DATA, 56, 20, 10
   e. 100   DATA   A = 5, B = 6, C = 7
   f. DATA 50, 60

Answers:
   a. In most systems, the values in DATA statements must be separated by commas.
   b. In most systems, the values must be separated by commas, not semicolons.
   c. The comma after the last value causes an error.
   d. The comma after the word DATA should be omitted.
   e. The DATA statement cannot contain variable names. The correct form is 100   DATA 5, 6, 7
   f. The DATA statement needs a line number.

2.5 What is the value of each variable as determined by the following READ-DATA statements?

```
a. 100    DATA 5, 10, -30.5, .05, 20, 30
   200    READ A, B
   210    READ X, Y
   220    READ P
   230    READ Q
b. 50     READ P, Q, R, S, T
   60     READ M, N
              .
              .
              .
   260    DATA -2, 36, 25.5, -0.002, 55, 6.0, 7.0
c. 10     READ G, H, I, J, K, L, M, N
   100    DATA 5.5, 2.8
   200    DATA 9.1, +3.2
   300    DATA 23.1
   310    DATA -9.5
```

Answers:

```
a. A = 5
   B = 10
   X = -30.5
   Y = .05
   P = 20
   Q = 30
b. P = -2
   Q = 36
   R = 25.5
   S = -0.002
   T = 55
   M = 6
   N = 7
c. G = 5.5
   H = 2.8
   I = 9.1
   J = +3.2
   K = 23.1
   L = -9.5
```

No value is provided for M and N. In this case, the computer prints the error message OUT OF DATA AT LINE 10.

The RESTORE Statement

The READ statement always reads a new value for a new variable. The reason is that whenever a value is read, a pointer marks that value automatically. Of course, when all the data are read, the pointer stays at the end of the data pool. The RESTORE statement allows the pointer to move back to the beginning of the data pool. Thus, the RESTORE statement makes it possible for the computer to read the same set of data again from the beginning. For example, the program

```
10 READ A, B, C
20 PRINT A, B, C
30 RESTORE
40 READ X, Y, Z
50 PRINT X, Y, Z
60 DATA 56.5, 2.3, 5.8, 93.2, 7.8
70 END
```

causes the following output:

```
56.5        2.3         5.8
56.5        2.3         5.8
```

The INPUT Statement

Whenever READ-DATA statements are used in a program, the computer reads the information without waiting. Many times, however, users want to input data on the terminal as a program is running. This capacity makes a program *interactive*; that is, the program pauses and accepts data from the user, directly through the terminal. In BASIC, the INPUT statement allows this interaction.

The form of the INPUT statement is the same as the form of the READ statement, but the difference is that the computer waits for the user to enter the data at the terminal rather than reading them from a DATA statement. Whenever the computer encounters an INPUT statement, the computer interrupts execution, displays a question mark, and waits for the user to input data. The following example demonstrates how INPUT works:

Example 2.14

Problem: Write an interactive program that accepts three numbers and displays the average of the numbers.

Program:
```
100    INPUT X, Y, Z
200    A = (X + Y + Z)/3
300    PRINT "THE AVERAGE OF "; X; Y; Z; " IS: "; A
400    END
```

Notes:

1. When it executes line 100, the computer automatically displays a question mark (?) and pauses until the user types in three numbers. Suppose, for example, the user types the following numbers after the question mark (input prompt) appears.

```
? 86.5, 78.5, 90
```

Immediately, the computer displays

```
THE AVERAGE OF 86.5   78.5   90   IS: 85
```

2. Because the computer displays only a question mark as the prompt, a person using the program may not know what to do in response. A PRINT statement requesting data at the beginning of the program improves the design. For example, the statements

```
90 PRINT "TYPE THREE NUMBERS SEPARATED BY COMMAS"
```

added at the beginning of the program cause the computer to print

```
TYPE THREE NUMBERS SEPARATED BY COMMAS
?
```

In this way, the user will know how to respond to the prompt.

Some BASIC systems allow a string of characters in the INPUT statement; thus the programmer can omit the PRINT statement giving the user instructions. A single line gives instructions and generates the prompt. For example,

```
100 INPUT "WHAT ARE A, B, AND C"; A, B, C
```

will cause this output

```
WHAT ARE A, B, AND C?
```

As before, the program pauses until the user types in the values.

SOME PROGRAMMING TECHNIQUES

Once data are input, and before they are output, normally they must be processed. The hallmark of computers, and their most useful feature, is their ability to process many data quickly and accurately. This section explores some programming techniques for processing data.

Looping

Looping allows a program segment to be repeated automatically many times. For example, if several sets of data are to be processed in the same way, you can use a loop to repeat the statements for each set instead of writing separate program segments for each. Thus, a *loop* is the automatic repetition of a program segment a certain number of times.

Looping is a very common practice in programming. It is simple, yet very important. Looping avoids the necessity of rewriting certain statements in a program. Several looping techniques exist in BASIC, and they will be discussed in Chapter 5. The simplest method of creating a loop is with the GOTO statement.

The GOTO Statement

Normally, a computer executes program statements in line-number order, one after another. The programmer, however, can change the normal sequence of execution by using a GOTO statement. A GOTO statement is called an *unconditional jump* because it can transfer control to any statement in the program at any time: there is no condition to satisfy before the jump is made. For example, a GOTO statement can be used to transfer control to the beginning of a program so that the program processes a new set of data, thereby making a loop. The following example demonstrates this technique:

Example 2.15

Problem: Write a program that reads a set of data consisting of three measurements. Calculate and print the sum of the set. Assume there is more than one set of data, each given by a DATA statement.

Solution Plan:

1. Read the set of data X, Y, Z.
2. Calculate the sum.
3. Print the sum.
4. Go to Step 1 to repeat the process for the next set of data.

Program:

```
100    READ X, Y, Z
200       S = X + Y + Z
300       PRINT "THE SUM OF "; X; Y; Z; " IS: "; S
400    GOTO 100
500    DATA 87.5, 79.5, 90.2
600    DATA 96.7, 98.6, 82.5
700    DATA 76.5, 86.3, 71.5
           .
           .
           .
900    DATA 94.5, 72.3, 82.5
1000   END
```

The printout will be

```
THE SUM OF   87.5   79.5   90.2   IS:   257.2
THE SUM OF   96.7   98.6   82.5   IS:   277.8
THE SUM OF   76.5   86.3   71.5   IS:   234.3
       :
THE SUM OF   94.5   72.3   82.5   IS:   249.3
OUT OF DATA IN LINE 100
```

Notes:

1. At the beginning, the READ statement causes the computer to read the first set of DATA, thus the values are X = 87.5, Y = 79.5, and Z = 90.2. The sum of the first set of data will then be calculated and printed. After the first sum is printed, the statement GOTO 100 transfers control to line 100, the READ statement, and a new set of data is read. Each time the READ statement is executed, the next set of data will be read automatically. Thus, the second time around the loop, the values are X = 96.7, Y = 98.6, and Z = 82.5.
2. The error message OUT OF DATA IN LINE 100 appears because the loop created for reading the data is infinite, and the computer expects an infinite number of values.
3. When a new set of data is read, the previous values of X, Y, and Z are erased.
4. The statements in the loop are indented for readability. Indention does not affect program execution because blank spaces are ignored in a BASIC line.
5. It is important to remember that each time the computer executes the READ statement, it automatically reads a new set of data.

Another use of the GOTO statement is to transfer control from one point in the program to another point in order to skip one or several instructions. This concept is illustrated below; there, a GOTO statement is used to control an infinite loop.

Controlling an Infinite Loop: IF-THEN

There are several ways to create loops in a program. You have seen one of the simplest—a loop created with a GOTO statement. However, the loop created in the previous example is an infinite loop. Of course, infinite loops are not desirable. Programmers need to control infinite loops—to tell the computer to keep repeating steps only until some condition becomes true. One way to do this is to use the conditional statements IF and THEN. Suppose you decide to signal the end of the data for a certain variable by using a predetermined value. For example, you may decide that after all the data for variable A are entered, a zero should signal the computer to get out of the loop. The statement

```
50    IF A = 0 THEN GOTO 100
```

does the job. It transfers control to line 100 if the value of A is equal to zero. This predetermined value is called a *sentinel value*.

IF statements are explained in detail in Chapter 4. However, the simple form of an IF statement shown above is sufficient at this time for terminating a loop. (Be careful when using IF-THEN statements. In some systems, you must drop the word THEN.)

The following example shows how to use IF-THEN and a sentinel value to end a loop:

Example 2.16

Problem: Write a program that calculates and reports the average of two test scores for five students. The data are

90	80
95.5	87.5
85	76.5
79	87.5
72	83

The sentinel value -99 indicates the end of data. Print FINISH at the end of the report.

Solution Plan:

1. Read Test 1, Test 2.
2. If Test 1 = -99, then go to Step 6.
3.   Calculate the average.
4.   Print the information.
5. Go to Step 1.

6. Print FINISH.
7. Give the data.
8. End the program.

Program:

```
10   READ T1, T2
20   IF T1 = -99 THEN GOTO 60
30       A = (T1 + T2)/2
40         PRINT "TEST 1 AND 2 ARE: "; T1; T2,
           "THE AVERAGE = "; A
50   GOTO 10
60   PRINT "FINISHED"
70   DATA 90, 80
80   DATA 95.5, 87.5
90   DATA 85, 76.5
100  DATA 79, 87.5
110  DATA 72, 83
120  DATA -99, 0
130  END
```

The output will be

```
TEST 1 AND 2 ARE 90 80      THE AVERAGE = 85
TEST 1 AND 2 ARE 95.5 87.5  THE AVERAGE = 91.5
    :
FINISHED
```

Note: The READ statement reads two data items. If the first item is -99, the loop ends because control passes to line 60.

String Variables

For some applications, we need to input or output characters or symbols such as names, Social Security numbers, addresses, and so forth. In BASIC, this type of data is called *alphanumeric* or *string data*. Alphanumeric data can contain alphabetic, numeric, or special characters such as dollar signs, periods, and blanks.

Alphanumeric data can have variable names just as numeric data do. However, a dollar sign suffix to the variable name indicates that the variable is alphanumeric. For example:

```
A$   N$   B1$   X$   ANAME$   ADDRESS$
```

are all variables for alphanumeric data. The following simple program shows how the character variable is used:

```
10 READ X$
20 PRINT X$
30 DATA "JOHN DOE BROWNSON"
```

The output will be

```
JOHN DOE BROWNSON
```

Alphanumeric variables are also called string variables. The following rules apply to alphanumeric data:

1. In most systems, a comma or a space separates the data items in DATA statements and in the responses to INPUT statements. The use of quotation marks is optional if the string does not contain a space or a comma. The following are some examples:

    Example 1:

    ```
    10   READ A$, B$
    20   DATA "JOHN", PATTY
    ```

    Example 2:

    ```
    10   PRINT "WHAT IS YOUR NAME"
    20   INPUT A$
    30   PRINT "HI "; A$
    ```

    The response can be either "JOHN" or JOHN.

2. If the data contain commas or spaces, then quotation marks are necessary to mark the beginning and end of the data.

    ```
    10   PRINT "TYPE YOUR ADDRESS"
    20   INPUT A$
    ```

The data must be typed inside quotation marks. For example:

"524 NORTH STREET, NEWARK, CA 96743"

Otherwise, the commas and spaces in the string will create a problem.

3. Alphanumeric data cannot be added or multiplied in a mathematical sense. We can, however, compare them, sort them, and transfer the contents of one variable to another.

4. A character constant may be assigned to a character variable. Here are some examples:

```
10   A$ = "GREAT"
20   G$ = "A"
30   B$ = "        "
100 LET X$ = "MY FIRST RUN"
```

5. If numeric data are stored as characters, they will be treated as characters, not numbers. For example, if

```
10   A$ = "25"
20   B$ = "3"
```

then

```
30   X$ = A$*B$
```

is not valid because 25 and 3 are considered characters in this example, not numerals.

For further examples, look at the following solved problems:

■ Solved Problems

2.6 What is the value of each variable after each of the following READ statements is executed?

a. ```
10   READ P, Q$, R$
200 DATA 3.9, "ROUTE 4", "MT. VERNON"
```

b. ```
10   READ A$, B$, C$
100  DATA "PAY", "MERRY", "4811 EAST DR., MI"
```

c. ```
50   READ Q$, M, G$
60   DATA 5632, 8931, "56 DAYTONA"
```

d. ```
100  READ Q, M$, P$
200  DATA 29, "MAY", JACK
```

e. ```
150 READ G$, H$, X$
200 DATA "   POOR", "   RICH", COLD
```
```

Answers:

a. P = 3.9
   Q$ = "ROUTE 4"
   R$ = "MT. VERNON"
b. A$ = "PAY"
   B$ = "MERRY"
   C$ = "4811 EAST DR., MI"
c. Q$ = "5632" (character)
   M = 8931 (numeric)
   G$ = "56 DAYTONA"
d. Q = 29
   M$ = "MAY"
   P$ = "JACK"
e. G$ = "   POOR"
   H$ = "   RICH"
   X$ = "COLD"

2.7 What is the value of the variables in each of the following statements?

	Statement	Data (Response)
a.	INPUT X$, Z, P	RATE, 9, 36.5
b.	INPUT X$, Y$, P$	ROUT3, MT.PLEASANT, MI
c.	INPUT Q, R$, S$	48, "MT. PLEASANT, MI", USA
d.	INPUT J$, K$	" PARK", CAR

Answers:

a. X$ = "RATE"
   Z = 9
   P = 36.5
b. X$ = "ROUT3"
   Y$ = "MT.PLEASANT"
   P$ = "MI"
c. Q = 48 (numeric)
   R$ = "MT. PLEASANT, MI"
   S$ = "USA"
d. J$ = "   PARK"
   K$ = "CAR"

2.8 Find the errors, if any, in the following statements:

   a. 10   INPUT A$, B$
      20   C$ = A$ * B$
      30   PRINT A$, B$, C$

b. 100 INPUT X, Y$
      200 G = X + Y$
      300 PRINT G, X, Y$
   c. G$ = BAY
   d. LET N$ = "CHUCK NEWCOMER, HAYWARD"
   e. X$ = "200 MILLBROOK", "CA"

Answers:

   a. Alphanumeric data cannot be multiplied in this manner.
   b. Numeric data and alphanumeric data cannot be added.
   c. If BAY is a character constant, it must be enclosed in quotation marks. If BAY is a character variable, it must suffix a dollar sign.
   d. This is correct.
   e. Two character constants cannot be assigned to a single variable.

Generating Sequence Numbers

It is easy to write program statements that generate a series of numbers in a fixed pattern, such as *sequence numbers*. The following example shows the technique:

Example 2.17

Problem: Print the sequence 1, 2, 3, ..., up to 85.

Program:
```
10   N = 0
20   N = N + 1
30       PRINT N
40       IF N = 85 THEN GOTO 60
50   GOTO 20
60   END
```

Notes:

1. The program needs no input data.
2. The initial value of variable N (zero) is assigned at the beginning of the program, outside the loop.
3. Line 20 (N = N + 1) generates numbers 1, 2, 3, and so on. It works as follows: The first time that the program is executed, N

equals 1 (N = 0 + 1), so a 1 is printed. After the 1 is printed, line 50 transfers control back to line 20. The second time around the loop, N equals 2 (N = 1 + 1), and 2 is printed. The third time, N equals 3 (N = 2 + 1), and so on.

4. The loop ends when N equals 85.

The example above illustrates a common technique of generating sequential numbers in a program. The statement N = N + 1 is called a *counter block* because it counts the number of times that the program goes through the loop.

Accumulating Data: Finding the Total

Often, we need to calculate the total of a series of data. It is quite simple to calculate the total of a series of numbers by accumulating the numbers in a program. The following program demonstrates the techniques.

Example 2.18

Problem: Write a program that reads a series of numbers one by one and finds the sum and the average of the numbers. The sentinel value zero indicates end of data. Sample data: 65, 82, 596, 29, 8, 53, 90, 93, 75.5, 82, 93, 91, 25, 0.

Solution Plan:
1. Set the counter N equal to zero.
2. Set the accumulator S equal to zero.
3. Read one item of data: A.
4. If the item is equal to zero go to Step 9.
5.   Add A to the accumulator by: S = S + A.
6.   Add 1 to the counter by: N = N + 1.
7.   Print the data.
8. Go to Step 3.
9. Calculate the average by: G = S/N.
10. Print the information.
11. Give the data.
12. End the program.

Program:

```
10   N = 0
20   S = 0
30   READ A
40     IF A = 0 THEN GOTO 90
50     S = S + A
60     N = N + 1
70     PRINT A
80   GOTO 30
90   G = S/N
100  PRINT "THE SUM IS "; S, "THE AVERAGE IS "; G
110  DATA 65, 82, 596, 29, 8, 53, 90, 93, 75.5, 82
120  DATA 93, 91, 25, 0
130  END
```

Notes:

1. The initial values of S and A (both zero) must be set outside the loop.
2. The statement S = S + A, inside the loop, accumulates the values of A.
   It works this way:

   new S = old S + a new data item (A)

   For example, when the first A is read,

   S_1 = 0 + A_1 or 0 + 65 = 65

   After the second data item is read,

   S_2 = S_1 + A_2 or 65 + 82 = 147

   After the third data item is read,

   S_3 = S_2 + A_3 or 147 + 596 = 743

   The program continues until all the data are read and the total is calculated.
3. N = N + 1 counts the number of data. We need to keep track of the number of data in order to calculate the average at the end.
4. After all the data are read, control passes to statement 90, where the average is calculated and printed. The signal that all data are read is the sentinel value.

Accumulating data in a loop with a statement such as

SUM = SUM + a new number

is a common programming technique. This kind of statement always works if the first sum is set equal to zero before the loop starts. Assigning an initial value to a variable is called *initializing*.

Fortunately, in BASIC all variables are initialized to zero when the program starts. Therefore, if the programmer fails to initialize variables, the program still works. However, to make the program understandable, you should initialize all the variables explicitly at the beginning of a program even though the BASIC system initializes all values to zero. Of course, you must initialize a variable if you want its first value to be other than zero.

A Complete Program

The following examples demonstrate the concepts you have learned in this chapter:

Example 2.19

Problem: Write a program that reads the name of a customer (assume less than 13 characters), the number of units of a product ordered, and the price per unit of the product, for several customers. The word FINISH, used instead of a customer name, indicates the end of data. The following are sample data:

```
JOHN DOE          12       13.99
PAT WILSON        18       15.99
KAY WILLIAMS       7       11.99
     .             .          .
     .             .          .
     .             .          .
FINISH             0          0
```

The program should print a report that shows (a) appropriate headings for the columns; (b) the sequence number, the customer's name, the number of units ordered, the price, and the total amount (price × number of units) for each customer in a report form; and (c) the total amount ordered by all the customers at the end of the report.

Program:

```
10   M = 0
20   S = 0
30   PRINT "SEQ#", "NAME", "UNITS", "PRICE", "TOTAL"
40   PRINT "-----------------------------------------"
40   PRINT
50   READ N$, U, P
60   IF N$ = "FINISH" THEN GOTO 120
70      T = U * P
80      M = M + 1
90      PRINT M, N$, U, P, T
100     S = S + T
110  GOTO 50
120  PRINT
130  PRINT "THE TOTAL ORDER:", S
140  DATA "JOHN DOE", 12, 13.99
150  DATA "PAT WILSON", 18, 15.99
160  DATA "KAY WILLIAMS", 7, 11.99
170  DATA "MAY JACKSON", 10, 20
200  DATA "FINISH", 0, 0
210  END
```

The output will be

SEQ#	NAME	UNITS	PRICE	TOTAL
1	JOHN DOE	12	13.99	167.88
2	PAT WILSON	18	15.99	287.82
3	KAY WILLIAMS	7	11.99	83.93
4	MAY JACKSON	10	20	200
THE TOTAL ORDER:		739.63		

Notes:

1. The loop ends after FINISH is read. Note that FINISH is enclosed in quotes in the IF statement.
2. M = 0 and S = 0 are set before the loop to initialize the counter and the total accumulator.

3. The heading is printed before the loop starts.
4. Each heading is printed separately. Notice that each is shorter than 14 characters so that it will fit in the zone and align with the data.
5. The following PRINT statement is also acceptable to print the headings.

```
10   PRINT "SEQ#    NAME    UNITS    PRICE    TOTAL"
```

An Interactive Program

The BASIC language allows you to write programs that give the illusion of letting you converse directly with the computer. This kind of processing is called *interactive,* and it is made possible by the PRINT and INPUT statements. The following program shows how the program in the previous example can be made interactive:

Example 2.20

Problem: Write an interactive program that accepts the names of customers, number of units ordered, and the price per unit. Print the sequence number, the customer's name, number of units ordered, price, and the total amount of order. If the word FINISH is entered instead of a customer's name, print the total amount for all customers at the end of the output.

Program:

```
10    M = 0
20    S = 0
30    PRINT "******* HI, THIS IS THE COMPUTER...HOW ARE YOU ******"
40    PRINT "I WILL CALCULATE THE TOTAL AMOUNT OF AN ORDER."
50    PRINT "TYPE THE DATA, SEPARATED BY COMMAS."
60    PRINT "WHEN FINISHED, TYPE:    FINISH, 0, 0"
70    PRINT "WHAT IS THE NAME, NO. OF UNITS ORDERED, AND PRICE"
80    INPUT N$, U, P
90    IF N$ = "FINISH" THEN GOTO 150
100       T = U * P
110       M = M + 1
120       PRINT "NO. = "; M; "FOR: "; N$; "NO. OF UNITS: "; U;
125       PRINT " PRICE: "; P; "TOTAL AMOUNT: "; T
130       S = S + T
140       GOTO 70
150   PRINT
160   PRINT "THE TOTAL ORDER: "; S
170   END
```

The first output will be

```
******* HI, THIS IS THE COMPUTER...HOW ARE YOU ******
I WILL CALCULATE THE TOTAL AMOUNT OF AN ORDER
TYPE THE DATA, SEPARATED BY COMMAS
WHEN FINISHED, TYPE:    FINISH, 0, 0
WHAT IS THE NAME,  NO. OF UNITS ORDERED,  AND PRICE
?
```

The user might then input these data:

```
? "JOHN DOE", 12, 13.99
```

Then the computer prints

```
NO. =   1 FOR: JOHN DOE NO. OF UNITS:   12 PRICE: 13.99
TOTAL AMOUNT = 167.88
WHAT IS THE NAME,  NO OF UNITS ORDERED,  AND PRICE
?
```

Notes:

1. The computer displays the input prompt, ?, each time around the loop. The process repeats until the user enters FINISH, 0, 0.
2. The output can be designed differently.

A Game Program

A game program is an interactive program that accepts input and simulates a process. Writing a game program is a good educational project because it is fun. Game programs, however, are normally complicated and require using simulation techniques, many IF statements, and graphics. These are the subject of the following chapters. At this time, however, try keying the following program and running it for a friend's birthday. Your friend may be amazed at the computer's capability!

Example 2.21

Problem: Develop and write an interactive program for a friend's birthday.

Program:

```
10 PRINT "************************************************************"
15 PRINT "~~~~~~~~~~~~~~~~~     H I   ~~~~~~~~~~~~~~~~~~~~~~~~~"
20 PRINT "THIS IS THE COMPUTER TALKING. I HAVE HEARD THAT"
25 PRINT "IT IS YOUR BIRTHDAY, TELL ME YOUR NAME."
30 PRINT "PLEASE TYPE YOUR FIRST NAME, THEN YOUR LAST NAME"
35 PRINT "SEPARATED BY A COMMA. HIT MY RETURN KEY AFTER"
40 PRINT "YOU ARE DONE."
45 INPUT A$, B$
50 PRINT " HI "; B$;" "; A$; " OOPS SORRY, I SHOULD BE SMARTER"
55 PRINT "THAN THAT AND GET YOUR NAME STRAIGHT "; A$; " "; B$
60 PRINT "SORRY FOR GOOFING, I KNOW SO MANY NAMES THAT"
65 PRINT "SOMETIMES IT IS HARD TO KEEP UP."
70 PRINT "ANYWAY "; A$; " HAPPY BIRTHDAY"
75 PRINT "HAPPY BIRTHDAY TO YOU....HAPPY BIRTHDAY TO YOU."
80 PRINT "LET ME GUESS YOUR AGE "; A$
85 PRINT "TO HAVE ME GUESS YOUR AGE, DO THE FOLLOWING"
90 PRINT "MAGIC FORMULA. I AM 10 YEARS OLD, JUST DO THIS"
95 PRINT "1. ADD MY AGE TO YOURS. 2. DIVIDE THE TOTAL BY 2."
100 PRINT "3. SUBTRACT MY AGE FROM IT.  NOW TYPE THE REMAINDER."
105 PRINT"DON'T FORGET TO HIT MY RETURN KEY AFTER YOU ARE THROUGH."
110 PRINT
115 INPUT R
120 Y = R*2 + 10
125 D = Y*365
130 H = D*24
135 PRINT "WELL ";A$;" YOU ARE ";Y;" YEARS OLD, OR ";D;" DAYS OLD"
140 PRINT "YOU WERE BORN "; H; " HOURS AGO "
145 PRINT "********* BYE, COME BACK TO SEE ME SOON ************"
150 END
```

Solved Problems

2.9 Write an interactive program that repeatedly accepts two numbers, then calculates and prints the sum and the product of the two numbers. Terminate the program and print BYE when zeros are entered.

2.10 Write a program that reads the variable K and then calculates the product: $1 \times 2 \times 3 \times 4 \ldots \times K$. Print the sequence numbers and the result of the multiplications at each stage.

2.11 What does the following program do? Is there a flaw in the program?

```
10   N = 0
20   I = 0
30   N = N + 2
40      I = I + N
50   GOTO 30
60   END
```

Answers:

2.9
```
10    PRINT "THIS PROGRAM CALCULATES THE SUM"
20    PRINT "AND THE PRODUCT OF TWO NUMBERS"
30    PRINT "TYPE TWO NUMBERS SEPARATED BY A"
40       PRINT "COMMA, TYPE ZEROS WHEN FINISHED"
50       INPUT A, B
60       IF A = 0 THEN GOTO 120
70       S = A + B
80       P = A*B
90       PRINT "THE NUMBERS ARE: "; A, B
100      PRINT "THE SUM IS: "; S,"THE PRODUCT IS: ";P
110   GOTO 30
120   PRINT "******* BYE *******"
130   END
```

2.10
```
 5    READ K
10    N = 0
20    M = 1
30    N = N + 1
40        M = M*N
50        PRINT "N = "; N, "PRODUCT = "; M
60        IF N = K GOTO 80
70    GOTO 30
75    DATA 9
80    END
```

2.11 The program adds up the even numbers 2, 4, 8, ..., etc. The flaws of the program include the infinite loop as well as the fact that no values are printed.

PROGRAM SPACING

Spaces in the program and in the output that the program generates play an important role in the readability of a program. This section explores some of the basic techniques of controlling the spaces.

Output Spacing

The PRINT statement can control the vertical spacing of a printout. For example, the program

```
10    A = 20
20    B = 30
30    PRINT A
40    PRINT
50    PRINT
60    PRINT B
70    END
```

prints the value of A, skips two lines, and then prints the value of B (on the fourth line).

Commas and Fixed Tabs

Horizontal spacing can be controlled by commas, semicolons, and TAB. PRINT USING, discussed in Chapter 6, also controls spacing. As mentioned earlier, a comma used as a separator in the PRINT statement causes the values to be printed at fixed intervals; that is, in positions 1, 16, 31, 46, 61, and so on. These positions can be considered fixed tabs. Example 2.19 showed how fixed tabs can be used to print a report with headings. The following is another example:

Example 2.22

Problem: Write a program segment that prints INTEREST TABLE starting in column 21 and then headings INVESTMENT, INTEREST, GROSS, and TOTAL on the next line, starting in colums 1, 16, 31, and 46, respectively.

Program Segment:
```
10   PRINT "                    INTEREST TABLE"
20   PRINT
30   PRINT "INVESTMENT, "INTEREST", "GROSS", "TOTAL"
      .
      .
      .
      .
```

The output will be

```
                    INTEREST TABLE
INVESTMENT      INTEREST       GROSS          TOTAL
```

Variable Tabs with the TAB Function

The TAB function in BASIC gives the programmer the ability to specify the exact position at which an item is to be printed. The TAB function is used in a PRINT statement of the form

line no.   PRINT TAB(i_1); item1; TAB(i_2); item2; . . .

where *i* is an argument indicating the starting position of the item to be printed. TAB works much as a typewriter does.

Example 1:
```
10 PRINT TAB(22); "XYZ COMPANY"
```

will print XYZ COMPANY starting at column 22.

Example 2:

    100 PRINT TAB(3); A; TAB(14); B; TAB(39); C

will print the value of A starting at column 3, the value of B starting at column 14, and the value of C starting at column 39.

In Standard BASIC, the argument *i* can be a numeric constant, a variable, or even a mathematical expression. The following is an example:

100 PRINT TAB(5); X; TAB(X); Y; TAB(A + B/C); Z; TAB(I + 1); K

If the argument is an expression, it will be evaluated and converted to an integer before the item is printed.

The TAB function can be also interpreted as controlling the position of the cursor. Thus, PRINT TAB(23); A causes the cursor to move to position 23 and the value of A to be printed there.

Spaces in the Program

In most BASIC systems blank spaces are allowed anywhere in a program line as long as they do not occur within BASIC terms. For example,

    10 P RINT A, B

is not allowed, but

    10   PRINT   X   ,   Y

is valid. To make a program readable, use blank spaces before and after a word or variable and after a line number. Also use spaces to indent a group of related statements, such as statements in a loop.

Multilines per Statement

In some versions of BASIC (such as BASIC-PLUS), a statement can be written in several lines with one line number. In this case, a special character (normally an ampersand) used at the end of the line indicates that the line continues. This feature is important for readability of a program because it allows you to break a long statement into several easy-to-read lines. Assume, for the purposes of this text, that the ampersand (&) indicates that the line continues. Thus

    100 PRINT "X IS EQUAL TO: "; X; "AND Y IS EQUAL: "; Y
    110 END

can be written conveniently as

```
100 PRINT "THE VALUE OF X IS EQUAL TO: "; &
         "AND Y IS EQUAL: "; Y
110 END
```

The following is another example. The line

```
100 IF X$ = "FINISH" THEN &
                    GOTO 999
```

is equivalent to

```
100 IF X$ = "FINISH" THEN GOTO 999
```

When you can use a character to indicate the continuation of a line, you need not use the FEED key or a statement number. It is a good idea to break the line after a comma or a semicolon rather than in the middle of a string in quotation marks.

Multistatements per Line

Some systems allow you to write several statements on one line with a single line number (see Appendix B). For example, in some systems a colon separates independent statements written in one line. Thus

```
10 PRINT X   :   PRINT Y   :   PRINT Z
```

is equivalent to

```
10 PRINT X
20 PRINT Y
30 PRINT Z
```

The following is another example. The line

```
100 N = N + 1   :   PRINT N   :   GOTO 59
```

is equivalent to

```
100 N = N + 1
110 PRINT N
120 GOTO 59
```

The statement separator varies with the system used. For example, in some BASIC systems you use a backslash (\) to separate multiple statements on one line (see Appendix B).

Multistatements should not be used unless the statements are logically related. Use no more than three statements per line. Some programmers do not use multistatements because they make editing difficult.

Multiassignments

Some BASIC systems (see Appendix B) allow you to assign a value to several variables with one statement, for example:

    100 X = Y = Z = 0

However, this is not a standard assignment statement, and some systems may interpret such a statement differently from others.

■ Solved Problems

2.12 Find the errors, if any, in the following statements. Assume the ampersand is the continuation symbol and the colon is the multi-statement symbol.

    a. `100 PRINT "THIS IS THE FINAL &`
                        `RESULT"`

    b. `200                 &`
          `PR              &`
             `INT, X`

    c. `30      LET X = P      &`
                  `+ Q      &`
                  `+ R`
       `40      PRINT X`

    d. `10 IF A = 0 THEN,            &`
                   `GOTO 99`

    e. `100 SUM = SUM + A            &`
        `110   GOTO 69`

    f. `55    IF X$ = "FINISH" THEN    &`
        `65            GOTO 99`

    g.
```
          .
          .
          .
     100 PRINT "A = "; A    : &
         PRINT "B = "; B    : &
         PRINT "C = "; C    : &
     110 END
```

    h. `50    S = S + A : 60 PRINT S`

    i. `10    IF X$ = "FINISH" THEN  :`
                            `GOTO 96`

Answers:

a. The statement is not incorrect, but it is not good practice to split a string of characters with the continuation symbol.
b. Splitting the word PRINT causes an error.
c. This is correct if the system allows the ampersand as a continuation character.
d. The comma causes an error.
e. The ampersand is not needed.
f. The line number "65" is not needed.
g. This is correct. Note that line 100 consists of three statements in three physical lines.
h. The second statement does not need a statement number (60 should be omitted).
i. A continuation character is needed in the first line instead of the colon.

EXERCISES

2.1 Find the errors in the following statements.

```
a.  10   A = $3600
b.  30   X = 36,000
c.  40   PRINT A B C
d.  15   PRINT; X; Y; Z
e.  50   LET A + B = C
f.  100  READ, A, P, Q
g.  90   DATA 50, 60, 90
h.  10   DATA: 5, 90, 53.5
i.  55   INPUT X Y Z
j.  65   IMPUT I, J, K
k.  100  GOTO READ
l.  50   A = "X=DOLLARS"
m.  90   N$ = PINE STREET
```

2.2 Explain the print position of each of the items in the following print statements:

a.
```
100   PRINT A, B, C
110   PRINT A; B; C
120   PRINT A, B; C
130   PRINT A; B, C
```

b.
```
100   PRINT "THE VALUE OF THE Q IS:", Q
110   PRINT "THE VALUE OF THE Q IS: "; Q
```

c.
```
100   PRINT P, Q, Z
110   PRINT TAB(1); P; TAB(16); Q; TAB(31); Z
```

d.
```
100   PRINT TAB(25); "COEFFICIENT TABLE"
110   PRINT
120   PRINT TAB(7); "E"; TAB(17); "F"; TAB(27); "G"
130   PRINT TAB(4); E; TAB(14); F; TAB(24); G
```

e. `100   PRINT TAB(12); X; Y, Z`

f. `100   PRINT A; B; TAB(27); C, D`

Programming Exercises:

Write a complete BASIC program for each of the following problems; include appropriate headings and descriptions for each. Use either a READ or INPUT statement, unless otherwise specified. Assume more than one set of data for each. If the data are not provided, make up your own.

2.3 Write a program that calculates and prints the sum, the average, and the product of a set of data. Each set consists of three numbers. The last set contains zeros, indicating the end of data. Test the program with the following data:

56	25	30
10	8	23
5	9	8
12	51	32
100	10	50
0	0	0

2.4 Write a program that prints the odd numbers 1, 3, 5, 7, . . . , up to 99.

2.5 Write a program that calculates and prints the sum of the numbers 1, 2, 3, 4, . . . , up to 99.

2.6 Write a program that reads the values of variables M and N (M smaller than N) and calculates the product of the numbers from M up to N;

that is, M × (M+1) × (M+2) × , , , × (N-1) × N. (Keep the values small, because the result of multiplication can become very large.)

2.7 Write a program that calculates the sum of the even numbers from 6 to 52.

2.8 Write a program that prints the sequence numbers 1 to 20 on one line.

2.9 An instructor would like to calculate the average of students' test scores. Write an interactive program that accepts the test scores, one by one, and prints the grand average after -99 is entered as the last test score.

2.10 Celsius temperature (C) can be calculated by $C = (5/9)(F-32)$, where F is the temperature in degrees Fahrenheit. Write an interactive program that accepts a Fahrenheit temperature and calculates and prints the equivalent temperature in Celsius. Terminate the program if -999 is entered.

2.11 Write an interactive program that asks for a customer's name, the number of units of a product ordered, and the unit price of the product. The sales tax is 4 percent of the gross sales. Calculate the gross sales for the item and the total charge (sales plus tax) for the customer. Print the customer's name, number of units ordered, price, gross sales, and total charge. Print the total of all gross sales when FINISH is entered as the customer's name.

2.12 Write an interactive program that asks for the name of a student and for that student's scores on two tests. Calculate the average of the two scores and print the information. Print the average of all students after FINISH is entered as a name.

2.13 If A dollars are invested at an annual interest rate of R (decimal), after N years the total amount of money compounded (TOT) can be calculated by

$TOT = A(1 + R)^N$

Write a program that calculates the total amount for each of the following data lines.

Amount	Interest Rate	Years
55.5	.05	5
565.5	.10	10
6960.0	.12	7
25.0	.04	20
100.0	.08	15
0.0	0.0	0

2.14 A classical programming example is the so-called Manhattan problem. In 1627, Manhattan Island was bought for $24. Write a simple program to calculate how much the $24 would be worth today if it had been placed in a savings account at the following annual interest rates

5%, 6%, 7%, 8%, 9%, 10%

Use the formula in the previous problem.

2.15 Write a complete program that calculates T from the formula

$$T = (U + V + W) \times (U - V) \times (U - W) \times (V - W)$$

2.16 The velocity (V) and the distance (X) traveled by an object are given by the formulas

$X = 1/2 \; at^2$
$V = at$

where a is the constant acceleration and t is the time in seconds. Write an interactive program which asks for a, and t, and prints a, t, X, and V.

2.17 Write a program for the following problem. Given are the data for several customers of a gas company. Each line contains the following information: customer's name, last meter reading, and current meter reading. The last line contains FINISH, 0, 0. Your program should:

a. Calculate amount of gas used.

b. Calculate cost at 23.5 per unit.

c. Print a report showing the sequence numbers, the customer's name, last meter reading, current meter reading, amount of gas used, and the cost for each customer.

d. Calculate the total gas used for all customers and the total cost to all users and print them at the end of the report. Use the following data to test the program.

```
PAT WHITESON    32983    33151
BILL HANSON     92182    92798
ROBIN ABBOTT    10329    10482
JOHN PARKER      9283    10001
MATT WILSON      0000      308
JOHN PAULSON     6789     6799
FINISH              0        0
```

2.18 Write a program to calculate kinetic energy (T) as

$$T = (1/2)PV^2$$

where P (mass) and V (velocity) are given as input.

2.19 An annuity in which the yearly payment at the end of each of N years is P has a present value of

$$T = P \times \frac{1 - (1 + R)^{-N}}{R}$$

where R is the annual interest rate (decimal). Write an interactive program that keeps asking for P, R, and N; calculates T; and prints the information.

Games:

2.20 Write a program that uses several PRINT statements to draw a kite on the screen. Make the length of the kite almost equal to the size of the screen. Then use a GOTO statement to transfer control to the beginning of the program. When you run this program, the kite should appear to fly on screen. The object of the game is to stop the kite so that the entire kite stays on the screen. (Find out what key to press to stop a running program. On some computers, the BREAK key interrupts a program; on others you must press CONTROL and S. See also Appendix B.) You may vary the program by drawing a rocket, airplane, planet, spaceship, several balloons, or several birds.

2.21 Develop a conversational program that asks a question, accepts a response, or tells a riddle or joke. For example, the program might ask

```
"WHAT IS BLACK AND WHITE AND RED ALL OVER?"
```

After accepting the response (R$), the terminal might display

```
"NO IT IS NOT "; R$; ".  IT IS A NEWSPAPER."
```

SUMMARY

You have learned:

1. In BASIC, a constant is a quantity that does not change; 53 is a numeric constant, and "YOUR TEST SCORE IS: " is a string constant. String constants must appear in quotation marks.
2. The PRINT statement can be used to print constants as well as the values of variables and expressions. An example of a PRINT statement is

```
10 PRINT "THE VALUE OF A IS "; A; "ITS SQUARE IS: "; A * A
```

3. When a comma is used as a separator in a PRINT statement, the values are printed at fixed intervals, in zones of about 15 spaces. When a semicolon is used as a separator in a PRINT statement, numeric values are printed with one space between them and string values are printed with no spaces between them.

4. The READ-DATA statements can be used to read values for variables. An example is

   ```
   10 READ A, B, C, D
   20 DATA 85.5, 30, 58.0, 3
   ```

5. The INPUT statement makes a program interactive. An example is

   ```
   10 INPUT X, Y, Z
   ```

   When the computer encounters an INPUT statement in a program, the computer displays a question mark and waits for the user to enter the values of the variables on the terminal.

6. A string variable can contain characters rather than a numeric value. A dollar sign suffix to a variable name indicates a string variable; for instance, A$. In summary, each variable has a name, a type, and a value. For example:

Name	Type	Value
A$	String	"CAT"
X	Numeric	3.12

7. Looping is a program structure used to repeat a program segment several times.

8. A GOTO statement is used for unconditional branching. It may be used for looping.

9. We can count the number of times that a loop is executed or generate sequence numbers in a program by using a statement of the form N = N + 1 in a loop.

10. We can accumulate the data in a loop by using a statement of the form SUM = SUM + A.

11. The TAB function, used with a numeric argument in a PRINT statement, causes values to be printed at the column named in the argument. The following is an example:

    ```
    PRINT TAB(31); "THE NAME IS: "; TAB(47); N$
    ```

    THE NAME IS will appear starting at column 31; the value of N$, at column 47.

REVIEW QUESTIONS/SELF-TEST

2.1 Which of the following statement is not correct?
```
a.   5    DATA X = 5, U1 = 10, J = "JOHN"
b.  50    READ X, U1, J$, K, L9
c.  95    INPUT U, P
d.  65    PRINT "X IS NOT", Y; "TRUE X IS "; TAB(I); X
e. 105    LET F = F + 5
```

2.2 What is the value of each variable in the following program?
```
10    READ X, Y
20    READ P, Q, R$
        .
        .
        .
200   DATA 53, 908, 32
210   DATA 5
220   DATA "MAIN STREET, CONN."
300   END
```

2.3 What is wrong with the following program?
```
 5   C = A + B
10   READ A, B
20   Q = 2*(A + B)/C
30   PRIT "A= " A "B= " B "C= " C "Q= " Q
40   END
```

2.4 Write an interactive program that asks the name and the age of the user. The program then prints the name of the person and his or her age in minutes. Use a loop so that the program keeps accepting data until FINISHED is entered instead of a name.

Answers:

2.1 Only a is not correct.

2.2
```
X = 53
Y = 908
P = 32
Q = 5
R$ = MAIN STREET, CONN.
```

2.3 The program has three errors. First, the READ statement must appear before line 5, because in its current position line 5 uses variables awaiting definition from the READ statement. Second, the program is missing a DATA statement. Third, PRINT must be spelled correctly. Also, the values in the PRINT statement need commas or semicolons, in some systems.

2.4
```
10 PRINT "HI, WHAT IS YOUR NAME"
20    INPUT A$
30    IF A$ = "FINISHED" GO TO 90
40    PRINT "HOW OLD ARE YOU "; A$
50    INPUT Y
60    X = Y * 365 * 60 * 24
70    PRINT A$; " YOU ARE "; X; " MINUTES OLD"
80 GOTO 10
90 END
```

Program Development and Structured Programming

3

In This Chapter:

Compilation
Compiler
Interpreter
Versions of BASIC
BASIC Statements

Error Detection
Syntax Errors
Execution Errors
Logical Errors
How to Debug a Program

Program Planning
Algorithms
Programming Tools
Programming Cycle

Writing Structured Programs
Sequence Structure
Selection Structure
Iteration Structure

How to Write a Structured Program
Structured Design
Readability
Reliability
Documentation

A Case—Printing a Report
Step 1: The Problem
Step 2: Input-Output Design
Step 3: Process Design
Step 4: Coding
Step 5: Running, Testing, and Debugging
Step 6: Documentation

Exercises

Summary

Review Questions/Self-Test

3

Program Development and Structured Programming

In the previous chapters, we discussed fundamental programming concepts in BASIC. By now, you should be able to write a simple BASIC program. However, to write an effective program to solve a specific problem, you must first develop an appropriate solution method and adopt a suitable programming technique. In this chapter, we take a look at the development process. In particular, you will learn:

- How English words in your program are translated for the computer
- What kinds of errors a program may have
- What tools to use when planning a program
- How a program should be planned
- How to use structured programming techniques to write better programs

COMPILATION

In this section we introduce some terminology with which you should be familiar. After reading this section, you should be able to define the following:

machine language
higher-level language
compiler
compilation
interpreter

machine-independent language
source program
object program
execution

Compiler

Each computer is designed to recognize special instruction codes. These codes can be executed only if they are in some predetermined numeric code. Instructions written in such a way are said to be in machine language. *Machine language is a series of instructions in numeric code that a computer can interpret.*

Machine languages are machine dependent. That is, a program written for one model cannot be processed by another model. Writing a program in machine language is extremely difficult and time-consuming.

However, higher-level languages allow programmers to write programs without knowing machine language. Such languages are machine independent and easy to learn. There are many higher-level languages currently in use. BASIC is one of them. It is somewhat like English, easy to learn, and general enough to handle a variety of problems. Also, it can be used on almost any computer.

You may be wondering how a computer can understand a higher-level language such as BASIC. The *source program* (the original program) is translated for the machine by a special program called the *compiler*. Thus, *compilation* is the process of translating a source program into a form that the computer can carry out.

The translated source program, which now is stated as a series of numeric codes the computer can interpret, is called the *object program*. The translator (the compiler) works without human intervention (see Figure 3.1). BASIC—or any higher-level language—is thus a *machine-independent* language because it does not have to be written for a specific computer model.

A successful program may be done in one run, but, normally, a program goes through a computer a couple of times (Figure 3.2).

1. The source program is translated, errors are identified, appropriate storage is allocated for the variables, and the machine code is produced.
2. If the program does not have serious problems, the object program goes through the computer to be executed; that is, the instructions are carried out.

Interpreter

A compiler translates an entire program. However, both translation into machine language and execution can be done line by line. This method of translation is very useful for programs that are run in an interactive environment because a user can quickly receive the response for each

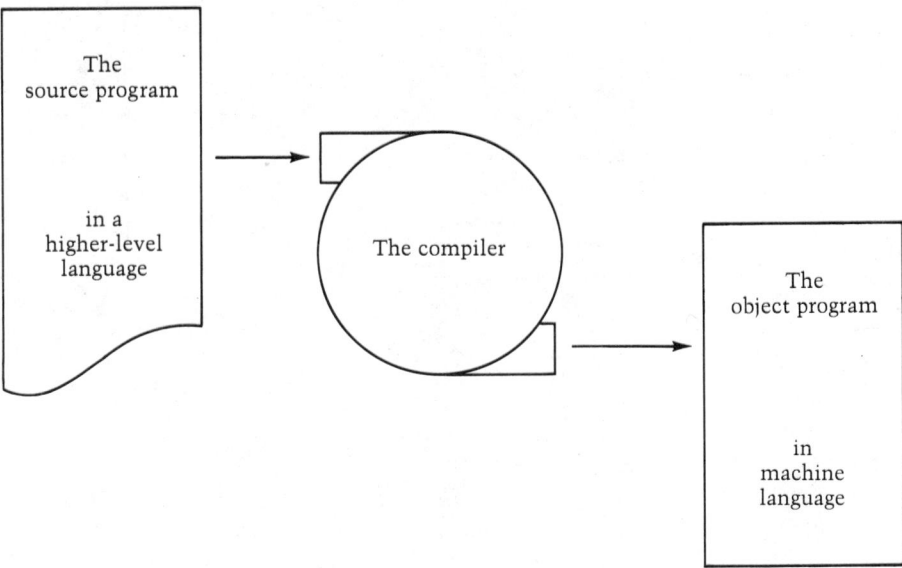

Figure 3.1 The compiler

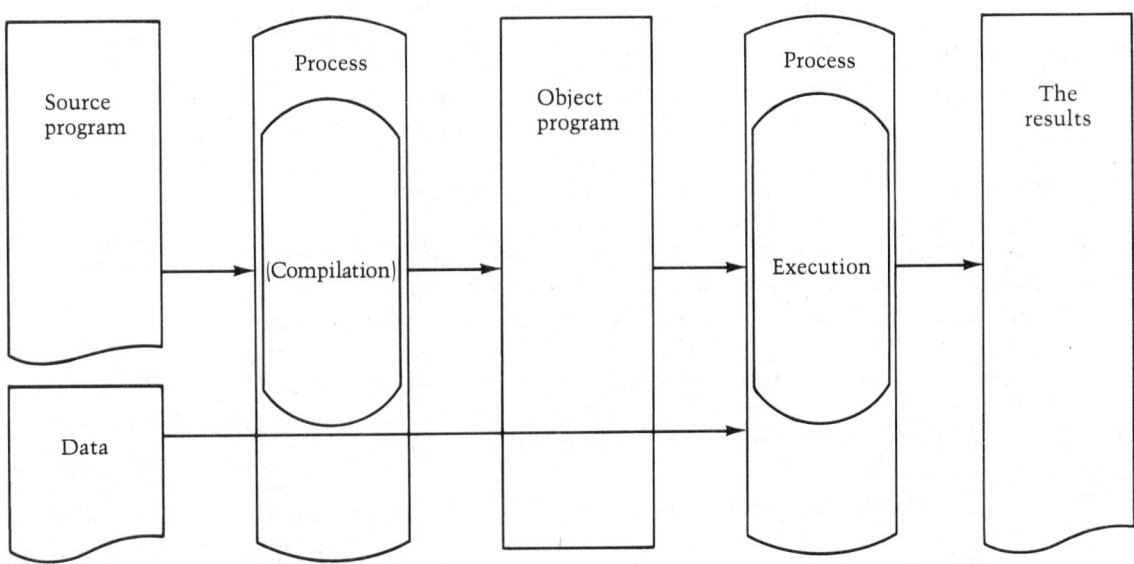

Figure 3.2 Compilation and execution

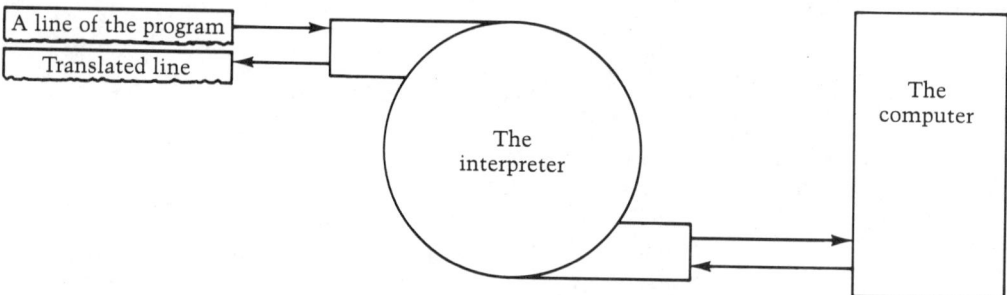

Figure 3.3 The interpreter

line. This is done with most BASIC programs, and the translator in this case is called the *interpreter* (See Figure 3.3). *An interpreter is a program that translates and causes execution of a program on a line-by-line basis.*

The precise interpretation process can not be generalized because it is complex and varies with the system being used. Some systems do no translation until the RUN command is given, while others may do partial translation and give error messages immediately after a line is typed.

Versions of BASIC

As you have learned, you need a BASIC compiler, or more commonly a BASIC interpreter, to run a BASIC program. BASIC was one of the first higher-level languages to be widely used. The first version of BASIC was developed in the early 1960s. Since then it has undergone many changes, improvements, and modifications. Although different versions of BASIC have many common characteristics, they may be rather different because of add-on features and other modifications. Furthermore, different computer manufacturers have developed their own versions of BASIC. Each such version has its own unique features and name. MBASIC, APPLE-BASIC, TRS-80 DOS BASIC, BASIC-PLUS, BASIC-PLUS-2, and BASIC-PLUS-EXTENDED are some versions of BASIC. For example, one of the features of the BASIC-PLUS-EXTENDED and BASIC-PLUS-2 is that a variable name can have from 1 to 30 characters—letters, digits, or embedded periods—the first of which must be a letter. Thus LAST.NAME, SOCIAL.SECURITY.NUMBER, A1, and SR are all valid variable names in these versions of BASIC.

Fortunately, the add-on features have been, for the most part, quite similar. Thus, after learning the principles, you will not have difficulties writing a BASIC program for any computer or converting from one version to another.

BASIC Statements

Some BASIC statements instruct the computer to carry out a specific task. For example, a READ statement causes the computer to read the data from the data section. Such statements are called *executable statements*.

Some statements, however, provide supportive information for the program and do not cause a task to be performed. For example, a DATA statement furnishes data for a READ statement. These statements are *nonexecutable*. Such nonexecutable statements do not result in machine instructions by the interpreter, whereas executable statements result in some kind of machine instruction.

Executable statements build the logical sequence of a program. By changing the order of an executable statement, you may change the entire program. But nonexecutable statements do not influence the logic of a program. Some of them—including DATA—may be placed anywhere in the program without affecting the logic of the program. Yet, the order of some nonexecutable statements is important. We will discuss the purpose and order of many kinds of nonexecutable statements as we progress.

ERROR DETECTION

After keying the BASIC statements into a terminal, you tell the computer to execute the program by typing the RUN command. If you have used the proper control statements, and if the program is correct, the output will be displayed as specified. A program, however, may have to be corrected and rerun several times before it is completely correct. Detecting and removing the errors (bugs) from a program is called *debugging*. Debugging is an important part of the programming process.

A program may have three types of errors:

1. Syntax errors
2. Execution errors
3. Logical errors

Syntax Errors

A syntax error is a grammatical error. (Syntax is the branch of grammar that deals with the interrelationship and order of words and phrases.) Remember that a language follows a series of grammatical rules. When you make a grammatical error in a statement, the interpreter cannot figure out what that statement is, only that there is an error. Some typical syntax errors are misspelling a key word; leaving out a key character, such as a separator; or typing an invalid constant, such as a number with a comma.

The interpreter detects syntax errors before execution. The computer does not correct any such error; instead the computer prints an error message when it detects the error. These messages, although not always straightforward, help you identify the errors and their location in the program. The form of the message also varies with the interpreter being used. Some interpreters print clearer messages than others, and some print only a question mark when an error is encountered.

Look at the following solved problems for examples of syntax errors:

■ **Solved Problems**

3.1 Find the syntax errors in the following statements. Can you guess what kind of message will be printed for each error?
   a. 100   A = 100,000
   b. X = P*.05
   c. 10   PRINT A B C D
   d. 10   X = 2(A+B)
   e. 100   Q = (A+B) (C-D)
   f. 100   X = $100.00
   g. 10   REED X, Y
   h. 100   (A+B) = C
   i. 100   THIS IS A COMMENT

   Answers:
   a. ILLEGAL NUMBER. Commas are not allowed in numeric constants.
   b. MISSING LINE NO. Line numbers are required except in immediate mode.
   c. ILLEGAL STATEMENT. Some systems require a comma as a separator; in others, this statement is correct.
   d. ILLEGAL STATEMENT. The arithmetic operator after 2 is missing.
   e. ILLEGAL EXPRESSION AT LINE 100. The arithmetic operator is missing.
   f. ILLEGAL NUMBER. Dollar signs are not allowed in numeric constants.
   g. ILLEGAL STATEMENT. READ is misspelled.

> **h.** `ILLEGAL STATEMENT.` The left side of an assignment statement cannot be an expression.
>
> **i.** `ILLEGAL STATEMENT.` This is not a BASIC statement.

Note: Some new BASIC compilers do not require line numbers.

Execution Errors

Unlike syntax errors, execution errors are detected during the execution of a program. Execution or run-time errors occur during the run of a program because of some mistake in programming. For instance, the infinite loop in the program segment below has an execution error:

```
10   N = N + 1
20      X = X + N
30   GOTO 10
```

If the above program segment is run on a large computer, the computer stops executing the program because of the limited computer time that is assigned to a user, and error codes will be printed. But in a microcomputer, the program runs infinitely, the cursor blinks, and nothing is displayed or printed.

It is more difficult to detect and locate an execution error than a syntax error. Often, execution errors are caused by logical errors.

Logical Errors

Logical errors exist when the program output is incorrect. Such a program contains no syntax errors and may run without execution errors. A logical error may be due to an omitted or misplaced statement or to an incorrectly specified action. For example, if a program does not print the desired output, it is possible that the appropriate `PRINT` statement is missing or that the appropriate variable is not included in the `PRINT` statement. The logical error can also be due to incorrect specification, incorrect design, or incorrect procedure. For example, if the average of three variables is calculated by

```
AVG = X + Y + Z/3
```

the result will not be correct because the expression is incorrect. The formula should be corrected to read

```
AVG = (X + Y + Z)/3
```

Some logical errors are easy to find, but others are not. If the printout, for instance, shows that the floor area of a room is a negative number, you know right away that something is wrong either with the calculations or the input data. If the program listing is correct and there is no execution error, but there is no output, the PRINT statements may be incorrect. Other logical errors are difficult to diagnose and correct. The computer may detect syntax (and sometimes execution errors), but it cannot detect logical errors, because a computer cannot understand the logical sequence of your program.

How to Debug a Program

Debugging a program can be challenging, rewarding, and sometimes frustrating. The first step is to find out whether the error is a syntax, execution, or logical error. Syntax errors are detected and corrected first. Detecting syntax errors is easy because the computer prints a message for a syntax error, and some of the errors are obvious. For example, it is very common to misspell a key word. Obviously, a misspelled key word is not an instruction the computer understands. Common syntax errors are:

1. Using a reserved word as a variable name
2. Misspelling key words (typographical errors)
3. Making variable names too long (more than the allowable number of characters)
4. Starting statements without a line number (except commands or statements in the immediate mode; also, some of the new compilers do not require a line number)
5. Omitting the left or right parenthesis in a pair
6. Omitting a necessary comma or semicolon, or using commas and spaces incorrectly
7. Typing a letter o instead of a zero, or a 1 instead of the letter l, and vice versa

Logical errors (and execution errors due to logical errors) are not always easy to detect. Finding them is time consuming and requires a lot of patience.

Basically, there are three methods of detecting errors: (1) using a structured walk-through, (2) tracing values, and (3) using the trace facilities of the system.

Structured Walk-Through

A structured walk-through is a review of the program step by step, line by line, and variable by variable. Using boxes to represent values and jotting down the values with a pencil is a great help. Most errors can be detected with this simple technique, which is used even by skilled programmers for simple or complex problems. The technique is very effective when the reviewer plays the role of the (very dumb) computer as it carries out the instructions.

Tracing Values

You can use a PRINT statement temporarily, such as

```
10   PRINT "A = "; A; "B = "; B
```

to trace the values of the variables in different parts of a program, especially when the values are critical. If the values are unexpected, you get an immediate clue about the error. You can also trace with a PRINT statement in the immediate mode. This technique allows you to find out what values are stored in memory for each variable. For example, consider this program.

```
10   READ A, B
20   X = A + B
30   PRINT A, B, S
40   DATA 10, 20
50   END
```

This program will display

```
10              20              0
```

The programmer probably does not expect this output. He or she can double-check the values after the program is executed by typing

```
PRINT A, B, X
```

The programmer will probably notice that the appropriate variable does not appear in the PRINT statement in line 30 (S is used instead of X).

Another useful technique for tracing the values is using the STOP and then CONT (continue) statements. The STOP statement in a program causes execution to stop, and CONT in the immediate mode causes execution to continue. For example, when you run the program

```
10   READ A , B
20   X = A + B
30   STOP
40   PRINT A , B , S
50   DATA 10 , 20
60   END
```

execution stops when the computer encounters line 30. The programmer then can check the values by using a PRINT statement in an immediate mode, such as

```
PRINT A , B , X
```

The program can be modified, if necessary. Then, if CONT is typed, the program continues. Of course, this simple five-line program does not show the value of using STOP-CONT statements for debugging. But if a program is complicated, this method is of great help.

Extra PRINT statements let you trace not only the changing values of the key variables, but also the flow of the execution. For example, if you run the program

```
5    PRINT "POINT 1, BEFORE THE LOOP"
10   Y = 10
20       S = X + Y
30   GOTO 10
40   PRINT "POINT 2, AFTER THE LOOP"
```

the output will be

```
POINT 1, BEFORE THE LOOP
```

The computer will never reach line 40 and print the message POINT 2, AFTER THE LOOP.

Tracing values with several temporary PRINT statements throughout the program helps you find most of the problems. Of course, all the extra PRINT statements can be dropped after the errors are found for the final copy of the program.

Trace or Dump Facilities

Most systems have an automatic trace facility that traces the flow of (and sometimes the values in) the program during execution. To activate the facility, you must include a special command in the program (or use that command in the immediate mode). When the trace facility is "on," the computer prints the line numbers as they are executed. The sequence of line numbers represents the flow of the program, and unexpected patterns in execution sequence give clues as to errors. For example, suppose the term TRON activates the facility and the term TROFF deactivates the facility in a system. If you run the program

```
5   TRON
10  Y = 10
20  S = X + Y
30  GOTO 10
40  PRINT S
50  TROFF
```

the output will be

```
[5] [10] [20] [30] [10] [20] [30] [10] [20] [30]
[10] [20] [30] . . .
```

As you see, the pattern [10] [20] [30] is repeated infinitely, so the trace indicates that the program contains an infinite loop. The trace facility features, the exact form of the trace statement (TRON in this case), and the information displayed on the screen during a trace are all system dependent. See appendix B.

PROGRAM PLANNING

Writing the BASIC statements that form a program is called *coding*. Certainly, before coding, the programmer must understand the problem, decide about the necessary output and input, and develop a detailed solution procedure—an algorithm.

Algorithms

An *algorithm* is a detailed set of solution procedures suitable for computer programming. Most of the time, developing an algorithm requires ample thought, research, and time. Each step of an algorithm will eventually be performed by BASIC statements. The following is an algorithm for finding whether an integer is even or odd:

1. Start.
2.   Read a number, K.
3.   Find the integer of K divided by 2.
4.   Find the remainder, R.
5.   If R = 0 then
           K is even
      Else
           K is odd
6. End.

A well-developed algorithm must be:

1. Sufficiently detailed to allow programming
2. Concise
3. Unambiguous
4. Flexible
5. Effective in solving the specified problem
6. Efficient in terms of resource usage

These characteristics are illustrated by the following algorithm for adding a series of data.

1. Start; identify a variable, SUM, which will accumulate the answer; set SUM equal to zero.
2. Read the number of data, N.
3. Repeat the following steps, N times:
      3.1 Read an item of data.
      3.2 Accumulate the data in SUM.
      3.3 Print the data item.
4. Print the accumulated data, the SUM.

    This algorithm is detailed enough to be coded as a program. It is unambiguous. It is flexible because it can handle a range of input data rather than solving for a specific set of data. The algorithm is effective because it provides an answer to the problem in a few steps.

    The efficiency of an algorithm depends on the total resources used for developing and implementing the algorithm—computer time and storage as well as human resources. The next section discusses tools for developing effective algorithms.

Programming Tools

Any program requires careful planning of the output, input, and solution procedure before BASIC statements are actually written. The print chart and screen chart are two useful tools for designing the output and input of a problem. Flowcharts, hierarchy charts, pseudocode, and logic charts are some tools for designing the solution procedure of the program from input to output.

These tools are used in the first step of writing a program. They serve several purposes:

1. They facilitate the development of the algorithm.
2. They make it easy to visualize the solution procedure.
3. They are a guide to actual programming.
4. They document the input, output, and logic of the program.
5. They facilitate communication among those involved in programming.

Print Charts

The output of a program should be designed so that the person using it can acquire information from the output easily. It should be simple, descriptive, straightforward, and readable. Each item should be sufficiently described, and the relationship between the items should be clear. If the output is a report, it typically includes (1) titles, (2) column headings, (3) detailed data lines, and (4) footings, which are the summary or totals.

A *print chart*, also called a printer spacing chart, is a preprinted, lined form used to design the output of a program. The form allows you to determine the exact location of each item of information, the centering of headings, the required spaces between columns, and other necessary information about a desired output. This information is necessary for writing the PRINT statements. Figure 3.4 shows a sample print chart.

When designing the output, you should be aware of the number of spaces allowed on a line. For example, if one line on the video terminal will equal a line of output, the maximum number of spaces available is normally 80, but some monitors allow only 40 characters per line.

The maximum number of spaces on a printer line is between 72 and 200, depending on the printer, but usually it is 80, 120, 132, 136, or 160. We assume in this text that the monitor allows up to 80 characters, and the printer allows at least 80 characters per printed line.

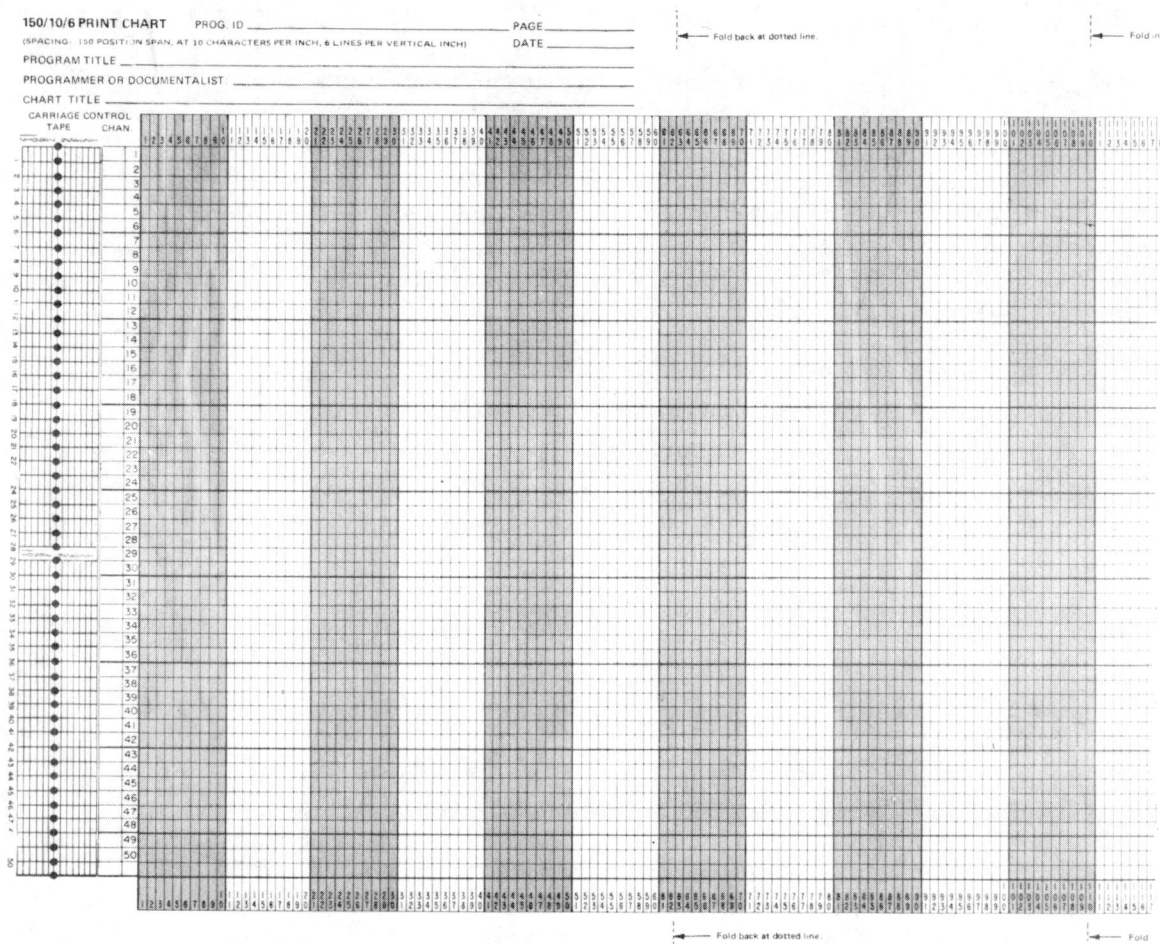

Figure 3.4 A typical print chart

Screen Charts

BASIC is an interactive language, and most of the outputs are displayed on the screen. Like printed outputs, screen output should be designed carefully. A screen chart is a preprinted, lined form used to design the information on the screen. The difference between a print chart and a screen chart is that the print chart is larger. Most screens are up to 80 columns wide and 24 lines long. Figure 3.5 shows a sample screen chart.

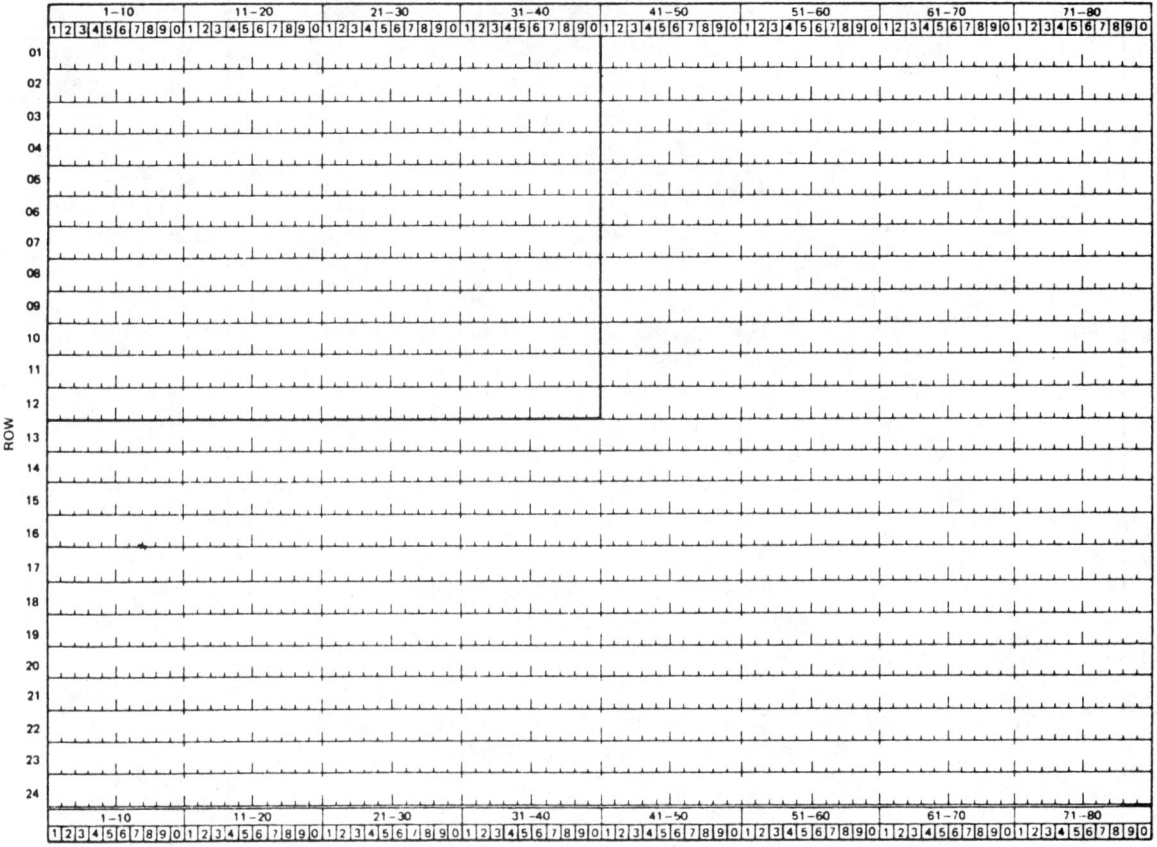

Figure 3.5 A typical screen chart

The screen chart is also important for input design, since the data are mostly input through the video terminal.

Flowcharts

A flowchart is an easy-to-read diagram of a program. It is a pictorial presentation of the steps in solving a problem. Each step, represented by a symbol, indicates a necessary action. The sequence of the steps is shown by arrows. The most important symbols used in flowcharts are shown in Figure 3.6.

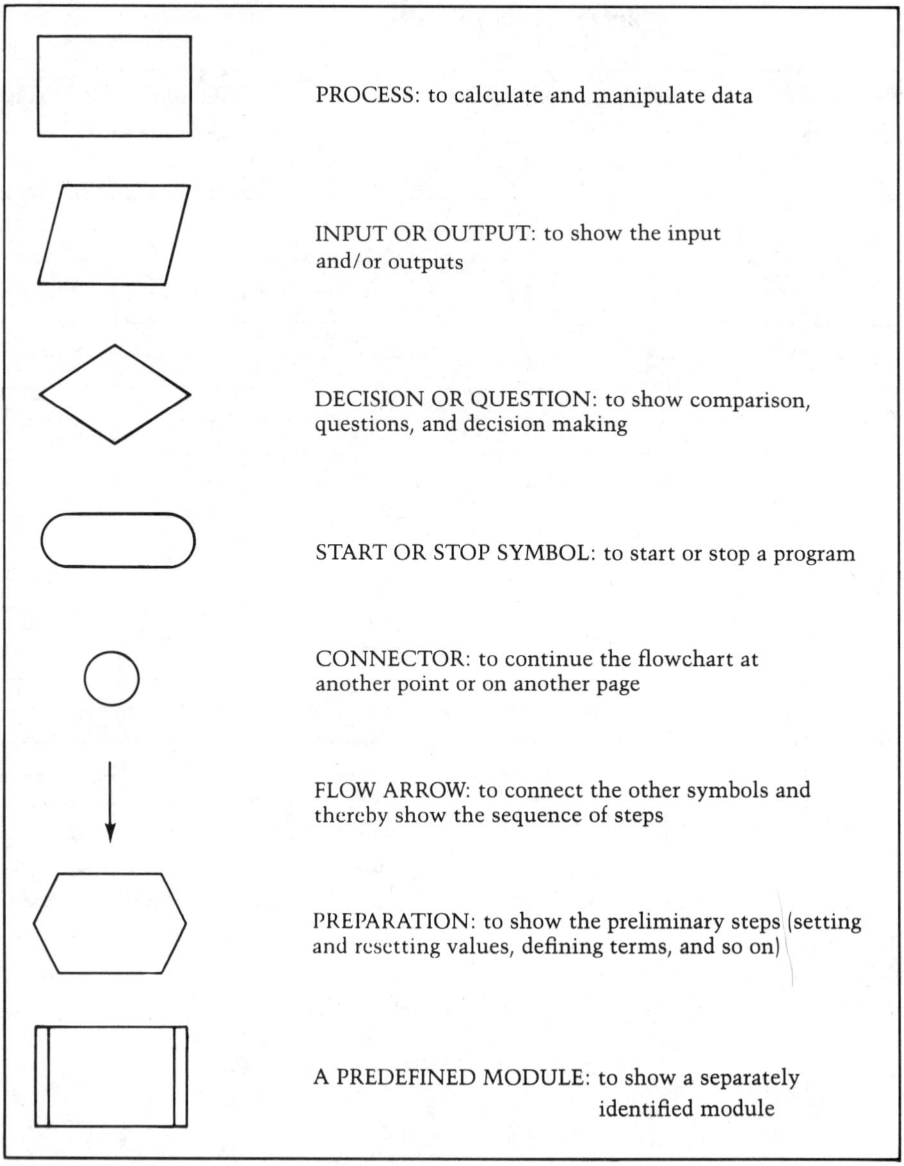

PROCESS: to calculate and manipulate data

INPUT OR OUTPUT: to show the input and/or outputs

DECISION OR QUESTION: to show comparison, questions, and decision making

START OR STOP SYMBOL: to start or stop a program

CONNECTOR: to continue the flowchart at another point or on another page

FLOW ARROW: to connect the other symbols and thereby show the sequence of steps

PREPARATION: to show the preliminary steps (setting and resetting values, defining terms, and so on)

A PREDEFINED MODULE: to show a separately identified module

Figure 3.6 Common flowchart symbols

The following examples demonstrate the use of a flowchart: The flowchart in Figure 3.7 shows how to find the floor area of a room. The inputs are two variables: length and width. The area is calculated by multiplying them. The output is length, width, and area.

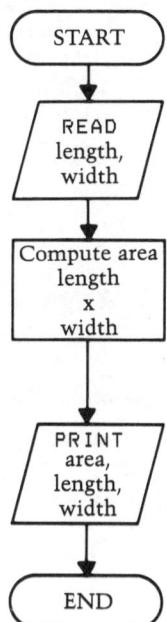

Figure 3.7 A simple flowchart

The flowchart in Figure 3.8 shows how to find the floor area of a room if there is more than one set of data, how to stop the loop, and how to print the heading.

These two examples are simplified flowcharts. You will see more examples of flowcharts throughout this text.

Flowcharting seems to be a time-consuming process; nevertheless, it is a very useful problem-solving tool. Some of the advantages of flowcharts are as follows:

1. Flowcharts are plans for solving problems.
2. They make it easy to code a program.
3. They are useful for finding logical errors.
4. They document how the program should work.
5. They are a medium of communication between the problem-solver and the programmer (if the two are not the same person).

Flowchart symbols can be hand drawn, but it is better to use a template. Flowcharting templates are available in most computer supply stores.

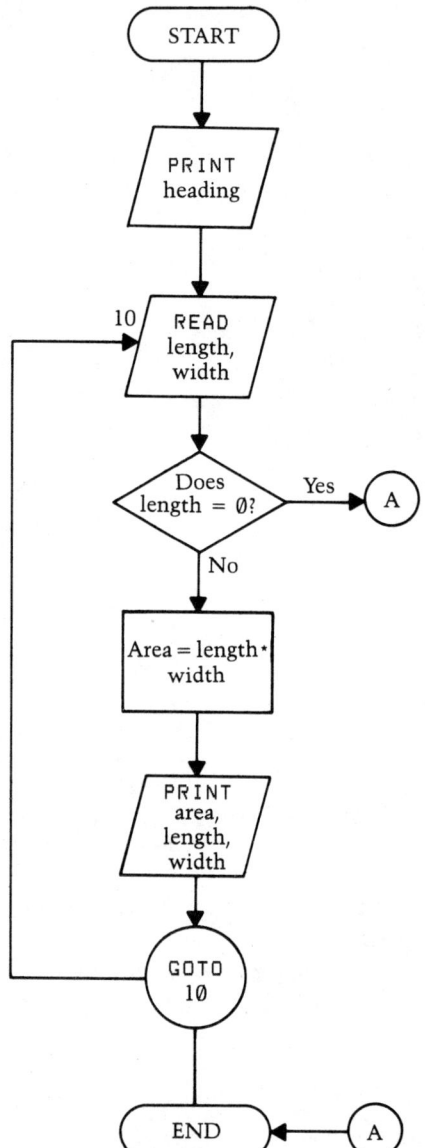

Figure 3.8 The flowchart for calculating the area of a room

Structured Flowcharts

A structured flowchart is a modular flowchart that shows the major steps or modules of a program. Each module is then expanded into smaller modules and finally into a detailed flowchart. Thus a structured flowchart

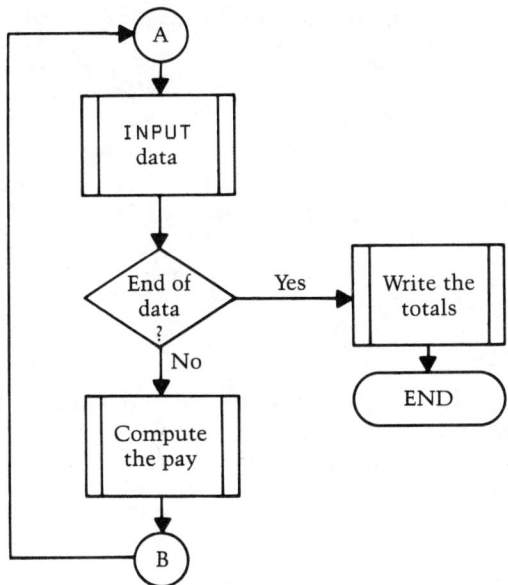

Figure 3.9 A structured flowchart

is a useful tool that allows programmers to concentrate on the major tasks of a problem first, and then work it through until they create a detailed flowchart for small modules. The detailed flowchart of a module shows actual coding. Figure 3.9 shows a structured flowchart.

Pseudocode

Pseudocode is a program design tool that, just like flowcharts, represents the solution of a problem. However, it does not use any symbols and is an informal way of expressing the plan. The programmer writes, in a narrative form, the necessary steps for solving a problem.

The following is a simple example of pseudocode:

```
READ length, width
Area = length * width
PRINT length, width, area
END
```

The following is a more complete form of the pseudocode above:

Write the headings
READ length, width
  Area = length * width
  PRINT length, width, area
IF more data, THEN
        goto read
ELSE
End the program

Pseudocode has not been standardized yet, and there are several variations. One of the advantages of pseudocode is that it can be written as modules and submodules (like the outline for a report, a chapter, or a paragraph). The following is an example:

1. Write headings
    1.1 Heading 1: company name
    1.2 Heading 2: employee number, pay, deductions, net
2. Initialize variables
    2.1 Total pay = 0
    2.2 Total deductions = 0
    2.3 Total net = 0
3. Begin the loop, repeat the following
4. Read data, at the end go to Step 8
    4.1 Read employee number, wage rate, hours worked
5. Calculate
    5.1 Pay = wage × hours
    5.2 Deduction = pay × .12
    5.3 Net = pay − deduction
    5.4 Calculate totals
        5.4.1 Total pay = total pay + pay
        5.4.2 Total deduction = total deduction + deduction
        5.4.3 Total nets = total nets + nets
6. Write employee number, pay, deductions, net
7. End the loop
8. Write total pay, total deduction, total nets
9. End the program

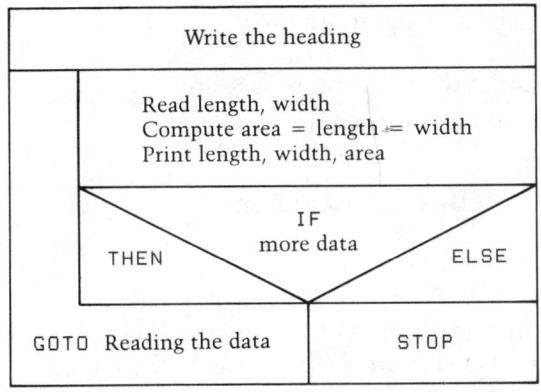

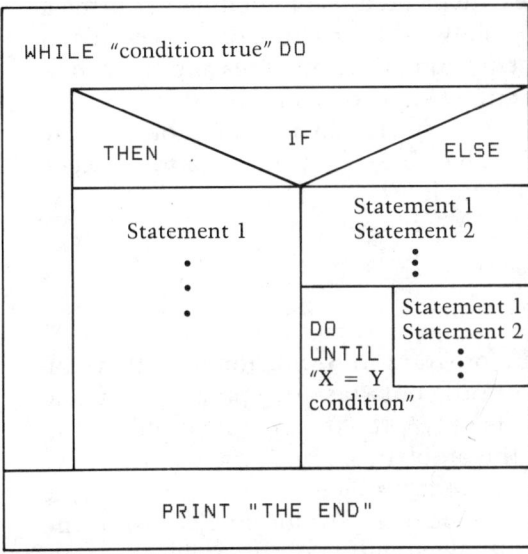

Figure 3.10 Examples of logic charts

A simple form of pseudocode has been used throughout the text in the examples under the title "Solution Plan." We continue to use this simple form in the following chapters.

Logic Charts

Logic charts (also called Nassi-Schneiderman charts, after their developers) are charts that show the logical structure of a program. A logic chart is a table of the steps, logic, and flow of the solution methods to a problem. Figure 3.10 shows two examples of this kind of chart.

The logic chart uses a combination of the following:

1. A table that shows the structure of the solution procedure
2. A rectangle diagram to show one or several statements
3. An L-shaped box to show a loop
4. Two triangles to show the IF-THEN-ELSE conditions

Hierarchy Charts

If a program is long, it cannot be managed unless it is broken down into smaller programs or modules. A good design starts at the top of the entire program, divides it into modules, and works down to the bottom until several small, manageable modules are created. Each module performs a specific function. A hierarchy chart shows the structure of a program and its modules. It is a pictorial representation of the modules and their relationships. Figure 3.11 shows a hierarchy chart of a simple program.

A hierarchy chart makes it easy to break down a big problem into smaller segments and makes it possible to explain the function of each module and the relationship among modules.

Programming Cycle

As mentioned previously, writing a program in BASIC (or any other language) is called coding. Coding is not the only task of a programmer, and BASIC (or any computer language) is only a tool for solving problems. In fact, coding is just a small part of the problem solving process. Before we start coding, we must first understand the problem to be solved, analyze it, break it down into modules or components, develop an algorithm, and plan the solution methods. A clear understanding of the problem, objectives, requirements, constraints, and solution procedure are necessary steps prior to coding.

Defining and designing a program is more important and more time consuming than writing BASIC codes. It is advisable to devote plenty of time and thought to the planning process. The following six general steps will help you in the analysis and the programming process.

Step 1. Problem Analysis and Definition

Analyze and understand the problem fully. Try to state the nature of the problem and list its objectives in writing. This phase clarifies what the problem is, how it can be solved by a program, what the expected outputs are, and how each output should look.

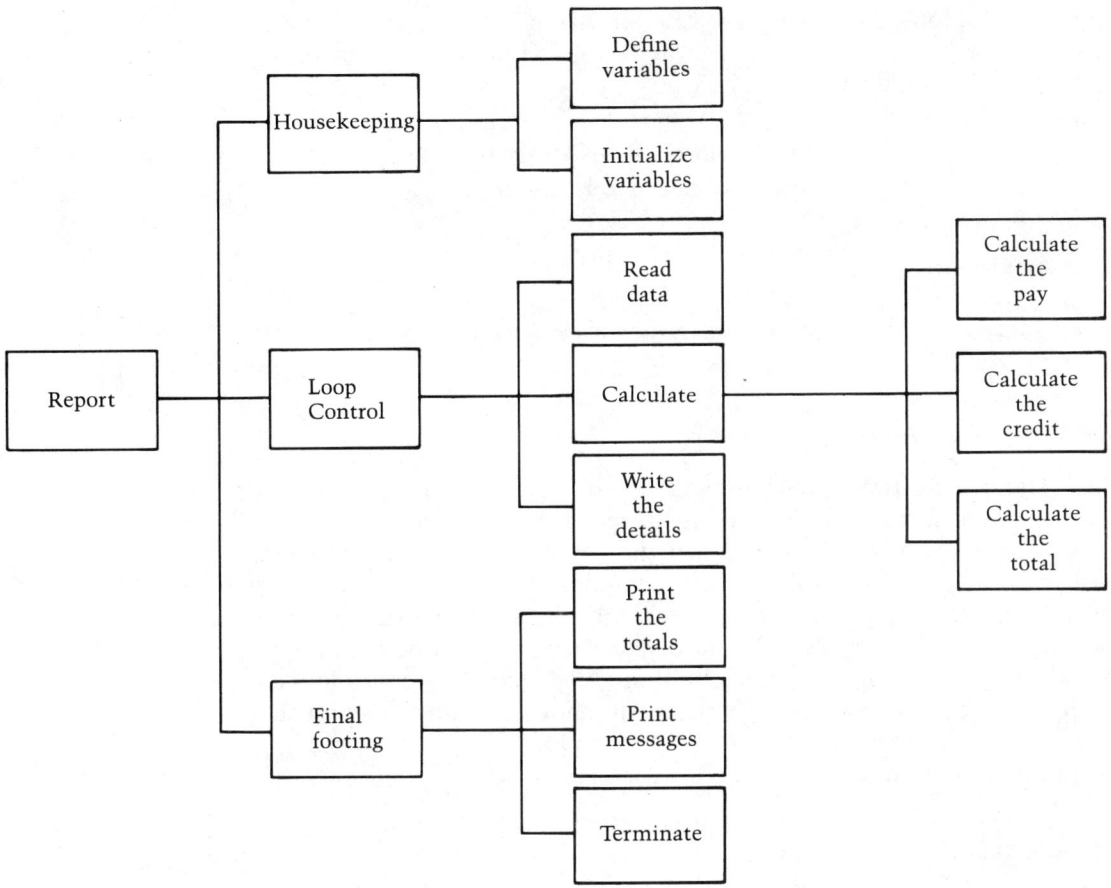

Figure 3.11 An example of a hierarchy chart

Step 2. Input-Output Design

Before any processing, you must know how the output will look and how the input should be prepared. The input-output design can be accomplished in two steps. First, list the items that must appear on the output as well as their types (numeric, character). Then, list the input items as well as their characteristics (length and type). Avoid unnecessary or redundant input. The input should be the information that is needed to produce the appropriate output. Remember that the items that the program will calculate or generate must not appear in the input list. For example, you can always calculate the average of the test scores or generate the sequence numbers in the program. Second, design the layout for the output and input using a printer spacing chart. The output layout shows how the output should look, along with the exact location of each item. The input layout shows the form and location of all input items. The summary of the steps for input/output design is:

1. List the variables that must appear on the output.
2. List the variables that must be included in the input.
3. Design the output layout.
4. Design the input layout.

It is important to design the output first because that is the objective of the program.

Step 3. Process Design

Formulate the solution procedures. This step defines the procedures or calculations necessary to arrive at the output from the inputs. To accomplish this step you must break down the entire problem into modules. Each module is a small, manageable component of the whole problem. For example, reading the data, making calculations, and printing the information can each be a module. Naturally, it is easier to define the required procedures and calculations for a small module than for the problem as a whole. A hierarchy chart is a good tool to show the modules and their relationship. Then either a flowchart or pseudocode is used as the blueprint of the program.

Step 4. Coding

Write the program in BASIC statements. Make sure to review the program carefully after coding to detect any logical or syntax errors.

Step 5. Execution, Testing, and Debugging

Key the statements into a terminal and run the program. After you correct syntax errors, make a first run of the program with test data for which you already know the correct output.

Step 6. Documentation

Describe the program, the solution procedure, and its limitations. This essential part of the programming process is necessary to document the problem and solution procedures for future reference. After a period of time, even the original programmer may refer to this documentation for the details of a program. In fact, documentation starts from the beginning of the programming cycle. The documentation includes flowcharts, pseudocodes, format specifications, and the program with comments within the source program. A final report explaining the nature of the problem, the solution methods, the way the program works, its limitations, and other important points about the program completes the documentation phase.

Sometimes the programmer is not the same person as the problem solver. In that case, the problem solver (the analyst) does Steps 1 through 3, and the programmer does Steps 4 through 6. In any case, the programmer should understand the problem and the solution procedures fully. The sample problem at the end of the chapter illustrates the process.

WRITING STRUCTURED PROGRAMS

Many reports show that the costs of maintaining and modifying a program are greater than the costs of producing it—in fact, three to five times more. Therefore, readable programs ultimately make data processing more efficient and less costly.

Structured programming is a method of designing and writing organized programs so that they are easier to code, easier to understand, and less prone to errors. The goal of structured programming is to avoid bad program organization and thus to produce programs that can be read, maintained, and modified easily by other programmers.

For example, a program with too many GOTO statements, an unclear pattern of instructions, or logic that is difficult to follow because of disorganized branching cannot be called structured. In theory, a structured program can be written by using only three elementary structures:

1. Sequence
2. Selection (decision)
3. Iteration (loop)

Sequence Structure

The sequence structure is the basic flow of a program, one statement follows another one in sequence as they are coded.

In sequence structure, there is no transfer of control to another point in the program. The entry point is the beginning of the sequence, the first statement; the exit point is the end of the sequence, the last statement (points A and B in the sequence structure shown in Figure 3.12).

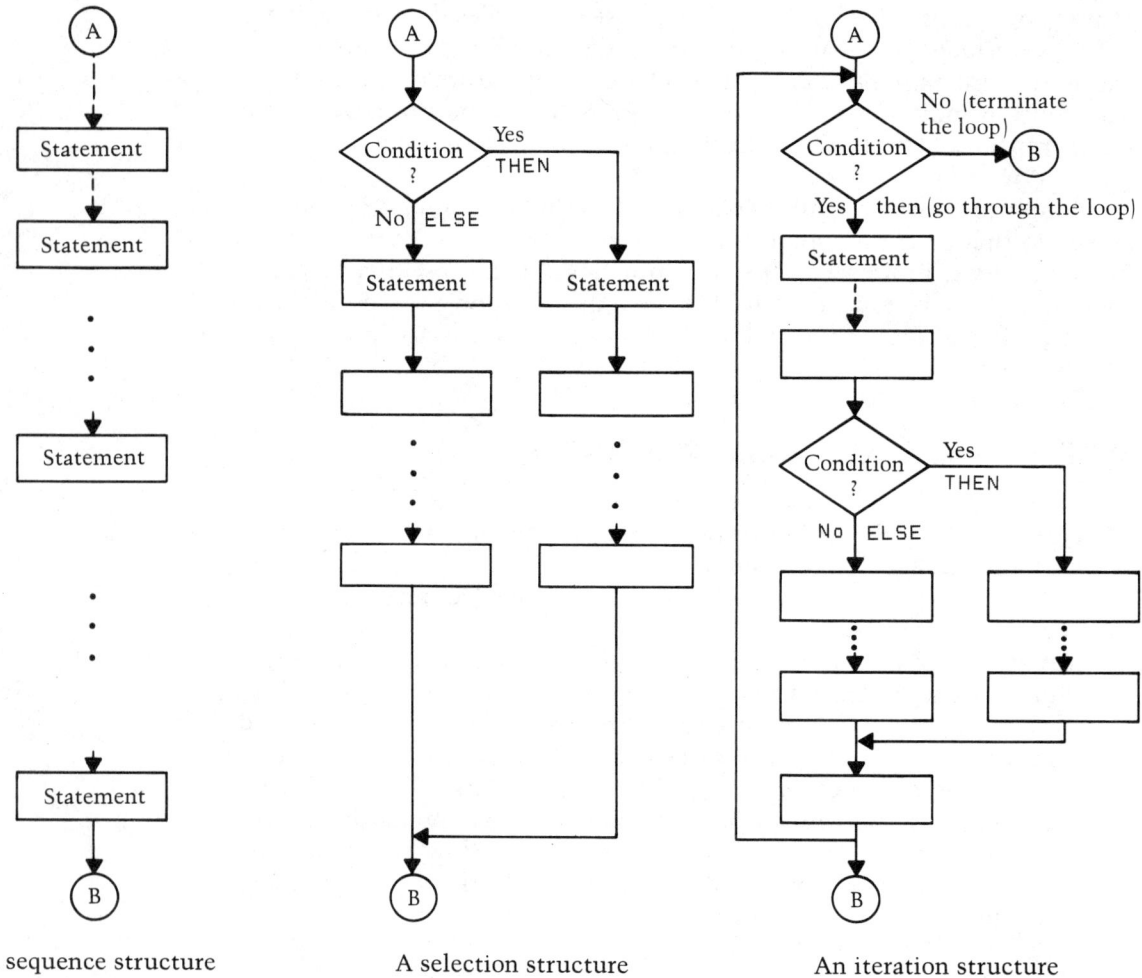

Figure 3.12 The control structures

Selection Structure

In the selection structure, there is a condition for executing one or several instructions. If the condition is true, a set of distinct and separate statements is executed; if the condition is false, another set of statements is executed. In a selection structure, there is a single entry to the structure and a single exit (points A and B in the selection structure shown in Figure 3.12). In BASIC, selection structure is achieved by using the IF statement. The IF statement is discussed in detail in Chapter 4.

Iteration Structure

In an iteration structure, certain statements are executed repeatedly as long as a given condition is true. The entry point is the beginning and the exit is the end of the structure (see points A and B of the iteration structure shown in Figure 3.12). The iteration structure can be implemented by the DO-WHILE statements in BASIC. Unfortunately, not all versions of BASIC offer this feature. The FOR-NEXT statements are another choice for this structure. These looping techniques are explained in detail in Chapter 5.

HOW TO WRITE A STRUCTURED PROGRAM

Structured programming simply means writing a program by systematic planning so that it is easy to produce, understand, debug, and maintain. A structured program exhibits the following characteristics:

1. Structured design
   a. Top-down design
   b. Modularity
2. Readability
3. Reliability
4. Full documentation

Structured Design

Before we give technical definitions of structured design, consider the simple analogy of a builder constructing a house. Building cannot start until the builder does a lot of planning. First, decisions must be made on how the house will be built: the size, style, number of the rooms, and so on. Also, many constraints must be considered, including the area of the building site, rules and regulations, and cost.

After these decisions have been made and the builder has a general plan as well as blueprints, he or she can break down the whole job into many separate tasks. For example:

1. Foundation
2. Framing
3. Exterior trim
4. Utilities
5. Interior trim

Looking at this more closely, we find that we can break down some of these jobs into even smaller jobs:

2. Framing
   - 2.1 Floors
   - 2.2 Exterior walls
   - 2.3 Interior walls
   - 2.4 Roof

We can break down the tasks into still smaller jobs:

2.2 Exterior walls
   - 2.2.1 Studs and plates
   - 2.2.2 Doors
   - 2.2.3 Windows

By now, you can see what we are leading to. We broke down a large job into many smaller ones. This is the main idea behind structured design. It is the first rule of structured programming, which we can express this way:

1. Plan before coding.
2. Look at the overall problem.
3. Break the problem down into a sequence of smaller, easier problems (modules).

No matter how big or small a program is, it can be broken down into modules, even if it consists of such simple steps as input, processing, and output. This approach is especially helpful today because many businesses use large, complex programs of many pages. If one breaks down these large programs into modules, writing them becomes a relatively easy task.

There is another important aspect to consider. Return to the construction example for a moment. You cannot build the walls until the foundation is complete, nor can you build the roof until the walls are complete. Parts are interrelated, and most parts depend on previous ones.

Top-Down Design

The concept of top-down design is very simple. The programmer focuses first on the overall structure of the problem and then designs the major modules of the program. Once that is done, he or she works on the next

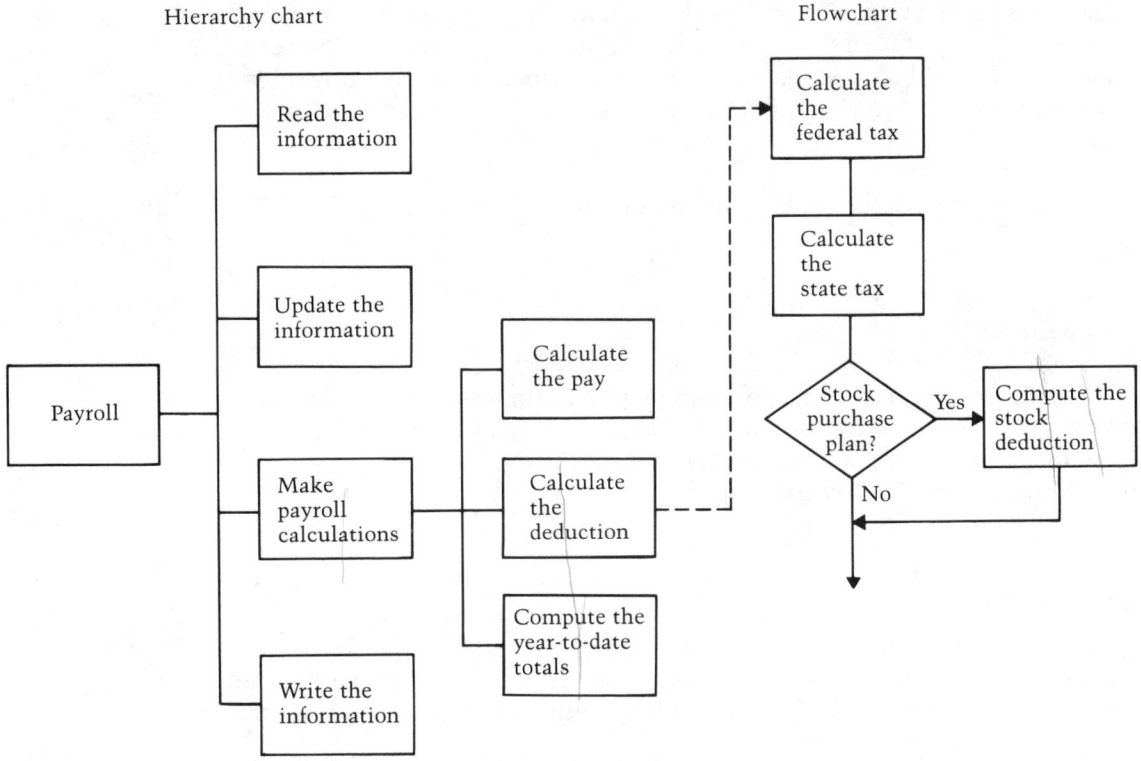

Figure 3.13 Comparison of a hierarchy chart and a flowchart

lower level. This process continues until the entire program is divided into functional modules and submodules.

A hierarchy chart is a useful tool in structured programming for getting an overview of the entire program. It shows the levels of abstraction in each stage. A hierarchy chart does not show decision making, logic, or flow of execution as a flowchart does. See Figure 3.13 for a depiction of the differences. Flowcharts show procedures; hierarchy charts show functions. A hierarchy chart allows the programmer to concentrate on *what* needs to be done before determining *how* it is to be done. The chart also groups related functions. The function of the top module is to summarize the lower modules. Each subsequent level of defined modules is less abstract.

Modularity

A module is a self-contained program unit that performs a task in support of the major function of the program. In terms of programming code, a module is a collection of logically related instructions that can be grouped together. However, a module is not just a chunk of the program, rather it is a well-defined body of logically related statements. By breaking down a big problem into small modules, a programmer can concentrate on the smaller units one at a time. The progression of modules reflects the organization of the entire program. Throughout the text, we will discuss the techniques, advantages, and desiderata of a module further.

Readability

The physical appearance of a program plays an important role in the readability of its logical structure. It is not difficult to make a BASIC program readable by following a few simple rules and using common sense. The following are some recommendations:

Descriptive Names

A descriptive variable name helps the reader recognize the purpose of that variable. Most versions of BASIC allow you to choose a variable name with more than one letter. Certainly, the meaningful name AREA is better than A, and the formula

```
AREA = WIDTH*LENGTH
```

is more readable than

```
A = B*C
```

We continue to use variable names with more than one character in this text to make the examples more readable. However, you must check the BASIC manual for your system to find out what rules govern symbolic names. If your system does not allow the multicharacter names we use, select names that are legal in your system. (When you run the programs in this text, simply drop all characters after the first one.)

Blank Spaces

Blank spaces help to make the statements and their purpose understandable. Blank spaces can also be used to group logically related statements. For example, it is very common to indent the statements inside the loop, as follows:

```
10 READ A, B
20 IF A = 0 GOTO 110
30          C = A + B
40          P = A*B
50          PRINT A, B, C, P
60 GOTO 10
70 DATA 10, 20
80 DATA 5, 6
90 DATA 10, 95
100 DATA 0, 0
110 END
```

Indention is very useful to show the relationship of a group of statements to others. You will see more examples of how useful indention is in later chapters. Follow these recommendations to make effective use of spaces in a program:

1. Use blanks to separate the components of a statement. Use a blank between a key word and the rest of the statement. A blank after a comma makes a line more readable. Also use a blank before and after the following characters:
   a. An equals sign (=)
   b. Addition and subtraction operators (+, −)
2. Do not use blanks before or after the multiplication, division, and exponentiation operators (*, /, ^). Example:
   X = (A + B − C*D)/E^2
3. Use a blank line or a REM followed by line of asterisks to separate a module from the rest of the program.

Comment Lines

You will find that describing the important points of a program is a great help. One way to do this is to write a comment about them. Comments are very useful in describing the sequence, logic, variables, and critical parts of a program. Furthermore, at the beginning of a program most programmers use a remark block that includes the following items:

1. The purpose of the program and a brief description of the algorithms used
2. The name of the programmer and the date the program was developed

3. The variables dictionary
4. The input and output files—the file names, the medium, and the record format

Further comments should be used judiciously throughout the program to explain the major steps. Comments are particularly necessary:

1. Before each branching
2. To explain the connections between modules
3. Before a statement that might seem obscure or confusing
4. Before a statement to which control is transferred from far away (explain how it is reached)
5. To show the layout of the data

Using too many comments (overcommenting) is not advisable either; it is especially important not to use comments that simply repeat a BASIC statement.

Other Readability Recommendations

The following is a list of further hints for making programs readable:

1. Always initialize the variables.
2. Do not use GOTO or IF-GOTO statements unless absolutely necessary. This is discussed further in Chapter 4.
3. Most BASIC systems allow several statements per line. However, it is best to put only one statement on a line, or at least to group the statements (no more than three on a line) so that they do not detract from the readability of the program.
4. DATA statements should be grouped and placed at the end or at the beginning of the program or module.
5. If you need to continue a statement on the next line, always break the statement after a comma. When you do, indent the continuation line so that it aligns under the key word in the line above, for example:
   ```
   200   DATA 45, 78, 23, 54, 65, 96,
               23, 45, 87, 43
   50 PRINT "THE PARAMETERS ARE EQUAL TO "; A, B, C,
            "THE SIDES ARE"; X, Y, Z
   ```
6. Avoid ambiguity in an arithmetic expression by using extra pairs of parentheses to group the variables.

Reliability

Reliability in a broad sense refers to minimizing the chance of errors in all aspects of program development, design, and coding. However, when we say a program is reliable, we usually mean that it works correctly under a wide range of conditions.

Thus, any program must go through extensive testing before it can be considered reliable and ready for use. Test data should be created for all cases, especially for critical values. It is particularly important that a program be tested with:

1. "Good" data: expected, normal data
2. "Bad" data: unexpected data
3. Flexible number of data:
   a. No data at all
   b. Only one datum
   c. The maximum possible number of data

Documentation

Documentation is the process of reporting how the program was developed, designed, coded, and tested. It also includes a report explaining how the program can be used. Documentation of a program is important for several reasons. First, almost all programs are eventually modified. If there is no documentation (or poor documentation), much time will be wasted determining how the program works. Second, most programs are used by someone other than the original programmer. If the program has no documentation, it is almost impossible for such users to do so. Documentation may be provided for:

1. The reviewer, who needs to maintain and modify the program
2. The user, to show how to use the program and how to enter data
3. The operator, to show what files are to be used, if necessary

Documentation is a continuing part of the development of a program. It should begin with the project and progress with it. One advantage of such documentation is that it provides a basis for continuing the project should there be a change in programmers. Documentation should include, but not be limited to:

1. What the program does, how it does it, and what its limitations are
2. The methods of computation (algorithms or processing)
3. A detailed, logical description of the program with the appropriate flowcharts, pseudocodes, or hierarchy charts
4. The planning documents, such as output and output layouts
5. A list of the codes, including the internal comments
6. Samples of the input and output and the results of the tests performed

The user document should include detailed instructions for using the program and entering the data. It should also state limitations on the number of variables and give an explanation of error messages, if any.

It is important that each organization develop and adopt standards for documentation. Standards greatly enhance efficiency by providing a uniform tool for further program development and maintenance. Without standards, reviewers cannot measure the quality of program work easily.

A CASE—PRINTING A REPORT

The following example demonstrates the general procedures for translating a problem into a program:

Step 1: The Problem

XYZ Gas Company's managers would like to see a monthly report showing the total gas consumption of their customers and the cost to each customer. Analysis shows that:

1. Billing rates are different (commercial rates, residential rates, and so on).
2. The last meter readings and the current meter readings are available.
3. The managers would like to see the information about each customer and the totals at the end of the report.

The objective is, therefore, to write a program that generates such a report.

Step 2: Input-Output Design

A detailed analysis shows that the variables listed in Table 3.1 are necessary for the output. The amount and the totals can be calculated if the rate is known. Therefore, we need the information shown in Table 3.2 for input.

The output should look like the layout shown in Figure 3.14.

Input design is next. It is a good idea to place each customer's data on one DATA line. The order of the data is ID number, previous meter reading, current meter reading, and rate.

The following sample data are used for this program.

```
DATA  54985,  562.26,   721.6,   .35
DATA  49822,  205.5,    296.75,  .38
DATA  36872,  911.5,    983.25,  .33
DATA  99995,   59.75,   295.9,   .39
DATA  45632,  199.5,    358.3,   .33
DATA  33333,    0.0,   1123.5,   .39
DATA  45678,  250.5,    332.5,   .38
DATA      0,    0,        0,     0
```

Table 3.1 Output Analysis Form for the Sample Program

Item	Variable Name	Type	Field Length
1. The customer's identification number	ID	Numeric	5 columns
2. The units of gas used by each customer	GASUSE	Numeric	6 columns
3. The billing rate	RATE	Numeric	6 columns
4. The total dollar amount charged to each customer	AMT	Numeric	7 columns
5. Total units of gas used by all customers	SUMGU	Numeric	7 columns
6. Total dollar amount for all customers	TOTAMT	Numeric	7 columns

Table 3.2 Input Analysis Form for the Sample Program

Item	Variable Name	Type	Field Length
1. The customer's identification number	ID	Numeric	5 columns
2. The previous meter reading	PREV	Numeric	6 columns
3. The current meter reading	CURRENT	Numeric	6 columns
4. The rate per unit	RATE	Numeric	6 columns

132 *Program Development and Structured Programming*

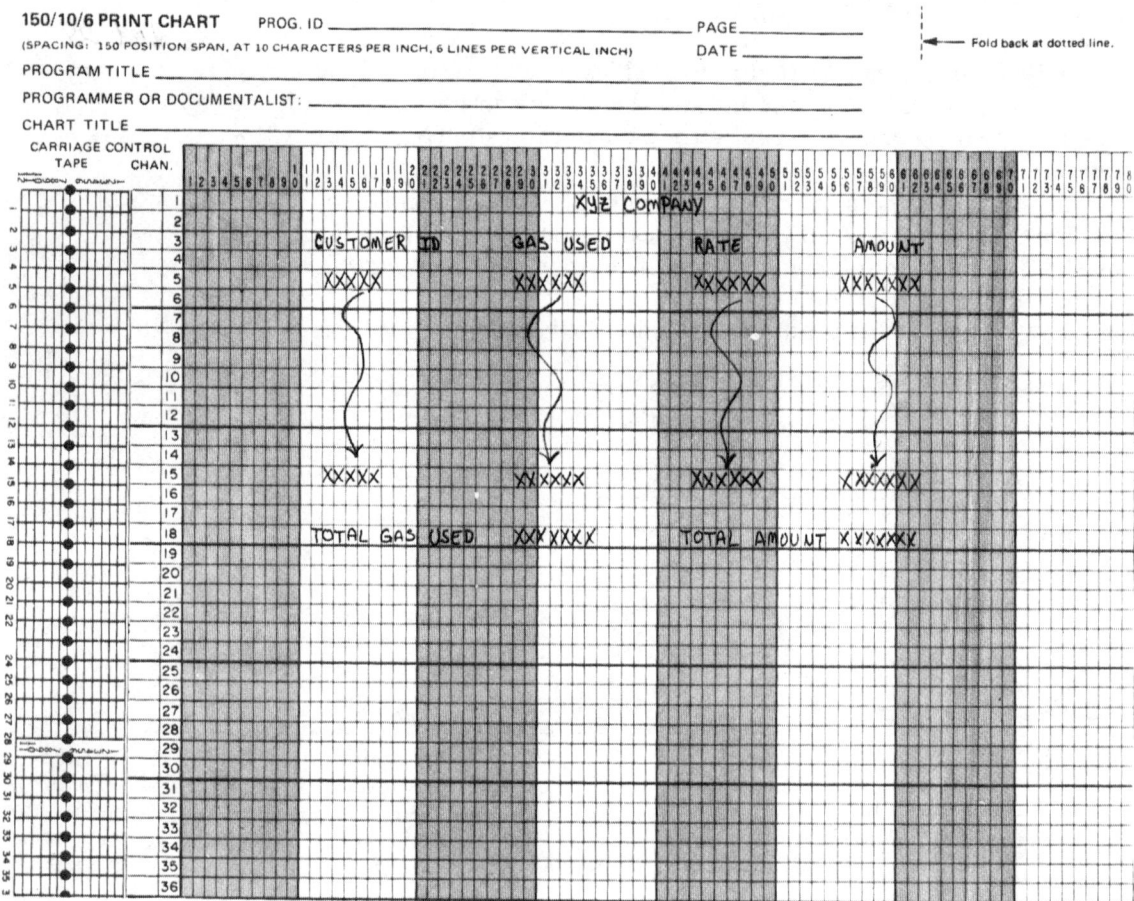

Figure 3.14 Output design for the sample problem

Step 3: Process Design

The program is broken down into the following modules:

1. Housekeeping
   1.1 Writing the headings
   1.2 Initializing variables
2. Input-process-output loop
   2.1 Reading data
   2.2 Calculating
   2.3 Printing the information

A Case—Printing a Report   **133**

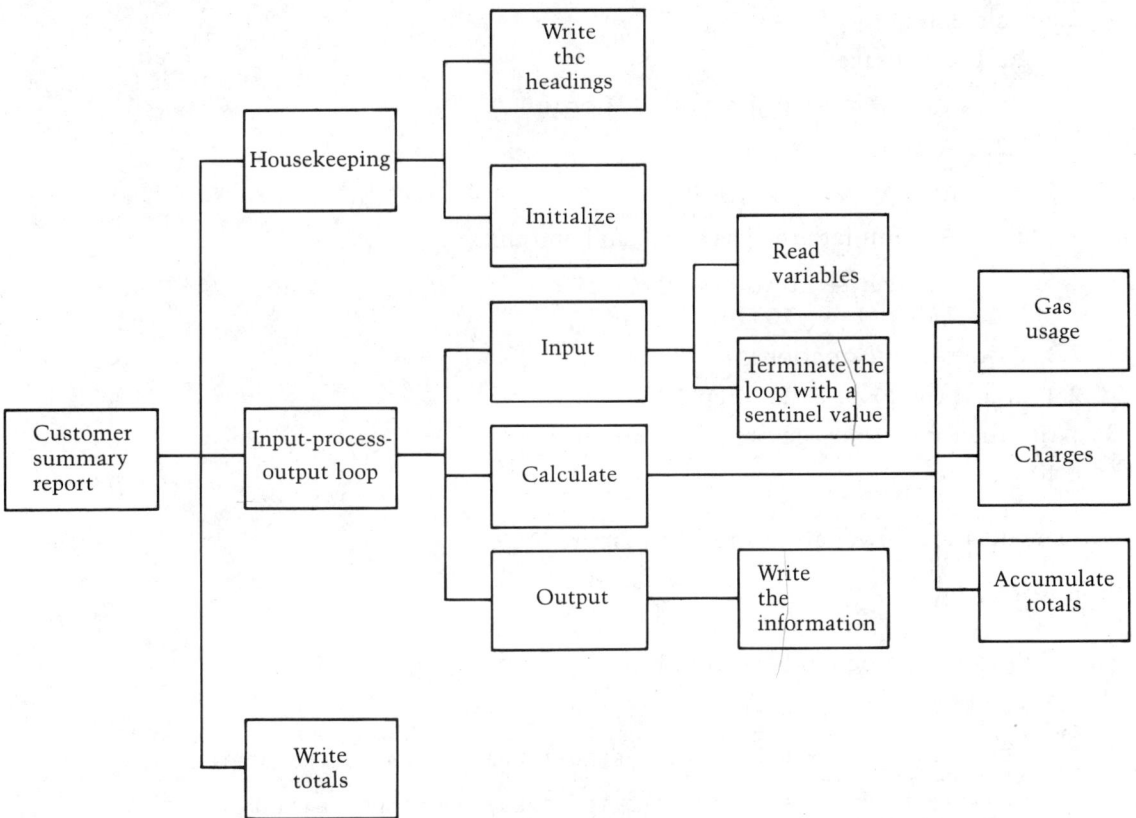

Figure 3.15 The hierarchy chart for the sample problem

3. Printing the totals

The hierarchy chart is shown in Figure 3.15, and the expanded outline is as follows:

1. Housekeeping
   - **1.1** Write headings
   - **1.2** Set:
     ```
     SUMGU = 0
     TOTAMT = 0
     ```
2. Input-process-output loop
   - **2.1** Read variables for each customer;
     ```
     IF ID = 0 terminate the loop, GO TO Step 3
     ```

- 2.2 Calculate:
    - 2.2.1 Gas usage:
        ```
        GASUSE = CURRENT - PREV
        ```
    - 2.2.2 Amount of charge:
        ```
        AMT = RATE*GASUSE
        ```
    - 2.2.3 Accumulate the gas usage and amount:
        ```
        SUMGU = SUMGU + GASUSE
        TOTAMT = TOTAMT + AMT
        ```
- 2.3 Write the information
- 2.4 End of the loop, GOTO Step 2.1
3. Write the total gas usages and total amounts
4. END

The detailed flowchart is shown in Figure 3.16.

Step 4: Coding

The coding of the program is as follows:

```
10  REM AUTHOR : T. J. WHITE, OCTOBER 15, 19--
20                                                                    REM
30  REM THIS PROGRAM GENERATES A REPORT FOR THE GAS USERS OF THE
40  REM COMPANY
50  REM THE INPUTS ARE CUSTOMER'S ID, PREVIOUS METER READING,
60  REM CURRENT METER READING, AND THE RATE FOR EACH CUSTOMER.
70  REM ***********************************************************
80  REM *   VARIABLE DICTIONARY:                                   *
90  REM *                                                          *
100 REM *      ID         =  THE CUSTOMER'S ID NUMBER              *
110 REM *      PREV       =  THE PREVIOUS METER READING            *
120 REM *      CURRENT    =  THE CURRENT METER READING             *
130 REM *      RATE       =  THE RATE                              *
140 REM *      GASUSE     =  THE GAS USAGE                         *
150 REM *      AMT        =  THE AMOUNT                            *
160 REM *      SUMGU      =  TOTAL GAS USED                        *
170 REM *      TOTAMT     =  THE TOTAL AMOUNT                      *
180 REM *                                                          *
190 REM ***********************************************************
200                                                                   REM
210 REM PRINTING THE HEADING
220     PRINT TAB(34);"XYZ COMPANY"
230     PRINT TAB(12); "CUSTOMER ID"; TAB(29); "GAS USED";
240         TAB(44); "RATE"; TAB(57); "AMOUNT"
250                                                                   REM
260     SUMGU = 0
270     TOTAMT = 0
300 REM ****** BEGINNING OF READ-PROCESS-WRITE MODULE ******
310     *** AN ID NUMBER EQUAL TO 0 TERMINATES THE LOOP ***
320     READ ID, PREV, CURRENT, RATE
330     IF ID = 0 THEN GOTO 450
340        GASUSE = PREV - CURRENT
350        AMT = RATE*GASUSE
```

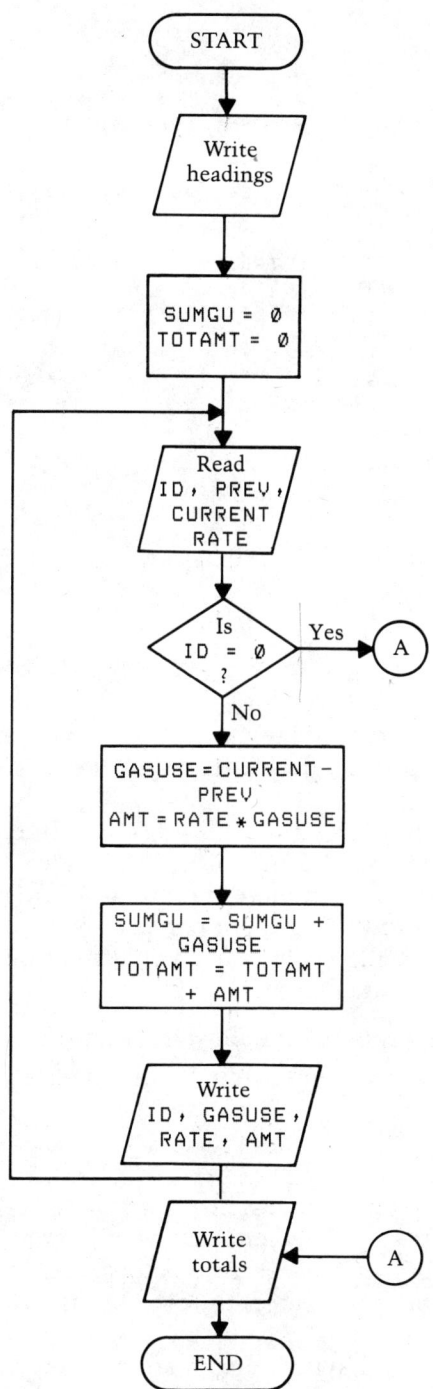

Figure 3.16 The flowchart for the sample problem

```
360                                                                       REM
370            SUMGU = SUMGU + GASUSE
380            TOTAMT = TOTAMT + AMT
390                                                                       REM
400            PRINT TAB(13); ID; TAB(29); GASUSE; TAB(44); RATE;
410            PRINT TAB(56); AMT
420         GOTO 300
430 REM ****** END OF THE READ-PROCESS-WRITE-MODULE ********
440                                                                       REM
450 REM WRITING THE FOOTINGS
460       PRINT TAB(12); "TOTAL GAS USED"; TAB(28); SUMGU;
470       PRINT TAB(43); "TOTAL AMOUNT"; TAB(56); TOTAMT
500 REM *************** D A T A **********************
510    DATA 54985, 562.26, 721.6,   .35
520    DATA 49828, 205.5,  296.75,  .38
530    DATA 36872, 911.5,  983.25,  .33
540    DATA 99995,  59.75, 295.9,   .39
550    DATA 45632, 199.5,  358.3,   .33
560    DATA 33333,   0.0,  1123.5,  .39
570    DATA 45678, 250.5,  332.5,   .38
580    DATA 0, 0, 0, 0
590 END
```

After the program is written, the flowchart and the program are carefully reviewed again for any logical or syntax errors.

Step 5: Running, Testing, and Debugging

After program is keyed into a terminal, listed, and reviewed, RUN is typed in. The run of the program, shown in Figure 3.17, has several syntax errors.

1. In line 240, the word PRINT is missing from the beginning of the line. This error has occurred because line 230 is terminated with the carriage return key, and line 240 should be a complete statement. In this example, it should start with the word PRINT. (You can use the feed key for continuation, or some systems allow you to use a continuation symbol, usually an ampersand, at the end of a line.)

2. Line 310 has the same kind of error. Line 310 should start with REM.

3. Line 370 has a typographical error. The statement should be corrected to read:

   `370 SUMGU = SUMGU + GASUSE`

Notice that the interpreter in this system catches the errors on a line-by-line basis. The lines will be executed up to where the syntax errors occur (note that the heading is printed). Then the execution stops, and an error message is displayed. After the line is corrected, the program is run again.

The program is run once more after all syntax errors are corrected. The listing and the output of the program is shown in Figure 3.18 on page 138. The program has several logical errors.

```
10  REM AUTHOR : T. J. WHITE, OCTOBER 15, 19--
20                                                                    REM
30  REM THIS PROGRAM GENERATES A REPORT FOR THE GAS USERS OF THE
40  REM COMPANY
50  REM THE INPUTS ARE CUSTOMER'S ID, PREVIOUS METER READING,
60  REM CURRENT METER READING, AND THE RATE FOR EACH CUSTOMER.
70  REM ***************************************************************
80  REM *    VARIABLE DICTIONARY:                                     *
90  REM *                                                             *
100 REM *       ID       =   THE CUSTOMER'S ID NUMBER                 *
110 REM *       PREV     =   THE PREVIOUS METER READING               *
120 REM *       CURRENT  =   THE CURRENT METER READING                *
130 REM *       RATE     =   THE RATE                                 *
140 REM *       GASUSE   =   THE GAS USAGE                            *
150 REM *       AMT      =   THE AMOUNT                               *
160 REM *       SUMGU    =   TOTAL GAS USED                           *
170 REM *       TOTAMT   =   THE TOTAL AMOUNT                         *
180 REM *                                                             *
190 REM ***************************************************************
200                                                                    REM
210 REM PRINTING THE HEADING
220     PRINT TAB(34); 'XYZ  COMPANY'
230     PRINT TAB(12); 'CUSTOMER ID'; TAB(29); 'GAS USED';
240         TAB(44); 'RATE'; TAB(57); 'AMOUNT'
250                                                                    REM
260     SUMGU = 0
270     TOTAMT = 0
300 REM ****** BEGINNING OF READ-PROCESS-WRITE MODULE ******
310     *** AN ID NUMBER EQUAL TO 0 TERMINATES THE LOOP ***
320     READ ID, PREV, CURRENT, RATE
330     IF ID = 0 THEN GOTO 450
340         GASUSE = PREV - CURRENT
350         AMT = RATE*GASUSE
360                                                                    REM
370         SUMGU + SUMGU = GASUSE
380         TOTAMT = TOTAMT + AMT
390                                                                    REM
400         PRINT TAB(13); ID; TAB(29); GASUSE; TAB(44); GRATE;
410         PRINT TAB(56); AMT
420     GOTO 300
430 REM ****** END OF THE READ-PROCESS-WRITE-MODULE ********
440                                                                    REM
450 REM WRITING THE FOOTINGS
460     PRINT TAB(12); 'TOTAL GAS USED'; TAB(28); SUMGU;
470     PRINT TAB(43); 'TOTAL AMOUNT'; TAB(56); TOTAMT
500 REM *************** D A T A **********************
510  DATA 54985,  562.26,  721.6,   .35
520  DATA 49828,  205.5,   296.75,  .38
530  DATA 36872,  911.5,   983.25,  .33
540  DATA 99995,   59.75,  295.9,   .39
550  DATA 45632,  199.5,   358.3,   .33
560  DATA 33333,    0.0,  1123.5,   .39
570  DATA 45678,  250.5,   332.5,   .38
580  DATA 0, 0, 0, 0
590 END


RUN
                              XYZ COMPANY
              CUSTOMER ID     GAS USED
SYNTAX ERROR IN 240

RUN
                              XYZ COMPANY
              CUSTOMER ID     GAS USED         RATE         AMOUNT
SYNTAX ERROR IN 310

RUN
                              XYZ COMPANY
              CUSTOMER ID     GAS USED         RATE         AMOUNT
SYNTAX ERROR IN 370
```

Figure 3.17 The sample program with syntax errors

```
10  REM AUTHOR : T. J. WHITE, OCTOBER 15, 19--
20                                                                          REM
30  REM THIS PROGRAM GENERATES A REPORT FOR THE GAS USERS OF THE
40  REM COMPANY
50  REM THE INPUTS ARE CUSTOMER'S ID, PREVIOUS METER READING,
60  REM CURRENT METER READING, AND THE RATE FOR EACH CUSTOMER.
70  REM ****************************************************
80  REM *    VARIABLE DICTIONARY:                           *
90  REM *                                                   *
100 REM *      ID        =   THE CUSTOMER'S ID NUMBER       *
110 REM *      PREV      =   THE PREVIOUS METER READING     *
120 REM *      CURRENT   =   THE CURRENT METER READING      *
130 REM *      RATE      =   THE RATE                       *
140 REM *      GASUSE    =   THE GAS USAGE                  *
150 REM *      AMT       =   THE AMOUNT                     *
160 REM *      SUMGU     =   TOTAL GAS USED                 *
170 REM *      TOTAMT    =   THE TOTAL AMOUNT               *
180 REM *                                                   *
190 REM ****************************************************
200                                                                         REM
210 REM PRINTING THE HEADING
220    PRINT TAB(34); 'XYZ  COMPANY'
230    PRINT TAB(12); 'CUSTOMER ID'; TAB(29); 'GAS USED';
240    PRINT TAB(44); 'RATE'; TAB(57); 'AMOUNT'
250                                                                         REM
260    SUMGU = 0
270    TOTAMT = 0
300 REM ****** BEGINNING OF READ-PROCESS-WRITE MODULE ******
310 REM *** AN ID NUMBER EQUAL TO 0 TERMINATES THE LOOP ***
320    READ ID, PREV, CURRENT, RATE
330    IF ID = 0 THEN GOTO 450
340      GASUSE = PREV - CURRENT
350      AMT = RATE*GASUSE
360                                                                         REM
370      SUMGU = SUMGU + GASUSE
380      TOTAMT = TOTAMT + AMT
390                                                                         REM
400      PRINT TAB(13); ID; TAB(29); GASUSE; TAB(44); GRATE;
410      PRINT TAB(56); AMT
420    GOTO 300
430 REM ****** END OF THE READ-PROCESS-WRITE-MODULE ********
440                                                                         REM
450 REM WRITING THE FOOTINGS
460    PRINT TAB(12); 'TOTAL GAS USED'; TAB(28); SUMGU;
470    PRINT TAB(43); 'TOTAL AMOUNT'; TAB(56); TOTAMT
500 REM *************** D A T A ***********************
510 DATA 54985, 562.26, 721.6,   .35
520 DATA 49828, 205.5,  296.75,  .38
530 DATA 36872, 911.5,  983.25,  .33
540 DATA 99995,  59.75, 295.9,   .39
550 DATA 45632, 199.5,  358.3,   .33
560 DATA 33333,   0.0, 1123.5,   .39
570 DATA 45678, 250.5,  332.5,   .38
580 DATA 0, 0, 0, 0
590 END

RUN
                            XYZ  COMPANY
         CUSTOMER ID     GAS USED        RATE            AMOUNT
            54985         -159.34          0             -55.769
            49828          -91.25          0             -34.675
            36872          -71.75          0             -23.6775
            99995         -236.15          0             -92.0985
            45632         -158.8           0             -52.404
            33333        -1123.5           0            -438.165
            45678          -82             0             -31.16
      TOTAL GAS USED    -1922.79     TOTAL AMOUNT       -727.949
```

Figure 3.18 The listing and output of the sample program with logical errors

A Case—Printing a Report

```
10  REM AUTHOR : T. J. WHITE, OCTOBER 15, 19--
20                                                              REM
30  REM THIS PROGRAM GENERATES A REPORT FOR THE GAS USERS OF THE
40  REM COMPANY
50  REM THE INPUTS ARE CUSTOMER'S ID, PREVIOUS METER READING,
60  REM CURRENT METER READING, AND THE RATE FOR EACH CUSTOMER.
70  REM *********************************************************
80  REM *   VARIABLE DICTIONARY:                                 *
90  REM *                                                        *
100 REM *      ID       =   THE CUSTOMER'S ID NUMBER             *
110 REM *      PREV     =   THE PREVIOUS METER READING           *
120 REM *      CURRENT  =   THE CURRENT METER READING            *
130 REM *      RATE     =   THE RATE                             *
140 REM *      GASUSE   =   THE GAS USAGE                        *
150 REM *      AMT      =   THE AMOUNT                           *
160 REM *      SUMGU    =   TOTAL GAS USED                       *
170 REM *      TOTAMT   =   THE TOTAL AMOUNT                     *
180 REM *                                                        *
190 REM *********************************************************
200                                                              REM
210 REM PRINTING THE HEADING
220     PRINT TAB(34); 'XYZ  COMPANY'
225     PRINT
230     PRINT TAB(12); 'CUSTOMER ID'; TAB(29); 'GAS USED';
240     PRINT TAB(44); 'RATE'; TAB(57); 'AMOUNT'
250     PRINT
260     SUMGU = 0
270     TOTAMT = 0
300 REM ****** BEGINNING OF READ-PROCESS-WRITE MODULE ******
310 REM *** AN ID NUMBER EQUAL TO 0 TERMINATES THE LOOP ***
320     READ ID, PREV, CURRENT, RATE
330     IF ID = 0 THEN GOTO 450
340         GASUSE = CURRENT - PREV
350         AMT = RATE*GASUSE
360                                                              REM
370         SUMGU = SUMGU + GASUSE
380         TOTAMT = TOTAMT + AMT
390                                                              REM
400         PRINT TAB(13); ID; TAB(29); GASUSE; TAB(44); RATE;
410         PRINT TAB(56); AMT
420     GOTO 300
430 REM ****** END OF THE READ-PROCESS-WRITE-MODULE *******
440                                                              REM
450 REM WRITING THE FOOTINGS
460     PRINT TAB(12); 'TOTAL '; TAB(28); SUMGU;
470     PRINT TAB(56); TOTAMT
500 REM ************* D A T A *************************
510 DATA 54985, 562.26,  721.6,  .35
520 DATA 49828, 205.5,   296.75, .38
530 DATA 36872, 911.5,   983.25, .33
540 DATA 99995,  59.75,  295.9,  .39
550 DATA 45632, 199.5,   358.3,  .33
560 DATA 33333,   0.0,  1123.5,  .39
570 DATA 45678, 250.5,   332.5,  .38
580 DATA 0, 0, 0, 0
590 END
RUN
```

```
                       XYZ  COMPANY

          CUSTOMER ID     GAS USED     RATE     AMOUNT

             54985         159.34       .35     55.769
             49828          91.25       .38     34.675
             36872          71.75       .33     23.6775
             99995         236.15       .39     92.0985
             45632         158.8        .33     52.404
             33333        1123.5        .39    438.165
             45678          82          .38     31.16

             TOTAL        1922.79              727.949
```

Figure 3.19 The final run of the sample program

1. The gas usage and the amount should not be negative. This error has occurred because the formula for the gas usage is incorrect. The formula should be corrected to read:

   ```
   340 GASUSE = CURRENT - PREV
   ```

2. The RATE should not be zero. The error is not due to a misreading of the value, because there is no zero in the DATA statements. Careful review shows that (in line 400) RATE is misspelled.

Furthermore, a PRINT statement is inserted at line 250 and at line 455. The first PRINT statement creates a blank line between the two headings, and the second one creates a blank line before the totals. Lines 460 and 470 are also combined to improve the readability of the output.

The final listing and the output for the test data are shown in Figure 3.19 on page 139. The figures still need to be aligned. The alignment of decimal points and other output editing can be accomplished with PRINT USING, discussed in Chapter 6.

Step 6: Documentation

The documentation of this program can be provided as follows:

1. The problem and the solution procedure (summary of Steps 1–5)
2. The flowchart, hierarchy charts, and the pseudocode for the program
3. The final run of the program (Figure 3.19)
4. Comments: This program generates a summary report using input data read in the program. This program does not print customers' bills nor does it store the data for later billing or processing.

EXERCISES

3.1 Find the errors in the following statements or programs. Identify the errors as syntax, execution, or logical errors.

   a. `10 PRINT A B C`
   b. `20 RAED P, Q, R`
   c. `100 T = (F-32)(A-B)`
   d. `LET P = Q*R`
   e.
   ```
   10 READ W, R
   20 PAY = WAGE*RATE
   30 PRINT WAGE, RATE, PAY
   40 DATA 5,5, 10
   50 END
   ```
   f.
   ```
   10 THIS IS THE BEGINNING OF THE PROGRAM
   20 INPUT X, Y
   ```

g. 10 READ A
   20 READ X, Y, Z
   30 DATA 5, 90, 30
   40 PRINT A, X, Y, Z
   50 END

h. 100 READ X
   200 T = T + X
   300 GOTO 100
   400 DATA 5, 6, 7
   500 DATA 10, 8, 5
   600 END

i. 10 READ R
   20 Q = R*.02
   30 IF R = 0 GOTO 99
   40 GOTO 10
   50 DATA 50, 92, 36, 82, 59, 0
   60 END

j. 50 READ F
   60 SUM = SUM + F
   70 IF F = 0 GOTO 110
   80 SUM = 0
   90 GOTO 50
   100 DATA 9, 18, 26, 15, 12, 6, 9, 0
   110 PRINT "TOTAL="; S
   120 END

k. 10 READ X, Y
   20 LET Z = Y/X
   30 PRINT "THE RATIO IS="; Z
   40 IF X = 0 THEN GOTO 99
   50 GOTO 10
   60 DATA 90, 30
   70 DATA 56, 29
   80 DATA 0, 29
   99 END

l. 10 READ A$, B
   20 C = A$ + B
   30 PRINT A$, B, C
   40 DATA JOHN, 50
   50 END

m. 10 READ N$, B, C
   20 DATA JOHN, PAT, KEY

n. 10 READ A, B
   20 N = 0
   30 IF A = 0 GOTO 99
   40 N = N + 1
     ⋮
   100 GOTO 10

o. 100 READ X, Y, Z, Q
   200 PRINT X, Y, Z, Q
   300 DATA 5, 10
   400 END

p. 50 READ A, B
   60 C = A + B
   70 END
   80 DATA 50, 60

q. 30 GOTO 99
     ⋮
   90 PRINT A
   100 END

3.2 Find out the following information about the computer you use:
  a. What is the name of the computer model?
  b. Who is the manufacturer?
  c. What version of BASIC is available?
  d. How do you use the printer to list your program or to print the output?

3.3 Suppose you would like to find the average heights and weights of the students in the BASIC course. Develop and design a program for this purpose. Follow the programming cycle explained in this chapter.

3.4 Suppose you would like to calculate the average percentages of the price increases of certain products in a grocery store. A simple way is to record the prices of certain products for one period, record the prices of the same products in another period (for example, after 6 months), and then calculate the average percentage price increase. Develop and design a program for this purpose. Follow the programming cycle explained in this chapter.

3.5 Develop an interactive program that accepts a series of numbers and, after -99 is typed, prints the average of all the numbers.

3.6 Suppose you buy a car on installment for T dollars to be paid off in N years. If the interest rate is R (expressed as a decimal), your monthly payment, P, can be calculated by the following formula:

$$P = T \times \frac{R/12}{1-(1+R/12)^{-12N}}$$

Develop an interactive program that accepts T, R, and N and calculates the monthly payment. Print the information. Hint: Change the formula to a shorter form by using different variables such as:

```
X = R/12
Y = 1 + X
Z = 1/(Y^(12*N))   this is the same as (1+R/12)^-12N
P = T*X/(1 - Z)
```

3.7 Write a program that accepts information about employees and prints a pay report.
  a. Input
     Name, ID number, wage rate, and the number of hours worked during a week.
  b. Processing
     The gross pay = hours * wage rate
     The deductions = Gross * .25

c. Output
      1. The sequence number, name, ID, wage rate, number of hours worked, gross pay, deduction, and the net in a report form.
      2. The total gross, deductions, and net for all employees at the end of the report.

      Place FINISH in the name field of the last record to indicate the end of the data.

SUMMARY

You have learned:

1. The meaning of the following terms:

execution	executable statement	interpreter
machine language	nonexecutable statement	compilation
higher-level language	debugging	BASIC-PLUS
source program	system command	BASIC-PLUS-2
object program	compiler	BASIC-PLUS-EXTENDED

2. A program may have to be rerun several times before it is completely correct. A program can have three kinds of errors:
   a. Syntax errors
   b. Execution errors
   c. Logical errors
3. An algorithm is the step-by-step procedure of solving a problem in precise detail.
4. A flowchart is a pictorial presentation of the necessary steps for solving a problem. You should be familiar with the flowcharting symbols and techniques.
5. A pseudocode represents in narrative form the necessary steps for solving a problem.
6. A programmer must understand the problem to be solved and plan the solution procedures. The programming cycle explained in the text should help you plan your program.
7. Structured programs are easy to follow and understand and thus easy to debug or modify. A structured program uses only three basic control

structures: (1) sequence structure, (2) decision structure, and (3) iteration structure. A structured program should be in top-down style, modular, readable, reliable, and well-documented.

REVIEW QUESTIONS/SELF-TEST

3.1 What is the difference between a machine language and a higher-level language?

3.2 What is the difference between the source program and the object program?

3.3 What is a compiler? What is compilation? What is an interpreter?

3.4 Standard BASIC is the newest version of BASIC. True or false?

3.5 The process of writing program statements is called _____ .

3.6 Removing errors from a program is called _____ .

3.7 A program can have three kinds of errors. What are they? Explain each briefly and give an example of each.

3.8 A programmer must know the solution procedure of a problem before programming. True or false? Discuss.

3.9 Several planning steps were explained as part of the programming cycle. Explain how each step is important in solving a problem.

3.10 Explain the following:
   a. An algorithm
   b. A flowchart
   c. A pseudocode

3.11 Which of the following BASIC statements has a syntax error?
   a. 10   D = A * 3B%
   b. 100 B + A * P = C
   c. 200 T = T + /B
   d. 100 RAED X, Y
   e. 200 PRNIT TAB 20 X
   f. all of the above

Decision Making, Comparing, Branching

In This Chapter:

The IF Statement

Problems Using the IF Statement
Finding the Largest Number
Terminating a Loop

Programming Style and Structured IF Block
GOTO Style
GOTO-Less Style
Structured Style

Structured Programming

Compound IF Statement: Logical Operators

Conditional Branching

Games

Menu in a Program

A Case—Generating a Report
Step 1: The Problem
Step 2: Input-Output Design
Step 3: Process Design
Step 4: Coding
Step 5: Execution, Testing, and Debugging
Step 6: Documentation

Exercises

Summary

Review Questions/Self-Test

4

Decision Making, Comparing, Branching

When writing programs, we often want the computer to take some action based on the outcome of the comparison of quantities or variables. For example, sometimes it is necessary to find out which quantity is larger, whether a value is less than zero, or whether a variable equals another. This chapter explains several alternative statements in BASIC for comparison and decision making. Understanding these statements and their applications is very important because the appropriate use of conditional statements directly affects problem-solving capability and programming style.

THE IF STATEMENT

The IF statement can be used to compare two variables or two values. A very simple form of this statement was used in previous chapters. Example 4.1 illustrates a more general use of the statement.

Example 4.1

Problem: The normal discount rate is 5 percent unless an amount is greater than $10,000, in which case the discount rate is 10 percent. Write a program that reads an amount; calculates the discount; and prints the amount, discount rate, and discount. Assume that there is more than one amount and that a zero indicates the end of data. Explain the solution procedure (the plan) and draw the flowchart before writing the program.

Solution Plan:

Start.
  Read AMT; at the end of data terminate the program
    Assume RATE = .05
      If AMT >10,000 Then RATE = .10
      Calculate the discount: DIS = RATE•AMT
      Print AMT, RATE, DIS
  Go to the beginning of the loop to read additional data
  End

Flowchart: See Figure 4.1.

Program:

```
10 READ AMT
20 IF AMT = 0 THEN GOTO 99
30   RATE = .05
40   IF AMT > 10000 THEN RATE = .10
50   DIS = RATE*AMT
60   PRINT "AMOUNT =";AMT;" RATE =";RATE;" THE DISCOUNT =";DIS
70 GOTO 10
80 DATA 25693.5, 7284.75, . . . 16955.4, 0
99 END
```

Notes:

1. The IF statement in line 40 compares the value of the variable AMT to $10,000 and checks whether AMT is greater than $10,000. If the statement is true, the value of RATE changes to 10 percent (note that it was 5 percent). If the comparison is not true, the next statement is ignored; that is, there is no change in the value of RATE. In either case, the statement in the line immediately following the IF statement is executed.
2. The statements in the loop are indented for readability. As you have learned, blank spaces do not affect the meaning of the statements.
3. The flowchart for this example, shown in Figure 4.1, aids in understanding the logic of the program. Note that the IF statement is used for the decision symbol.
4. The output will be

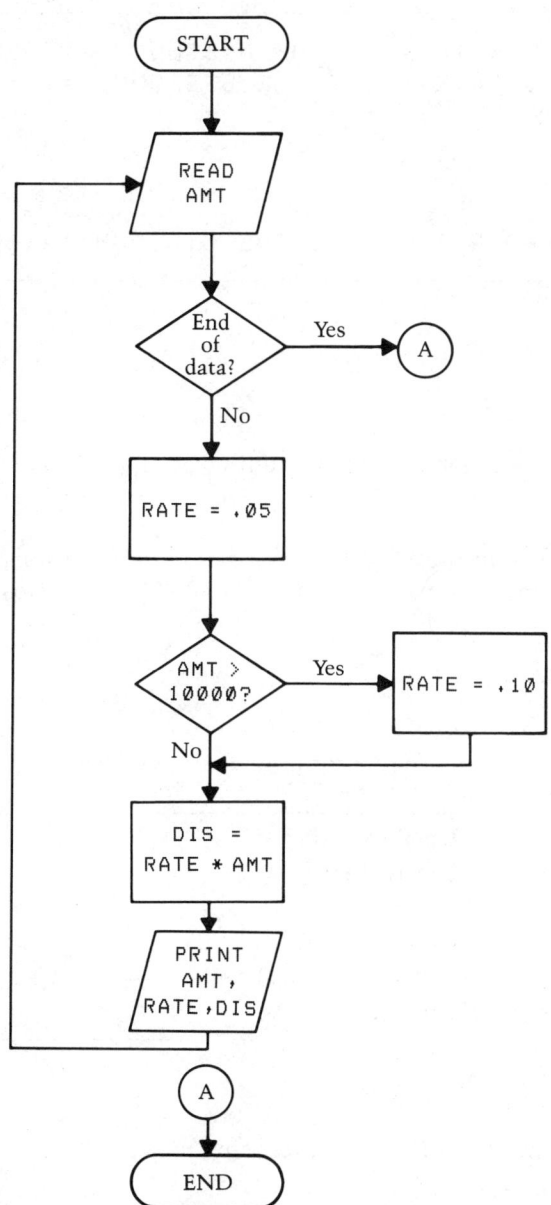

Figure 4.1 The flowchart for Example 4.1

```
AMOUNT = 25693.5 RATE = .1 THE DISCOUNT = 2569.35
AMOUNT = 7284.75 RATE = .05 THE DISCOUNT = 364.23

    :          :       :            :

AMOUNT = 16955.40 RATE = .10 THE DISCOUNT = 1695.54
```

The output design can be improved by including an appropriate heading.

The symbol *greater than*, >, in the above example is called a *relational operator*. A variety of such comparisons are permitted in BASIC. The most commonly used are shown in Table 4.1.

Table 4.1 Relational Operators

Relational Operator	Meaning
=	Equal to
>	Greater than
<	Less than
>=	Greater than or equal to
<=	Less than or equal to
<>	Not equal to

The following are some examples of the IF statement:

```
100  IF A > B THEN GOTO 999
99   IF X >= Y THEN GOAL = ACE
55   IF A + B <= 2*A*C THEN GOTO 100
65   IF ANSWER$ <> "YES" THEN GOTO 500
80   IF RESPONSE$ = "NO" THEN ANSWER$ = "YES"
50   IF LOSS = 9999 THEN PRINT "COME ON"
```

The general form of the logical IF statement is as follows:

```
line no.    IF logical-expression THEN statement
               ↑            ↑                ↑
               ①            ②                ③
```

It has four components:

1. The word IF.
2. A logical expression whose outcome is either true or false.
3. An executable BASIC statement. This executable statement is performed if the expression is true; otherwise it is ignored. In either case, execution normally proceeds to the next line after IF (unless there is a GOTO statement).

Again, the statement to the right of the IF statement is executed only if the expression is true, otherwise it is ignored. Pay attention to the following important points when you use a logical IF statement:

1. The statement to the right of the IF statement (after the THEN) must be executable. A DATA statement, for example, cannot be to the right of the IF statement.
2. You can construct a simple logical expression by using a relational operator with variables, constants, or arithmetic expressions, but the expression must be capable of being evaluated as either true or false. For example

   ```
   55   IF A < Y = Z THEN PRINT "CORRECT"
   ```

   is not valid because the expression is not capable of being evaluated as either true or false. (In many systems, any expression that is evaluated as a nonzero value is considered true, whereas an expression evaluated as zero is false. Thus IF A<>0 THEN ... and IF A THEN ... are equivalent in such systems.)
3. In most versions of BASIC, you are allowed to write only one statement after the word THEN (see statement A in Figure 4.2). If the program requires that there be several statements after IF, you must branch to a block of statements with a GOTO statement (see block n_1 in Figure 4.2).

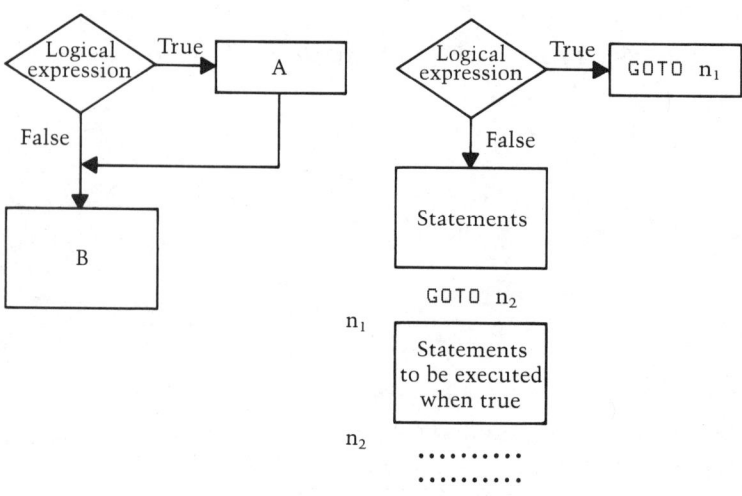

Figure 4.2 The logical IF

4. Two character strings can be compared in an IF statement. For example

   IF ANAME$ < "JOHN" GOTO 100

   is valid. A character is stored by its numeric code, and the value of a letter in the first part of the alphabet is less than the value of a letter in the latter part. In BASIC characters are compared according to their numeric codes. Two strings are equal only if their length, characters, and order of characters are the same. If either of the two strings contains more than one character, they are scanned and compared from left to right. The code of a blank has the lowest value. The following are some examples:

First Field		Second Field	Outcome
"ABC"	<	"ACC"	True
"ABC"	<	"ABD"	True
"AB "	<	"ABC"	True
"ABC"	<	"ABC"	False
"ABC899"	<	"ABC9"	True

5. It is best not to test the equality of a value to another value if one of them is achieved by computation. Because of the way the computer stores numbers, two seemingly equivalent numbers may not be judged as equal if one is stored under different conditions (for instance, when it is the result of a computation). For example, the expression in

```
100  IF X/2 = 1 THEN...
```

may never be true.

6. In most versions of BASIC, the word THEN or the word GOTO can be omitted. (In fact, in some systems the word THEN *must* be omitted.) For example, the three following statements are equivalent.

```
99   IF A > 5 THEN GOTO 30
55   IF A > 5 GOTO 30
75   IF A > 5 THEN 30
```

The following two statements are also equivalent.

```
55   IF X < Y THEN PRINT "X="; X
45   IF X < Y PRINT "X="; X
```

Again, this rule is not standard, and you should check the BASIC manual for your system concerning this rule.

PROBLEMS USING THE IF STATEMENT

The IF statement is used in problems with conditional situations: conditional branching, terminating, comparing, sorting, decision making, or rule making. The following are some examples.

Finding the Largest Number

It is very common to compare some values in a program to find the largest or the smallest value among a set of data. The following examples show some of the techniques. In each of the following examples, it is assumed that there is more than one data item and that zero indicates the end of data.

Example 4.2

Problem: Develop an algorithm, draw a flowchart, and write a program that reads a pair of numbers and prints the larger one.

Flowchart: See Figure 4.3.

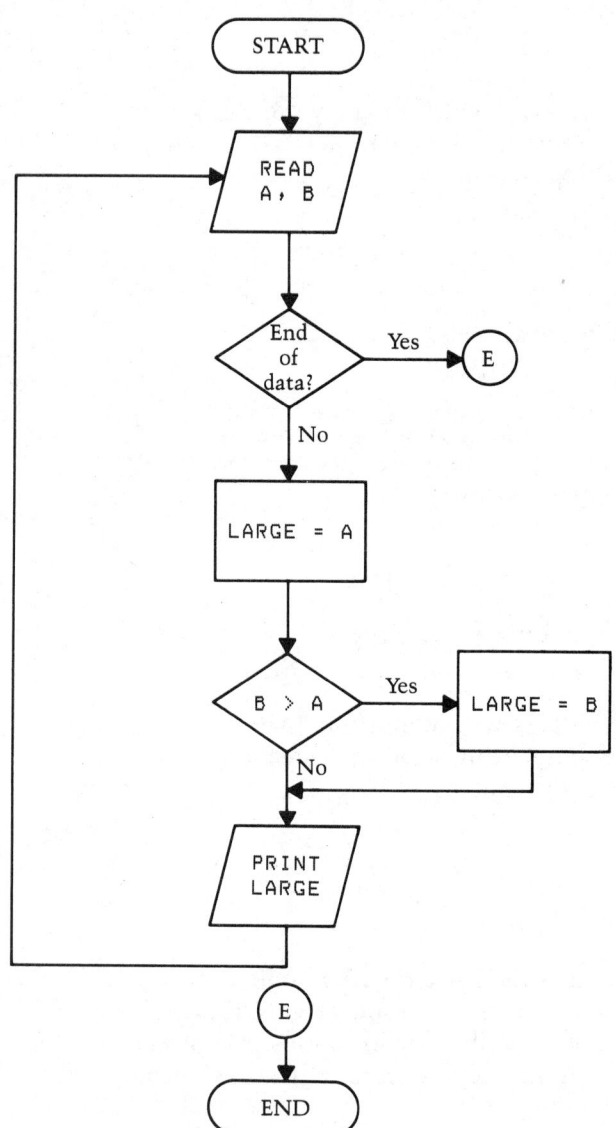

Figure 4.3 The flowchart for Example 4.2

Program:

```
10    READ A, B
20    IF A = 0 THEN GOTO 99
30      LARGE = A
40      IF B > A THEN LARGE = B
50      PRINT "THE LARGER NUMBER IS = "; LARGE
60    GOTO 10
70    DATA 92.2,61.5,  -8.3,-5.5,  -3, 0, , , , +3,6, 0,0
99    END
```

Notes:

1. When a pair of numbers (A, B) is read, it is assumed that A is the greater. Then A and B are compared. If B is greater, the value of LARGE changes to B; otherwise LARGE remains A.

2. The output will be

```
THE LARGER NUMBER IS =   92.2
THE LARGER NUMBER IS =  -5.5
THE LARGER NUMBER IS =   0
           ⋮
THE LARGER NUMBER IS =   6
```

3. The output design is deficient because it does not give a picture of the input. If the PRINT statement is changed to

   50 PRINT "THE LARGER OF "; A; " AND "; B; " IS "; LARGE

   then the output will be

```
THE LARGER OF  92.2 AND  61.5 IS  92.2
THE LARGER OF -8.5 AND -5.5 IS -5.5
THE LARGER OF -3 AND  0 IS  0
        ⋮
THE LARGER OF  3 AND  6 IS  6
```

Example 4.3

Problem: Write an interactive program that reads a series of numbers and prints the largest number among the data. Draw the flowchart before writing the program.

Flowchart: See Figure 4.4.

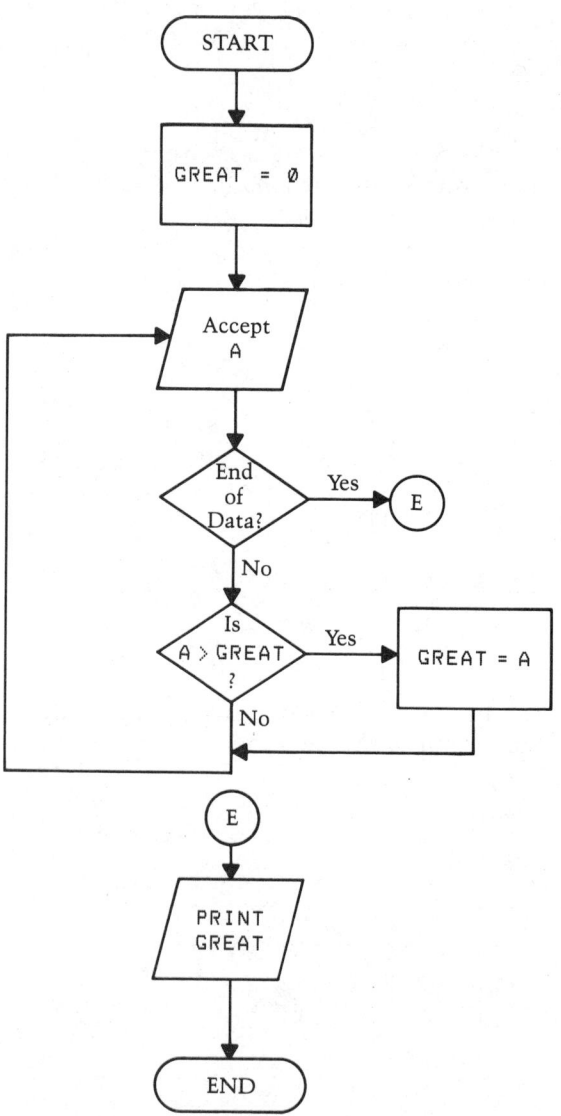

Figure 4.4 The flowchart for Example 4.3

Program:

```
10   PRINT "I WILL FIND THE LARGEST NUMBER"
20   PRINT "TYPE THE NUMBERS ONE BY ONE. TYPE ZERO AT END."
30   GREAT = 0
40   INPUT A
50   IF A = 0 THEN GOTO 100
60       IF A > GREAT THEN GREAT = A
70   GOTO 40
100  PRINT "THE LARGEST NUMBER IS "; GREAT
999  END
```

Notes:

1. At the beginning, it is assumed that the greatest number equals zero. Each time a new number (A) is read, it is compared to GREAT, the largest number up to that point. If A is greater than GREAT, then GREAT is changed to the new number; otherwise GREAT remains the same. The program continues until all the data are read, then the largest number is printed.
2. It is assumed that all the numbers are greater than zero. Otherwise, GREAT = 0 at the beginning of the program must be changed accordingly.

Terminating a Loop

An infinite loop created by a GOTO statement can be terminated by an IF statement. The following examples show several techniques.

Example 4.4

Problem: Calculate and print the weekly pay of several employees. Each data record contains wage rate and hours worked. There are exactly 15 records.

Program:

```
10   N = 0
20   PRINT "WAGE RATE", "HOURS WORKED", "PAY"
30   READ WAGE, HOURS
40       N = N + 1
50       PAY = WAGE*HOURS
60       PRINT WAGE, HOURS, PAY
70   IF N < 15 THEN GOTO 30
101  DATA 5.9, 40
102  DATA  ,  ,
         ⋮        ⋮
115  DATA  ,  ,
999  END
```

Notes:

1. The statement N = N + 1, the counter block, counts the number of times that the program goes through the loop, thus counting the number of data records.
2. If N (the number of repetitions or loops) is less than 15, control passes to the beginning of the program; otherwise, if the number of loops is equal to or greater than 15, the loop is terminated.

Header Value

The program in Example 4.4 works only if there are exactly 15 records in the data file. If there are more or fewer records, the program must be modified. We would like, however, to write a program that works with any number of data without requiring change. A better method is to have the number of data placed at the beginning of the data set. This value, which is called a *header value,* can then be read at the beginning of the program. The following example demonstrates this technique:

Example 4.5

Problem: The program in Example 4.4 is repeated. However, the number of records (15, for example) is placed at the beginning of the data.

Program:

```
10   N = 0
20   PRINT "WAGE RATE", "HOURS WORKED", "PAY"
30   READ K
40   READ WAGE, HOURS
50       N = N + 1
60       PAY = WAGE*HOURS
70       PRINT WAGE, HOURS, PAY
80   IF N < K GOTO 40
100  DATA 15
101  DATA 5.9, 40
         :    :
115  DATA , , ,
200  END
```

Notes:

1. The first READ statement reads the first value (15 in this case). This number is a header value showing how many data records follow.
2. If N (the number of times that the loop is repeated) is less than K (the number of records), the loop is repeated; otherwise the loop ends.

Sentinel Value

The program in Example 4.5 is independent of the number of data. To change the number of data, we need only change the first data item, the header value. However, the disadvantage of this method is that the number of data records must be precisely counted and entered.

Another way to terminate a loop is to place a number that is out of the range of the regular data as the last data record in the data file. We take this number to mean "end of data," and an IF statement can terminate the loop after that number is read. This value is called a *sentinel value* or *trailer record*. This technique was used in several programs in the previous chapters. The following program is another example:

■ Example 4.6

Problem: Calculate the average of the scores of students in a BASIC course. A negative number, such as -99, indicates the end of the data set.

Program:

```
10   N = 0     :    TOT = 0
30   READ SCORE
40      IF SCORE < 0 THEN GOTO 100
50      N = N + 1
60      TOT = TOT + SCORE
70   GOTO 30
100  AVG = TOT/N
110  PRINT "THE AVERAGE IS = ", AVG
120  DATA 95.5, 75.1, 85.4, . . . ,-99
999  END
```

Notes:

1. The READ statement reads each number. A negative number signals that all data have been read; the loop is then terminated.
2. N = N + 1 counts how many data items have been read. Note that the counter is placed after the sentinel testing statement so that the last item (the sentinel value) will not be counted. We need N to calculate the average.
3. The testing for the sentinel value occurs before any calculation in the loop.
4. The data are read in the loop, and the sum is accumulated in the loop as well. The average is calculated and printed after the loop.

Solved Problems

4.1 Write the following statements in BASIC.

  a. If N, the number of loop repetitions, still is not equal to K (the number of data lines), GOTO the beginning of the loop, statement number 5.

  b. If the number just read for X is negative, terminate the loop. The statement right after the loop is labeled 95.

  c. If the value of variable A is negative, make it positive.

  d. If X is not equal to Y, make it equal.

  e. If N is greater than M, stop execution.

  f. If X^3 is less than $3*X$, GOTO statement number 50.

  g. If X - Y is greater than X*Y, GOTO statement number 100.

  h. There are two variables, A and B. Calculate the square of the smaller number and the cube of the larger number.

Answers:

```
a. 100    IF N < K THEN GOTO 5
b. 200    IF X < 0 THEN GOTO 95
c. 300    IF A < 0 THEN A = -A
d. 400    IF X <> Y THEN X = Y
e. 100    IF N > M THEN STOP
f. 100    IF X^3 < 3*X THEN GOTO 50
g. 200    IF X - Y > X*Y THEN GOTO 100
h.  10    IF A < B THEN GOTO 100
    20    SS = B*B
    30    Q = A*A*A
    40    GOTO 200
   100    SS = A*A
   110    Q = B*B*B
   200    ....
```

4.2 Factorial N means $1 \times 2 \times 3 \times \ldots \times N$. For example, factorial 5 is: $1 \times 2 \times 3 \times 4 \times 5 = 120$. Write an interactive program that accepts N, calculates factorial N, and prints the data.

Answer:

```
10 PRINT "I WILL CALCULATE THE FACTORIAL OF A
   NUMBER IN A FLASH"
15 PRINT "WHAT IS THE NUMBER"
20 INPUT N
30 FACT = 1  :  K = 0
40    K = K + 1
50       FACT = FACT*K
60    IF K < N THEN GOTO 40
70 PRINT "FACTORIAL OF = "; N; " IS "; FACT
99 END
```

PROGRAMMING STYLE AND STRUCTURED IF BLOCK

As you have noticed, a program can be written in different ways to solve the same problem. Programming is not merely a technique; it is an art, science, and skill as well. When two programmers write a program to solve the same problem, chances are their designs and algorithms will be different. This will become apparent to you as your programs become longer. A good style, though, structures programs so that they are easy for the programmer or others to understand and modify if necessary.

Frequent use of the GOTO statement tends to make programs unstructured. To show this point, three programming styles are presented in the following sections. In the first and second sections, logical IF and GOTO statements are used. In the third section, you will be introduced to the IF-THEN-ELSE structure.

GOTO Style

A program may have many GOTO statements. The following is an example:

Example 4.7

Problem: Calculate the discount for an amount where the discount rate is

 5 percent   if the amount is up to $10,000
10 percent   if the amount is up to $20,000
20 percent   if the amount is equal to or more than $20,000

Assume that there are several data and that zero indicates the end of data.

Program:

```
10    READ AMT
20    IF AMT = 0 THEN GOTO 999
30      IF AMT < 10000 THEN GOTO 80
40      IF AMT < 20000 THEN GOTO 110
50        RATE = .2
60        DIS = RATE*AMT
70      GOTO 140
80        RATE = .05
90        DIS = RATE*AMT
100     GOTO 140
110       RATE = .1
120       DIS = RATE*AMT
140    PRINT "AMOUNT = "; AMT; " RATE = "; RATE; " DISCOUNT = "; DIS
150 GOTO 10
160 DATA 7562, 21395, . . . . . . . . . . . . . . . , 0
999 END
```

Notes:

1. The IF and GOTO statements are used to branch to a particular block of statements.
2. Some statements are indented to make the program readable and to make the logic of the program apparent. Indention does not affect the statements.
3. The program is broken down into blocks. Each block can contain one or several statements, which are executed or not, depending on whether an IF statement is true or false. For example, the block that starts at statement 80 is executed only when AMT is less than 1000.

GOTO-Less Style

The following example demonstrates another way to write a program that solves the same problem.

Example 4.8

Problem: The same as in Example 4.7.

Program:
```
10 READ AMT
20 IF AMT = 0 THEN GOTO 999
30   RATE = .05
40   IF AMT > 10000 THEN RATE = .1
50   IF AMT > 20000 THEN RATE = .2
60   DIS = RATE*AMT
70   PRINT "AMOUNT = ";AMT,"RATE = ";RATE,"DISCOUNT = ";DIS
80 GOTO 10
90 DATA . . . .
999 END
```

Note: The style is the same as that used in Example 4.1. The discount rate is assumed to be .05 at the beginning. If the amount is greater than 10000, the rate is changed to .10; if not, the rate remains .05. If the amount is greater than 20000, the rate is changed to .20.

164 *Decision Making, Comparing, Branching*

The GOTO style, which has many GOTO statements, seems easier to understand than the GOTO-less style. Although GOTO-less style is simpler, its logic is not as easy to follow. Which style is chosen depends on the programmer. Now, consider the following style as well.

Structured Style

In this section, the same problem is solved. This time, however, an IF-THEN-ELSE structure is used. Look at the example before we explain this method.

Example 4.9

Problem: The same as in Example 4.7. Draw a flowchart or a logic chart before coding, and use structured IF.

Flowchart: See Figure 4.5.

Logic chart: See Figure 4.6.

Program:

```
10 READ AMT
20 IF AMT = 0 THEN GOTO 999
30    IF AMT < 10000 THEN              &
                RATE = .05             &
       ELSE IF AMT < 20000 THEN        &
                RATE = .10             &
            ELSE                       &
                RATE = .20             &
40    REM END-OF-IF
50    DIS = RATE*AMT
60    PRINT "AMOUNT = ";AMT,"RATE = ";RATE,
            "DISCOUNT = ";DIS
70 GOTO 10
80 DATA . . .
999 END
```

Notes:

1. When the logical expression is true (that is, if the amount is less than $10,000), then the statement between THEN and the corresponding ELSE statement is executed, and the rest of the state-

Programming Style and Structured IF Block **165**

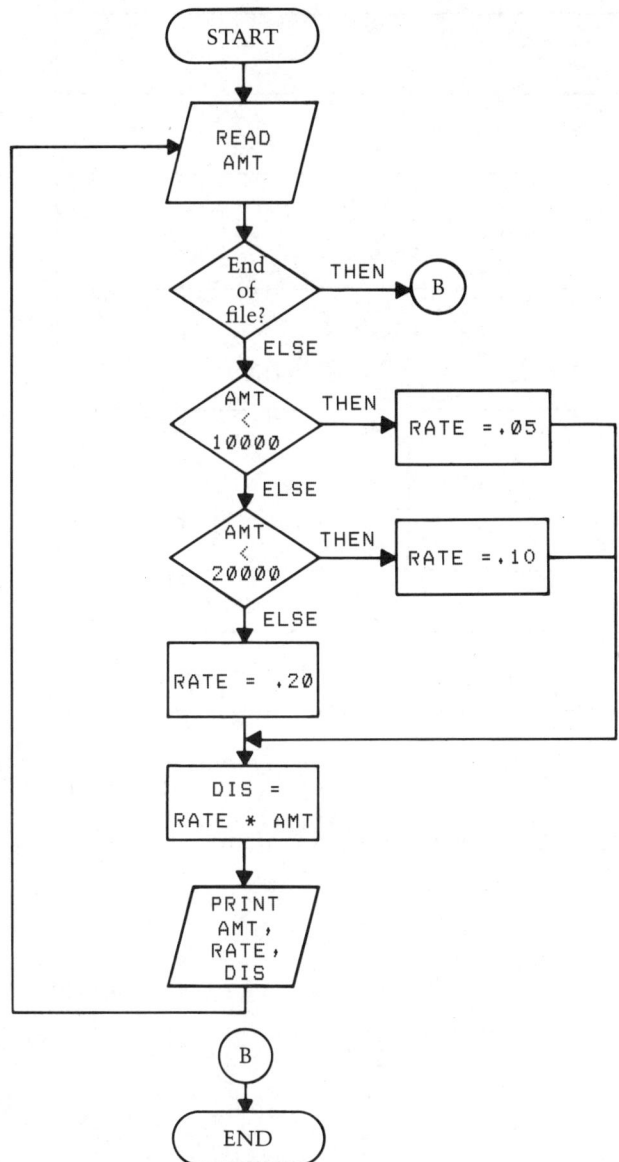

Figure 4.5 The flowchart for Example 4.9

ments up to END-OF-IF are ignored. Otherwise, (if false) the statement after the ELSE statement is executed.
2. The entire IF block is one statement, and the continuation character (&) is used here to divide it into several physical lines. Some lines are indented to make the pattern of the logic apparent.

166 *Decision Making, Comparing, Branching*

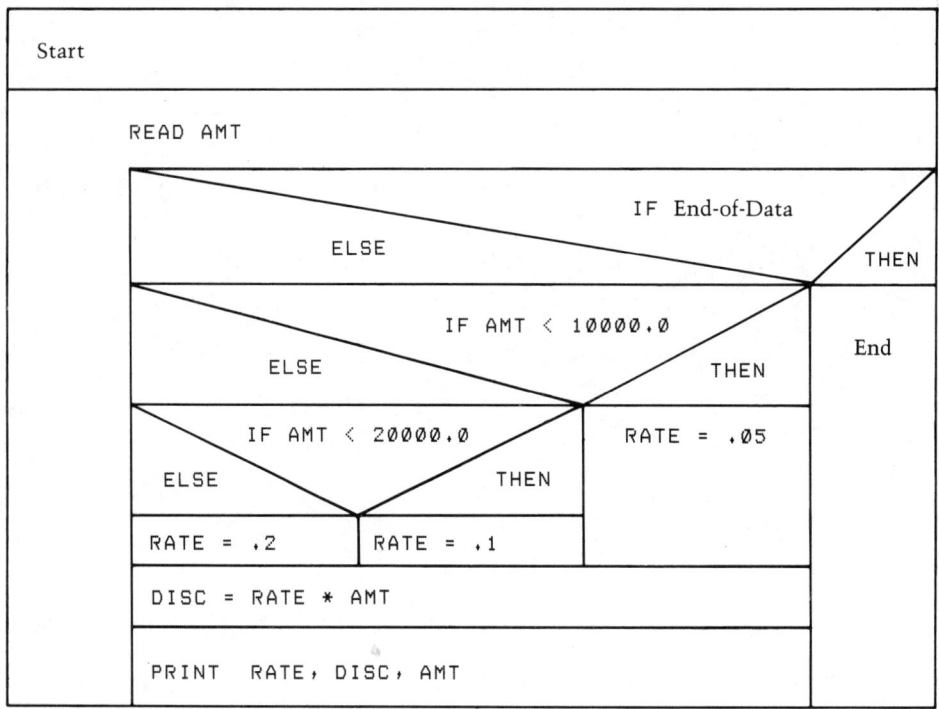

Figure 4.6 The logic chart for Example 4.9

Most versions of BASIC support the IF-THEN-ELSE statement. The general form of this statement is:

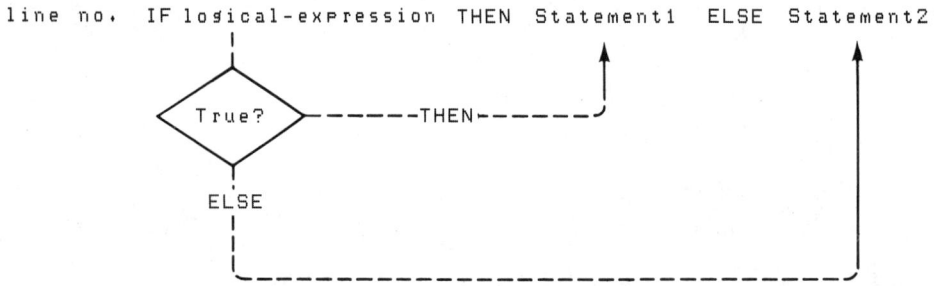

If the result of the expression is "true," Statement 1 is executed and Statement 2 is ignored. When the logical expression is false, Statement 2 is executed and Statement 1 is ignored. The following are some examples:

```
50 IF X = Y PRINT "X EQUALS TO Y" ELSE PRINT "X NOT EQUAL TO Y"
100 IF P < Q THEN END ELSE GOTO 300
```

An `IF` statement can be used in the range of `THEN` or `ELSE`. An `IF` within an `IF` is called *nested* `IF`. We used nested structured `IF` in Example 4.9.

As mentioned before, the `IF-THEN-ELSE` statement is a single statement. However, in some systems, it can be divided into several physical lines. For example:

```
10      IF X < 10 THEN                  &
            P = .10                     &
        ELSE                            &
            P = .50                     &
20 REM END-OF-IF
```

In this example, the & character indicates the line is continued. Some systems allow you to use another character or the feed key instead of the ampersand. In other systems the entire statement must be on one line.

STRUCTURED PROGRAMMING

You have seen the variety of programming styles that different uses of the `IF` statement create, and probably you agree that `IF-THEN-ELSE` statements make programs easier to understand and follow. The decision structure, in fact, is one of the most important control structures in a structured program. In structured programming, a decision structure has only one entry to and one exit from the decision block. When you use `IF` statements, it is desirable to write a structure that matches the pseudocode in Figure 4.7.

A structured `IF`, however, can have any of the three basic structures shown in Figure 4.8.

1. If the condition is true, then all the statements after `THEN` are executed. If the condition is false, all the statements after `ELSE` are executed.
2. All the statements after `THEN` are executed only if the condition is true. Otherwise, they are ignored.
3. The set of statements are executed only if the condition is false.

Notice that there is only one entry and one exit in all three structures.

Unfortunately, some BASIC interpreters do not allow the use of this structured `IF`. Other interpreters have `IF-THEN-ELSE` features, but allow

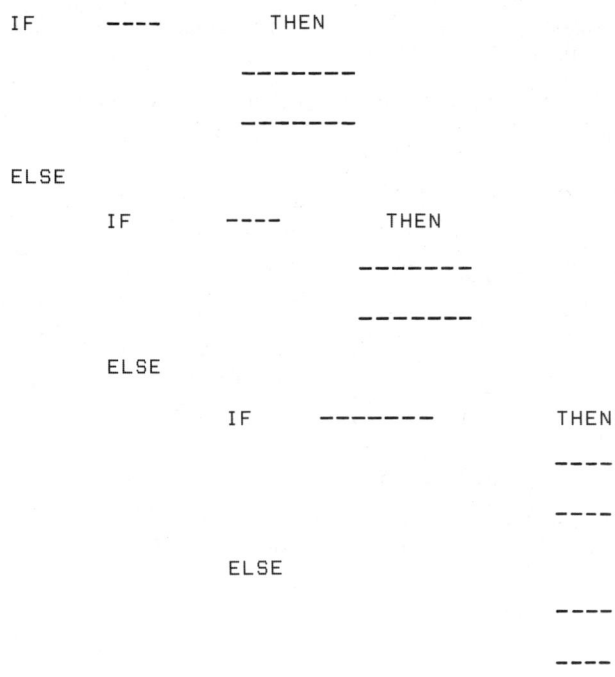

Figure 4.7 A pseudocode for an IF block

only one statement between THEN and ELSE and offer no END-IF statement. Other systems allow multistatements (separated by colons) in the range of THEN or ELSE, but the entire IF block must be limited to one line (see Appendix B). Programs using the structured IF shown in the previous pseudocode (or flowcharts) are:

- Easier to understand (with more apparent logic)
- Easier to code
- Easier to review at a later time
- Less prone to error
- Less time-consuming
- Easier to modify and document

These are the objectives of structured programming. What do you do if your system does not allow the structured IF? One way to implement the previous code is to use GOTO statements and remarks in a block of statements. An example follows:

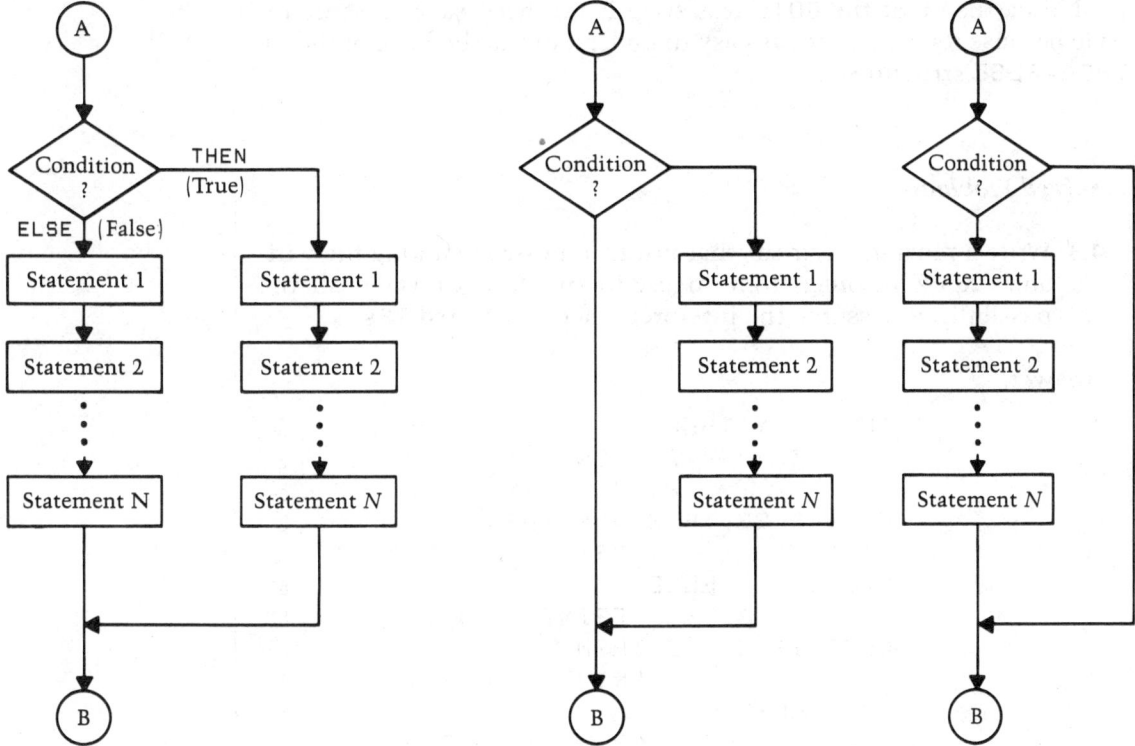

Figure 4.8 Correct decision structures

```
10              IF X > Y  THEN GOTO 100 ELSE GOTO 200
100     REM              THEN
110                        PRINT "X IS GREATER THAN Y"
120                        LET P = Q
130                        SEQ1 = SEQ1 + 1
140                      GOTO 300
200     REM     ELSE
210                        PRINT "X IS LESS THAN Y"
220                        LET P = R
230                        SEQ2 = SEQ2 + 2
240     REM     END-OF-IF
300     . . . . . . . . (next statement)
```

Notice that indention and remarks are necessary elements in artificial IF-THEN-ELSE blocks. Of course, GOTO statements are not recommended in structured programming. The above example is good for systems that do not offer IF-THEN-ELSE structure with multistatements in the range of THEN or ELSE.

170   *Decision Making, Comparing, Branching*

Notice also that the GOTO-less style is not necessarily a structured style because its logic is not as easy to understand as the logic of the IF-THEN-ELSE structure.

■ **Solved Problems**

4.3 Write a program segment that prints a message ranking the variables X,Y,Z in order from largest to smallest. Consider all the possibilities. Assume the interpreter accepts nested IFs.

Answer:

```
100             IF X > Y THEN                           &
                    IF Y > Z THEN                       &
                        PRINT "X > Y > Z"               &
                    ELSE IF Z > X THEN                  &
                            PRINT "Z > X > Y"           &
                         ELSE                           &
                            PRINT "X > Z > Y"           &
                ELSE IF X > Z THEN                      &
                        PRINT "Y > X > Z"               &
                     ELSE                               &
                        PRINT "Y > Z > X"               &
200             REM END-OF-IF                           &
```

4.4 Write a structured IF statement equivalent to the following:

```
a. 10    IF HOUR > 40 GOTO 50
   20    GROSS = HOUR*RATE
   30    GOTO 60
   50    GROSS = (HOUR - 40)*1.5*RATE + 40*RATE
   60    ........
b. 10    IF A < 1000 GOTO 50
   20    IF A < 2000 GOTO 70
   30       RATE = R
   40       GOTO 80
   50    RATE = P
   60       GOTO 80
   70    RATE = Q
   80    ........
```

```
     c.  10     IF X > 50000 GOTO 40
         20     IF X > 40000 GOTO 80
         30     GOTO 110
         40     RATE = 13
         50        IF I = 1 RATE = 15
         60        IF I = 2 RATE = 14
         70        GOTO 110
         80     RATE = 10
         90        IF I = 1 RATE = 12
        100        IF I = 2 RATE = 11
        110     ........
```

Answers:

```
  a. 10 IF HOUR > 40 THEN                              &
           GROSS = (HOUR-40)*1.5*RATE + 40*RATE        &
        ELSE                                           &
           GROSS = HOUR*RATE
     50 REM END-OF-IF
     60 ........
  b. 10     IF A < 1000 THEN                           &
                RATE = P                               &
            ELSE IF A < 2000 THEN                      &
                       RATE = Q                        &
                    ELSE                               &
                       RATE = R
     50 REM END-OF-IF
     60     ........
  c. 40     IF X > 50000 THEN                          &
                IF I = 1 THEN                          &
                       RATE = 15                       &
                ELSE IF I = 2 THEN                     &
                       RATE = 14                       &
                    ELSE                               &
                       RATE = 13                       &
            ELSE IF X > 40000 THEN                     &
                    IF I = 1 THEN                      &
                       RATE = 12                       &
                    ELSE IF I = 2 THEN                 &
                       RATE = 11                       &
                        ELSE                           &
                       RATE = 10
     50 REM END-OF-IF
    110     ........
```

4.5 Are the following IF statements correct?

a.
```
10         IF A < 5 THEN                &
              KODE = 1                  &
              GOTO 50                   &
           ELSE IF A < 10 THEN          &
              KODE = 2                  &
              GOTO 50                   &
           ELSE                         &
              KODE = 3                  &
              GOTO 50                   &
20 REM     END-OF-IF
50         ........
```

b.
```
10      IF SCORE > 90 GOTO 50
20      IF SCORE > 80 GOTO 60
30      IF SCORE > 70 GOTO 70
40      IF SCORE > 60 GOTO 80
45      IF SCORE < 60 GOTO 90
50      GRADE$ = "A"
60      GRADE$ = "B"
70      GRADE$ = "C"
80      GRADE$ = "D"
90      GRADE$ = "E"
100     PRINT GRADE$
```

Answers:

a. Not only are the GOTO 50 statements unnecessary, but they also create syntax errors in those systems that allow only one statement after each THEN or ELSE.

b. The program segment is not logically correct because some of the statements, such as the one in line 90, will be executed in all cases.

4.6 Does Structure A or Structure B, shown in Figure 4.9, conform to structured programming techniques?

Answers:

Structure A does not conform; it has many entries and many exits. Structure B conforms to structured programming technique.

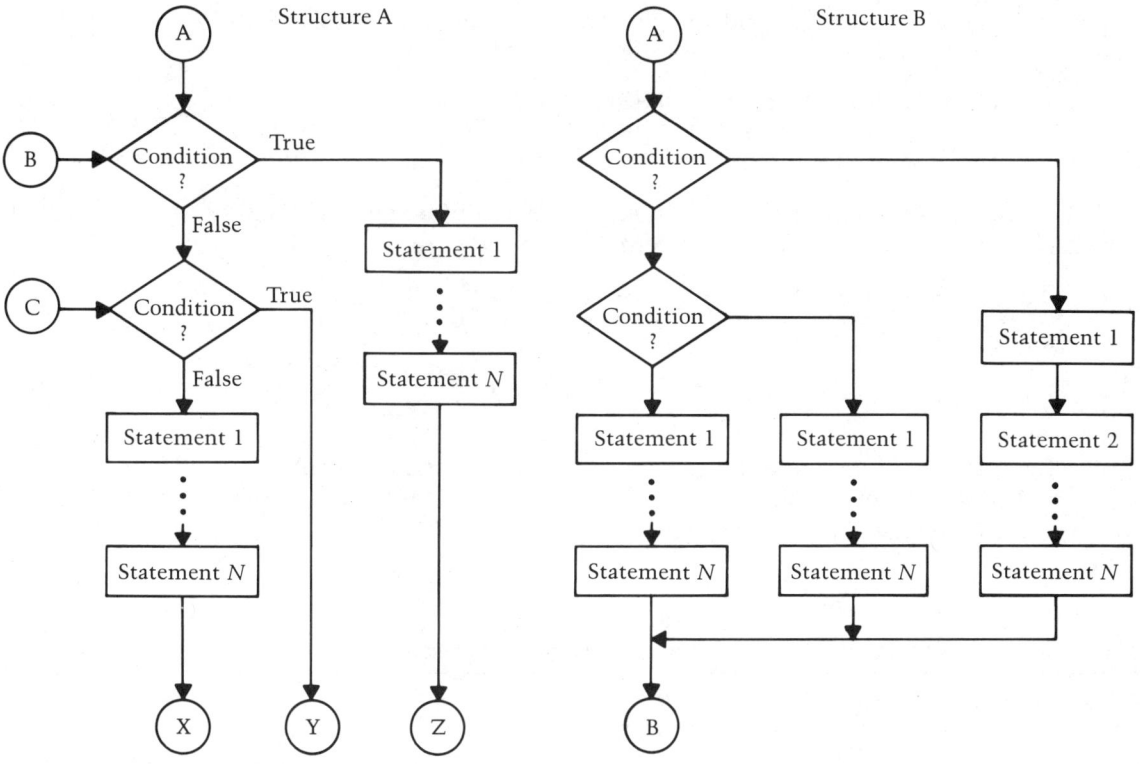

Figure 4.9

COMPOUND IF STATEMENT: LOGICAL OPERATORS

A simple logical expression can consist of values, constants, variables, or mathematical expressions and a relational operator—=, <, >, and so on. For example, all of the following are simple logical expressions:

```
56 < 39
 X >= 30
A+B < 2*C*D**2
```

A compound IF statement uses an IF statement and one or more logical expressions linked with a logical operator. (Although most systems allow compound IF statements, a few do not.) The most common logical operators are NOT, AND, OR, and EQV (equivalent). The following are all compound IF statements:

```
10 IF A > B AND B > C THEN RATE = .05
100 IF P = 30 OR Q < 3 THEN GOTO 900
500 IF X = 0 AND NOT Y < 35 THEN P = 3
```

Logical operators cannot be used in sequence except when the second operator is NOT. For example, the statement

```
55  IF A < B AND NOT A > C THEN GOTO 10
```

is valid. But, the statement

```
55  IF X < Y AND OR X > Z THEN GOTO 10
```

is not valid.

The outcome of a compound logical expression depends on the outcomes of the logical expressions used. Table 4.2 summarizes the outcomes of simple compound logical expressions.

Table 4.2 The Outcome of Simple Compound Logical Expressions

Log. exp. 1	Log. exp. 2	Log. exp. 1 AND Log. exp. 2	Log. exp. 1 OR Log. exp. 2
True	True	True	True
True	False	False	True
False	True	False	True
False	False	False	False

	Log. exp.	NOT Log. exp.
	True	False
	False	True

For example, if A = 1, and B = 2, then the outcome of the logical expression

```
A > B AND A > 0
```

is false because

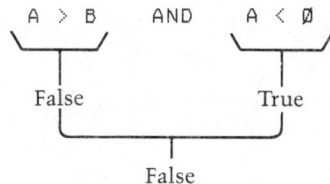

If a logical expression contains two or more logical operators, the priority of execution is as follows.

First: NOT   highest
Second: AND
Third: OR
Fourth: EQV   lowest

The priority of operations can be changed through the use of parentheses. Expressions within parentheses are evaluated first. It is recommended to group the expressions with parentheses.

Solved Problems:

4.7 Identify errors, if any, in the following IF statements:
 a. 10   IF (X < 30.5 AND X > 10.5) THEN STOP
 b. 100 IF AMT < 1000 AND > 100 THEN RATE = .05
 c. 200 IF IQ < 70 OR > 190 THEN GOTO 700
 d. 150 IF PAY = 500 AND KODE = 2 THEN GOTO 30
 e. 10   IF NET > 600 AND K = 5 OR NET < 60
         AND K = 4 THEN GOTO 300
 f. 50   IF CLASS = 1 AND OR SEX$ = "F" THEN N = N + 1

Answers:

 a. This is correct.
 b. The second logical expression is not complete. The statement can be corrected as follows:
    IF AMT < 1000 AND AMT > 100 THEN RATE = .05

c. Again, the second logical expression is not complete.
d. This is correct.
e. This is also correct, but a complex statement like this is not recommended.
f. The operators AND and OR cannot be used in immediate sequence.

4.8 Some systems differentiate between lowercase and uppercase letters. Assume you are accepting a response that should be either yes or no. Write a statement that transfers control to statement 999 if the response is yes, typed either in uppercase or lowercase letters.

Answer:

```
10   IF RESPONSE$ = "YES" OR RESPONSE$ = "yes" THEN GOTO 999
```

CONDITIONAL BRANCHING

With the logical IF statement or the IF block, you can write almost any program segment that involves comparison, decision making, and conditional branching. But BASIC also allows you additional choices. The ON GOTO statement is another feature for this purpose.

Like GOTO, ON GOTO is used for branching. But ON GOTO transfers control to one of several statements, depending on the values of an integer variable. By contrast, a simple GOTO statement transfers control to only one statement. Look at an example before we explain this topic further.

Example 4.10

Problem: Suppose the grade code for each student in a BASIC course is recorded as 1, 2, 3, 4, or 5, where 1 equals F, 2 equals D, 3 equals C, 4 equals B, and 5 equals A. Write a program that reads a student's name and his or her code. Calculate the number of each grade code and print the name and the letter grade. Print the number of each grade code at the end. Assume there are several students. E-O-R indicates end of data.

Program:

```
10   A = 0 : B = 0 : C = 0 : D = 0 : F = 0
20   READ ANAME$, KODE
30   IF ANAME$ = "E-O-R" GOTO 700
40      ON KODE GOTO 100, 200, 300, 400, 500
50                                              REM
100        GRADE$ = "F"
110        F = F + 1
120        GOTO 600
190                                             REM
200        GRADE$ = "D"
210        D = D + 1
230        GOTO 600
240                                             REM
300        GRADE$ = "C"
310        C = C + 1
320        GOTO 600
330                                             REM
400        GRADE$ = "B"
410        B = B + 1
420        GOTO 600
430                                             REM
500        GRADE$ = "A"
510        A = A + 1
530                                             REM
600      PRINT "STUDENT:"; ANAME$; "GRADE:"; GRADE$
610  GOTO 20
700  PRINT "NO. OF A'S: "; A, "NO. OF B'S: "; B, "NO. OF C'S: ";
705  PRINT   C, "NO OF D'S:"; D, "NO. OF F'S:"; F
800  DATA "PAT BROWN", 3, "JOE JOHNSON", 4 , . . , "E-O-R", 0
999  END
```

Notes:

1. ON KODE GOTO 100, 200, 300, 400, 500 transfers control to the block that starts with line number:

   100 if KODE = 1 (to assign an F and count the number of Fs)
   200 if KODE = 2 (to assign a D and count the number of Ds)
   300 if KODE = 3 (to assign a C and count the number of Cs)
   400 if KODE = 4 (to assign a B and count the number of Bs)
   500 if KODE = 5 (to assign an A and count the number of As)

2. The control is transferred out of each block by GOTO 600.
3. At the end of the data, the number of As, Bs, Cs, Ds, and Fs are printed by line number 700.
4. Note that NAME$ is not chosen because it is a reserved word for some systems.

The general form of an ON GOTO statement is:

    Line no.   ON   exp   GOTO N1, N2, N3, . . ., Nn

where N1, N2, N3, . . ., Nn are integers representing a line number and exp is an integer variable, a constant, or an expression. The ON GOTO statement works this way:

    IF   exp = 1   GOTO N1
    IF   exp = 2   GOTO N2
    IF   exp = 3   GOTO N3
    IF   exp = 4   GOTO N4
         :   :   :
    IF   exp = i_n GOTO N_n

For example,

    ON M GOTO 400, 6, 280, 99

means

    IF M = 1 GOTO 400
    IF M = 2 GOTO 6
    IF M = 3 GOTO 280
    IF M = 4 GOTO 99

If the value of exp is less than 1 or greater than n, then the action depends on the version of BASIC used. Some interpreters print an error message; others ignore the ON GOTO statement totally. If exp is a noninteger or an expression, it is evaluated to an integer value first.

The ON GOTO statement is very useful when you need to establish several independent blocks for different values of a variable. Each block can be a set of statements written for a particular value of that variable. For example, this technique is very common in the program that starts with a menu. Control is transferred to a particular block according to the code value of an item in the menu. Blocking is also very common in applications that require different calculations for different values of a code (a variable identifying an item), especially when the code takes on sequential integer values.

■ Solved Problems

4.9 Rewrite the following program segments. Use ON GOTO statements in your answers.

```
a. 10   IF K = 5 GOTO 100
   20   IF K = 4 GOTO 200
   30   IF K = 3 GOTO 300
   40   IF K = 2 GOTO 200
   50   IF K = 1 GOTO 100
b. 10   IF KODE = 1 THEN                &
             GOTO 100                   &
        ELSE IF KODE = 2 THEN           &
             GOTO 200                   &
        ELSE IF KODE = 3 THEN           &
             GOTO 300                   &
        ELSE                            &
             GOTO 400                   &
   20   REM  END-OF-IF
c. 100  IF I = 50 GOTO 600
   110  IF I = 51 GOTO 500
   120  IF I = 52 GOTO 700
d. 5    IF SCORE < 6 GOTO 50
   10   IF SCORE < 7 GOTO 60
   15   IF SCORE < 8 GOTO 70
   20   IF SCORE < 9 GOTO 80
   25   IF SCORE < 10 GOTO 90
   50   ......................
```

Answers:

```
a. 10   ON K GOTO 100, 200, 300, 200, 100
b. 10   IF KODE > 3 GOTO 400
   20   ON KODE GOTO 100, 200, 300
c. 100  J = I - 49
   110  ON J GOTO 600, 500, 700
```
Note the technique for converting the value of I to sequential values 1, 2, and 3.
```
d. 10   J = SCORE - 4
   20   IF J < 1 THEN GOTO 50
   30   IF J > 5 THEN GOTO 50
   40   ON J GOTO 50, 60, 70, 80, 90
   50   ...............................
```

180 *Decision Making, Comparing, Branching*

GAMES

In a game program, several variables interact to simulate a real or imaginary situation. These variables may represent policies, strategies, and rules. The imponderable "luck" can also be included in the program through the use of random numbers, a topic discussed in Chapter 10. Sophisticated games incorporate luck and use graphics. Developing a game is a creative and challenging job limited only by the imagination of its creator.

The following simple program is an example of a game:

Example 4.11

Problem: Develop a simple maze game that accepts some input and uses many IF-GOTO statements to branch to a particular block of statements. There should be only one way to reach the solution.

Program:

```
10   PRINT "**** WELCOME TO THE WORLD OF MAZE ****"
20   PRINT"IF YOU GET IN, I DO NOT GUARANTEE THAT YOU WILL GET OUT"
30   PRINT "ARE YOU WILLING TO TAKE A RISK"
40   INPUT A$
50   IF A$ = "NO" THEN GOTO 500
60   PRINT"TYPE A DIRECTION 1 = NORTH, 2 = EAST, 3 = WEST, 4 = SOUTH"
70   INPUT X
80   ON X GOTO 90, 110, 150, 90
90   PRINT " GOOD...GO ON, TYPE A NEW DIRECTION"
100  GOTO 70
110  PRINT " YOU CAN'T GO THAT WAY, TRY AGAIN."
120  GOTO 70
140  PRINT " YOU JUST WERE RESCUED FROM DEATH."
150  PRINT " YOU ARE TURNING ON ANOTHER ROAD NOW"
155  PRINT " YOU MAY GO ON, BE CAREFUL,  TYPE A DIRECTION"
160  INPUT Z
170  ON Z GOTO 180, 110, 150, 220
180  PRINT " NOBODY HAS BEEN THIS FAR BEFORE."
190  PRINT "YOUR SCORE IS 100% SO FAR. TYPE A NEW DIRECTION."
200  INPUT X
210  ON X GOTO 180, 300, 220, 140
220  M = 1
230  PRINT TAB(M); "DEAD"
240  M = M + 1
250  IF M < 30 GOTO 230
260  GOTO 400
300  N=1
310  PRINT TAB(N); "YOU ARE THE WINNER"
320  N = N + 1
330  IF N<30 GOTO 310
400  PRINT "WOULD YOU LIKE TO TRY AGAIN"
410  GOTO 20
500  PRINT "***YOU CHICKEN, CALL ME WHEN YOU GOT SOME GUTS***"
510  END
```

Note: The program style (called spaghetti style) itself is a maze. See if you can follow the winning pattern. Try to run the program with whatever system you have available. Note that at the beginning the program asks if the player would like to take a risk. It accepts YES in any language (try it)!

MENU IN A PROGRAM

Sometimes a program can do several things. Listing the choices and asking the user to select a choice is very common in interactive programs. A menu is a list of options available to the user of the program.

In terms of programming techniques, any time that a choice is selected, control should pass to one or several modules of the program that perform that task. The following simple program shows this concept. However, a menu-driven program for more sophisticated tasks requires a good modular programming approach. This concept is discussed further in Chapter 9, where subprograms are presented.

Example 4.12

Problem: Write a program that converts one of the following standard U.S. measures to its metric equivalent, according to a menu:

1. Inches to centimeters
2. Feet to centimeters
3. Inches to meters
4. Feet to meters
5. Fahrenheit to centigrade

Program:

```
10  PRINT " HI THIS PROGRAM CONVERTS THE FOLLOWING U.S."
15  PRINT " MEASURES TO THIER METRIC EQUIVALENTS."
20  PRINT
25  PRINT "1.   INCHES TO CENTIMETERS"
30  PRINT "2.   FEET TO CENTIMETERS"
35  PRINT "3.   INCHES TO METERS"
40  PRINT "4.   FEET TO METERS"
45  PRINT "5.   FAHRENHEIT TO CENTIGRADE"
50  PRINT "6.   END THE PROGRAM"
75  PRINT "PLEASE SELECT 1, 2, 3, 4, 5, OR 6"
80  INPUT OPTION
85  IF OPTION > 6 OR OPTION < 1 THEN GOTO 75
90  ON OPTION GOTO 100, 200, 300, 400, 500, 600
95  REM ***********************************************
100 REM *    THIS IS THE INCH TO CENTIMETER MODULE    *
110    INPUT "TYPE THE INCHES"; INCHES
120    CENTI = INCHES*2.54
130    PRINT INCHES; "INCHES ARE EQUAL TO:"; CENTI; "CENTIMETERS"
140 GOTO 20
150 REM ********** END OF INCH TO CENTIMETER MODULE**************
200 REM ***              FEET TO CENTIMETER MODULE              ***
210    INPUT "TYPE THE FEET"; FEET
220    CENTI = FEET*12*2.54
230    PRINT FEET; "FEET ARE EQUAL TO:"; CENTI; "CENTIMETERS"
240 GOTO 20
250 REM ********* END OF FEET TO CENTIMETER MODULE ************
300 REM ***              INCH TO METER MODULE              ***
310    INPUT "TYPE INCHES"; INCHES
320    METER = 2.54*INCHES/100
330    PRINT INCHES; "INCHES ARE EQUAL TO "; METER; " METERS"
340 GOTO 20
350 REM ************* END OF INCH TO METER MODULE *************
400 REM ***              FEET TO METER MODULE              ***
410    INPUT "TYPE FEET"; FEET
420    METER = FEET*12*2.54/100
430    PRINT FEET; "FEET ARE EQUAL TO "; METER; " METER"
440 GOTO 20
450 REM ************* END OF FEET TO METER MODULE *************
500 REM ***         FAHRENHEIT TO CENTIGRADE MODULE         ***
510    INPUT "TYPE DEGREES IN FAHRENHEIT:" ; XFAR
520    YCENT = (XFAR - 32)*5/9
530    PRINT XFAR; " DEGREES OF FAHRENHEIT EQUALS ";
535    PRINT  YCENT; " CENTIGRADES"
540 GOTO 20
550 REM ****** END OF FAHRENHEIT TO CENTIGRADE MODULE **********
600 PRINT "*************** C A L L   B A C K *****************"
999 END
```

A CASE—GENERATING A REPORT

The following problem demonstrates the application of the material covered so far. We will use the problem-solving concepts outlined in Chapter 3 to solve this problem.

Step 1: The Problem

XYZ Company would like a summary report showing the weekly pay and insurance deductions for each employee. Further analysis shows that:

- The insurance deductions depend on the number of dependents.
- The hours worked and wage rate data are available.
- Overtime (over 40 hours) is paid at 1.5 times the regular rate.
- The manager wants to see the total pay and total deductions at the end of the report.

The objective is to write a program to generate such a report.

Step 2: Input-Output Design

Output

After careful analysis, it is determined that the variables listed in Table 4.3 are necessary for the output.

Table 4.3 Output Analysis Form for the Sample Program

Item	Variable Name	Length
1. Employee's name	NAMES$	15 columns
2. Hours worked	HOURS	7 columns
3. Wage rate	WAGE	7 columns
4. Pay for the period	PAY	6 columns
5. Number of dependents	XDEPEND	1 columns
6. Deductions	DEDUCT	5 columns
7. Pay after deductions (net pay)	NET	7 columns
8. Total pay to all employees	TOTPAY	9 columns
9. Total deductions	ALLDED	9 columns
10. Total pay after deductions	SUMNET	9 columns

Input

To calculate the pay, deductions, pay after deductions, and totals, we need the input information shown in Table 4.4.

Table 4.4 Input Analysis Form for the Sample Program

Item	Variable Name
1. Employee's name	NAMES$
2. Hours worked	HOURS
3. Wage rate	WAGE
4. Number of dependents	XDEPEND

The Output Layout

The output design is shown in Figure 4.10.

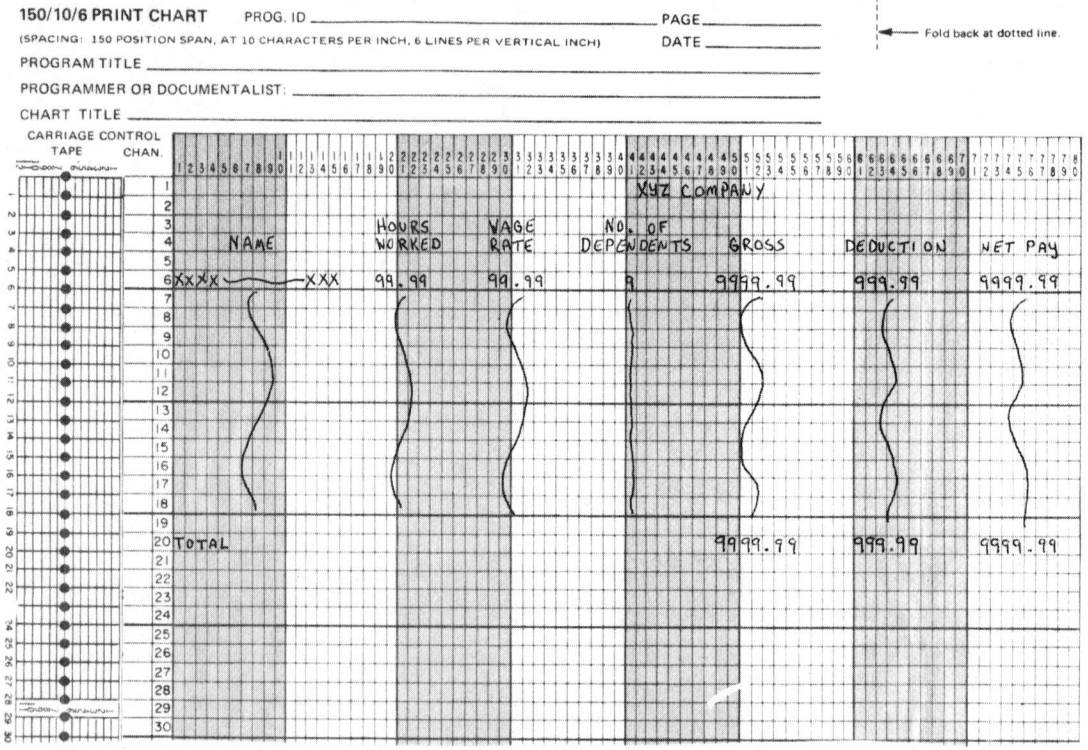

Figure 4.10 The output design for the sample problem

The Input Layout

It is determined that the input data for each employee will be entered as follows:

1. Employee's name
2. Hours worked for the period
3. Wage rate
4. Number of dependents

The words END-OF-DATA, entered instead of the employee's name, indicate the end of the data. The number of dependents is typed directly as input and changed to a code in the program. The following sample input data will be used for the program:

```
"JOHN JOHNSON",        38.50,  12.50,  2
"SUE SPENCER",         52.50,   9.50,  1
"MARY MANDELL",        29.25,  11.50,  3
"LORI LOTT",           40.00,  15.78,  2
"RANDY RAYBURN",       60.00,   6.75,  5
"DIANE DONALDSON",     72.00,   8.36,  3
"BARBARA BENTLY",      58.25,   5.20,  7
"END-OF-DATA",          0,       0,    0
```

Step 3: Process Design

The program is broken down into the following modules and submodules:

1. Housekeeping
   a. Printing the heading
   b. Initializing the variables
2. Reading the input information; sentinel value is: END-OF-DATA
3. Calculating
   a. Calculating the pay
   b. Calculating the deductions
   c. Calculating the pay after the deductions (the net)
   d. Calculating the totals

186 Decision Making, Comparing, Branching

4. Printing the information
   a. Writing the data about each employee in the loop created for reading the data
   b. Writing the totals after the loop

The process requirements for the calculation module are:

1. To calculate the pay (PAY) for the period, the following formulas are used:

   a. If employee worked 40 hours or less:

   PAY = HOURS*WAGE

   b. If employee worked more than 40 hours:

   PAY = WAGE*40 + 1.5*(HOURS - 40)*WAGE

2. Analysis shows that the deduction depends directly on the number of dependents as follows:

   12 percent of the pay if there are 3 or more dependents

   11 percent of the pay if there are 2 dependents

   10 percent of the pay if there is 1 dependent

   It is decided to use the variable CODE for deduction calculations. The value of CODE will be set equal to the number of dependents. However, if it is more than 3, CODE will be set equal to 3.

3. The pay after deduction will be calculated as

   NET = PAY - DEDUCT

4. The totals can be accumulated as

   TOTPAY = TOTPAY + PAY
   ALLDED = ALLDED + DEDUCT
   SUMNET = SUMNET + NET

   in the loop created for reading the data.

The flowchart for this problem is shown in Figure 4.11.

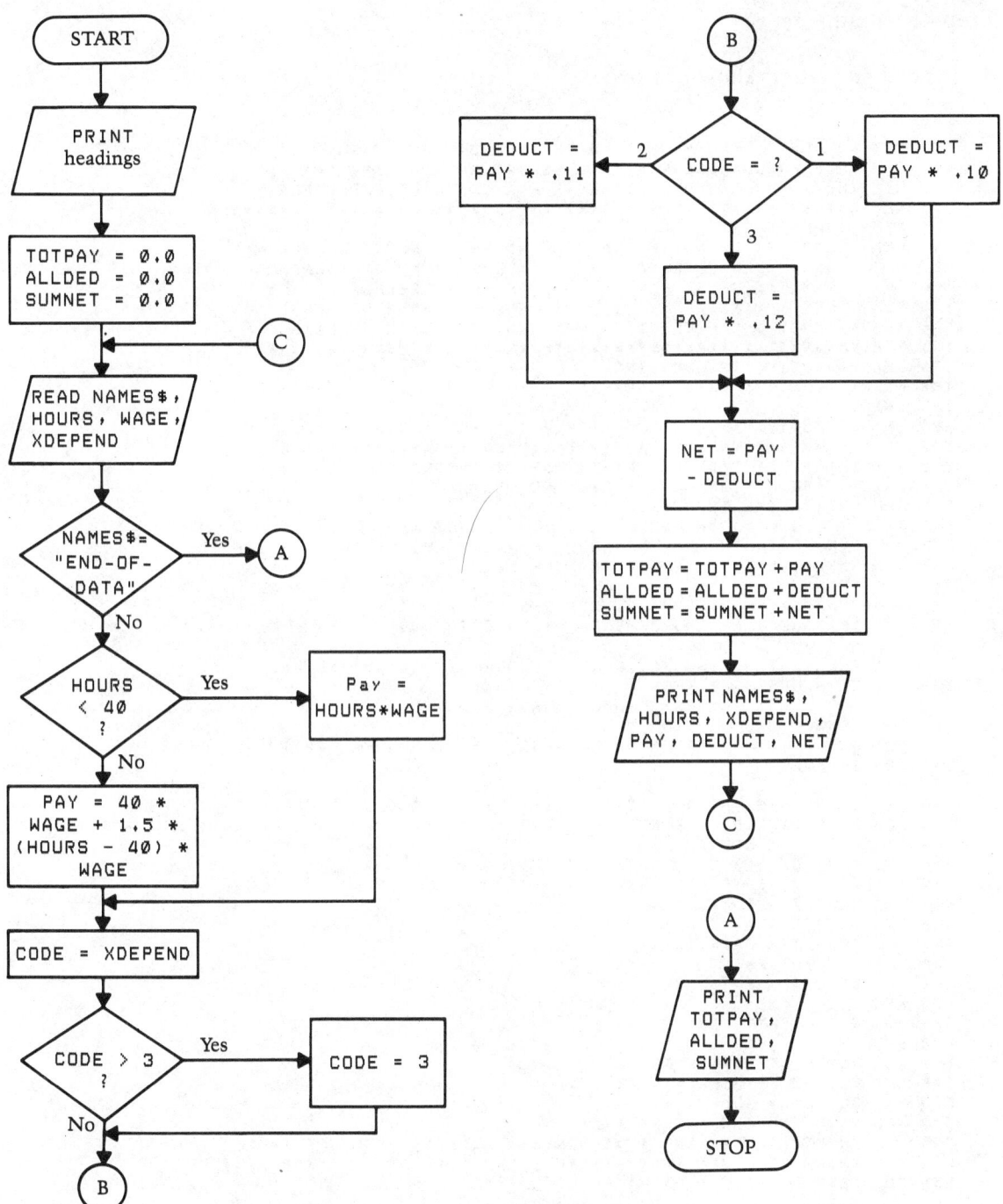

Figure 4.11 The flowchart for the sample problem

Step 4: Coding

The coded program is shown below:

```
10  REM AUTHOR:  RICH WARREN   DATE: AUGUST, 8, 19--
20  REM THIS PROGRAM GENERATES A REPORT SHOWING THE PAY AND
30  REM THE INSURANCE DEDUCTIONS FOR A GROUP OF EMPLOYEES
40  REM ***********************************************************
50  REM    VARIABLES:
60  REM    NAMES$: EMPLOYEE'S NAME   HOURS  : HOURS WORKED
80  REM    WAGE  : WAGE RATE         XDEPEND: NO. OF DEPENDENTS
100 REM    PAY   : GROSS PAY         DEDUCT : DEDUCTION
120 REM    NET   : NET PAY           ALLDED : SUM OF DEDUCTIONS
130 REM    SUMNET : SUM OF NETS      TOTPAY : SUM OF PAYS
140 REM ***********************************************************
170 REM  PRINTING THE HEADINGS:
180 PRINT TAB(30); 'XYZ COMPANY'
185 PRINT
190 PRINT TAB(19);'HOURS'; TAB(29); 'WAGE'; TAB(39); 'NO. OF'
200 PRINT TAB(6);'NAME'; TAB(19);'WORKED'; TAB(29); 'RATE';
210 PRINT TAB(35); 'DEPENDENTS'; TAB(50); 'GROSS'; TAB(60);
220 PRINT  'DEDUCTION'; TAB(72); 'NET PAY'
230 REM INITIALIZE TOTALS TO ZERO
240 TOTPAY = 0  :    ALLDED = 0   :   SUMNET = 0
250 REM THE BEGINNING OF THE LOOP, READING END-OF-DATA AS THE
260 REM EMPLOYEE NAME TERMINATES THE LOOP
265                                                           REM
270 READ NAMES$, HOURS, WAGE, XDEPEND
280     IF NAMES$ = 'END-OF-DATA' THEN GOTO 560
300                                                           REM
310 REM CALCULATING THE PAY, OVER 40 HOURS IS PAID TIME AND A HALF
330     IF HOURS < 40 THEN                                      &
                    PAY = HOURS*WAGE                            &
         ELSE                                                   &
                    PAY = HOURS*WAGE + 1.5*(HOURS - 40)*WAGE    &
340 REM END-OF-IF
350 REM
360 REM CALCULATE THE DEDUCTIONS: 10%, 11%, OR 12% OF THE PAY
370 REM DEPENDING ON THE XDEPEND, AND THE NET
375     CODE = XDEPEND
380     IF CODE > 3 THEN CODE = 3
390     ON CODE GOTO 400, 420, 440
400     DEDUCT = PAY*.10
410        GOTO 470
420     DEDUCT = PAY*.11
430        GOTO 470
440     DEDUCT = PAY*.12
450 REM
470     NET = PAY - DEDUCT
480 REM
490 REM CALCULATING THE TOTALS
500     TOTPAY = TOTPAY + PAY   :    ALLDED = ALLDED + DEDUCT
510     SUMNET = SUMNET + NET
520 REM PRINTING THE INFORMATION
530     PRINT NAMES$; TAB(19); HOURS; TAB(29); WAGE; TAB(40);
540     PRINT XDEPEND; TAB(49); PAY; TAB(60); DEDUCT; TAB(71); NET
550 GOTO 270
```

```
560 REM END OF THE LOOP, WRITING THE TOTALS
565 PRINT
570 PRINT 'TOTAL'; TAB(49); TOTPAY; TAB(61); ALLDED; TAB(72); SUMNET
600 REM ********** D A T A **********
620 DATA 'JOHN JOHNSON', 38.50, 12.50, 2
630 DATA 'SUE SPENCER', 52.50, 9.50, 1
640 DATA 'MARY MANDELL', 29.25, 11.50, 3
650 DATA 'LORI LOTT', 40.00, 15.78, 2
660 DATA 'RANDY RAYBURN', 60.00, 6.75, 5
670 DATA 'DIANE DONALDSON', 72.00, 8.36, 3
680 DATA 'BARBARA BENTLY', 58.25, 5.20, 7
690 DATA 'END-OF-DATA', 0, 0, 0
700 END
```

Step 5: Execution, Testing, and Debugging

The program is keyed into a terminal and each line is reviewed carefully for typing errors. The version of the BASIC used for this program is called MBASIC, which allows variable names with more than two characters.

After the program is typed carefully and saved, the program is executed by typing RUN. This BASIC interpreter checks each line for syntax errors line by line. If the interpreter finds an error, a message indicating the incorrect line is printed immediately. Then the line can be corrected. The first run of the program, shown in Figure 4.12, reveals a syntax error in line 170 due to the missing REM at the beginning of the remark statement. Although the program was carefully typed and checked, the error in line 170 was not caught. The missing REM is added and the program is run again.

The program is run for the second time (Figure 4.12), but after the headings are printed, the program stops and signals a syntax error in line 330. The error occurs because this version of BASIC does not accept the multiline statement (the IF statement) separated by the & symbol. Furthermore, the interpreter drops any line that has no line number. Line 330 is corrected by eliminating the continuation symbol and putting the entire IF block in one physical line.

When the program was reviewed again, a logical error was found. Line 390 was typed as

```
390 ON XDEPEND GOTO 400, 420, 440
```

This is not correct because CODE is used to indicate deduction code. The variable XDEPEND is replaced with CODE in this line.

After the errors are corrected, the program is executed by typing RUN. The program and the output is shown in Figure 4.13.

190 Decision Making, Comparing, Branching

A)
```
10   REM AUTHOR: RICH WARREN   DATE: AUGUST, 8, 19--
20   REM THIS PROGRAM GENERATES A REPORT SHOWING THE PAY AND
30   REM THE INSURANCE DEDUCTIONS FOR A GROUP OF EMPLOYEES
40   REM ****************************************************
50   REM    VARIABLES:
60   REM    NAMES$: EMPLOYEE'S NAME    HOURS  : HOURS WORKED
80   REM    WAGE  : WAGE RATE          XDEPEND: NO. OF DEPENDENTS
100  REM    PAY   : GROSS PAY          DEDUCT : DEDUCTION
120  REM    NET   : NET PAY            ALLDED : SUM OF DEDUCTIONS
130  REM    SUMNET: SUM OF NETS        TOTPAY : SUM OF PAYS
140  REM ****************************************************
170       PRINTING THE HEADINGS:
180  PRINT TAB(30); "XYZ COMPANY"            : PRINT
190  PRINT TAB(19);"HOURS": TAB(29); "WAGE"; TAB(39); "NO. OF"
200  PRINT TAB(6);"NAME"; TAB(19);"WORKED"; TAB(29); "RATE";
210  PRINT TAB(35); "DEPENDENTS"; TAB(50); "GROSS"; TAB(60);
220  PRINT   "DEDUCTION"; TAB(72); "NET PAY"
230  REM INITIALIZE TOTALS TO ZERO
240  TOTPAY = 0    :    ALLDED = 0    :    SUMNET = 0
250  REM THE BEGINNING OF THE LOOP, READING END-OF-DATA AS THE
260  REM EMPLOYEE NAME TERMINATES THE LOOP
265                                                          REM
270  READ NAMES$, HOURS, WAGE, XDEPEND
280       IF NAMES$ = "END-OF-DATA" THEN GOTO 560
300                                                          REM
310  REM CALCULATING THE PAY, OVER 40 HOURS IS PAID TIME AND A HALF
330       IF HOURS < 40 THEN                                 &
340  REM END-OF-IF
350  REM
360  REM CALCULATE THE DEDUCTIONS: 10%, 11%, OR 12% OF THE PAY
370  REM DEPENDING ON THE XDEPEND, AND THE NET
375       CODE = XDEPEND
380       IF CODE > 3 THEN CODE = 3
390       ON CODE GOTO 400, 420, 440
400       DEDUCT = PAY*.10
410         GOTO 470
420       DEDUCT = PAY*.11
430         GOTO 470
440       DEDUCT = PAY*.12
450  REM
470       NET = PAY - DEDUCT
480  REM
490  REM CALCULATING THE TOTALS
500       TOTPAY = TOTPAY + PAY   :   ALLDED = ALLDED + DEDUCT
510       SUMNET = SUMNET + NET
520  REM PRINTING THE INFORMATION
530       PRINT NAMES$; TAB(19); HOURS; TAB(29); WAGE; TAB(40);
540       PRINT XDEPEND; TAB(49); PAY; TAB(60); DEDUCT; TAB(71); NET
550  GOTO 270
560  REM END OF THE LOOP, WRITING THE TOTALS
565  PRINT
570  PRINT "TOTAL"; TAB(49); TOTPAY; TAB(61); ALLDED; TAB(72); SUMNET
600  REM ********** D A T A **********
620  DATA "JOHN JOHNSON", 38.50, 12.50, 2
630  DATA "SUE SPENCER", 52.50, 9.50, 1
640  DATA "MARY MANDELL", 29.25, 11.50, 3
650  DATA "LORI LOTT", 40.00, 15.78, 2
660  DATA "RANDY RAYBURN", 60.00, 6.75, 5
670  DATA "DIANE DONALDSON", 72.00, 8.36, 3
680  DATA "BARBARA BENTLY", 58.25, 5.20, 7
690  DATA "END OF DATA", 0, 0, 0
700  END

RUN
SYNTAX ERROR IN 170

RUN
                         XYZ COMPANY

              HOURS   WAGE    NO. OF
     NAME     WORKED  RATE   DEPENDENTS      GROSS      DEDUCTION    NET PAY
SYNTAX ERROR IN 330
```

Figure 4.12 The run of the sample problem with syntax errors

A)
```
10 REM AUTHOR: RICH WARREN   DATE: AUGUST, 8, 19--
20 REM THIS PROGRAM GENERATES A REPORT SHOWING THE PAY AND
30 REM THE INSURANCE DEDUCTIONS FOR A GROUP OF EMPLOYEES
40 REM **************************************************
50 REM   VARIABLES:
60 REM   NAMES$: EMPLOYEE'S NAME    HOURS  : HOURS WORKED
80 REM   WAGE   : WAGE RATE         XDEPEND: NO. OF DEPENDENTS
100 REM  PAY    : GROSS PAY         DEDUCT : DEDUCTION
120 REM  NET    : NET PAY           ALLDED : SUM OF DEDUCTIONS
130 REM  SUMNET : SUM OF NETS       TOTPAY : SUM OF PAYS
140 REM **************************************************
170 REM  PRINTING THE HEADINGS:
180 PRINT TAB(30); "XYZ COMPANY"    :    PRINT
190 PRINT TAB(19);"HOURS"; TAB(29); "WAGE"; TAB(39); "NO. OF"
200 PRINT TAB(6); "NAME"; TAB(19);"WORKED"; TAB(29); "RATE";
210 PRINT TAB(35); "DEPENDENTS"; TAB(50); "GROSS"; TAB(60);
220 PRINT "DEDUCTION"; TAB(72); "NET PAY"
230 REM INITIALIZE TOTALS TO ZERO
240 TOTPAY = 0   :   ALLDED = 0   :   SUMNET = 0
250 REM THE BEGINNING OF THE LOOP, READING END-OF-DATA AS THE
260 REM EMPLOYEE NAME TERMINATES THE LOOP
265                                                         REM
270 READ NAMES$, HOURS, WAGE, XDEPEND
280    IF NAMES$ = "END-OF-DATA" THEN GOTO 560
300                                                         REM
310 REM CALCULATING THE PAY, OVER 40 HOURS IS PAID TIME AND A HALF
330    IF HOURS < 40 THEN PAY = HOURS*WAGE ELSE PAY = 40*WAGE
340 REM END-OF-IF
350 REM
360 REM CALCULATE THE DEDUCTIONS: 10%, 11%, OR 12% OF THE PAY
370 REM DEPENDING ON THE XDEPEND, AND THE NET
375    CODE = XDEPEND
380    IF CODE > 3 THEN CODE = 3
390    ON CODE GOTO 400, 420, 440
400    DEDUCT = PAY*.10
410      GOTO 470
420    DEDUCT = PAY*.11
430      GOTO 470
440    DEDUCT = PAY*.12
450 REM
470    NET = PAY - DEDUCT
480 REM
490 REM CALCULATING THE TOTALS
500    TOTPAY = TOTPAY + PAY    :    ALLDED = ALLDED + DEDUCT
510    SUMNET = SUMNET + NET
520 REM PRINTING THE INFORMATION
530    PRINT NAMES$; TAB(19); HOURS; TAB(29); WAGE; TAB(40);
540    PRINT XDEPEND; TAB(49); PAY; TAB(61); DEDUCT; TAB(72); NET
550 GOTO 270
560 REM END OF THE LOOP, WRITING THE TOTALS
565 PRINT
570 PRINT "TOTAL"; TAB(49); TOTPAY; TAB(61); ALLDED; TAB(72); SUMNET
600 REM ********** D A T A **********
620 DATA "JOHN JOHNSON", 38.50, 12.50, 2
630 DATA "SUE SPENCER", 52.50, 9.50, 1
640 DATA "MARY MANDELL", 29.25, 11.50, 3
650 DATA "LORI LOTT", 40.00, 15.78, 2
660 DATA "RANDY RAYBURN", 60.00, 6.75, 5
670 DATA "DIANE DONALDSON", 72.00, 8.36, 3
680 DATA "BARBARA BENTLY", 58.25, 5.20, 7
690 DATA "END OF DATA", 0, 0, 0
700 END
```

```
RUN
                        XYZ COMPANY

                HOURS    WAGE    NO. OF
     NAME       WORKED   RATE    DEPENDENTS   GROSS      DEDUCTION   NET PAY
JOHN JOHNSON    38.5     12.5      2          481.25     52.9375     428.313
SUE SPENCER     52.5     9.5       1          380        38          342
MARY MANDELL    29.25    11.5      3          336.375    40.365      296.01
LORI LOTT       40       15.78     2          631.2      69.432      561.768
RANDY RAYBURN   60       6.75      5          270        32.4        237.6
DIANE DONALDSON 72       8.36      3          334.4      40.128      294.272
BARBARA BENTLY  58.25    5.2       7          208        24.96       183.04
END OF DATA     0        0         0          0          0           0

OUT OF DATA IN 270
```

Figure 4.13 The run of the sample problem with logical errors

There are several errors in the program:

1. The last record, which is a sentinel value, is printed, but the totals are not printed and the message OUT OF DATA in 270 is displayed. This happened because the sentinel value END OF DATA is not recognized. After the program and the data were checked, it was noticed that END OF DATA was keyed without hyphens (line 690). The data line should be corrected to match the statement in line 280:

    IF NAMES$ = "END-OF-DATA" THEN GOTO 570

2. The heading DEPENDENTS should be adjusted for a better alignment. This is corrected by using TAB(37) instead of TAB(35). Furthermore, a line of space between the headings and the data will make the output more readable. A PRINT statement is added to line 220 for this purpose.

3. The most important logical error lies in the calculation of PAY. For example, if an employee works 60 hours and the wage rate is 6.75, the gross pay must be

    $40 \times 6.75 + 1.5 \times 20 \times 6.75 = 472.50$

    However, the output shows the pay is 270. This kind of error is difficult to detect without test data. Using test data, one would notice immediately that there is something wrong with one of the formulas. The formulas are checked, and an error is found in the calculation of gross pay with overtime (line 330). This formula is corrected to read:

    PAY = 40*WAGE + 1.5*(HOURS - 40.0)*WAGE

One more adjustment was necessary before the final run. The tabs in line 570 were adjusted so that the totals would align with the detailed data lines.

After all errors were corrected, the program was run again. The final run and the output is shown in Figure 4.14.

It is important to print the figures in the financial reports so that the two decimal places representing cents align in columns and a dollar sign appears in the appropriate place. In BASIC, it is easy to do this kind of output editing with PRINT USING statements. This technique is discussed in Chapter 6.

Step 6: Documentation

This program is simple and straightforward. The documentation would include:

```
10  REM AUTHOR: RICH WARREN  DATE: AUGUST, 8, 19--
20  REM THIS PROGRAM GENERATES A REPORT SHOWING THE PAY AND
30  REM THE INSURANCE DEDUCTIONS FOR A GROUP OF EMPLOYEES
40  REM ***********************************************
50  REM    VARIABLES:
60  REM      NAMES$: EMPLOYEE'S NAME    HOURS  : HOURS WORKED
80  REM      WAGE  : WAGE RATE          XDEPEND: NO. OF DEPENDENTS
100 REM      PAY   : GROSS PAY          DEDUCT : DEDUCTION
120 REM      NET   : NET PAY            ALLDED : SUM OF DEDUCTIONS
130 REM      SUMNET: SUM OF NETS        TOTPAY : SUM OF PAYS
140 REM ***********************************************
170 REM PRINTING THE HEADINGS
180 PRINT TAB(30); "XYZ COMPANY"      : PRINT
190 PRINT TAB(19);"HOURS"; TAB(29); "WAGE"; TAB(39); "NO. OF"
200 PRINT TAB(6);"NAME"; TAB(19);"WORKED"; TAB(29); "RATE";
210 PRINT TAB(37); "DEPENDENTS"; TAB(50); "GROSS"; TAB(60);
220 PRINT "DEDUCTION"; TAB(72); "NET PAY"  : PRINT
230 REM INITIALIZE TOTALS TO ZERO
240 TOTPAY = 0  :  ALLDED = 0  :  SUMNET = 0
250 REM THE BEGINNING OF THE LOOP, READING END-OF-DATA AS THE
260 REM EMPLOYEE NAME TERMINATES THE LOOP
265                                                       REM
270 READ NAMES$, HOURS, WAGE, XDEPEND
280     IF NAMES$ = "END-OF-DATA" THEN GOTO 560
300                                                       REM
310 REM CALCULATING THE PAY,OVER 40 HOURS IS PAID TIME AND A HALF
330     IF HOURS<40 THEN PAY=HOURS*WAGE ELSE PAY=40*WAGE+1.5*(HOURS-40)*WAGE
340 REM END-OF-IF
350 REM
360 REM CALCULATE THE DEDUCTIONS: 10%, 11%, OR 12% OF THE PAY
370 REM DEPENDING ON THE XDEPEND, AND THE NET
375     CODE = XDEPEND
380     IF CODE > 3 THEN CODE = 3
390     ON CODE GOTO 400, 420, 440
400     DEDUCT = PAY*.10
410       GOTO 470
420     DEDUCT = PAY*.11
430       GOTO 470
440     DEDUCT = PAY*.12
450 REM
470     NET = PAY - DEDUCT
480 REM
490 REM CALCULATING THE TOTALS
500     TOTPAY = TOTPAY + PAY  :  ALLDED = ALLDED + DEDUCT
510     SUMNET = SUMNET + NET
520 REM PRINTING THE INFORMATION
530     PRINT NAMES$; TAB(19); HOURS; TAB(29); WAGE; TAB(40);
540     PRINT XDEPEND; TAB(49); PAY; TAB(60); DEDUCT; TAB(71); NET
550 GOTO 270
560 REM END OF THE LOOP, WRITING THE TOTALS
565 PRINT
570 PRINT "TOTAL"; TAB(48); TOTPAY; TAB(59); ALLDED; TAB(70); SUMNET
600 REM ********** D A T A **********
620 DATA "JOHN JOHNSON", 38.50, 12.50, 2
630 DATA "SUE SPENCER", 52.50, 9.50, 1
640 DATA "MARY MANDELL", 29.25, 11.50, 3
650 DATA "LORI LOTT", 40.00, 15.78, 2
660 DATA "RANDY RAYBURN", 60.00, 6.75, 5
670 DATA "DIANE DONALDSON", 72.00, 8.36, 3
680 DATA "BARBARA BENTLY", 58.25, 5.20, 7
690 DATA "END-OF-DATA", 0, 0, 0
700 END
RUN
```

                         XYZ COMPANY

| | HOURS | WAGE | NO. OF | | | |
| | WORKED | RATE | DEPENDENTS | GROSS | DEDUCTION | NET PAY |
NAME						
JOHN JOHNSON	38.5	12.5	2	481.25	52.9375	428.313
SUE SPENCER	52.5	9.5	1	558.125	55.8125	502.313
MARY MANDELL	29.25	11.5	3	336.375	40.365	296.01
LORI LOTT	40	15.78	2	631.2	69.432	561.768
RANDY RAYBURN	60	6.75	5	472.5	56.7	415.8
DIANE DONALDSON	72	8.36	3	735.68	88.2816	647.398
BARBARA BENTLY	58.25	5.2	7	350.35	42.042	308.308
TOTAL				3565.48	405.571	3159.91

Figure 4.14 The listing and final run of the sample problem

1. Summary of Steps 1 through 4
2. The flowchart
3. The coded program, which includes internal comments
4. A report telling how to place the data, how to use the program, and what the limitations of the program are

EXERCISES

4.1 Find the errors in the following IF statements:
```
a.  10    IF A$ = B GOTO 10
b.  100   IF X IS EQUAL TO Y STOP
c.  30    IF P < Q THEN REM P IS SMALLER
d.  40    IF , B = 0, GOTO 99
e.  50    IF A*B*C = 5, RATE = 25%
f.  100   IF P - Q THEN GOTO 100
g.  30    IF A = B, 10, 30, 40
h.  40    IF A OR B < G GOTO 100
i.  50    IF P < = Q THEN PRINT "P IS SMALLER", END
j.  30    IF A < 1000, RATE = .05, DIS = A*RATE
k.  10    IF A = B THEN
    20            RATE = .05
    30            X = 2*Y + 3
    40            Q = A*B
    50    ELSE
    60            RATE = .10
    70            X = 5*Y - 2
    80            P = A*B
```

4.2 Find the errors in the following ON GOTO statements:
```
a.  100   GOTO, 10, 20, 30, I
b.  200   IF X, GOTO 300, 400, 500
c.  50    ON A, 10, 50, 80, 90
d.  40    ON K GOTO 10 REM THIS IS A REMARK
e.  100   ON K = 3 GOTO 100
f.  100   IF J = 1 THEN ON K GOTO 100, 200, 300
```

4.3 Find the errors in the following compound IF statements:
- **a.** `10  IF RATE < .30 AND > .20 THEN PRINT "MEDIUM"`
- **b.** `100 IF CODE = 2 AND OR CODE = 20 THEN STOP`
- **c.** `200 IF MONTH$ = "APRIL" OR "JUNE" THEN DAY = 30`
- **d.** `100 IF X > 30.5 AND NOT < 100 THEN Y = 2*X`
- **e.** `300 IF PAID < 500 THEN RATE = .15 AND DIS = PAID*RATE`

4.4 Find the logical errors in the following programs or program segments:
- **a.**
    ```
    10   INPUT A
    20   IF A < 1000.0 THEN DISC = A*.05
    30   DISC = A*.1
    40   PRINT "A=", A, "DISCOUNT = ", DISC
    50   END
    ```
- **b.**
    ```
    10   INPUT A,B
    20   IF A < B PRINT "THE SMALLER NO. IS:", A
    30   PRINT "THE SMALLER NO. IS:", B
    40   END
    ```
- **c.**
    ```
    150  ON I GOTO 10, 20, 30
    160  PRINT A
    170  PRINT B
    180  PRINT C
    ```
- **d.**
    ```
    90   ON JAY GOTO 100, 200, 300
    100  X = A*B
    200  X = B*C
    300  X = A*C
    ```
- **e.**
    ```
    10   IF A < 10 GOTO 30
    20   B = A*A
    30   B = X*X
    40   PRINT B
    ```
- **f.**
    ```
    100  IF AMT < 1000 THEN RATE = .05
    200  RATE = .08
    300  DISC = AMT*RATE
    400  PRINT AMT, RATE, DISC
    ```

Programming Exercises:

Write a complete BASIC program for each of the following problems. Assume more than one data record in each of the problems. Use appropriate loops, headings, and spaces.

4.5 Write a program that calculates letter grades for students in a course. Input is the student's name, ID number, and the average of the exam scores. The grade is determined as follows:

Average	Grade
0 through 60	F
more than 60 through 70	D
more than 70 through 80	C
more than 80 through 90	B
more than 90 through 100	A

Print the name, ID, average, and the grade for each student. Print the number of As, Bs, Cs, Ds, and Fs at the end. Write the segment of the program that calculates the grade with

a. IF statement using GOTO style
b. IF statement using GOTO-less style
c. IF-THEN-ELSE statement

and then compare them. Which method do you find easiest? Use the following test data:

```
"PAT DOE"        , 56238 , 79.5
"JIM JOHNSON"    , 49587 , 85
"ANNA MOSES"     , 30984 , 100
"MARY WILSON"    , 28756 , 71.3
"HARRY ROSEN"    , 66958 , 45.5
"LEE ANDERS"     , 97846 , 90
"PAUL THOMAS"    , 63549 , 77
"BETTY SMITH"    , 33894 , 61
"FINISH"         , 0     , 0
```

4.6 Write an interactive program that accepts the name, ID, and a test score for several students and then prints the name, the ID, and the score of the student who has the highest score.

4.7 Write an interactive program that accepts values for four variables, A, B, C, and D, and prints

EQUAL	if A/B = C/D
NOT EQUAL	if A/B ≠ C/D
UNDEFINED	if either B or D is equal to zero

4.8 Write a program that inputs the value of a variable and then outputs the absolute value of that variable. The absolute value of a number is its numeric value without regard to its sign. For example, the absolute value of -3 is 3 and the absolute value of 4 (that is, $+4$) is 4.

4.9 Write an interactive program to calculate the roots of the equation

$$ax^2 + bx + c = 0$$

where a, b, and c are input. If $a = 0$, (and $b \neq 0$) the root of the equation is

$$x = -c/b$$

Otherwise, the equation has two roots. The roots are calculated by

$$x_1 = \frac{-b + \sqrt{b^2 - 4ac}}{2a}$$

$$x_2 = \frac{-b - \sqrt{b^2 - 4ac}}{2a}$$

Notice that if $(b^2 - 4ac)$ is negative, the equation does not have a real root; and if $b^2 - 4ac$ is zero, the equation has two identical roots of

$$x = \frac{-b}{2a}$$

4.10 The following information about students in a course is available: name, ID number, test score 1, and test score 2. Write a program that reads the information and prints the following for each student in a report form.

  a. Sequence number
  b. Student's ID
  c. Student's name
  d. Test scores
  e. Student's average
  f. Grade (see Exercise 4.5)

Also print the name and ID number of the students with the highest and the lowest average at the end. Make sure to design the output and draw a flowchart before writing the program.

4.11 Write an interactive program that reads an amount, then calculates and prints a discount based on the following rates:

If the amount is up to $200, the discount is 6 percent.
If the amount is up to $500, the discount is 8 percent.
If the amount is up to $1000, the discount is 10 percent.
If the amount is more than $1000, the discount is 12 percent.

Design your own output.

4.12 Write a program that reads series of numbers, the first of which is a header value indicating the number of data. Calculate and print the average, the largest number, the smallest number, and the variance of the data. The variance (VAR) can be calculated by the formula

$$VAR = \frac{\text{the sum of the square of each number}}{\text{number of data}} - (\text{average})^2$$

4.13 The tuition in a college is calculated as

Up to 11 hours	$35 per hour
12 to 16 hours	$420
Over 16 hours	$420 + $30 per hour over 16 hours

Write a program that reads the names of the students and the number of hours each student takes. Calculate the tuition. Print the name and the tuition. Use the following input data to test the program:

Name	Number of Hours Taken
Pat Brownson	10
John Doe	12
Marta Baanie	11
Wayne Ng	15
Betty Barrett	9
Clare Johnny	16
Olive Aceite	18
No-More	0

Write the segment of the program that calculates the tuition according to the three styles explained in the text: GOTO style, GOTO-less style, and structured style.

4.14 The commission paid to a salesperson is calculated as

Sales up to $1,000	2 percent of the sales
Sales up to $5,000	3 percent of the sales
Sales up to $10,000	4 percent of the sales

Write a program that reads the name and ID of a salesperson and the amount each sold. Calculate and print the name, ID, sales, commission rate, and commission for each salesperson. Assume there are several data records. Terminate the program if the ID is 9999.

4.15 Suppose tax withheld is calculated as shown in the following table:

Gross	Tax Rate
Less than $5,000	0
$ 5,000 to $10,000	5%
$10,000 to $15,000	8%
$15,000 to $20,000	12%
$20,000 to $30,000	17%
More than $30,000	25%

Write a program that calculates the tax deduction for the employees of a company. Input is the employee's name, ID number, and yearly gross income. Output is the name, ID number, gross income, tax deduction, and net pay of each employee. The tax deduction is progressive; for example, if the employee's income is $18,000, the tax is

```
TAX = 5000.0*0.0 + 5000.0*.05 + 5000.0*.08 + 3000.0*.12
```

Print the total of the gross incomes, deductions, and net salaries at the end. Use a trailer value to terminate the loop.

4.16 Write a program that counts how many books were checked out from a library in one day and shows from which sections those books came. The input is the book number, the section code (1, 2, 3, 4, and 5), and the due date. The output is:

a. The book number, the section code, and the due date for each book

b. The total number of books checked out

c. The number of books checked out from each section

4.17 Write a program to handle students' grade information.
Input

a. Student's name

b. Code for sex
   M for male
   F for female

c. Code for class
   1 for undergraduate
   2 for graduate

d. Score for four exams
      Exam 1
      Exam 2
      Exam 3
      Exam 4

Output

   a. The following information for each student in a report form: A sequence number followed by the student's name, sex code, class code, exam scores, average of the scores, and letter grade, as follows:

      A   90–100
      B   80–89
      C   70–79
      D   60–69
      F   less than 60

   b. The following at the end of the report:
      1. The number of As, Bs, Cs, Ds, and Fs
      2. The grand average of all students
      3. The average of the graduate students
      4. The average of the undergraduate students

SUMMARY

You have learned:

1. An IF statement can be used to compare values. Two forms of the `IF` statement are the logical `IF` and the structured `IF`.

   a. The logical `IF` statement has the general form

      `IF X > Y THEN statement`

      where X or Y is a variable, a constant, or an arithmetic expression. We can use not only > (greater than) but also other relational operators such as <, >=, <=, =, and <>. The statement to the right of "THEN" is executed only if the outcome of the logical expression is true. If it is not true, the statement is ignored. In some BASIC systems, only one statement is allowed after "THEN." If several statements are necessary, you must use a `GOTO` statement to branch to a block of statements.

b. The structured `IF` block has the general form

```
IF logical expression THEN statement 1 ELSE statement 2
```

If the logical expression is true, statement 1 is executed; otherwise statement 2, after `ELSE` is executed.

2. A compound logical expression consists of logical operators (`AND`, `OR`, `NOT`) and logical expressions. Example:

```
99 IF YEAR = 1985 OR MONTH = 6 THEN Q = P
```

3. The `ON GOTO` statement has the general form

```
55  ON K GOTO N1, N2, N3, ...., Nn
```

Control is transferred to N1, N2, N3, ... Nn depending on whether the value of K (a variable or an arithmetic expression) is 1, 2, 3, or n. The `ON GOTO` statement is suitable when, depending on the value of a variable, control must pass to a different part of a program. It is especially useful when the variable is a code that can take sequential values and when certain calculations must be done for each value of the code.

4. A header record, or header value, is a value at the beginning of the data file that shows how many data records will follow. A trailer, or sentinel value, is a value at the end of the data file indicating the end of the data by a number that is out of the range of the regular data. Either a header or a trailer value can be used to terminate a loop.

5. Some typical uses of `IF` or `ON GOTO` statements include:
   - Calculating discounts for different rates, commissions for different criteria, grades for different standards, and the results of an equation for different values or the value of a function under different conditions
   - Terminating loops
   - Finding the largest or the smallest number among a set of data
   - Solving any other problems that require comparison and decision making

6. You also learned that:
   - A good programming style is one which makes a program easy to follow and understand.
   - Overuse of `GOTO` statements makes programs unstructured and hard to follow.
   - Indention is necessary for the readability of a program.
   - Structured programming requires the use of the structured `IF` block. Structured programming makes programs more readable, easier to code, and less time consuming.

REVIEW QUESTIONS/SELF-TEST

4.1 Which of the following statements is not correct?
    a. 10   IF A = B THEN GOTO 10
    b. 20   IF Q < P THEN PRINT "Q SMALLER"
    c. 15   IF X < 100 THEN RATE = .1, GOTO 10
    d. 20   IF A$ = "FINISH" THEN STOP

4.2 Are the following program segments syntactically and logically correct?
    a.   10   IF X < Y THEN PRINT "X IS SMALLER"
            20   PRINT "Y IS SMALLER"
    b. 100   IF A < B THEN   &
                               PRINT X   &
                               GOTO 200   &
                     ELSE   &
                               PRINT Y   &
                               GOTO 200   &
        200   ....

4.3 Write a program segment that calculates D = A*RATE, where
            RATE is .10, if A is less than 200
            RATE is .20, if A is greater than 200 but less than 300
            RATE is .30, if A is more than 300
   Use:
    a. IF statement
    b. Structured IF block

4.4 A company pays salary and commission to its salespeople as follows:
    a. $500 plus 6 percent of the amount sold if the amount is less than $5000
    b. $750 plus 7 percent of the amount sold if the amount is less than $10000 but more than $5000
    c. $1000 plus 8 percent of the amount sold if the amount is more than $10000

Write a complete program using headings, appropriate loops, and a trailer record to calculate and print the salary and commission for each salesperson. Print totals at the end. Follow the general programming cycle explained in Chapter 3. Use salesperson's ID and monthly amount as input.

Answers:

4.1 c

4.2 a. The segment has a logical error because line number 20 will always be executed no matter what the value of X is.

b. Not only is GOTO 200 unnecessary (because control will pass to line 200 in any case), but also it creates an error for the systems which do not allow multistatements after THEN or ELSE.

4.3 a.
```
10        IF A < 200 THEN GOTO 50
20        IF A < 300 THEN GOTO 70
30            RATE = .30
40        GOTO 80
50            RATE = .10
60        GOTO 80
70            RATE = .20
80        D = A*RATE
          ⋮
```

b.
```
10        IF A < 200 THEN                 &
              RATE = .10                  &
          ELSE IF A < 300 THEN            &
              RATE = .20                  &
              ELSE                        &
              RATE = .30                  &
20 REM END-OF-IF
30        D = A*RATE
          ⋮
```

4.4 The coded program follows:

```
10   REM XYZ SALARY-COMMISSION REPORT
20   REM
30   REM AUTHOR S.H. WHITE, AUGUST 29, 19--
35   REM ************************************************
40   REM VARIABLES ARE:      ID: SALESPERSON'S ID
50   REM                     AMT: AMOUNT SOLD BY SALESPERSON
60   REM                     SAL: SALARY-COMMISSION
70   REM                  TOTAMT: TOTAL AMOUNT
80   REM                  CUMSAL: TOTAL SALARY
90   REM ************************************************
100  REM HEADINGS
110  PRINT TAB(50); 'XYZ COMPANY'
120  PRINT
130  PRINT TAB(25); 'SEQ #'; TAB(33); 'SALESMAN ID#';
135  PRINT TAB(50); 'THE AMOUNT'; TAB(65); 'SALARY-COMMISSION'
140  PRINT
150  TOTAMT = 0
160  CUMSAL = 0
170  N = 0
180  READ ID, AMT
190  IF ID = 0 THEN GOTO 400
195      N = N + 1
200      IF AMT < 5000 THEN                      &
                  SAL = 500 + AMT*.06            &
             ELSE IF AMT < 10000 THEN            &
                  SAL = 750 + AMT*.07            &
                ELSE                             &
                  SAL=1000 + AMT*.08             &
210  REM  END-OF-IF
300      PRINT TAB(26); N; TAB(35); ID; TAB(52); AMT; TAB(70); SAL
310      TOTAMT = TOTAMT + AMT
320      CUMSAL = CUMSAL + SAL
330  GOTO 180
400    PRINT
410    PRINT TAB(40); 'TOTALS:'; TAB(51); TOTAMT; TAB(68); CUMSAL
420    DATA 56734, 5795, . . . . .
430    DATA . . . . .
999    END
```

Looping

5

In This Chapter:

The FOR-NEXT Loop
The General Form of the FOR-NEXT Loop
Loop Flowcharting
Rules of a FOR-NEXT Loop

Nested Loop

The WHILE Loop

Writing Better Programs

Exercises

Summary

Review Questions/Self-Test

5

Looping

Automatic repetition of a segment of a program several times is called *looping*. Loops are essential in all aspects of programming. Every higher-level language offers special methods to facilitate this important feature. The FOR-NEXT loop is the most common method of looping in BASIC. The WHILE loop is another looping technique available in some versions of BASIC. We discuss these looping techniques in this chapter.

THE FOR-NEXT LOOP

The following section demonstrates two methods of looping. In Example 5.1, a GOTO statement is used. In Example 5.2, the FOR-NEXT loop is presented.

Example 5.1

Problem:

Write a program that prints a two-column table. The first column shows the numbers from 1 to 100; the second column shows the squares of the numbers in the first column.

Program:

```
10    N = 0
20    N = N + 1
30    IF N > 100 THEN GOTO 99
40       M = N^2
50       PRINT "N = "; N, "ITS SQUARE = "; M
60    GOTO 20
99    END
```

The output will be

```
N = 1          ITS SQUARE = 1
N = 2          ITS SQUARE = 4
  :              :
  :              :
N = 100        ITS SQUARE = 10000
```

Notes:

1. The statement N = N + 1 generates the sequence numbers from 1 to 100. This statement counts the number of times that the loop is executed.
2. The loop is repeated 100 times; an IF statement is used to stop the loop after 100 times. If the value of N, the control variable, is less than or equal to 100, the loop is repeated. If N is greater than 100, the loop is terminated.
3. Four statements are essential parts of the loop: (1) the statement initializing the control variable (N = 0), (2) the statement incrementing the control variable (N = N + 1), (3) the testing and transferring statement (IF-GOTO), and (4) the returning statement (GOTO 20).
4. The range of the loop is from line 20 through line 60.
5. The statements in the loop are indented for readability. As discussed in Chapter 4, indention is necessary for the readability of a program.

We can also use a FOR-NEXT loop to solve the problem in Example 5.1. Before we explain a FOR-NEXT statement, compare the following program with the previous one:

Example 5.2

Problem: The same as in Example 5.1: print the numbers from 1 to 100 and their squares.

Program:

```
10   FOR N = 1 TO 100
20      M = N^2
30      PRINT "N = "; N, "ITS SQUARE = "; M
40   NEXT N
50   END
```

The output will be

```
N = 1          ITS SQUARE = 1
N = 2          ITS SQUARE = 4
    ⋮              ⋮
N = 100        ITS SQUARE = 10000
```

Notes:

1. The statements FOR and NEXT substitute for the following four statements: (1) N = 0, (2) N = N + 1, (4) IF-GOTO, and (4) GOTO 20 in Example 5.1.
2. The range of the loop is from the FOR statement up to the NEXT statement.
3. The statements in the FOR-NEXT loop are indented for readability.

The FOR loop in the example looks like the following:

```
10   FOR N = 1 TO 100
        ⋮
40   NEXT N
```

The loop starts with the FOR statement and ends with the NEXT statement. The variable N, called the *control variable* or the index variable, controls the loop. The value of the control variable in this example starts with 1 and increases by 1 each time around the loop until its value is more than 100. All the statements inside the loop are repeated 100 times as well.

The control variable in the previous example started from 1 and was incremented by 1; that is, the value of the control variable was increased by 1 each time that the loop was executed. The following example shows that the increment and the initial value can be other than 1:

Example 5.3

Problem: Write a program that prints a two-column table. The first column shows odd numbers from 11 to 99; the second column shows the squares of the numbers in the first column.

Program:
```
10    FOR J = 11 TO 99 STEP 2
20      K = J^2
30        PRINT "THE NO.: "; J, " ITS SQUARE = "; K
40    NEXT J
99    END
```

Notes:

1. The starting value of the control variable (J) is equal to 11, and the loop terminates when the value of J is more than 99.
2. The increment of the control variable is 2; that is, the value of J is increased by 2 each time around the loop.

The General Form of the FOR-NEXT Loop

The general form of a FOR-NEXT loop is shown below:

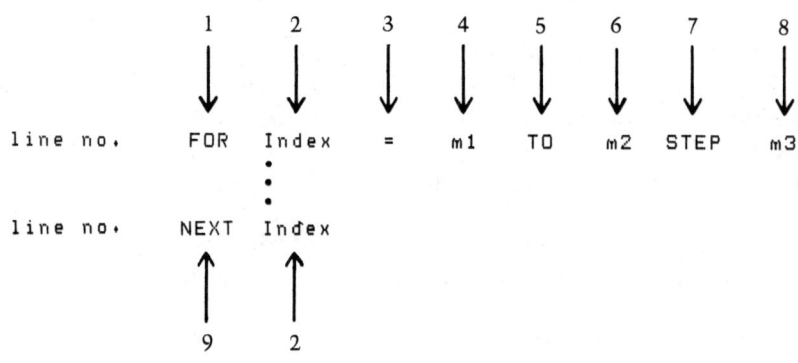

It has nine important components:

1. The word FOR
2. The control or index variable
3. An equals sign (=)
4. The initial value of the control variable
5. The word TO
6. The upper limit of the control variable
7. The word STEP
8. The increment of the control variable
9. The word NEXT, followed by the control variable

Furthermore, a FOR statement does the following tasks:

1. It starts a loop with the word FOR.
2. It establishes the range of the loop. That range is from the word FOR through the word NEXT.
3. It initializes the index variable.
4. It increments the control variable by m3 each time the loop is executed. If the increment is +1, STEP m3 can be omitted.
5. It tests the control variable. If the new value is less than or equal to the upper limit, execution is repeated; if it is greater than the upper limit, the statement directly after NEXT is executed, assuming m3 is positive.

The following are two more examples of FOR loops:

Example 5.4

The following program prints numbers 10 through 99 in intervals of 3.

Program:

```
10    FOR N = 10 TO 99 STEP 3
20        PRINT N
30    NEXT N
99    END
```

Example 5.5

The following program reads two numbers and prints (1) a sequence number, (2) the data, (3) the product of the data, and (4) the sum of the products at the end of the program. The loop is repeated 49 times.

Program:

```
10    TOT = 0
20    FOR SEQ = 1 TO 49
30       READ A, B
40       C = A*B
50       TOT = TOT + C
60       PRINT SEQ, A, B, C
70    NEXT SEQ
80    PRINT TOT
90    DATA .......
100   DATA .......
999   END
```

Loop Flowcharting

We use two symbols to indicate the FOR loop, as shown in Figure 5.1. The first symbol shows the beginning of the loop, and the second one shows the end of the loop. The flowchart for the previous example is shown in Figure 5.2.

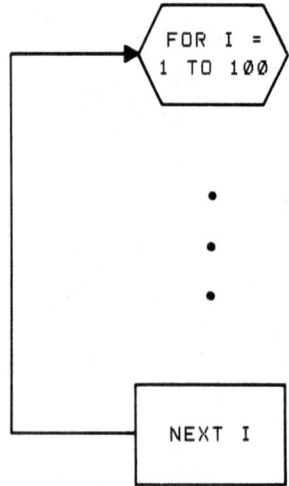

Figure 5.1 FOR-NEXT loop flowcharting

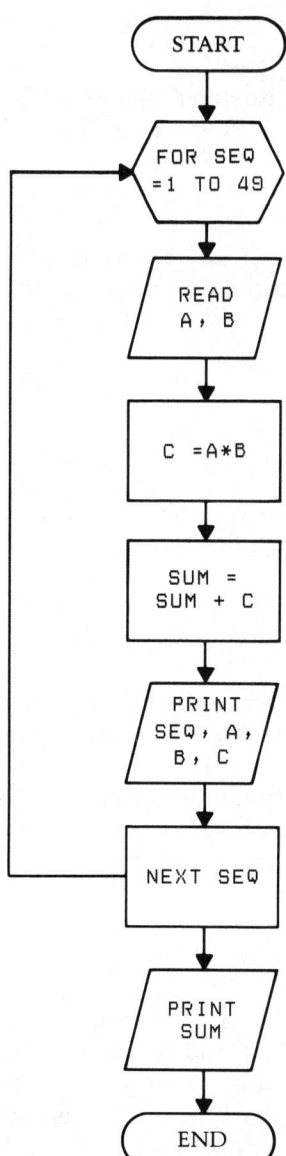

Figure 5.2 The flowchart for a simple FOR-NEXT loop

214 *Looping*

Rules of a FOR-NEXT Loop

You should become familiar with certain rules for using FOR loops. These rules will be explained through examples in the following section.

The Control Variable

The control variable is tested each time that the FOR statement is executed. If $m3$ is positive, a FOR loop will be executed as long as the value of the control variable is equal to or less than its upper limit. For example, the following loop is executed once.

```
10    FOR I = 1 TO 1 STEP 1
20        PRINT I
30    NEXT I
```

The following loop, however, will not be executed because the initial value of the control variable is greater than its upper limit.

```
100   FOR I = 2 TO 1 STEP 1
200       PRINT I
300   NEXT I
```

(This is true in most of the systems. However, some of the systems will execute the above loop once because they test the value of the control variable after each loop execution.)

Furthermore, the initial, final, and increment values need not be constants (numbers). All or any of the values can be variables or expressions, if the variables are defined before the loop. The following is an example:

Example 5.6

Problem: Each of several employee data records contains the employee's ID number, number of hours worked, and the wage rate. The first record is a header indicating the number of employee records. Draw a flowchart and write a complete program that reads the data and prints the (1) sequence number, (2) employee number, (3) hours worked, (4) wage rate, and (5) pay to each employee. Print the total pay to all employees at the end of the report.

Flowchart: The flowchart is shown in Figure 5.3.

The FOR-NEXT Loop **215**

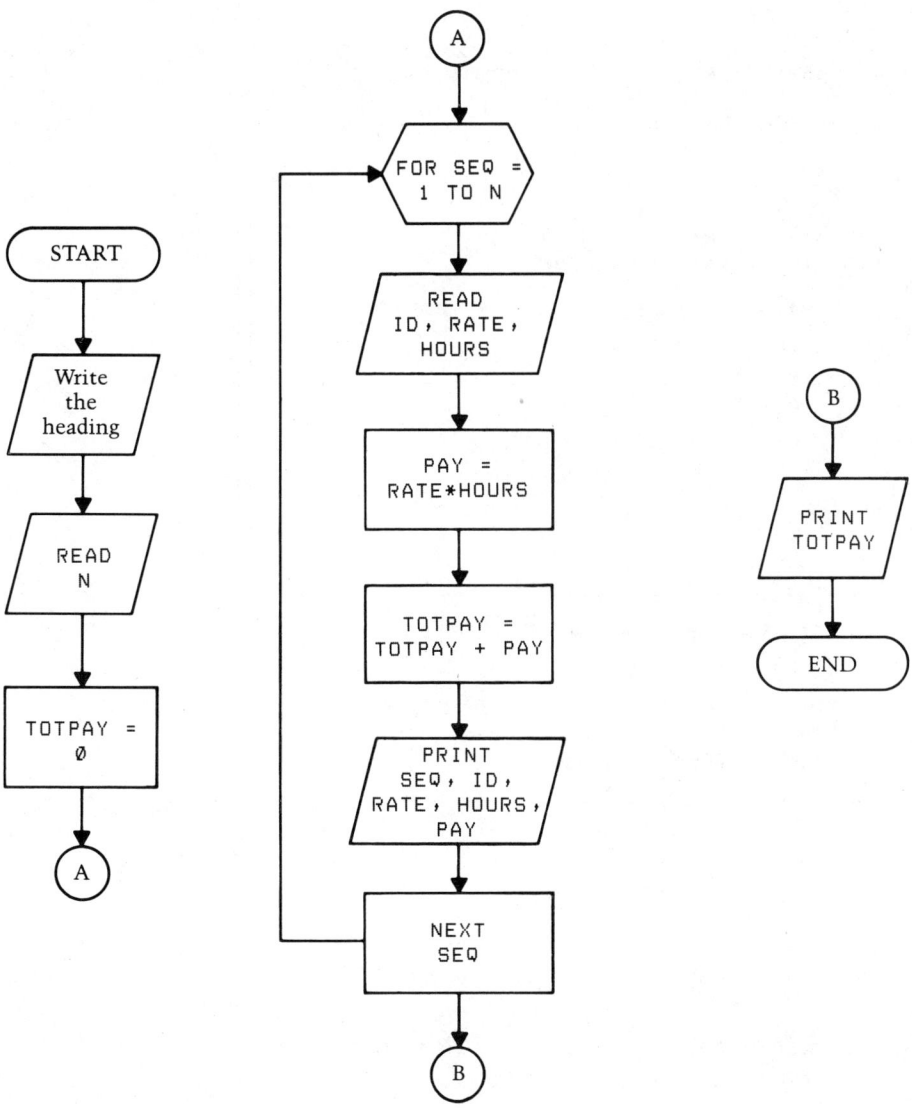

Figure 5.3 Flowchart for Example 5.6

Program:

```
10   PRINT "SEQ. NO.", "EMPLOYEE #", "HOURS", "RATE", "PAY"
20   READ N
30   REM  N IS THE SENTINEL VALUE
40   TOTPAY = 0
50   FOR SEQ = 1 TO N
60      READ ID, RATE, HOURS
70      PAY = RATE*HOURS
80      TOTPAY = TOTPAY + PAY
90      PRINT SEQ, ID, HOURS, RATE, PAY
100  NEXT SEQ
110  PRINT "TOTAL PAY TO ALL EMPLOYEES: "; TOTPAY
120  DATA 3
130  DATA 5628, 5.85, 40
140  DATA 2382, 9.15, 39
150  DATA 5823, 8.40, 39.5
999  END
```

The output will be

```
SEQ. NO.    EMPLOYEE #     HOURS     RATE      PAY
   1           5628         40       5.85      234
   2           2382         39       9.15      329.55
   3           5823         39.5     8.4       331.8
TOTAL PAY ALL EMPLOYEES: 895.35
```

Notes:

1. The first READ statement reads the number of records (N), 3 in this example.
2. The upper limit of the control variable in the FOR statement is set to N. The value of N has been previously defined.

In most versions of BASIC, the increment value of a FOR statement can be negative as well as positive. If the increment value is positive, the control variable increases in value after each loop. This also implies that the initial value of the control variable must be less than the upper limit. If the increment value is negative, the control variable decreases in value, and the loop will be executed while the value of the control variable is equal to or greater than the upper limit. The following example demonstrates this:

The FOR-NEXT Loop

Example 5.7

Problem: Write a program that prints the numbers from 99 to 1.

Program:
```
10    FOR COUNT = 1 TO 99
20       DCOUNT = 100 - COUNT
30       PRINT DCOUNT
40    NEXT COUNT
50    END
```

or

```
10    FOR DCOUNT = 99 TO 1 STEP -1
20       PRINT DCOUNT
30    NEXT DCOUNT
40    END
```

Note: If the increment value is negative, the control variable decreases in value after each loop. The upper limit must be less than or equal to the initial value.

Two other important rules about the control variable are:

1. The value of the control variable cannot be changed in the range of the loop. For example:

```
10    FOR K = 1 TO 10 STEP 2
20       K = K + 5
30       PRINT K
40    NEXT K
```

is not valid because the value of K is changed in the loop.

2. The value of the control variable after a FOR loop is completely executed is not always equal to the upper limit. The value can be predicted and used in most versions of BASIC. For example, the following program

```
10    FOR NO = 1 TO 10 STEP 2
20    NEXT NO
30    PRINT NO
40    END
```

will print 11 as the final value of NO. Note that the values of NO are 1, 3, 5, 7, 9, and 11. When the value is 11, the loop will not be executed, but will be terminated instead. (*Note:* This is true in most versions, but not in all. Check your manual or run the example to see what number is printed.)

Normal and Abnormal Termination

A FOR loop can be terminated before it is completely executed. The following is an example:

Example 5.8

Problem: A car rental agency rents about 100 cars each day. Write a program that reads the mileage of the rented cars, then calculates and prints the average mileage of the cars rented. The sentinel value is a negative number.

```
10   NUMBER = 0     :     SUM = 0
20   FOR CAR = 1 TO 100
30      READ MILES
40      IF MILES < 0 THEN GOTO 80
50      NUMBER = NUMBER + 1
60      SUM = SUM + MILES
70   NEXT CAR
80   AVG = SUM/NUMBER
90   PRINT "AVERAGE: "; AVG
110  DATA 349.5, ......
120  DATA ........................,-99
130  END
```

Notes:

1. The FOR loop will be terminated when a negative value is read.
2. NUMBER = NUMBER + 1 keeps track of the number of cars. We need this figure to calculate the average.
3. SUM = SUM + MILES adds the mileages.
4. The average is calculated and printed after the loop is terminated.

There are two ways to terminate a FOR loop:

1. *Normal termination* occurs when the FOR loop ends after complete execution and control passes to the first statement after the loop. In this case, if the increment value is positive, the final value of the control variable is greater than its upper limit after the loop is terminated. If the increment value is negative, the final value of the control variable is less than its lower limit after the loop is completely executed.

2. *Abnormal termination* occurs when a GOTO or an IF-GOTO statement transfers control outside of the loop, regardless of the value of the control variable. The current value of the control variable after abnormal termination stays in memory and can be used at later points in the program. For example, the program

```
10    FOR JAY = 1 TO 50
20       IF JAY = 3 GOTO 40
30    NEXT JAY
40    PRINT JAY
50    END
```

will print 3, the current value of JAY. As another example, the average in Example 5.8 could be calculated by

```
AVG = SUM/(CAR-1)
```

(CAR-1) is used because the last value must not be counted when the average is calculated.

Transferring within and from a FOR Loop

Syntactically, control can always pass from one point in the FOR loop to another point in the same loop. But control cannot be transferred from a point outside the loop into a FOR loop.

Of course, control can be transferred to the beginning of a FOR loop from any point in the program any time. Remember, however, that when you do so the control variable is set to its initial value. Because of this fact, you must branch to the NEXT statement first when you need to transfer control from a point inside the FOR loop to the beginning of the loop. Otherwise, you may create an infinite loop. As an example, assume you want to write a program that prints all the numbers from 1 to 20 except 13. Consider the following loop for this purpose:

```
10    FOR I = 1 TO 20
20       IF I = 13 GOTO 10
30       PRINT I
40    NEXT I
```

This loop is infinite because whenever control passes to the beginning, the control variable is set equal to 1 (the initial value) and never reaches 20 (the upper limit). The loop can be corrected as follows:

```
10    FOR I = 1 TO 20
20       IF I = 13 GOTO 40
30       PRINT I
40    NEXT I
```

Figure 5.4 shows some valid and invalid uses of GOTO in a FOR loop. However, transferring control from one point in a loop to another creates an unstructured iteration module and is thus not recommended.

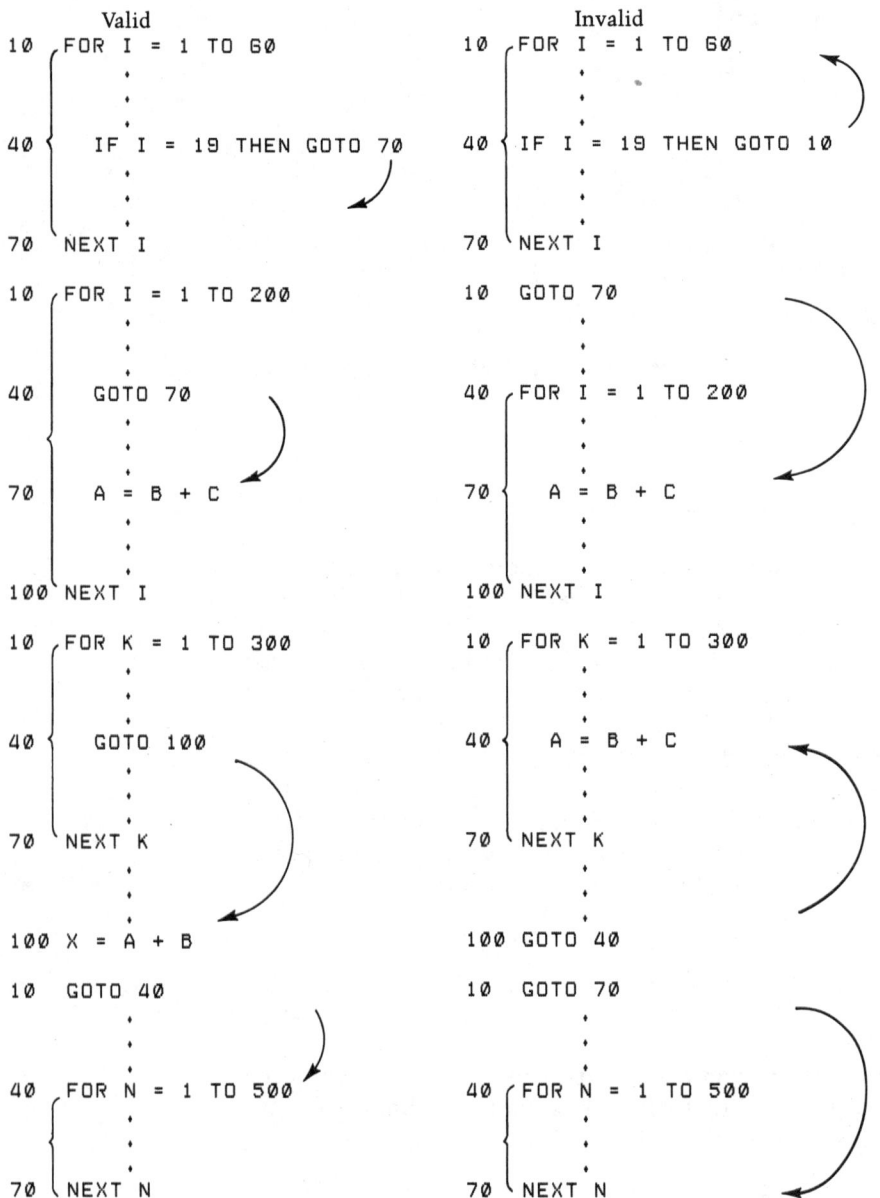

Figure 5.4 Examples of valid and invalid loops

Summary of the Rules about FOR-NEXT Loops

1. The initial value and the upper limit of the control variable must be present in the FOR statement. However, if the increment (STEP) value is not present, it is assumed to be 1.
2. Any initial value, upper limit, or increment value of the control variable (a) can be positive, negative, or zero (but the increment cannot be zero) and (b) can be a variable or an expression as long as the variables are defined.
3. If the increment value in a FOR statement is positive, the control variable increases in value. That is, the upper limit of the control variable must be greater than or equal to the initial value. If the increment is negative, the control variable decreases in value, and its upper limit must be less than or equal to the initial value. The increment may not be zero.
4. The value of the control variable cannot be changed inside the FOR loop. For example,

    ```
    10   FOR X = 1 TO 10
    20     X = X + 2
    30     PRINT X
    40   NEXT X
    ```

    is not valid since X, the control variable, is changed inside the loop.
5. If the increment value is positive, a FOR loop is executed as long as the current value of the control variable is less than or equal to its upper limit. If the increment value is negative, a FOR loop is executed as long as the current value of the control variable is greater than or equal to its upper limit.
6. If any variable representing the initial value, upper limit, or increment value in a FOR statement is undefined, the loop cannot be executed.
7. The last statement in a FOR-NEXT loop must be a NEXT statement. (Some systems let you drop the control variable after the word NEXT. Dropping the variable is not recommended because of readability considerations.)
8. Syntactically, it is possible to transfer control out of the loop by using a GOTO statement or an IF-GOTO statement. From the standpoint of structured programming, however, branching in a loop structure is not recommended.
9. To skip the remaining statements in a FOR loop and continue the loop, control must always be transferred to the end of the loop, the NEXT statement, rather than directly to the beginning, the FOR statement.

222 *Looping*

10. In normal termination, the value of the control variable is not always equal to its upper limit after the FOR loop ends. For instance,

    ```
    10   FOR N = 1 TO 6 STEP 2
              ⋮
    40   NEXT N
    50   PRINT "N = "; N
    60   END
    ```

    prints 7 for N in most versions of BASIC. Nevertheless, if control passes outside the loop in the case of abnormal termination, the control variable retains its current value.

11. Designate the control variable as an integer value if possible. Thus, for example, if % denotes an integer variable,

    FOR X% = 1% TO 100%

    is more efficient than

    FOR X = 1 TO 100.

Solved Problems

5.1 Find the errors, if any, in the following statements:
   a. 10   FOR III = 1, 50, STEP 3, DO
   b. 20   FOR N = 99 TO 1, 2, 3
   c. 30   FOR INDEX% = M% TO N% STEP Q%
   d. 30   FOR QUE = 5
   e. 20   FOR K = 95 TO 1
   f. 30   FOR NONE = 1 TO 100 STEP 0
   g. 10   FOR M = -2 TO 100 STEP -3
   h. 100 FOR K = 2*N^3/3 TO 5*M*N/J STEP 3*M

Answers:
   a. The correct form is

      100   FOR III = 1 TO 50 STEP 3

   b. The form of the FOR statement is not correct.
   c. This is correct, assuming % defines the variables as integers.
   d. There must be at least two values after the equals sign.

e. The initial value must be less than the final value because 1 is the default increment value. (This is syntactically correct, but the loop will not be executed correctly.)

f. The increment value cannot be zero.

g. The initial value must be greater than the final value if the increment is negative.

h. This is correct.

5.2 Are the following loops correct? If not, find the errors.

```
a. 10   FOR K = 1 TO 100 STEP 2
        ⋮
   100  NEXT IF K < 100 GOTO 10

b. 100  FOR COUNT = 1 TO 100 STEP 3
   110     PRINT COUNT
   120     IF COUNT = 13 THEN COUNT = 33
   130  NEXT COUNT

c. 10   FOR J = 1 TO 10
   20      GAMA = E^J
   30   NEXT J
   40   PRINT GAMA
   50   IF GAMA < 100 THEN GOTO 20

d. 10   FOR X = 1 TO 100
   20      IF X = 7 THEN GOTO 10
   30      PRINT X
   40   NEXT X
```

Answers:

a. The last statement of a FOR loop cannot be a NEXT-IF-GOTO statement.

b. The value of the control variable cannot be changed in the range of the loop.

c. Control cannot be transferred into a loop.

d. Control must be transferred to the NEXT statement, line 40, not to the beginning, line 10.

5.3 As mentioned in Chapter 4, factorial N, represented by N!, is defined as:

$1 \times 2 \times 3 \times \ldots \times N-1 \times N$

Write an interactive program that reads N and prints the factorial of N.

Answer:

```
10   PRINT "I WILL CALCULATE THE FACTORIAL OF";
20   PRINT "A NUMBER IN A FLASH"
30   PRINT "TYPE YOUR NUMBER"
40   INPUT N
50   FACT = 1
60   FOR COUNT = 1 TO N
70      FACT = FACT*COUNT
80   NEXT COUNT
90   PRINT "FACTORIAL OF: "; N; " IS: "; FACT
100  END
```

Note: If you run this program, keep the value of N less than 10, because the factorial of a number can become very large.

5.4 Write a program that prints numbers 1 through 99, three numbers to a row, as shown below.

```
1    2    3
4    5    6
7    8    9
:    :    :
```

Answer:

```
10   B = 0  :  C = 0
20   FOR A = 1 TO 99 STEP 3
30      PRINT A, A + 1, A + 2
40   NEXT A
50   END
```

5.5 Write a program that prints the integers from 1 to 80, one per line, so that each line starts one space farther to the right than the previous line, as shown below:

```
1
 2
  3
   .
    .
     .
```

Answer:

```
10 FOR I = 1 TO 80
20     PRINT TAB(I); I
30 NEXT I
40 END
```

NESTED LOOP

Sometimes it is necessary to use one or more loops inside another loop. Loops arranged in this way are called *nested loops*. The following problem is an example.

■ *Example 5.9*

Problem: Write an interactive program that shows how many words (meaningful or not) can be made from N letters. The program should accept a number continuously until zero is typed in. (Factorial N shows the number of ways, defined as: $1 \times 2 \times 3 \times \ldots \times N$. See Solved Problem 5.3).

Program:

```
10   PRINT "I WILL TELL IMMEDIATELY HOW MANY WORDS, MEANINGFUL"
15   PRINT "OR NOT, YOU CAN MAKE FROM N LETTERS"
20   FOR ROUND = 1 TO 1000
30     PRINT "TYPE THE NO. OF LETTERS, TYPE 0 WHEN DONE"
40     INPUT N
50     IF N = 0 THEN GOTO 120
60     FACT = 1
70     FOR K = 1 TO N
80         FACT = FACT*K
90     NEXT K
100    PRINT "OUT OF ";N;"LETTERS YOU CAN MAKE UP TO ";
               FACT;" WORDS"
110  NEXT ROUND
120  PRINT ".........* * * BYE * * *........."
130  END
```

Note: There are two loops in the example. The first loop attempts to read 1000 numbers, while the second one (the inner loop) calculates and prints the factorial of each number read.

The rules for FOR-NEXT loops given previously also apply to any nested loop. In addition, the ranges of the loops must not "cross"; that is, the inner loop must lie completely inside the outer loop. For example,

```
 10  FOR J = 1 TO 100
      .
      .
      .
100  FOR K = 1 TO 100
      .
      .
      .
200  NEXT J
      .
      .
      .
300  NEXT K
```

is not valid because the loops overlap. Figure 5.5 shows examples of valid nested loops.

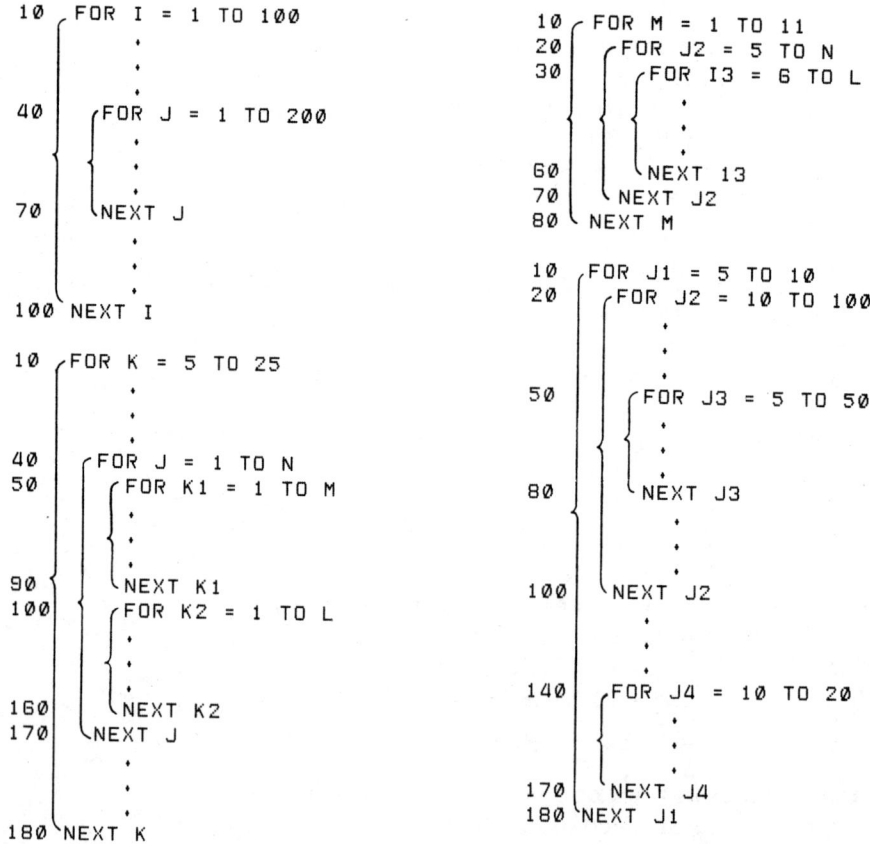

Figure 5.5 Some valid nested loops

Nested Loop 227

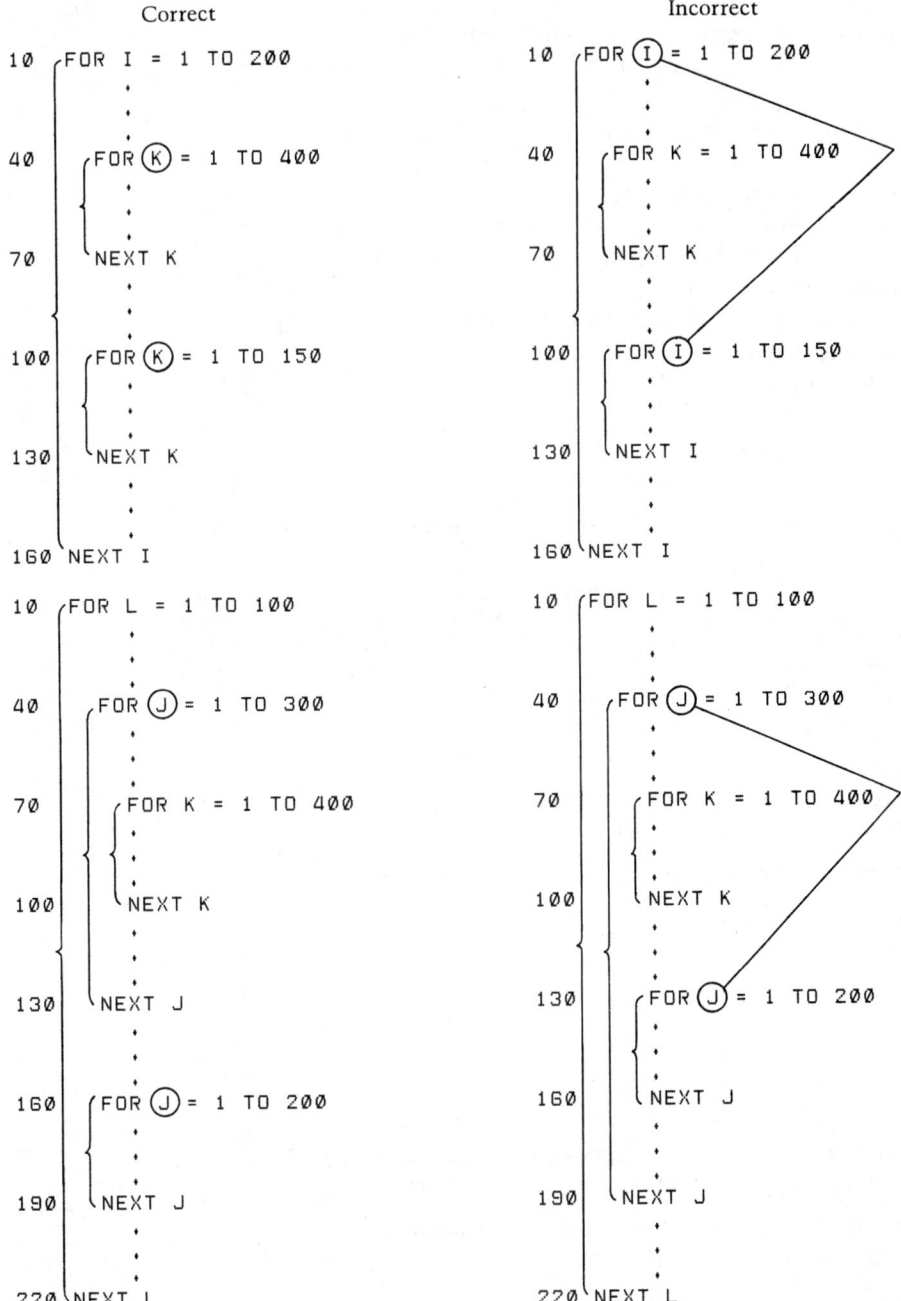

Figure 5.6 Identical control variables in a nested loop

The same control variable cannot be used in two nested loops unless one of the loops is completed before the other starts. Figure 5.6 shows when you can use identical control variables in two loops.

The following is another example of a nested loop.

Example 5.10

Problem: Suppose the compound interest on an amount is to be calculated. One way to compound interest is to compute the interest on the previous year's total and accumulate the totals and interests. Write an interactive program that continuously accepts an amount, an interest rate, the year of initial investment, and the year of withdrawal. Calculate the compound interest and print the information. Zero indicates the end of data.

Program:

```
10   PRINT"I WILL CALCULATE THE COMPOUNDED INTEREST ON AN AMOUNT."
20   FOR TIME = 1 TO 1000
25       PRINT
30       PRINT "TYPE THE AMOUNT, INTEREST RATE (IN DECIMAL), YEAR"
40       PRINT "THE AMOUNT WAS INVESTED, AND YEAR IT WAS WITHDRAWN,"
50       PRINT "EACH SEPARATED BY A COMMA.  TYPE ZEROS WHEN THROUGH"
60       INPUT AMT, R, N1, N2
70       IF AMT = 0 GOTO 170
80       XTOT = AMT
90       FOR YEAR = N1 TO N2
100          INTRST = XTOT*R
110          XTOT = XTOT + INTRST
120      NEXT YEAR
130      PRINT "       AMOUNT: "; AMT, "RATE: "; R
140      PRINT "DEPOSITED IN: "; N1, "WITHDRAWN IN: "; N2
150      PRINT "TOTAL PRINCIPAL AND INTEREST IS: "; XTOT
160  NEXT TIME
170  PRINT "**** GOOD LUCK ****"
200  END
```

Notes:

1. The outer loop (the first loop) attempts to read 100 data records, but the sentinel value (when AMT is 0) terminates the loop.
2. The inner loop calculates the interest of an amount and accumulates the total amount and interest.

Solved Problems

5.6 Find the errors, if any, in the following loops:

    a. 10   FOR KAY = 1 TO 50
            ⋮
        100   FOR JAY = 1 TO 50
            ⋮
        200   NEXT KAY
            ⋮
        300   NEXT JAY

    b. 10   FOR ROUND = 1 TO 100
            ⋮
        110   FOR ROUND = 1 TO 50
            ⋮
        200   NEXT ROUND
            ⋮
        300 NEXT ROUND

    c. 10   FOR N = 1 TO 100
            ⋮
        100   IF N = J THEN GOTO 270
            ⋮
        250   FOR M = 1 TO 200
        260   PRINT M
        270   PRINT N
        280   NEXT M
        290 NEXT N

Answers:

    a. The loops overlap.
    b. The same control variable cannot be used for both loops in this example.
    c. Control cannot be transferred into a loop (into the inner loop).

5.7 Write a program that prints the following sequence of numbers:

    1   1
    1   2
    1   3
    2   1
    2   2
    2   3
    3   1
    3   2
    3   3

Answer:

```
10    FOR I = 1 TO 3
20      FOR J = 1 TO 3
30        PRINT I, J
40      NEXT J
50    NEXT I
60    END
```

5.8 Write a program that prints the following sequence of numbers:

    1   1 2 3 4 5 6 7 8 9
    2   1 2 3 4 5 6 7 8 9
    3   1 2 3 4 5 6 7 8 9
    ⋮
    50   1 2 3 4 5 6 7 8 9

Answer:

```
10    FOR I = 1 TO 50
20      PRINT I,
30      FOR K = 1 TO 9
40        PRINT K;
50      NEXT K
60      PRINT
70    NEXT I
80    END
```

THE WHILE LOOP

The WHILE loop is another feature of some versions of BASIC. It serves the combined structured functions of the IF-GOTO and FOR-NEXT statements. The following example demonstrates the form of the WHILE loop:

Example 5.11

Problem: Use the following function to find *y* for values of *x* from -7.5 to $+7.5$ in increments of .25.

$Y = 5X^3 + 2X^2 - 3$

Program:

```
10   X = -7.5
20   WHILE X <= 7.5
30      Y = 5*X^3 + 2*X^2 - 3
40      PRINT "X = ";X, "Y = ";Y
        X = X + .25
50   WEND
70   END
```

Note: The statements in the loop are repeated as long as the logical expression X <= 7.5 is true.

The general form of the WHILE loop is

```
line no.    WHILE a logical expression
               ⋮
            loop statements
               ⋮
line no.    WEND
```

The logical expression used here is the same as that used in the logical IF statement. The expression is tested first. If it is true, the statements in the loop are executed. If the expression is false, control passes to the statement right after the WEND statement. The variable that controls the loop (X in Example 5.11) must be updated (incremented) within the loop. Otherwise, any WHILE is an infinite loop. The WHILE loop is useful when the loop is to be repeated only while a condition remains true, rather than a certain number of times.

Not all versions of BASIC have the WHILE loop feature. Moreover, the forms can be slightly different from system to system. For example, some of the systems use NEXT instead of WEND. In Microsoft BASIC, exp can be any numeric expression. As long as exp is not zero (for true), MBASIC executes the statement in the loop. The WEND statement marks the end of the loop.

WRITING BETTER PROGRAMS

Loop structures are the most important part of a program. Improper looping technique can make a program completely unstructured. To be structured, a program should have distinct iteration structures. These can be either DO-WHILE or DO-UNTIL loops. In a DO-WHILE loop, a condition is tested first; the statements in the loop are executed only if the condition is true. In a DO-UNTIL loop, the condition is tested after the statements are executed (see Figure 5.7). In a FOR-NEXT loop, the condition is the counter (the control variable). Thus a FOR-NEXT loop is repeated a certain number of times.

In BASIC, FOR-NEXT and WHILE statements offer a way to implement the iteration structure. Pay attention to the following points when you use loops:

1. Always use FOR-NEXT or DO-WHILE, rather than IF-GOTO, to create loops in a BASIC program.
2. All the statements inside the loop should be indented. Furthermore, if a loop is nested, indent to make the range of each loop clear; that is, indent the statements of the inner loop relative to those of the outer loop.
3. Do not violate the rule of single entry and single exit. The entry point to a FOR loop is the FOR statement and the exit point is the NEXT statement. (The entry point for a WHILE loop is the WHILE statement.) It is important to avoid branching inside, to, or from a loop.
4. Consider readability when you write loop statements. For example, use a space before or after an equals sign and a space before and after the index values.
5. Structured programming requires that the condition for continuing a loop be tested before any statement in a loop is executed. However, if you do not use a DO-WHILE loop for the reading-processing-writing segment of your program, you need to check the sentinel value (end-of-file marker) after a READ statement is executed. The technique shown in Figure 5.8 on page 234 violates the rules of structured programming

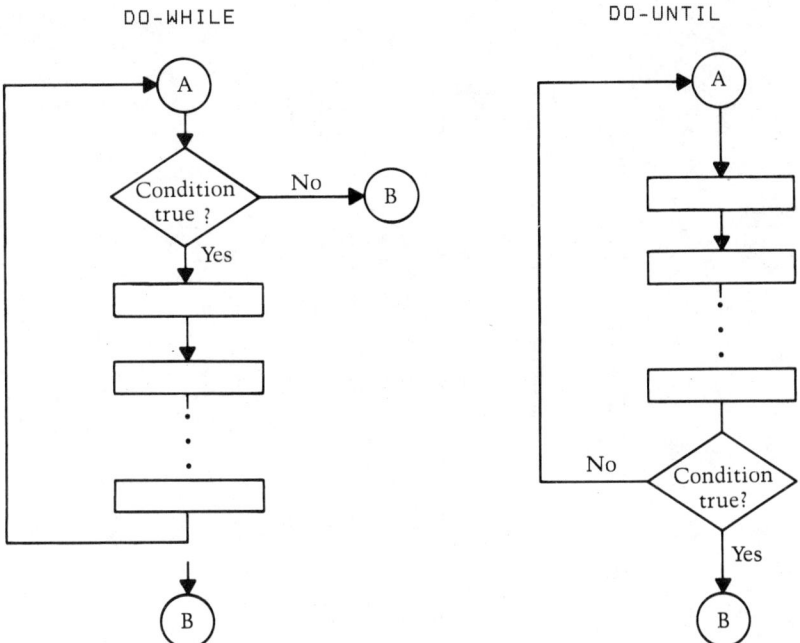

Figure 5.7 Iteration structures

because the first statement is not a decision statement. One way to correct the structure is shown in Figure 5.9 on page 234. Notice that in this structure, the first record is read (the first READ statement) before the loop begins. The READ statement at the bottom of the loop causes all records after the first to be read.

EXERCISES

5.1 Identify errors in the following FOR statements:
   a. FOR J FROM 1 TO 100
   b. FOR K = FROM 5 TO 100
   c. FOR P = 1 TO 75 DO
   d. FOR X = M, N, Q
   e. FOR A = A TO B
   f. FOR H = M TO 2*N + 3 DO
   g. FOR INDEX = 1 TO 100 STEP 0
   h. FOR COUNT = 1 TO 100 STEP -2
   i. FOR TALLY = 99 TO 1 STEP 3

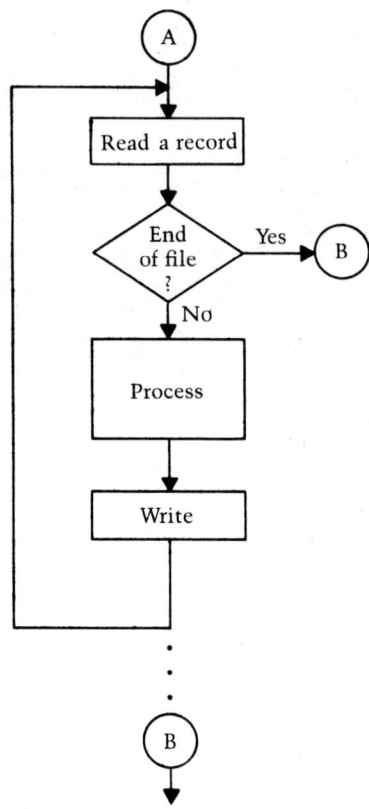

Figure 5.8 An unstructured read-process-write loop

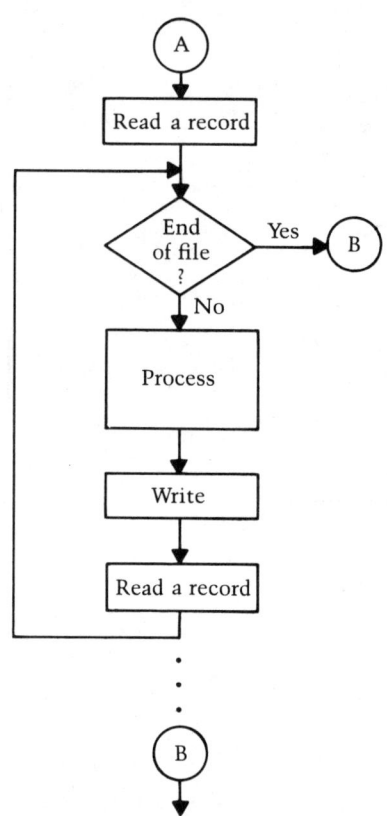

Figure 5.9 A structured read-process-write loop

5.2 Identify errors in the following loops:

    a. `100 FOR KAY = 1 TO N`

           ⋮

       `150    IF KAY = 13 THEN GOTO 100`

           ⋮

       `200 NEXT KAY`

b. 100 FOR TALLY = 1 TO 100 STEP 3
      ⋮
    150   TALLY = TALLY + 2
      ⋮
    200 NEXT TALLY

c. 10 FOR K = 1 TO 100
    20   PRINT " K = "; K
    30 END

d. 10   IF A = 0 THEN GOTO 150
       ⋮
    50   FOR N = 1 TO 100
       ⋮
    150   PRINT N
       ⋮
    200 NEXT N

e. 10   FOR PA = 1 TO 200
    20   FOR KA = 1 TO 300
    30   IF KA = 25 GOTO 10
    40   PRINT KA
    50   NEXT KA
    60   NEXT PA

f. 10   FOR COUNT = 1 TO 50
    20   FOR COUNT = 51 TO 150
    30   PRINT COUNT
    40   NEXT COUNT
    50   NEXT COUNT

g. 50   FOR RX = 1 TO 300 STEP 3
    75   IF RX = 75 THEN GOTO 200
    100   FOR EX = 1 TO 75
    200   SSS = SSS + EX^2
    250   PRINT EX, SSS
    300   NEXT EX
    350 NEXT RX

Programming Exercises:

Write a complete BASIC program for any of the following problems. Use FOR-NEXT statements to create the loop. Pay attention to appropriate headings, formats, and spaces.

5.3 Print

```
THIS IS A BASIC COURSE
```

100 times. Start each line one space farther right than the previous line.

5.4 Add the integers from 1 to N, where N is to be given as input.

5.5 Print the odd numbers from 1 to N with 5 numbers to a line. The input is N, and the output will look like the numbers below.

```
 1    3    5    7    9
11   13   15   17   19
 :    :    :    :    :
```

5.6 Print a table of three columns. The first column shows the numbers from 1 to N, the second column shows the squares of the numbers, and the third column shows the cubes of the numbers. N is to be read as an input. Place asterisks around the table. The printout should look like the table below.

```
**********************************************
*    NUMBERS    *    SQUARE    *    CUBE     *
**********************************************
*       1       *       1      *      1      *
*       2       *       4      *      8      *
*       .       *       .      *      .      *
*       :       *       :      *      :      *
*       N       *      N^2     *     N^3     *
**********************************************
```

5.7 The sine of x can be calculated approximately by summarizing the first n terms of the infinite series

$$\text{Sin } x = x - \frac{x^3}{3!} + \frac{x^5}{5!} - \frac{x^7}{7!} + \cdots$$

Write a program that calculates and prints the sine of X. X and N will be read in as input data (! is a factorial sign.)

5.8 Combination of N and M can be calculated by

$$C_M^N = \frac{N!}{M!(N-M)!}$$

where C is the combination of N items taken M at a time (number of ways that a subgroup of size M can be selected from a group of size N), and

$N! = 1 \times 2 \times 3 \times \cdots \times N$
$M! = 1 \times 2 \times 3 \times \cdots \times M$
$(N-M)! = 1 \times 2 \times 3 \times \cdots \times (N-M)$

Write an interactive program that calculates and prints C, where N and M are to be accepted as input (with N larger than M). Keep the values of M and N below 10 because their factorials can become very large.

5.9 Write an interactive program that calculates the average of a set of numbers. The number of data (N) is to be read at the beginning, followed by the data.

5.10 Write an interactive program that calculates the mean, variance, and the largest and smallest number of a set of data. The number of data (N) is read at the beginning and followed by the data. The variance, VAR, can be calculated as

$$VAR = \frac{\text{Sum of the square of each datum}}{N} - (\text{mean})^2$$

5.11 Write a program that prints the numbers and the square of the numbers from M to N in increments of I. The starting value (M), the final value (N), and the increment (I) are to be read. For example, if M = 6, N = 20, and I = 2, the printout will be

NUMBERS	SQUARES
6	36
8	64
10	100
⋮	⋮
20	400

5.12 Write the program in the previous exercise (5.11) so that it accepts several sets of data (instead of one) and prints the numbers and their squares. Use a trailer value to indicate the end of data. Assume there are fewer than 10 sets of data.

5.13 Write a program that calculates the volume of several cylinders with heights of 10, 20, 30 and radii of 1, 2, 3, 4, 5, 6, 7, 8, 9, 10. The volume can be calculated by the formula

$$V = 3.14 r^2 h$$

5.14 If X dollars are deposited in an account earning interest compounded annually at rate R, the total money after N years is

$$T = X(1 + R)^N$$

Write a program that calculates the total money for X dollars, N years, and different interest rates. The input is X and N. The output is a table of two columns. The first column shows different interest rates starting from .03 in increments of .01 up to the point where the money is doubled (T = 2*X). The second column shows T.

5.15 Write a program that finds values of Y for values of X in the equation

$$Y = 5X^2 + 3X - 2$$

from A to B in increments of C. A, B, and C are to be read in.

5.16 If a component has an average life of T hours, the probability (P) of running without failure at least A hours can be calculated by

$$P = \frac{1}{2.718^{A/T}}$$

Write a program that calculates the probability (P) for a component. The input is the product ID number and the average life (T) of the component. The output is a two-column table. The first column shows different values of A at intervals of 2.5 starting at 1 up to 5*T, and the second column shows the corresponding probabilities.

5.17 Write an interactive program that accepts a word and an integer N. The program then prints the word 1000 times. Each line should have N more spaces at the beginning than the previous line until there are more spaces than the screen will accommodate (assume a screen of 70). In this case, the printed line should have N spaces fewer than the preceding line until there is only one space before the word. The cycle then repeats.

5.18 Write a program that will balance the checking accounts of the customers of a bank. The input is each customer's name, account number, and current balance on one record, followed by that customer's deposits, which are positive, and withdrawals, which are negative. A deposit of 0 indicates the end of deposits/withdrawals for the customer. Assume that the number of withdrawals and deposits per customer is less than 10 and that there are fewer than 100 customers. Zero for the ID number indicates the end of the data. Design your own output. Make sure to print the totals at the end. (*Hint:* You can use two loops. Read the account numbers and current balances in the first loop, and the deposits/withdrawals in the second one.)

5.19 Write a complete interactive program that calculates the average scores for N exams taken by a student. There are many students, and the number of exams varies from student to student. However, the student's name, student's ID number, and the number of exams taken by the student are to be accepted, followed by the student's scores. There are about 100 students. The ID number −9999 indicates the end of the data. Print the grand average and the number of students at the end.

5.20 Assume that you have bought a car and that your monthly payment is PAY. Write an interactive program that prints a table giving the following output:

   a. The date
   b. The sequence numbers as the payment number
   c. The payments (the transaction amount)
   d. The interest
   e. The payments applied to the principal (or the amortization amount)
   f. The remaining balance

The input is:

   a. Beginning balance (BAL)
   b. Interest rate (R) in percentage form
   c. Monthly payments (PAY)
   d. The number of periods to be included in the table (N)
   e. The initial date, input in month, day, year format. You can use the following formulas:
   XR: monthly interest rate = R/1200
   INT: the interest for each period = BAL*XR
   AP: the payment applied to the principal = PAY − INT
   New BAL = Previous BAL − AP
   For example, if

```
BAL = 6589.5
PAY = 139.5
R = 13.5
N = 3
Date: 1,1,85
```

Then the output is:

```
DATE        PAY #    PAYMENT    INTEREST    APPLIED    BALANCE
1/ 1/85      1        139.5      74.1319    65.3681    6524.13
2/ 1/85      2        139.5      73.3965    66.1035    6458.03
3/ 1/85      3        139.5      72.6528    66.8472    6391.18
```

SUMMARY

You have learned:

1. The FOR-NEXT statements are an important way to create loops in BASIC. The general form of the FOR loop is:

   ```
   line no.    FOR Index = m1 TO m2 STEP m3
                 ⋮
   line no.    NEXT Index
   ```

   Index is a variable that controls the loop. Its value starts at m1 and changes by m3 each time around the loop until the value of Index exceeds m2. The most important rules governing the FOR-NEXT loop are:

   a. The initial value, upper limit, and increment of the control variable must be defined.

   b. Control cannot be transferred into a loop, but control can be transferred out of a loop.

   c. The value of the control variable cannot be changed inside the loop.

2. One loop used inside another is called a nested loop. If loops are nested, the range of one loop must not be interrupted by the other. In other words, the loops must not "cross." The rules governing FOR-NEXT loops apply to each loop in a group of nested loops.

REVIEW QUESTIONS/SELF-TEST

5.1 Which of the following statements is not correct?

   a. 10 FOR INDEX = M TO N STEP Q
   b. 10 FOR COUNT = 2*A + 3 TO 5^2 STEP M^3
   c. 10 FOR JAY = 5 TO 10 STEP 0
   d. 10 FOR PA = 100 TO 1 STEP -3
   e. 10 FOR K = 1 TO 3

5.2 Find the errors in the following loops:

a.
```
100 FOR J = 1 TO 99 STEP 2
110     PRINT J
120     J = J + 1
130 NEXT J
```

b.
```
100 FOR K = 1 TO 301
110     IF K = 101 THEN GOTO 100
120     PRINT K
130 NEXT K
```

c.
```
10 FOR I = 1 TO 45
20     FOR I = 46 TO 100
30         PRINT I
40     NEXT I
50 NEXT I
```

5.3 Write an interactive program that repeatedly accepts a number (N) and calculates the sum of the odd numbers from 1 to N. Print the result. Entering a negative number for N should terminate the program. Use FOR-NEXT loops.

Answers:

5.1 c

5.2 a. The value of the control variable cannot be changed inside the loop.

b. Control should be transferred to line 130 instead of line 100.

c. The same control variable cannot be used in the outer loop and the nested loop.

5.3
```
10  PRINT 'I WILL CALCULATE THE SUM OF THE ODD NUMBERS';
20  PRINT ' FROM 1 TO N'
30  FOR ROUND = 1 TO 1000
40      PRINT 'TYPE N, TYPE A NEGATIVE NUMBER IF THROUGH'
50      INPUT N
60      IF N < 0 THEN GOTO 140
70      SUM = 0
80      FOR K = 1 TO N STEP 2
90          SUM = SUM + K
100     NEXT K
110     PRINT 'THE SUM OF ODD NUMBERS FROM 1 TO '; N;
120     PRINT ' IS: '; SUM
130 NEXT ROUND
140 PRINT '*** BYE, CALL BACK ***'
999 END
```

Editing, Data Type, Strings

In This Chapter:

Output Editing
PRINT USING Statement
The Format
Printing Strings with PRINT USING
Editing Symbols

Data Form
Numeric Data
Character Data

Control Design

Exercises

Summary

Review Questions/Self-Test

6

Editing, Data Type, Strings

The first part of this text introduces you to fundamental programming techniques and to BASIC in general. In the following chapters, we discuss advanced features of BASIC. In this chapter, the following important topics are discussed:

1. Output editing
2. Data forms: numeric and character data
3. Control design

The general forms of statements are presented. However, you should check the variations and special features of the system you are using. The BASIC reference manual for your system is a good reference source for this purpose.

OUTPUT EDITING

Output editing is the process of getting the computer to print data in a desired format. Output editing is important for business reports, which need to be presented in a coherent and easily read format.

The editing features of BASIC allow you to specify the length of the data to be printed, to specify the desired number of decimal digits, to align numbers on the decimal point, or to insert symbols, such as dollar signs or commas. These important features of BASIC are explained in detail in the following sections.

246 *Editing, Data Type, Strings*

PRINT USING Statement

Output editing is accomplished with a PRINT USING statement followed by a series of symbols. Before we explain PRINT USING, look at the following example:

Example 6.1

Problem: Assume the computer has stored the value of the average of a test score as

    AVG = 092.52410

Write a program segment that prints the value with two whole digits and one digit after the decimal point.

Program Segment:

    100 PRINT USING "##.#"; AVG

The output will be

```
92.5
```

Notes:

1. The pound sign (#) signifies a desired digit.
2. PRINT USING is a special statement for printing a variable in a desired format.
3. The format of the data—that is, the form, length, and decimal point position—is indicated by the string "##.#".

The general form of the PRINT USING statement is

    line No.   PRINT USING   Format ; VarList

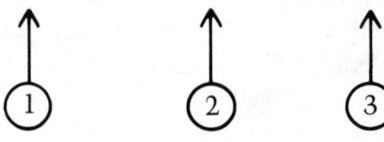

Its components are:

1. The term PRINT accompanied by USING
2. The *format*, explained below
3. The *list* of variables, constants, or expressions

The Format

The information in a line can be printed according to a format. The format can be in any of the following forms:

1. A string constant that contains the desired format specifications. The string can contain descriptors for more than one variable. For example

    ```
    100 PRINT USING "####.### ##"; A; B
    ```

    will print the value of A with four digits to the left of the decimal point and three to the right, and then the value of B with two digits and no decimal point. There will be one space between the printed values of A and B.

2. A string variable that contains the format specifications. For example

    ```
    50  S$ = "####.### ##"
    100 PRINT USING S$; A; B
    ```

    is equivalent to the example above.

3. A line number that refers to the format statement. The format statement contains a line number, a colon, and the specifications. The following is an example:

    ```
    100 PRINT USING 200; A; B
          ⋮
    200 :####.### ##
    ```

Not all systems, however, accept this form.
    The format specifications determine the arrangement of information in a printed line. Each item must have its own field descriptor.

Printing Strings with PRINT USING

String constants can be printed with the PRINT USING statement by placing the string in the format specification. The following examples demonstrate this method:

Example 6.2

Problem: Write a program that calculates the average of two numbers.

Program:

```
100 READ X,Y
110 Z = (X + Y)/2
120 PRINT USING "X: ##.## Y: ##.##   AVERAGE: ##.##"; X; Y; Z
130 DATA 87.5, 92.3
140 END
```

The output will be

```
X: 87.50 Y: 92.30   AVERAGE: 89.90
```

Example 6.3

Problem: Suppose that B = 39.37924. Write a program segment that prints THE VALUE OF B:, and then the value of B with two decimal places.

Program Segment:

```
10 B = 39.37924
20 X$ = "THE VALUE OF B: ##.##"
30 PRINT USING X$, B
```

The output will be

```
THE VALUE OF B: 39.38
```

Example 6.4

Problem: Suppose A = 5.69328. Write a program segment that prints the phrase THE AVERAGE IS and then the value with two decimal places.

Program Segment:
```
100 A = 5.69328
110 THE AVERAGE IS : ##.##
120 PRINT USING 110, A
130 END
```

The output will be

```
THE AVERAGE IS : 5.69
```

Note: This example is similar to Example 6.3 except that it uses a format line which is system dependent.

Example 6.5

Problem: Write a program segment that prints

```
A IS EQUAL TO    B IS EQUAL TO
```

Program Segment:
```
100 A$ = "A IS EQUAL TO    B IS EQUAL TO"
110 PRINT A$
```
The output will be

```
A IS EQUAL TO    B IS EQUAL TO
```

Note: In this example, the string is printed without PRINT USING.

Those examples show how to print a heading, ending, or description in an appropriate place and order. Example 6.6 shows this technique further:

Example 6.6

Problem: Write a program that reads two measurement results and calculates the average of the measurements for several products. Print each measurement with a total of four digits, two before and two after the decimal point. Print the grand average at the end. A negative measurement indicates the end of data.

Program:

```
90   NUM = 0
100  A$ = "         FIRST TEST     SECOND TEST    THE AVERAGE"
110  B$ = "           ##.##           ##.##          ##.##"
120  C$ = "                     GRAND AVERAGE        ##.##"
130  PRINT A$
140  READ T1, T2
150  IF T1 < 0 THEN GOTO 210
160    NUM = NUM + 1
170    AVG = (T1 + T2)/2
180    PRINT USING B$, T1, T2, AVG
190    SUM = SUM + AVG
200  GOTO 140
210  GAVG = SUM/NUM
220  PRINT USING C$, GAVG
230  DATA 76.5, 82.3, 93, 81.67, . . . , -1, 1
300  END
```

The printout will be

```
    FIRST TEST     SECOND TEST     THE AVERAGE
      76.50           82.30           79.40
      93.00           81.67           87.33
        :               :               :
                  GRAND AVERAGE        79.55
```

Notes:

1. Writing the heading is the first step in the program logic and should come before the loop.
2. The editing symbols for the data are aligned under the headings by the formats in the program itself (lines 100, 110, 120).

Editing Symbols

As explained before, output for both numeric and string data can be edited with PRINT USING. The features of the format specification and the symbols for each descriptor are explained next.

Digits and the Decimal Point

The pound symbol (#) represents a digit, and a period represents the place of the decimal point in the printed data. Table 6.1 presents examples.

Several important features of # and . are listed below:

1. The number of digits to the left and/or right of the decimal point is determined by the # symbols.
2. The decimal points in a column of data with the same descriptor align automatically because the data are right-justified (printed to align at the right) with spaces on the left if the number has fewer digits than specified.
3. The printed data are rounded off if necessary. Rounding means that the rightmost digit to be printed remains the same if it is followed by a number less than 5 but is incremented by 1 if the following digit is 5 or greater.
4. The sign of a negative number takes up one of the spaces allotted for a digit.
5. If the number is too large to fit in the specified format field, some systems print the entire number and a symbol indicating overflow (% in some systems). Other systems print asterisks instead of the number.

Table 6.1 Using Editing Symbols # and .

Internal Value	Format Descriptor	Printed Result	Comments
005623.5	####.###	5623.500	
45.89452	###.##	45.89	Note the leading blank.
362.3762	###.##	362.38	The output is rounded off.
-023.32600	###.#	-23.3	The sign takes the place of a digit.
6293.5	###.#	*****	The number is too large for the field.
38.571	###	39	The output is rounded off.

Comma Insertion

When a numeric value is large, it is common to print the number with one or more commas. For example, it is easier to read 3,524,567 than 3524567. If you use PRINT USING and a field descriptor containing commas, you can print numbers with commas. The comma is printed at the specified position unless all the digits before the comma are zeros. A comma must have digits on either side. It cannot, for example, appear before a decimal point. Table 6.2 provides examples.

Dollar Sign Insertion

Financial reports often contain figures with dollar signs. To include dollar signs in the output, insert a $ character in a descriptor. For example, the descriptor $###.## will cause the value 325.69 to be printed as $325.69. The dollar sign can be printed in a fixed position or immediately adjacent to the number. If immediately adjacent, it is called a floating dollar sign and also causes zero suppression. A floating sign can be accomplished by using several $ symbols in the descriptor. (Microsoft BASIC (IBM-PC) uses a double dollar sign ($$) for the floating dollar sign.) A dollar sign, however, cannot appear after a decimal point. Table 6.3 provides some examples.

Table 6.2 Comma Insertion

Internal Value	Format Descriptor	Printed Result	Comments
0062389.324	###,###.##	62,389.32	Note the leading space.
26.5198	###,###.##	26.52	No comma is printed; note leading spaces.
1234567.6372	#,###,###.##	1,234,567.64	Rounded *
5006.68	#,###	5,007	Rounded

*This is a very large number, and, depending on the system, all the digits may not be printed. See the section "Precision of Data," later in this chapter.

Table 6.3 Dollar Sign Insertion

Internal Value	Format Descriptor	Printed Result	Comments
032.56	$####.##	$ 32.56	Fixed $ sign
000389.276	$$$$$.##	$389.28	Zero suppression, floating sign
54328.32	$$,$$$.##	$54,328.32	Insertion of both $ and ,

Sign Insertion (+ and −)

Sometimes it is critical to print the sign of a numeric value. In such cases, inserting a + symbol in the descriptor will ensure that a plus sign is printed if the value is positive or a minus sign is printed if the value is negative. The + can be inserted to the right or left of the number, as desired. Furthermore, if you wish to print the sign of only negative values (and a blank for the positive values), you may do so by inserting a − sign in the descriptor.

If the number has fewer digits than specified in the descriptor, the sign is printed before the leading spaces. To move the sign as close as possible to the digits, you can use a floating sign, that is, more than one + (or −) in the descriptor. A floating sign causes zero suppression. A plus or minus sign, however, cannot be surrounded by other symbols. Table 6.4 provides examples.

Table 6.4 Using Sign Insertion Editing

Internal Value	Format Descriptor	Printed Result	Comments
56.23	+##.##	+56.23	
026.89	###.##+	26.89+	
−89.32	###.##+	89.32−	
−68.9	++++#.##	−68.90	Floating +, zero suppression
+238.50	−####.##	238.5	No sign printed
−68.9	−####.##	− 68.90	Two leading spaces

String Descriptors

Character variables or constants, as well as numeric data, can have descriptors. Symbols in the descriptors indicate the position, form, spacing, or other formats of a character string. However, the symbol used as a descriptor of the character varies with the system being used. For example, in CDC-BASIC, a < or > followed by any number of # symbols is the descriptor of a string. The following is an example for this system:

```
10   X = 67.8034
20   :>############### ##.##
30   B$ = "X IS EQUAL TO :"
40   PRINT USING 20, B$, X
```

This program segment will print

```
X IS EQUAL TO : 67.80
```

Again, the symbol used to represent string descriptors varies from system to system. The symbols >, " ", %, or \ are used for this purpose in various systems. For example, Microsoft BASIC (IBM-PC) and BASIC-PLUS use blanks inside a pair of backslashes to indicate the position and the length of a string field. In Microsoft, n spaces in a pair of backslashes specifies n + 2 characters to be printed. The following is an example:

```
10   X = 67.8341
20   Y$ = "X IS EQUAL TO :"
30   A$ = "\              \ ##.#"
40   PRINT USING A$; Y$; X
```

This program segment will print

```
X IS EQUAL TO : 67.8
```

The following is another example. This program segment will print PATTY HAS AN AVERAGE OF: 91.5.

```
10   X$ = "PATTY"
20   Y = 91.523
30   A$ = "\    \ HAS AN AVERAGE OF: ##.#"
40   PRINT USING A$, X$, Y
```

Note that it is important to specify the length of the string variable. Microsoft BASIC uses an "&" to specify an unknown length for printing a string variable. For example

```
10  X$ = "ABCDEF"
20  PRINT USING "&"; X$
```

will print

```
ABCDEF
```

Again, check your reference manual for the exact form. Regardless of the symbol used in the descriptor of the string data, the descriptor should be sufficiently long; otherwise, truncation occurs.

Notes about Descriptors

1. The format specification provides information about the layout of the data. If the format is given in a separate line and referenced by the line number (in BASIC-PLUS, for example), you can place the format anywhere in the program and not change the logical sequence of instructions. In fact, it is good programming practice to separate the format lines from the rest of the program in order to make the logic of the program apparent. Placing all the format lines together also gives you a clear picture of the final output. Format lines can be placed near the beginning of the program.
2. A format variable, or the format line, can be used more than once.
3. There are restrictions on the use of some editing symbols. Some of these follow:
   a. Plus and minus signs, if present, must come before or after any other editing characters.
   b. There can be only one decimal point per descriptor, and it must be placed after a leading sign, if present.
   c. Dollar symbols, if present, must appear following a positive or negative symbol, if present.
4. There are some other editing symbols, which vary with the system being used. For example, some systems allow you to insert asterisks, commonly used before the dollar figure in checks.
5. A summary of the editing symbols for numeric data is presented in Table 6.5.

Table 6.5 Editing Symbols for Numeric Data

Symbol	Meaning	Comment
#	a numeric digit	
.	decimal point	Only one per field
,	inserting comma	No limit on number used; can be used only before the decimal
$	inserting $	Using more than one in descriptor causes dollar sign to float
*	inserting *	Using more than one in descriptor causes symbol to float
+	inserting + sign	Using more than one in descriptor causes sign to float
−	inserting − sign	Using more than one in descriptor causes sign to float

Solved Problems

6.1 Are the following statements correct? If not, correct the errors.

a. `100 PRINT USING "TOTAL = $$#,###.##", X`

b. ```
100 A = 53.2
110 B = 98.3
120 C = A*B
130 PRINT USING "##.##"; C
```

c. ```
90  A$ = "##.##"
100 PRINT A$, B
```

d. `100 PRINT USING "##.####.#", A, B`

e. `90  PRINT USING A, B, C`

f. `100: ###.##.#`

g. `200 A$ = "##$$.##"`

h. `90  B$ = "-###.##-"`

i. `100 C$ = "###.##$"`

Answers:

a. This is correct; however, the legality of using a comma, semicolon, or space as a separator after the format specification depends on the system being used.

b. The descriptor for C is too small.

c. If the purpose is to use A$ as a format specification, then the word USING is missing. (This is syntactically correct. What does it print?)
d. Some systems require a space separating the descriptors for A and B.
e. The format specification is missing.
f. Two decimal points cannot be used in a descriptor. (Also, few systems allow format lines.)
g. The $ cannot appear between digits.
h. The − cannot be on both sides.
i. The $ cannot appear after the decimal point.

DATA FORM

As discussed in Chapter 2, there are two types of data in BASIC: numeric data and string data. The details are explained in this section.

Numeric Data

Although numeric data can contain only numeric values, they can be presented in the following forms:

1. Real
2. Integer
3. Exponential
4. Double-precision

Real Numbers and Integers

Real numbers and integers are two important types of numeric data.

1. A *real number* is a numeral with a fractional part, such as 93.56, 8.1, 932.12, −56.29. Real values are also referred to as *decimal* or *floating point* values.
2. An *integer* is a whole number without a decimal point, such as 53, 193216, 131, or −92

These are further examples of real numbers:

562.1234	32.19	+8000.0	5.0
−1.0	60.	12000.	0.0

These are further examples of integers:

−621	+123	10001	1
600196	10000	−52	0

An integer variable is a variable that can accept integer data, and a real variable is a variable that can accept real data.

In BASIC, numeric values are normally processed as real, even if the programmer does not specify them as such. For example, the statement A = 30 implicitly causes the value of A to be stored as real (30.0). Some systems, however, allow a quantity to be defined as an integer explicitly, if desired. For example, in BASIC-PLUS the suffix % indicates an integer quantity, thus, the statement A% = 30% causes the variable A to be defined as integer, and the integer value 30 to be assigned to it. (In MBASIC only the integer variable can be defined by suffixing the variable name with %.)

If a system allows this feature, it is important to specify an integer as such in a program because integers are processed more efficiently than other types of data. BASIC handles real data differently from integer data. The programmer, therefore, should separate integers from real numbers for more efficient processing.

To take advantage of the computer's efficiency in processing integer values, the programmer must take care not to use mixed modes. The term *mixed mode of operation* applies to the use of both integers and real numbers in the same statement. For example, all the statements

```
10   A% = 32.5 + 5%
30   X = B% + C%
100  D% = 3*A
```

are examples of mixed modes, assuming % defines integer values. For more examples, look at the following solved problems:

▮ Solved Problems

In the following problems, we assume % defines integer values.

6.2 Which of the following statements are in mixed mode? Explain how each could be corrected to take advantage of integer processing efficiency.

  a. 10   A = 52% + 285
  b. 20   X = 91% + Y

c. 55   P% = 32
   d. 100 N% = N% + 1
   e. 45   R = A%*P
   f. 35   M% = G*F% + 3

Answers:

All of the lines contain mode mixing. The correction depends on the intention of the programmer. The following are possibilities:

   a. 10   A% = 52% + 285%
   b. 20   X% = 91% + Y%
   c. 55   P% = 32%
   d. 100 N% = N% + 1%
   e. 45   R% = A%*P%
   f. 35   M% = G%*F% + 3%

6.3 What is the value of A% in each of the following statements?

   a. 10   A% = 5628.675
   b. 20   A% = 2*3.4
   c. 10   N% = 2%
      20   A% = 15%/N%
   d. 100 A% = 31.9 + 2.9

Answers:

   a. 5628
   b. 6
   c. 7
   d. 34

Exponential Form

In BASIC, often E-notation (scientific notation) is used to represent a very large or small real number. In E-notation, the decimal point is displaced to the left or right. For example, 5720000 may be written as 57.2E5 (the decimal point moves five places to the left). An obvious advantage of this notation is that a large number can be written (and stored in the memory of a computer) in a shorter form. For example, the number

   2659000000000000000000000000000000

can be written and stored as

   26.59E32

Table 6.6 Presenting Data in E-Notation

Data in E-Notation	Mathematical Values	
	Exponent Form	Numeric Form
1.0E0	1.0×10^0	1.0
.999999E+15	$.999999 \times 10^{15}$	999999000000000
−632.5213E+9	-632.5213×10^9	−632521300000
8925.5E−7	8925.5×10^{-7}	.00089255
+5623.527E09	$+5623.527 \times 10^9$	5623527000000

The number 57.2E5 means "57.2 times 10 to the fifth power," or 57.2×10^5. Table 6.6 provides additional examples of numbers written in E-notation. Notice that when the number after E is negative, the decimal point moves to the left.

Precision of Data, Double Precision

The number of digits in a real number, regardless of the decimal point and the leading or trailing zeros, are referred to as significant digits (that is, the number of digits of the whole part plus the number of digits in the fraction part). For example

    493.5632

has seven significant digits, and

    0098236.20

has six significant digits.

Because the size of a memory cell (called a *memory word*) that holds a piece of data is limited, the magnitude and the number of significant digits to be stored are also limited. The maximum number of significant digits that can be stored, as well as the largest number that can be stored, varies among the computer systems. Most computer systems can store at least six significant digits and numbers up to a magnitude of E−75 to E+75 (10^{-75} to 10^{75}).

If, for example, a computer can store seven significant digits and numbers of the magnitude up to E±75, then the following are invalid numbers:

5619.3259E+5	More than seven significant digits
325.52E022	More than two digits in the exponent

0.982578987E4	More than seven significant digits
2153.25E85	Exponent larger than 75
621.52E−82	Exponent smaller than −75
5.32IE12.5	Decimal point is illegal in exponents

If a number has more significant digits than allowable (n), the number is rounded off internally. That is, all the digits after the nth digit are discarded. However, if the first discarded digit is 5 or greater, 1 is added to the last significant digit. For example, the following numbers are rounded off to seven significant digits:

Number	Rounded
65.6327829512	65.63278
5.69283681	5.692837
3657823.2515	3657823.

Some computer systems, however, truncate the number rather than rounding it off.

In some numeric applications, limited significant digits may create serious problems because of rounding-off errors. Some systems allow variables to be defined as *double-precision* values. Double-precision values are represented internally by two memory cells. Thus, the maximum number of significant digits of double-precision data is approximately twice that of single-precision data. The way variables are defined as double-precision values varies among systems. For example, in EXTENDED-BASIC, a double-precision value is so defined by the suffix #. The following segment is an example of how double-precision variables are used:

```
10   READ A#, B#
20   C# = A#/B#
30   PRINT C#
40   DATA 5.6, 369.893283
50   END
```

This program prints the value of C with more than 14 significant digits.

Input/Output of Data in E-Notation

Data can be input in exponential form, as the following example illustrates:

```
100 READ A, B, C
110 D = A + B + C
120 PRINT A, B, C, D
130 DATA 562.87E+15, 62.8, -2.389E5
```

The form of the printed data, however, depends on the internal values. The following rules apply to most systems:

1. Printed negative values are preceded by a minus sign, and printed positive values by a blank.
2. Leading zeros and trailing zeros (zeros after a decimal point) are suppressed.
3. If there are too many significant digits, that is, more digits than the system allows, the last digit is obtained by rounding off.
4. The data are normally printed in regular form (not in E-notation) except when the number is either too big or too small. The following rules apply:
    a. If the value to be printed is too small (smaller than .01, depending on the system), then the data are printed in exponential form.
    b. If the number of significant digits to be printed is greater than the system allows, the data are rounded off and printed in exponential form.

The following is an example:

Example 6.7

Problem: What does the following program print? (Assume the computer prints six significant digits.)

Program:

```
10   A = -235
20   B = 123456789.321
30   C = .008321
40   D = 123456
50   PRINT A, B, C, D
60   END
```

The output will be

```
-235            1.23456E+8           8.321E-3              123456
```

Character Data

Character data were introduced in Chapter 2, and have been used in the programs throughout the text. The following list is a summary of the most important features of character data discussed so far:

1. *String variables* A string variable is a variable that can contain character data. It is defined by adding the suffix $ to the variable name. For example:

    A$ ANAME$ ADRES$

    are string variables. (Keep in mind that some BASIC systems do not accept a name with more than a letter and a digit.)
2. *String input/output* When entering character data, for instance, in response to an INPUT prompt, you may place the character strings inside quotation marks, but they are not necessary. However, if the string contains special characters, such as blanks or commas, quotation marks are necessary.
3. *String assignment* A string of characters can be assigned to a string variable if the string constant is placed in quotation marks.
4. *String comparison* String constants or variables can be compared in an IF statement. For example:

    100 IF ANAME$ < "ABC"

    is valid. A letter occurring late in the alphabet has a higher value than a letter occurring early in the alphabet, and digits have lower values than letters. If strings contain more than one character, they are compared by alphabetical order. For example, AB has a lower value than AC.

Some other features of character data are discussed in the following sections.

Solved Problems

6.4 Specify the type and form of the data in each of the following statements:
  a. 10   X$ = "ABC"
  b. 100   Q$ = "39.5"
  c. 50   K = 50
  d. 75   M = 3856.2E+29
  e. 60   J# = 32.893#

Answers:

a and **b.** Character

c. Numeric, real

d. Numeric, exponential-form

e. Numeric, double precision (assuming # defines double-precision data)

Character Codes—ASCII Table

The computer stores characters in memory by their numeric codes. The most common BASIC coding system is the ASCII code. (Pronounced Ask-key, ASCII is an acronym for American Standard Code for Information Interchange.) For example, the ASCII code of capital A is 065 (in decimal). Table 6.7 lists the most important ASCII codes. As you see from the table, the ASCII codes reflect the alphabetical order of the letters they represent, and the character-code values of digits are lower than those of letters.

Of course, there is no need to memorize the ASCII codes. The BASIC system translates the characters to codes automatically without the programmer's being aware of it. If a programmer wants to convert a character to its code or vice versa, two functions, ASC and CHR$, are useful. The forms of these two functions are

```
Line no. k = ASC(a$)
Line no. x$ = CHR$(n)
```

where ASC converts the character a$ to its ASCII code (k), and CHR$ converts an ASCII code n to its character (x$). For example, the statements:

```
100   M = ASC("B")
110   PRINT M
```

will print

```
66
```

The program

```
100   Q$ = CHR$(65)
110   PRINT Q$
120   END
```

Table 6.7 ASCII Codes

Control Characters			Letters and Special Characters					
ASCII value		Meaning	ASCII value	Character	ASCII value	Character	ASCII value	Character
000	NUL	Null	032	(space)	064	@	096	`
001	SOH	Start of heading	033	!	065	A	097	a
002	STX	Start of text	034	"	066	B	098	b
003	ETX	End of text	035	#	067	C	099	c
004	EOT	End of transmission	036	$	068	D	100	d
005	ENQ	Enquiry	037	%	069	E	101	e
006	ACK	Acknowledge	038	&	070	F	102	f
007	BEL	Bell	039	'	071	G	103	g
008	BS	Backspace	040	(	072	H	104	h
009	HT	Horizontal tab	041	)	073	I	105	i
010	LF	Line feed	042	*	074	J	106	j
011	VT	Vertical tab	043	+	075	K	107	k
012	FF	Form feed	044	,	076	L	108	l
013	CR	Carriage return	045	-	077	M	109	m
014	SO	Shift out	046	.	078	N	110	n
015	SI	Shift in	047	/	079	O	111	o
016	DLE	Data link escape	048	0	080	P	112	p
017	DC1	Device control 1	049	1	081	Q	113	q
018	DC2	Device control 2	050	2	082	R	114	r
019	DC3	Device control 3	051	3	083	S	115	s
020	DC4	Device control 4	052	4	084	T	116	t
021	NAK	Negative acknowledge	053	5	085	U	117	u.
022	SYN	Synchronous idle	054	6	086	V	118	v
023	ETB	End of transmission block	055	7	087	W	119	w
024	CAN	Cancel	056	8	088	X	120	x
025	EM	End of medium	057	9	089	Y	121	y
026	SUB	Substitute	058	:	090	Z	122	z
027	ESC	Escape	059	;	091	[	123	{
028	FS	File separator	060	<	092	\	124		
029	GS	Group separator	061	=	093	]	125	}
030	RS	Record separator	062	>	094	∧	126	~
031	US	Unit separator	063	?	095	—	127	DEL

will print

```
A
```

The functions can also be used in PRINT statements. For example, 10 PRINT CHR$(65) is valid. (The functions are explained in detail in Chapter 9.) If you wish to see which characters correspond to the ASCII codes in your system, run the following program:

```
10   FOR I = 1 TO 255
20       PRINT "CODE=": I, "CHARACTER =": CHR$(I)
30   NEXT I
40   END
```

This program prints all the characters. However, some of the characters are not printable, rather they cause some action. For example

```
PRINT CHR$(7)
```

activates the beep. These characters are called control characters because they are used for control purposes.

Control Characters

ASCII codes 1 through 31 are control characters, and their action depends on the system used. The control characters have interesting applications. They can be used to move the cursor, clear the screen, sound the beep, control the communication system, or control the output format. The following application uses the beep.

Example 6.8

Problem: It is common to test input data for correctness. Assume that a number to be input should not be greater than 1000. Write a program segment that prints BET TOO LARGE and sounds the beep if the number is greater than 1000.

Program Segment:

```
100  INPUT A
110  IF A > 1000 THEN PRINT CHR$(7); "BET TOO LARGE"
     ⋮
```

For more examples, look at the following solved problems:

Solved Problems

The action of control characters depends on the system used. For the following problems, assume the ASCII control characters have the effect shown in the table below.

Code	Function
7	Sounding the beep
11	Moving the cursor up one line
26	Clearing the screen and moving the cursor to the top.
30	Moving the cursor "home" (to the top of the screen) without clearing the screen

6.5 Write a program segment that:

a. Prints the word BEEP and sounds the beep ten times.

b. Creates a variable name that clears the screen whenever it is used, uses the name to clear the screen, and then prints TYPE YOUR NAME on the fifth line of the screen. (In many systems, there is a special term for clearing the screen. CLS, HOME, and CLEAR are examples. See Appendix B.)

c. Prints WHAT IS YOUR NAME: XXXXXXXXX, and then accepts a name. The cursor should move to the beginning of XXXXXXXXX before the name is accepted.

Answers:

```
a. 110 FOR I = 1 TO 10
   120    PRINT "BEEP"; CHR$(7)
   130 NEXT I
b. 90  CLEAN$ = CHR$(26)
   100 PRINT CLEAN$
   110 FOR I = 1 TO 4
   120    PRINT
   130 NEXT I
   140 PRINT "TYPE YOUR NAME"
```

c.
```
100 PRINT "WHAT IS YOUR NAME: XXXXXXXXXX"
120 PRINT TAB(18); CHR$(11);
130 INPUT A$
```

Character Expressions

Some programming techniques require that character strings be joined. In BASIC, string characters are joined by the concatenation operator, which, in most systems, is the plus sign. (It varies, however, among systems, see Appendix B.) For example,

```
A$ = "A" + "B" + "C" + "D"
```

is equivalent to

```
A$ = "ABCD"
```

The following are further examples:

Example 1: The program segment

```
10 X$ = "JACK"
20 Y$ = "BROWN"
30 Z$ = X$ + " " + T$
40 PRINT Z$
```

will print

```
JACK BROWN
```

Example 2: The program segment

```
10 C$ = "UNITED STATES O"
20 D$ = "F AMERICA"
30 E$ = C$ + D$
40 PRINT E$
```

will print

```
UNITED STATES OF AMERICA
```

Substring Reference

Sometimes we need to extract one or more characters from a string. In BASIC, the MID$ function is used for this purpose. In most systems, the form of the function is

$$\text{MID\$(a\$, n1, n2)}$$

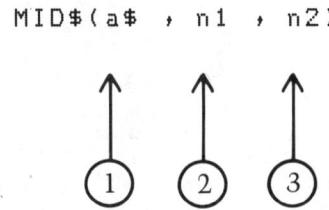

Its components are:

1. The variable name a$, or a string constant
2. The first character to be extracted (n1)
3. The number of characters to be extracted (n2)

For example, if

    100 A$ = "ABCDEFGHIJKLMN"

then each of the following X$ is a substring of A$:

    200 X$ = MID$(A$,1,5)   Value: "ABCDE"
    300 X$ = MID$(A$,2,10)   Value: "BCDEFGHIJK"
    400 X$ = MID$(A$,6)   Value: "FGHIJKLMN"

Notice that when no value is given for n2, the computer returns all characters from n1 to the end of the string.

Other important functions for referencing a part of a character string are RIGHT$ and LEFT$. In most systems, LEFT$ and RIGHT$ functions allow you to reference M characters of the leftmost or rightmost parts of the string. For example, if again

    100 A$ = "ABCDEFGHIJKLM"

then each of the following X$ is a substring of A$:

    500 X$ = LEFT$(A$,3)   Value: "ABC"
    600 X$ = RIGHT$(A$,5)   Value: "IJKLM"

MID$, LEFT$, RIGHT$ can all be used to extract a part of a string.

Table 6.8 Some Character Functions

Function	Purpose	Example
INKEY$	Accepts a single character from the keyboard	A$ = INKEY$
LEN(a$)	Returns the length of a character string	B = LEN(A$)
VAL(a$)	Returns the numeric value of a number stored as a character string	D = VAL("12")
STR$(x)	Changes the numeric value to a character string	A$ = STR$(23) B$ = STR$(D)

Other String Functions

Table 6.8 lists some other useful string functions. Unfortunately, these functions are not standard, and their forms vary slightly from system to system. The following examples demonstrate how these functions can be used. (Make sure to check the manual for your system before using these functions.)

■ **Example 6.9**

The INKEY$ Function

Problem: The INKEY$ function is very useful. It accepts a character from the keyboard. INKEY$ is normally used in an assignment statement, such as 100 X$ = INKEY$. This statement tells the computer to assign the code value of the key just pressed, if any, to X$. The statement, however, does not cause the computer to wait for a key to be pressed. Therefore, the null string (" ") is assigned to X$ (no key is pressed). The program then continues to the next line. Using INKEY$, write a loop that causes execution to stop until a key is hit.

Program Segment:

```
 90 PRINT "HIT ANY KEY TO CONTINUE"
100 X$ = INKEY$
110 IF X$ = "" THEN GOTO 100
120 . . . . .
```

Example 6.10

The LEN Function

Problem: Assume a program asks the user to input a five-character code for a product. Write a program segment that prints a message if the code is longer than five characters.

Program Segment:
```
100 INPUT CODE$
110 A = LEN(CODE$)
120 IF A > 5 THEN PRINT "CODE TOO LONG"
```

Example 6.11

The VAL Function

Problem: Suppose that in response to the statement
```
100 INPUT ADRES$
```
the user is expected to type string data such as
```
"123 HIGH STREET"
```
Write a program segment that prints the number portion of the address in numeric form.

Program Segment:
```
100 INPUT ADRES$
110 X = VAL(ADRES$)
120 PRINT X
```

Example 6.12

The STR Function

Problem: Suppose a Social Security number, such as 123456789, is read as a numeric datum. Write a program segment that prints the number in the form 123-45-6789.

Program Segment:

```
100 X$ = STR$(SSN)
110 A$ = LEFT$(X$,3)
120 B$ = MID$(X$,4,2)
130 C$ = RIGHT$(X$,4)
140 D$ = A$ + "-" + B$ + "-" + C$
150 PRINT D$
```

■ **Solved Problems**

6.6 Write a program or program segment that accomplishes each of the following tasks.

    a. Accept a word, such as BASIC, and print it in this format:

```
B
 BA
  BAS
   BASI
    BASIC
```

    b. Suppose a person's first name, middle name, and last name are stored in A$, with each name separated by a space. Print each part of the name on a separate line.

    c. Accept Y (for yes) or N (for no) without waiting for the user to press the RETURN key after he or she types the letter. Branch to line 200 if the response is Y and to line 300 if the response is N.

Answers:

    a.
```
100 INPUT A$
110 FOR I = 1 TO LEN(A$)
120     PRINT TAB(I), LEFT(A$, I)
130 NEXT I
```

    b.
```
100 FOR I = 2 TO LEN(A$)
110     IF MID$(A$, I, 1) = " " THEN GOTO 130
120 NEXT I
130 F$ = LEFT (A$, I)
140 FOR J = I+1 TO LEN(A$)
150     IF MID$(A$, J, 1) = " " THEN GOTO 170
160 NEXT J
170 N = J - I
180 M$ = MID$(A$, I+1, N)
190 L$ = MID$(A$, J)
200 PRINT F$
210 PRINT M$
220 PRINT L$
```

c. ```
100 PRINT "WOULD YOU LIKE TO CONTINUE?"
110 A$ = INKEY$
120   IF A$ = "Y" THEN GOTO 200
130   IF A$ = "N" THEN GOTO 300
140 GOTO 110
```

### LINE INPUT Statement

The LINE INPUT statement causes a BASIC system to accept a record as the value of a single string variable. The form of the statement is

   line no.   LINE INPUT var$

Again, the form of the statement is not standard and depends on the system being used. Table 11.1 in Chapter 11 presents some examples of the form of the statement in several systems.

A record is considered to be a line that is terminated by a carriage return. The record can contain any character, such as a letter, a comma, or a quotation mark. This feature allows flexibility in input data. Often, this statement is used to read records from a file, a topic discussed in Chapter 11. In any case, the record can be separated easily into fields by the MID$, LEFT$, or RIGHT$ functions. The following is an example:

### Example 6.13

*Problem:* A record contains the following fields:

| An ID number | positions 1 to 5 |
| A name | positions 6 to 20 |
| A telephone number | positions 21 to 26 |

Write a program segment that accepts a record and prints each field in the record separately.

*Program Segment:*
```
100 LINE INPUT X$
110 ID$ = LEFT$(X$, 5)
120 ANAME$ = MID$(X$, 6, 15)
130 PHONE$ = MID$(X$, 21, 6)
140 PRINT ID$
150 PRINT ANAME$
160 PRINT PHONE$
```
```

CONTROL DESIGN

Control design consists of the provisions that ensure correct data are accepted, processed, and reported. The objective of control design is twofold: (1) to ensure the correct processing and (2) to prevent fraud. A well-designed BASIC program should check the validity of information at each of the three stages:

1. Input
2. Processing
3. Output

At each stage, necessary testing provisions should be included to detect improper information and to indicate possible corrective action. Testing the data for accuracy and completeness when they are entered is called *input editing, validation,* or simply *editing*.

The following is a list of simple techniques that can be incorporated into a BASIC program for control purposes.

1. *String size check*   Sometimes the input fields must not have more than a certain number of characters. String size can be checked easily with an IF statement and the LEN function.
2. *Value check*   Sometimes a value must be equal to a constant. If so, the field can be checked for a correct value. For example, if the response to a question should be either YES or NO, then an IF statement can easily test whether this condition is satisfied. Other responses should be considered "invalid input."
3. *Data type check*   Sometimes the input value must be either numeric or string data. Data type can be checked easily with an IF and the VAL function.
4. *Sign test*   Numeric values can be positive or negative. Sometimes it is inappropriate to process a positive or a negative value. For example, the net pay to an employee after all deductions must not be negative, and the program should print an error if it is negative.
5. *Limit check*   The value of a numeric field can be checked against a predetermined maximum value. If, for example, the weekly pay to an employee paid by the hour must not exceed $1000, this condition can be checked easily in an IF statement.
6. *Range test*   The range test ensures that the value of a variable lies within some predetermined values. For example, assume the input data for the variable YEAR must not be greater than 1984 or smaller than 1971. Satisfaction of this condition can be checked in an IF statement.

7. *Presence check* Sometimes a data field must have a value. In this case, the field can be checked against spaces or the null character.

EXERCISES

6.1 Find all the errors in the following PRINT USING statements.
   a. `100 PRINT USING A, B, C`
   b. `70  PRINT "THE VALUE OF X IS: ##.##"; X`
   c. `110 PRINT USING "##.###"; A; B`
   d. `150 PRINT USING A$, B$, "/      /, /     /"`
   e. `90  PRINT USING "##--.--"; X, "+++.++"; Y`
   f. `50  PRINT USING "###."; A`
   g. `100 PRINT USING "-###.##-"; X`
   h. `90  PINT USING "9999.99"; X`
   i. `100 PRINT USING`

6.2 Express the following numbers in E-notation with two decimal places. Assume that the computer will not accept more than seven significant digits or a number larger than 10^{75}. State which numbers should be defined as double-precision values.
   a. 562389500000
   b. -362897
   c. $+368.5623 \times 10^{35}$
   d. $59322859283 \times 10^{36}$
   e. $52453923258 \times 10^{36}$
   f. .052839823
   g. .000000082
   h. 2569000000000000000

6.3 What do the following statements accomplish or print? Use Table 6.7 as a reference.
   a. ```
      100 A$ = CHR$(72) + CHR$(73)
      110 PRINT A$
      ```
   b. ```
      500 Z$ = CHR$(72) + CHR$(73) + CHR$(32) + "HOW ARE YOU"
      510 PRINT Z$
      ```
   c. ```
      90 X$ = CHR$(51) + CHR$(57) + CHR$(53)
      100 PRINT "X IS = " ; X$
      ```
      ```

d.
```
50  INPUT R$
60  IF R$ = "NO" THEN PRINT CHR$(7)
```
e.
```
100  INPUT A$
110  IF LEN(A$) > 15 THEN PRINT "NAME TOO BIG"
120  PRINT CHR$(7)
```
f.
```
60  INPUT X$
70  IF X$ = "CLEAN" THEN PRINT CHR$(7)
```

6.4 Write a program to accomplish each of the following tasks:

   a. Accept a word, and print it in a two-triangle form so that the first line contains the first character of the word, the second line contains the first and second characters, and so on. The second triangle should be the mirror image of the first one. For example, if the word is BASIC, the output is

```
B            B
BA          AB
BAS        SAB
BASI      ISAB
BASICCISAB
```

   b. Accept a word, such as BASIC, and print it as

```
BASICBASIC
 BASI BASI
  BAS BAS
   BA BA
    B B
```

   c. If you are using a video terminal, write a loop to repeat the program in either a or b above 1000 times. The resulting pattern pleases the eye.

   d. Accept a word and find N, the number of characters in the word. Print the word 1000 times so that each new line has N spaces more at the beginning than the previous line. If, however, the line has more spaces at the beginning than the screen will accommodate (assume a screen width of 80 or 40), then the next line will have N spaces fewer at the beginning than the previous line. Use this program to create a pleasing design on the monitor. (*Note:* Compare this exercise to Exercise 5.17 in Chapter 5. Here, you should use a function to find the length of the word.)

6.5 Write a program to accomplish each of the following tasks:

   a. Accept a string value. If the value is numeric, sound the beep and print a message saying that a string value is expected.

b. Assume a long report is to be displayed. Write a program segment that stops the report after every 20 lines and continues it if the user presses any key.

c. Accept a word and check the word to see if it contains a double letter.

d. Accept a name, then print the name and the number of characters in the name. Sound the beep if the name is longer than 20 characters.

e. Accept a yes or no response. If the response is "no" print

********* CALL BACK ***********

However, the user should not have to press the RETURN key. (Hint: Use the INKEY$ function to accept the characters one by one.)

f. Accept a title and print it at the center of the screen.

g. Accept a sentence and count the number of commas in the sentence. If there is more than one comma, replace each comma with a space and print a message saying there are too many commas. Print the sentence after editing.

6.6 Assume you would like to send the following letter to 20 of your friends. Design and develop a program that first accepts the letter, then accepts the names and addresses and finally generates the letters.

    [Address]
    Dear [Johnny]
      Surprise!
      I will have a surprise party for Jim Nopaz in my house this coming Friday. You and your [guest/spouse] are cordially invited.
      Jim will be here at 6:30. Make sure you are here before he arrives.
                           Sincerely,
                             Your name

Note that the items in the brackets are given as input.

6.7 Write a program that accepts a name, scrambles the letters, and prints the scrambled name.

6.8 Write a program that accepts a name and prints each letter of the name on a different line, diagonally. For example, if the name is GUSTAV, the program should print

```
G
 U
  S
   T
    A
     V
```

6.9 Assume you want to send a secret message. One approach is to convert each character of the message to its ASCII code.

  a. Write a program that accepts a message, encodes it, and prints the coded message.

  b. Write a program that accepts a coded message, decodes it, and prints the message. Test the program with the following coded message.

  8979853265826932787463279786 9

  Assume every two digits stand for a letter of the message.

  c. A better encoding method is to add a constant number to each letter's ASCII code. Repeat a and b, above, using this new technique.

6.10 Write a program that prints an invoice for a customer.

  a. Input
  Identify the customer in the first record

	Columns
Customer's name	1–20
Customer's street address	21–40
Customer's state	41–60
Customer's account no.	61–66

  The transaction records follow

Name of the product	1–30
Unit ordered (such as 99)	31–32
Unit price (such as 999.99)	33–38

  b. Processing
  1. The amount of each order is calculated as

  units ordered × unit price

  2. The tax is 6.5 percent of the amount.
  3. The total amount for each item is the amount plus the tax.

  c. Output
  Design an invoice, print the address so that the invoice is ready for mailing, and make sure the invoice has the following parts:
  1. Company logo
  2. Customer's name and address
  3. Headings for the transactions records
  4. Details of the transaction records, including the amount, the tax, and the total amount

5. The total tax and the total sales, for all products, at the end of the invoice

Use a fixed dollar sign and inserted commas for the transaction items. Use a floating dollar sign and inserted comma for the totals.

6.11 Write a program that reads an employee's name, ID number, hours, and wage rate. Calculate the pay. The overtime is 1.5 times the regular wage rate. Print the name, ID number, hours, wage rate, and the pay to each employee. Print an asterisk next to the pay if the employee has worked more than 60 hours (to get management's attention). Also, print the total pay to all employees at the end. Use fixed dollar signs and inserted commas for the pay, and floating dollar signs and inserted commas for the total. A trailer record terminates the loop that reads the data.

6.12 A construction company's weekly pay to its employees is based on the following formula:

```
PAY = HOURS*RATE + EXTRA*HOURS, IF HOURS <= 40
```

Otherwise

```
PAY = 40.0*RATE + 1.5*(HOURS - 40)*RATE + EXTRA*HOURS
```

EXTRA is calculated according to the number of years an employee has worked for the company.

0–5 years	$2.00
6–10 years	$3.00
11–20 years	$4.00
over 20 years	$5.00

Write a program that generates the pay report. The input is the employee's name, hours worked during a week, number of years employed, and the base wage rate. The output is the input information and the pay to each employee in report form. Also print the total pay, the total overtime, and the total pay for overtime at the end. Use fixed dollar signs and inserted commas for the pay, and floating dollar signs and inserted commas for the total. The last record contains FINISHED for the employee's name. The control design of the program should check the following items:

a. Overtime must not be more than 20 hours.
b. No one's pay should be more than $1500.00.
c. No one has worked for more than 30 years.

Print asterisks next to any item violating the above conditions.

6.13 The end-of-year bonus to the employees of the GHM Company is based on the following plan:

5 percent of income for single employees (KODE = 1)

7 percent of income for married employees with no children (KODE = 2)

9 percent of income for married employees with children (KODE = 3)

In addition, the following lump sum is added to the bonus:

$1,000 if income is less than $10,000

$750 if income is $10,000 to $20,000

$500 if income is more than $20,000

Write a program that generates the bonus report and the totals. Design the inputs, controls, and outputs. Use fixed dollar signs and inserted commas for the pay, and floating dollar signs and inserted commas for the totals.

6.14 The Consumer Gas Company charges its customers by the number of units used during the billing period according to the following schedule:

a. For residential use (KODE = 1)

0 to 50.00 units at $.55 per unit

From 50 to 100.00 units at $.49 per unit

From 100 to 500.0 units at $.39 per unit

From 500 to 800.0 units at $.30 per unit

More than 800 units at $.26 per unit

b. For industrial use (KODE = 2)

0 to 400 units at $.49 per unit

From 400 to 1000 units at $.35 per unit

More than 1000 units at $.29 per unit

The charges are progressive. That is, if a residential customer uses 120 units, the charge is

```
CHARGE = 50*.55 + 50*.49 + 20*.39
```

Write a program to generate a report for customer's charges. Design the input and output. Use the customer's ID, last reading, and current reading as input. Make sure to print the totals at the end. Use fixed dollar signs and inserted commas for the charges, and floating dollar signs and inserted commas for the totals.

6.15 Write a program that prints weekly check stubs for employees of the XYZ company. The input is:

Employee ID	Columns 1 to 5
Hours worked for the week	Columns 7 to 11
Wage rate	Columns 13 to 17
Employee's name	Columns 19 to 30
Employee's address (number and street)	Columns 32 to 51
Employee's address (city and state)	Columns 53 to 72

Let the deductions be 15 percent of the gross pay. Hours over 40 are paid at 1.5 times the regular rate. The last record is a trailer with the sentinel value −9999 as the ID number. An example of the output is shown below.

```
*************************************************************
*                      XYZ COMPANY                           *
*       EMPLOYEE # 99999              JOHN DOE               *
*                                     4899 AUDUBON ST.       *
*       HOURS WORKED XX.XX            MT. PLEASANT, MI 48858 *
*       TOTAL PAY $9999.99            DEDUCTIONS $999.99     *
*                      NET PAY $9999.99                      *
*************************************************************
```

6.16 Rewrite the previous program so that it prints two check stubs side by side. (*Hint:* You should use two READ statements to read the information for two employees).

SUMMARY

You have learned:

1. Printing values in a desired form, length, and place is called output editing. Output editing is accomplished through PRINT USING in BASIC. The following symbols can be used to describe a field:

Symbol	Function
# and .	Locates a digit and sets the position of the decimal point
,	Inserts a comma
$	Inserts a dollar sign
+ or −	Gives the sign of the field

2. There are two types of data in BASIC: numeric data and string data.
3. Numeric data can be in any of the following forms:
   a. Real
   b. Integer
   c. Exponential
   d. Double-precision
4. Character data can contain a letter, digit, or any other symbol. The following are some properties of character strings:
   a. Any character is stored in the form of a code. A common coding system is the ASCII code. The ASCII code value of a character can be invoked by the ASC function, and a numeric code can be converted to its character by the CHR$ function. Some ASCII codes are used for control purposes and have interesting applications.
   b. Strings can be joined together by the concatenation operator.
   c. A part of a string can be extracted by the MID$, LEFT$, and RIGHT$ functions.
   d. The numeric value and the length of a character string can be determined by a character function.
5. Control design should be included in a program to ensure data are accurately accepted, processed, and delivered.

REVIEW QUESTIONS/SELF-TEST

6.1 Are the following statements correct? Also, identify which statements contain character data.
   a. `100 X% = 29%`
   b. `200 Y = 56.328E-23`
   c. `300 A$ = "43"`
   d. `100 K# = 999#`
   e. none of the above

6.2 Assume ASCII code 7 sounds the beep. Write a program segment that pauses execution and asks the user to type an X. As soon as an X is typed, execution continues; there should be no need for the user to press the RETURN key. If a character other than X is typed, the program should sound the beep and wait until an X is typed.

6.3 Develop and write a program that reads and prints information about check deposits to an account. The input is the check number and the amount of the check. The output is a report including the amount of each check and the total. Include fixed dollar signs in the amounts, and floating dollars and inserted commas in the totals.

Answers:

6.1 All of the statements are correct and c contains character data (assuming % defines integer data and # defines double-precision data).

6.2
```
100 PRINT "TYPE X"
110     B$ = INKEY$
120     IF B$ = "X" THEN GOTO 150
130     PRINT CHR$(7)
140 GOTO 100
150 ..........
```

6.3
```
10  TOT = 0
20  A$ = '            CHECK NUMBER          AMOUNT'
30  B$ = '            ------------          ---------'
40  C$ = '                ###               $####.##'
50  D$ = '            ------------          ---------'
60  E$ = '                TOTAL             $$,###.##'
70  PRINT A$
80  PRINT B$
100 FOR I = 1 TO 100
110     READ N, A
120     IF A <= 0 THEN GOTO 200
130     TOT = TOT + A
140     PRINT USING C$; N ;A
150 NEXT I
200 PRINT D$
210 PRINT USING E$; TOT
220 DATA 562, 3695.36, 643, 2192.55, 652, 78, . . . ,0, -99
999 END
```

One-Dimensional Arrays

7

In This Chapter:

Array Techniques
Subscripted Variables
The Dimension Statement
Reason for Arrays: An Example
Arithmetic Expressions with Arrays
Array Input-Output
Printing Values on One Line
Mirror Printing
Summary of Important Points About Arrays

Some Examples of Arrays and Programming Techniques
Exercises
Summary
Review Questions/Self-Test

7

One-Dimensional Arrays

Many programs in the previous chapters used loops. In these loops, the same variable name could be used in a repeated operation. However, when a new variable value is read, the previous value is erased. The technique is fine as long as we do not need to store all the values. Arrays in a program allow us to store all the values. An *array* is a series of variables that all have the same name. A particular *element* in an array is identified by a subscript. In BASIC, we can use one- or two-dimensional arrays. One-dimensional arrays are explained in this chapter. Two-dimensional arrays are discussed in Chapter 8.

ARRAY TECHNIQUES

For some applications, it is necessary to read and store all the data before they are processed. To do this, you must give each piece of data a variable name, as the following example shows:

Example 7.1

Problem: An instructor would like to compare individual students' test scores against the class average. Write a program that accepts and stores ten test scores, then calculates the average of the scores. Print each score and the average on one line.

Solution Plan:

1. Accept all the data.
2. Calculate the average.
3. Print each score and the average.

Program:

```
10  REM ********** ACCEPT THE DATA *************
20  PRINT "TYPE TEN TEST SCORES, ONE PER LINE"
100 INPUT T1
110 INPUT T2
120 INPUT T3
130 INPUT T4
140 INPUT T5
150 INPUT T6
160 INPUT T7
170 INPUT T8
180 INPUT T9
190 INPUT T10
200 REM ********** CALCULATIONS ***************
210 SUM = T1 + T2 + T3 + T4 + T5 + T6 + T7 + T8 + T9 + T10
250 AVG = SUM/10
300 REM ********** PRINT THE DATA **********
305 PRINT "TEST #1"; T1; "AVERAGE:"; AVG
310 PRINT "TEST #2"; T2; "AVERAGE:"; AVG
315 PRINT "TEST #3"; T3; "AVERAGE:"; AVG
320 PRINT "TEST #4"; T4; "AVERAGE:"; AVG
325 PRINT "TEST #5"; T5; "AVERAGE:"; AVG
330 PRINT "TEST #6"; T6; "AVERAGE:"; AVG
335 PRINT "TEST #7"; T7; "AVERAGE:"; AVG
340 PRINT "TEST #8"; T8; "AVERAGE:"; AVG
345 PRINT "TEST #9"; T9; "AVERAGE:"; AVG
350 PRINT "TEST #10"; T10; "AVERAGE:"; AVG
999 END
```

Notes:

1. Variable names T1, T2, T3, ..., T10 represent test score 1, test score 2, and so on.
2. Because we would like to calculate the average after all data are read, we must choose a different variable name for each score. The following program, for instance, cannot be used because it does not store the scores individually.

```
10   SUM = 0
20   FOR I = 1 TO 10
30      INPUT A
40      SUM = SUM + A
50      PRINT A
60   NEXT I
70   AVG = SUM/10
80   PRINT AVG
100  END
```

The program in Example 7.1 is not only unduly long but also impractical if there are many data. Imagine writing this type of program for 1000 records. Fortunately, BASIC allows us to write the same program as follows:

Example 7.2

Problem: Same as in Example 7.1: read and store ten test scores, calculate the average, then print the scores and the average.

Program:

```
10   DIM  T(10)
20   SUM = 0
30   REM *********** ACCEPT THE DATA ************
100  PRINT 'TYPE TEN TEST SCORES, ONE PER LINE'
110  FOR I = 1 TO 10
120      INPUT T(I)
130  NEXT I
200  REM *********** CALCULATIONS **************
210  FOR I = 1 TO 10
220      SUM = SUM + T (I)
230  NEXT I
250  AVG = SUM/10
300  REM *********** PRINT THE DATA **********
310  FOR I = 1 TO 10
320      PRINT 'TEST '; I; T(I); 'AVERAGE:'; AVG
330  NEXT I
999  END
```

Notes:

1. T(I) is used to represent the variables in the loop; as I changes from 1 to 2, from 2 to 3, and so on, the program creates T(1), T(2), and so on up to T(10). T1, however, is not the same as T(1); they are two different kinds of variables.
2. The dimension statement (DIM) declares that T can have ten elements: T(1), T(2), T(3), ..., T(10).
3. The program is written in three small modules:
   a. Reading the data
   b. Calculating the average
   c. Writing the data and the average

Although we could have used a single loop in the program for all the modules, writing the program in smaller modules is preferable. The value of this technique becomes apparent when a program is long and complicated.

4. The module that calculates SUM accomplishes the same purpose as

```
SUM = 0.0
SUM = SUM + T(1)
SUM = SUM + T(2)
      ⋮
SUM = SUM + T(10)
```

Subscripted Variables

Instead of labeling a series of variables A, B, C, and so on, we can call them $A_1, A_2, A_3, \ldots, A_n$. These are called *subscripted variables*. In mathematics, subscripted symbols denote the elements of a set, that is, individual elements in a group of related items.

In most programming languages, subscripts must be written in parentheses: A(1), A(2), A(3), and so on. The complete set of these variables is called an array; each subscripted variable is then an element of the array. *Thus an array is a group of elements, identified by a single name, that are treated as a whole.* In other words, an array refers to the collection of the elements of a group of variables. Each variable is called a *subscripted variable* or simply an *element*.

An array whose elements are specified by one subscript is called a *linear* or *one-dimensional array*. In BASIC, we may also have two-dimensional arrays whose elements have two subscripts, such as B(2,3).

When the computer creates an array, it assigns a certain number of consecutive memory cells to the specified array name (see Figure 7.1).

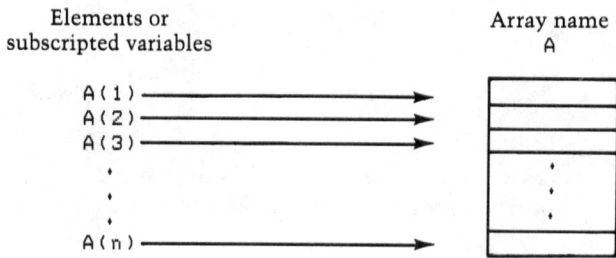

Figure 7.1 An array and its elements

Each individual element can be referred to by its *index*—the subscript. Thus, *an array is a group of memory cells that collectively have the same name; each element in the array can be located by its index*, *the subscript*. In BASIC, if there are more than ten elements in an array, you must use the DIM statement in the program to define the array and the number of its elements.

The Dimension Statement

Used in a program, the DIM statement defines an array and its size. That statement instructs the computer to reserve a certain number of consecutive memory locations for the elements of the array. More than one array can be defined in a single DIM statement. The simple form of the DIM statement for a one-dimensional array is

```
line no. DIM var1(n1), var2(n2), ...
```

where var1, var2, ... are the array names, and n1, n2, ... are unsigned integers representing the number of elements in each array. For example

```
100 DIM X(500), AMOUNT(100), JOY(50), N$(100)
```

declares that X, AMOUNT, JOY, and N$ are arrays having 500, 100, 50, and 100 elements, respectively. Note that there is no comma after the word DIM but that the arrays are separated by commas.

The appropriate dimension statement must appear in the program before an array is used. However, certain features concerning the placement of the dimension statement and the definition of an array vary among systems, as follows:

1. In some systems, dimension statements defining arrays must be placed at the very beginning of the program; in others, the DIM statement can be placed anywhere in the program as long as it appears before the array is used.
2. The number of elements in each array (the array size) must be a positive integer value. However, some interpreters allow you to use a variable as a dimension size. For example,

```
100 READ N
110 DIM X(N)
    ⋮
```

is valid in those systems. This important feature makes it possible to allocate memory locations dynamically in a program.

3. The lower boundary of an array is normally equal to zero by default instead of 1. Thus, for example,

   ```
   DIM A(10)
   ```

   creates these 11 elements: A(0), A(1), A(2),..., A(10).
4. The lower boundary of an array can be defined with the OPTION BASE statement. For example,

   ```
   5  OPTION BASE 1
   10 DIM X(100)
   ```

   creates an array X with 100 elements, starting from 1 up to 100. If allowed, this feature is a useful way to eliminate all zero subscripts in a program, thus saving some storage space. However, the space occupied by the zero elements is inconsequential. Furthermore, some algorithms must have a zero element.
5. If you do not define an array with a DIM statement, the computer creates an array with only ten elements by default as soon as you use a subscripted variable. For example, the program segment

   ```
   10 FOR J = 1 TO 10
   20    READ A(J)
   30 NEXT J
   ```

   is valid as long as the value of the subscript is below 10. It is good programming practice, however, to define all arrays explicitly.
6. If a system allows you to define values as integers, it is efficient to define all the subscripts as integers, for example,

   ```
   10 DIM X(50%)
   50 X(I%) = ...
   100 KAY%(J%) = 5%
   ```

The DIM statement provides information about the maximum number of elements needed. The entire array, however, need not be used in a program. The following is an example,

```
10 DIM M(100)
20 FOR K = 1 TO 5
30    READ M(K)
40    PRINT M(K)
50 NEXT K
60 DATA 5, 10, 6, 30, 20
70 END
```

When you define the size of an array, estimate the maximum number of necessary elements. Avoid unnecessarily large sizes because they are inefficient in terms of memory usage. If an array occupies more memory than is available, the program will not run, and the computer will print error messages.

Solved Problems

7.1 Write a dimension statement to define the following arrays:

  a. Array COUNT with 30 elements and array SEQ with 1000 elements.
  b. Array TABLE, which can contain 65 elements, and array LIST, which can contain 110 numeric values.
  c. Array NAME to store the names of the students in a course, array ADRES for their addresses, and array TEST for their test scores (assume 62 students).
  d. Character array NAME with 100 elements, array ADRES with 100 elements, array ID with 100 elements for integers, and array SCORE with 100 elements for real numbers. Assume % defines integer values.
  e. Arrays ID, PRICE, and UNITS, each with 50 elements. Assume that array ID is for integer data and that % indicates integer values. Define all the subscript values as integers.

Answers:

  a. 10 DIM COUNT(30), SEQ(1000)
  b. 50 DIM TABLE(65), LIST(110)
  c. 30 DIM NAME$(65), ADRES$(65), TEST(65)
  d. 10 DIM NAME$(100), ADRES$(100), ID%(100), SCORE(100)
  e. 10 DIM ID%(50%), PRICE(50%), UNITS(50%)

7.2 Find the errors in the following statements:

  a. 10 DIM X(-5), Y(M), Z(10)
  b. 100 DIM, YR(60), ZR(70), K(100),
  c. 50 DIM X(100) Y(50) Z(200)
  d. 10 DIM (300), JAY(30)
  e. 70 DIM (100 + 2), Y(N + 1)

f. 10 DIM X%(5%), KAY%(100%), NAME$(100%), PIE(50%)
g. 5 DIM X(100)
   10 DIM X(150)

Answers:

a. The array size can never be a negative number. The use of the variable M to define array size is allowed only in some systems (and only if the value of M is defined).
b. The commas after DIM and after K(100) must be omitted.
c. In most systems, commas must separate array names in DIM statements. (However, in some systems a space is also a separator; thus, for such systems this statement is correct).
d. The name of the first array is missing.
e. The array name is missing, and, in most systems, the array dimension can be neither 100 + 2 nor N + 1.
f. This is correct if % indicates integer values. Note that all the subscripts are defined as integers; furthermore, the contents of arrays X and KAY will be integers.
g. The array is defined twice.

Reason for Arrays: An Example

As we saw in Example 7.1, sometimes the nature of the problem requires that we use an array. The following is another example:

Example 7.3

Problem: Draw a flowchart and write an interactive program that accepts the names of N companies and their stock prices. (Assume these are sample stocks with similar prices.) Print the names of companies with below-average stock prices and the prices. There are fewer than 100 companies.

Flowchart: See Figure 7.2.

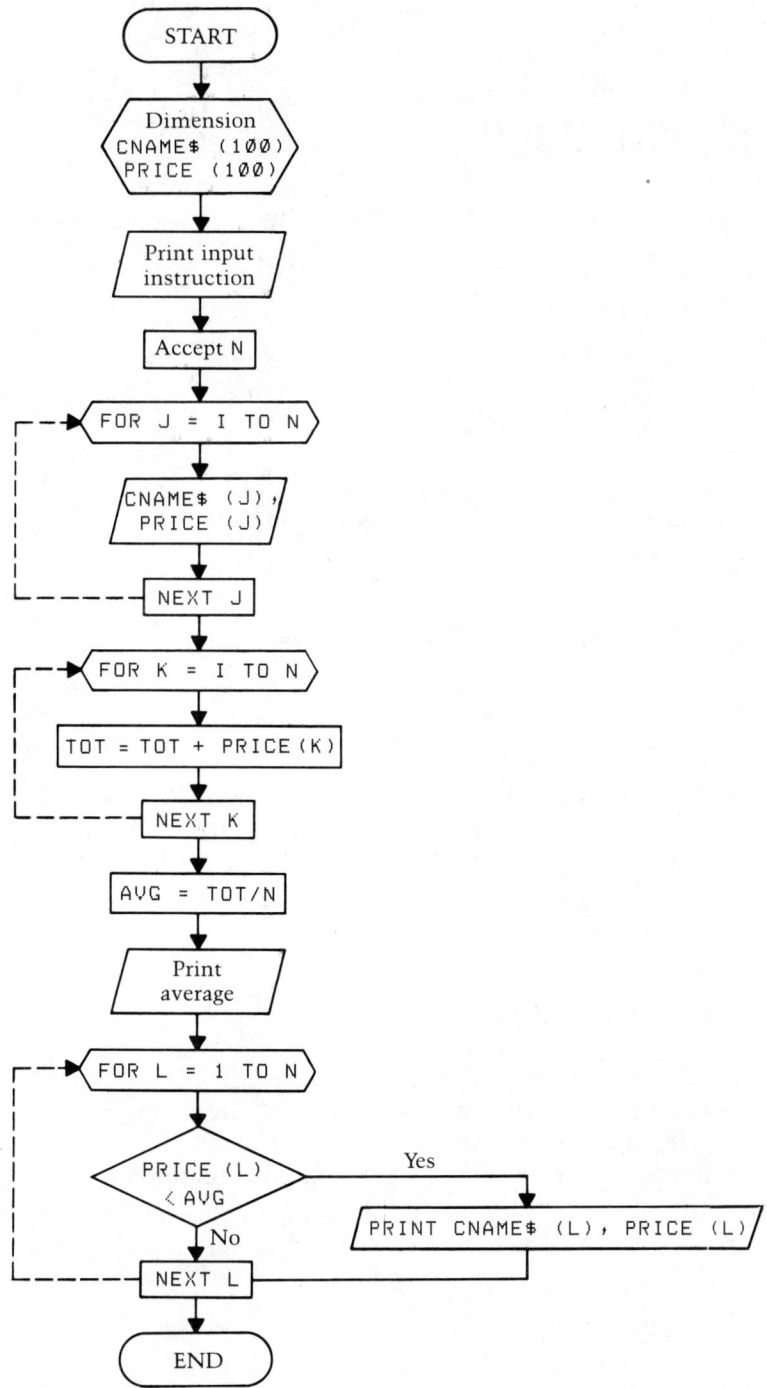

Figure 7.2 The flowchart for Example 7.3

Program:

```
10   DIM CNAME$(100), PRICE(100)
20   PRINT "THIS PROGRAM PRINTS BELOW-AVERAGE STOCK PRICES"
30   PRINT "HOW MANY COMPANIES ARE THERE"
40   INPUT N
50   PRINT "TYPE COMPANY NAMES AND STOCK PRICES, ONE PER LINE"
60   TOT = 0
70   REM ------------------------------------------
100  FOR J = 1 TO N
110      INPUT CNAME$(J), PRICE(J)
120  NEXT J
130  REM ------------------------------------------
200  FOR K = 1 TO N
210      TOT = TOT + PRICE(K)
220  NEXT K
230  REM ------------------------------------------
240  AVG = TOT/N
250  PRINT "THE AVERAGE PRICE IS: "; AVG
300  PRINT "BELOW-AVERAGE PRICES AND NAMES ARE: "
310  FOR L = 1 TO N
320      IF PRICE(L) < AVG THEN PRINT CNAME$(L), PRICE(L)
330  NEXT L
400  END
```

Notes:

1. The program's modules are:
   a. Read the data
   b. Calculate SUM and AVG
   c. Write the average and the prices that are below average
2. The control variables in each FOR loop were chosen to show that the variable representing the subscript does not have to be the same in all the modules.

Arithmetic Expressions with Arrays

The array name refers to all the elements in the complete array. However, the array name followed by a subscript refers to a specific element of the array and can be considered as a single variable.

Any calculation must be performed with the individual elements of the array, that is, with subscripted variables. The following are some examples (assume A, B, and C are defined as arrays).

```
100  C(6) = B(2)*A(9)/2
90   A(5) = A(5) + B(4)
150  C(10) = .04*A(7) + 2*B(5)
```

A variable or even an arithmetic expression can represent the subscript in a program as long as the values of the variables in the subscripts have been defined. For example, if the value of I and M are defined, all of the following subscripts are valid:

```
A(I) = B(I) + C(I) + B(I)
SUM(I+1) = TOT(I-1)
A(5*N+2) = X(M+3)
NET(3*M-6) = MAY(2*M)
```

If the subscript is a real number or an expression, it will be evaluated and converted as necessary to an integer value first. For example, A(2.3) becomes A(2), or A(2*3.2) becomes A(6). (Some systems truncate a noninteger value rather than rounding it off.) After conversion, however, each value must not be less than the lower limit or greater than the upper limit of the dimension.

It is important to remember that only the individual elements of an array can be used in an expression. For example, the program segment

```
10 DIM A(100)
20 A = 0
```

is not valid. If the intention in this case is to set all the elements of the array equal to zero, then the individual elements must be used in a loop:

```
10 FOR I = 1 TO 100
20     A(I) = 0
30 NEXT I
```

Solved Problems

7.3 Find any errors in the following program segments:

```
a. 10 DIM X(10), Y(10), Z(10)
   20 FOR I = 1 TO 10
   30    READ X(I), Y(I)
   40    Z = X + Y
   50 NEXT I
b. 10 DIM X(100)
   50 FOR J = 1 TO 105
   60    X(J) = 3.3
   70 NEXT J
c. 10 DIM X(30)
   50 FOR K = 1 TO 30
   60    X(K+1) = K
   70 NEXT K
```

d.
```
10   DIM IY(65)
100  FOR L = 1 TO 30
110     IY(L - 2) = L
120  NEXT L
```

e.
```
10   DIM K(100)
20   FOR I = 1 TO 100
30      K(J) = I
40   NEXT I
```

f.
```
10   DIM JOY%(50)
20   X = 0
30   FOR M = 1 TO 50
40      X = X + 1
50      JOY%(M) = X
60   NEXT M
```

g.
```
10   DIM SUM(100)
20   SUM(1) = 0
30   X = 0
40   FOR I = 2 TO 100
50      X = X + 1
60      SUM(I) = SUM(I-1) + X
70   NEXT I
```

h.
```
10   DIM A(100)
        .
        .
        .
100  IF A = 0 THEN GOTO 30
```

Answers:

a. If one intends to add the elements of X and Y, then they must be subscripted. The arithmetic expression, therefore, should be corrected to

```
Z(I) = X(I) + Y(I)
```

b. Array X is defined as having up to 100 elements; therefore, the subscript J cannot be greater than 100.

c. The subscript cannot be greater than 30. (K + 1 will be 31 when K reaches 30.)

d. When the starting value of L is 1, L - 2 is negative, which is illegal.

e. The subscript of array K in the loop is not defined (zero will be assumed for J).

f. Array JOY is an integer array, but it is assigned real values. The statements can be corrected to

```
X% = X% + 1%
JOY%(M) = X%
```

g. This is correct.

h. Individual elements of array A must be used in the IF statement. If the intention is to check for the element that contains zero, then the following loop can be used:

```
100 FOR I = 1 TO 100
110     IF A(I) = 0 THEN GOTO 30
120 NEXT I
```

Array Input-Output

The elements of an array can be read or written individually:

```
100 DIM A(10)
110 READ A(1), A(2), A(3)
        ⋮
```

However, this method is neither efficient nor practical, especially when the subscripts become larger.

As we have seen in previous examples, the FOR loop is a convenient way to input or output the elements of an array. The following is another example:

Example 7.4

Problem: Read and print array A composed of 100 elements.

Program:

```
10   DIM A(100)
20   FOR I = 1 TO 100
30       READ A(I)
40   NEXT I
100  FOR J = 1 TO 100
110      PRINT A(J)
120  NEXT J
200  DATA ....
210  DATA ....
500  END
```

Note: The loop

```
20 FOR I = 1 TO 100
30     READ A(I)
40 NEXT I
```

will perform the same functions as

```
READ A(1)
READ A(2)
READ A(3)
    ⋮
READ A(100)
```

In the previous programs, we could have used one FOR-NEXT loop for both reading and writing data. It is good programming practice, however, to write a program in smaller modules (input can be considered one module and output another, although the modules in these examples are too small). Modular structure makes programs easy to code, understand, debug, and document.

Often a header or a trailer value is used to read an appropriate number of data in a loop. A sentinel value is particularly useful when the number of data is unknown. When a sentinel value is used, a counter block must keep track of the number of data for later use. The following is an example:

Example 7.5

Problem: Write an interactive program that accepts and then prints a report about the merchandise ordered by customers of a store during a given period.

Input:

Customer's name
Number of units ordered
Price of each unit

The sales tax is 4 percent of the cost of the amount ordered. Print the input information, tax, and total amount of the order for each customer in a report form. Also print the information about customers whose total order is above average. There are fewer than 100 customers. However, the last record should indicate end of data.

Program:

```
10  DIM CUS$(100), UNORD(100), PRICE(100)
15  DIM AMTORD(100), TAX(100), ORD(100)
20  SUM = 0        :        N = 0
30  PRINT "THIS PROGRAM PRINTS THE CUSTOMER ORDERS REPORT."
60  PRINT "TYPE THE CUSTOMER'S NAME, UNITS ORDERED, AND THE PRICE"
70  PRINT "SEPARATED BY A COMMA, ONE CUSTOMER PER LINE."
80  PRINT "TYPE E-O-R, 0, 0 WHEN THROUGH."
100 FOR K = 1 TO 100
110    INPUT CUS$(K), UNORD(K), PRICE(K)
120    IF CUS$(K) = "E-O-R" THEN GOTO 200
130    N = N + 1
140 NEXT K
200 FOR L = 1 TO N
210    AMTORD(L) = UNORD(L)*PRICE(L)
220    TAX(L) = .04*AMTORD(L)
230    ORD(L) = AMTORD(L) + TAX(L)
240    SUM = SUM + ORD(L)
250 NEXT L
260 AVG = SUM/N
300 REM PRINT THE INFORMATION: FIRST LINE IS A HEADING
305 REM (WIDTH OF THE PAPER: AT LEAST 90)
310 PRINT "NAME", "UNITS ORDERED", "PRICE", "AMOUNT", "TAX", "TOTAL"
320 PRINT
330 FOR M = 1 TO N
340    PRINT CUS$(M), UNORD(M), PRICE(M), AMTORD(M), TAX(M), ORD(M)
350 NEXT M
360 PRINT TAB(60); "TOTAL ORDER: $"; SUM
400 PRINT "CUSTOMERS WITH ABOVE-AVERAGE ORDERS"
410 PRINT "NAME", "UNITS ORDERED", "PRICE", "AMOUNT", "TAX", "TOTAL"
420 FOR M = 1 TO N
430    IF TOTORD(M) > AVG THEN PRINT CUS$(M), UNORD(M), PRICE(M),
                                     AMTORD(M),TAX(M),ORD(M)
440 NEXT M
999 END
```

Notes:

1. The FOR loop is used to manipulate the individual elements of arrays. The sentinel value E-O-R terminates the loop that accepts the data. The statement N = N + 1 keeps track of the number of elements read. Each loop will then be repeated N times.

2. The amount ordered (AMTORD), tax (TAX), and total amount of order (ORD) for each customer are each calculated in arrays. The appropriate arrays are defined at the beginning of the program.

3. The DIM statement defines the maximum number of elements, 100 in this case. Only N elements (N < 100) are read and processed.

Printing Values on One Line

In the previous examples, the PRINT statements in the loop print one element per line. If it is desirable to print the elements of an array on one line, then semicolon (or comma) can be used at the end of the PRINT statement. For example,

```
100 FOR K = 1 TO 10
110     PRINT X(K);
120 NEXT K
```

will print all the elements on one line. If the elements do not fit on one line, a new line will be started automatically.

Mirror Printing

Incorrect results may be obtained if the input data are not read correctly. To check the input data for errors, you can place an extra PRINT statement immediately after each READ statement. The variables in these statements should be identical. This technique is called *mirror printing* or *echo printing*. It is good programming practice to use mirror printing in the first run of a program. Once you confirm that the input data are being transmitted correctly, you can remove the extra PRINT statements easily.

It is useful to use mirror printing not only with arrays but also with all the READ statements in a program.

Summary of Important Points About Arrays

1. Each array name and its size must be declared in a DIM statement. Two important features of the DIM statement vary with the system used:
   a. The size of the array can be a variable as well as a constant.
   b. If an array is not defined, the system defines it with 10 elements by default.
2. If the exact size of an array is not known, it should be defined to be

larger than appears necessary. However, an unreasonably large size is costly.

3. Obviously, one cannot use a subscript larger than the dimension size. If the subscript is negative or larger than the specified size, the computer aborts the program.

4. The DIM statement specifies the number of memory locations needed for the array. The statement must appear in the program before the array is used. Normally, it appears before any executable statement.

5. The type of an array element is determined by the array name just as the type of a variable is determined by its name (real, integer, character, and so on). All the elements of an array must be of the same type.

6. The elements of an array are stored under the array name by subscript order. The subscript is a reference number identifying a specific element. It is important to differentiate between the array subscript and the content of the element of an array. The subscript is only an index—a reference number—for a particular element. The content of an element can be any piece of data.

7. To refer to a specific element, use the name of the array followed by a subscript in parentheses. A typical subscript is an integer constant or variable. For example, if J is defined, then X(J) refers to the Jth element of the array X.

8. An arithmetic expression can be used as a subscript, for example:

    ANAME$(I+3)
    AAA(3*I+2)

9. The array name without a subscript refers to the complete array with all its elements. The array name alone cannot appear in a statement (except in a MAT statement, discussed in Chapter 8).

10. Elements of an array can be manipulated just as a single variable can be. Only one element (array name with a subscript) at a time can be used in arithmetic expressions.

11. Array input-output can be accomplished in a FOR-NEXT loop.

12. If a subscript is not an integer value, it will automatically be rounded off to an integer value. However, the rounding off process varies among systems.

SOME EXAMPLES OF ARRAYS AND PROGRAMMING TECHNIQUES

Arrays, though sometimes challenging, give programmers flexibility and programming power. Some algorithms are impossible or extremely difficult to implement without arrays. However, the programming techniques, data manipulations, and algorithms with arrays are somehow different from nonarray techniques.

This section contains some simple examples. In Chapter 10 you will see how arrays can be used to solve advanced problems. To understand the techniques used in the following examples, you must think through each problem before looking at the solution procedure given. Write down your own solution method and then compare it to the method outlined in the text. The procedure given is only one of several possible algorithms—yours could be better.

Example 7.6 Storing the Sum in an Array

Problem: Write a program that reads a series of 89 numbers and calculates the sum of the numbers in an array so that SUM(1) contains the value of A(1), SUM(2) contains A(1) + A(2), and so on. Print the data in subscripted form, and print the sum at each stage.

Program:

```
10    DIM A(100), SUM(100)
20    N = 89
100   FOR I = 1 TO N
110       READ A(I)
120   NEXT I
130                                                       REM
200   SUM (1) = A(1)
210   FOR J = 2 TO N
220       SUM (J) = SUM(J-1) + A(J)
230   NEXT J
240                                                       REM
300   FOR K = 1 TO N
310      PRINT "A("; K; ") = "; A(K), "SUM("; K; ") = "; SUM(K)
320   NEXT K
400   DATA 6.1, 5.2, 9.3, . . .
999   END
```

The output will be

```
A(1) = 6.1    SUM(1) = 6.1
A(2) = 5.2    SUM(2) = 11.3
      ⋮              ⋮
```

Example 7.7 *Direct Access to Factorial* N

Problem: Write a program that stores factorial 1 through 10 in ten elements of integer array FACT—factorial 1 in the first element, factorial 2 in the second, and so on. Then, after accepting an integer N in interactive mode, the program prints factorial N directly from the array FACT.

Program:

```
10   DIM FACT(10)
20   FACT(1) = 1
100  FOR K = 2 TO 10
110     FACT(K) = K*FACT(K-1)
120  NEXT K
200  PRINT 'I WILL CALCULATE THE FACTORIAL OF A NUMBER IN A FLASH.'
205  FOR TRY = 1 TO 200
210     PRINT 'TYPE A NUMBER LESS THAN 10; IF THRU, TYPE ZERO'
220     INPUT N
220     IF N = 0 THEN GOTO 300
230     PRINT 'FACTORIAL '; N; ' IS '; FACT(N)
240  NEXT TRY
300  PRINT '******** BYE ********'
310  END
```

Example 7.8 Searching

Problem: Write an interactive program that reads a series of names and corresponding phone numbers. Then, the program should accept a name and print the corresponding phone number. Assume there are fewer than 100 names and that E-O-F indicates end of data.

Program:

```
10   DIM N$(100), PHONE(100)
20   FOR I = 1 TO 100
30      READ N$(I), PHONE(I)
40      IF N$(I) = 'E-O-F' THEN GOTO 100
50      N = N + 1
60   NEXT I
100  PRINT 'THIS PROGRAM DISPLAYS THE PHONE NUMBERS'
105  FOR ROUND = 1 TO 200
110  PRINT 'WHAT IS THE NAME, TYPE NO-MORE IF THROUGH'
120     INPUT ANAME$
130     IF ANAME$ = 'NO-MORE' THEN GOTO 500
140        FOR J = 1 TO N
150           IF N$(J) = ANAME$ THEN GOTO 190
160        NEXT J
170     PRINT 'THE NAME IS NOT IN MY LIST'
180     GOTO 200
190     PRINT 'PHONE NUMBER OF '; ANAME$; ' IS '; PHONE(J)
200  NEXT ROUND
300  DATA 'JOHN NEWMAN', 7734300, 'PAUL NOWAK', 698555
310  DATA 'PAT BALUCCHI',2383356 , . . . . .
        :
390  'E-O-F', 0
500  PRINT '******** SEE YOU *********'
999  END
```

Note: The search starts with the first element of the array. All elements are checked sequentially until the desired name is found. If the name is not found after all the elements are searched, the program prints a message. This search method, called *sequential searching*, is not efficient for a large list. A more efficient method, binary search, is explained in Chapter 10.

Example 7.9 Direct Access to a Table, Table Look-Up

Problem: Write a program that reads a product code and prints the price of the product. The price is based on the following table:

Product Code	Price
1	5.50
2	6.50
3	7.75
4	9.10
5	10.90
6	12.90
7	14.00

Program:

```
10   DIM PRICE(7)
20   DATA 5.5, 6.5, 7.75, 9.1, 10.9, 12.9, 14
30   FOR I = 1 TO 7 : READ PRICE(I) : NEXT I
100  PRINT "I WILL PRINT THE PRICE IMMEDIATELY."
105  FOR TIMES = 1 TO 200
110     PRINT "TYPE THE PRODUCT CODE (1 TO 7)";
             "TYPE ZERO WHEN THRU"
120     INPUT CODE
130     IF CODE = 0 THEN GOTO 160
140     PRINT "THE PRICE IS : "; PRICE(CODE)
150  NEXT TIMES
160  PRINT "** SEE YOU SOON **"
999  END
```

Notes:

1. The term *table look-up* describes the procedure of accessing a particular piece of data in the table. If the key (the product code) is known, the price can be accessed directly.
2. To be practical, the program needs several modifications:
   - It should print the name of the product.
   - It should print a message if CODE is out of range.
   - It should accommodate more than seven products.

Example 7.10 Frequency Distribution

Problem: A frequency distribution shows the number of occurrences of some values. Write an interactive program that accepts 100 integers between 1 and 10 and then prints the frequency distribution of each integer.

Program:

```
10   DIM COUNT(10)
20   FOR I = 1 TO 10   :    COUNT(I) = 0   :    NEXT I
100  PRINT "I WILL PRINT THE FREQUENCY DISTRIBUTION OF UP TO 100"
110  PRINT "MEASUREMENTS BETWEEN 1 AND 10. TYPE ONE NUMBER PER LINE"
120  PRINT "TYPE ZERO WHEN THROUGH"
130  FOR I = 1 TO 100
140     INPUT MEASURE
150     IF MEASURE = 0 THEN GOTO 250
200         REM COUNT THE NUMBER OF OCCURRENCES
230     COUNT(MEASURE) = COUNT(MEASURE) + 1
240  NEXT I
250  PRINT
300  REM WRITE THE FREQUENCY DISTRIBUTION
310  PRINT "MEASUREMENT", "NO. OF OCCURRENCES"
320  FOR K = 1 TO 10
330     PRINT K, COUNT(K)
340  NEXT K
350  PRINT "**************** BYE ********************"
400  END
```

Note: Line 230 causes each element of array COUNT to accumulate the number of occurrences of each integer; for example, if the first measurement is the number 3, then

COUNT(3) = COUNT(3) + 1 = 0 + 1 = 1

If the number 3 is included in the data again, then COUNT(3) = 2. This accumulation process works for all the elements of array COUNT.

Example 7.11 Locating the Smallest Element in an Array

Problem: Write a program that finds the position of the smallest number in an array. There are fewer than 100 numbers, and the first is a header value. Print the smallest number and its subscript.

Program:

```
10  DIM A(100)
20  READ N
30  FOR I = 1 TO N
40      READ A(I)
50  NEXT I
60  REM ASSUME THE SUBSCRIPT OF THE
        SMALLEST NO. IS 1
70  K = 1
80  FOR J = 2 TO N
90      IF A(J) < A(K) THEN K = J
100 NEXT J
110 PRINT "THE SMALLEST NO. IS: "; A(K),
          "ITS SUBSCRIPT IS: "; K
120 DATA 5
130 DATA 39.6, 83.1, 52.8, 98.3, 42.3
200 END
```

Note: It is assumed at the beginning that the first value is the smallest number (K = 1). Each value is then compared with A(K) in the loop. If the value is smaller than A(K), K will change to the subscript of the smaller value; otherwise, K will not change.

Example 7.12 Inserting a Value into an Array

Problem: Suppose that array X is defined as having 100 elements and that data are already stored in N elements of the array (N < 100). The goal is to insert a value (D) into the first element of array X while maintaining the existing data in the same order. Find a solution method and then write the program segment.

Solution Methods: To insert a value into the first element of array X, the data already in the array must be shifted up by one element.

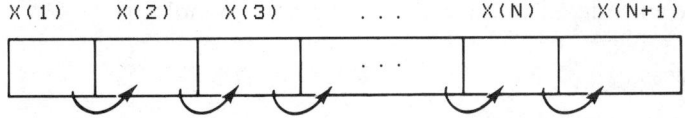

However, the program segment
```
100 FOR K = 1 TO N
100    X(K+1) = X(K)
120 NEXT K
```
will not work because when the contents of the first element are moved to the second, the original contents of the second element are erased. This also happens to the third, fourth, and finally all elements, and the value of A(1) is assigned to all the elements of array X. Three solution methods are presented below:

Method 1:

1. Copy all elements of array X into a new array Y.
2. Transfer the contents of array Y back to the original array X, but one element up the list.

Program Segment:
```
100 FOR J = 1 TO N
110    Y(I) = X(I)
120 NEXT I
130 FOR J = 1 TO N
140    X(J+1) = Y(J)
150 NEXT J
160 X(1) = D
```

Note: Method 1 requires 100 additional memory locations.

Method 2:

Store the contents of each element of X in a temporary memory location (TEMP) before assigning any value to it; for example, assign X(1) to TEMP before assigning D to it. Then, when exchanging the content of each X with TEMP, use another temporary memory location. Therefore, two additional memory cells are needed. The variable D can be used as the second temporary memory.

Method 2 requires three steps:

1. Assign X_i into a temporary memory TEMP.
2. Assign the value of D into X_i.
3. Assign TEMP to D (to be considered a new value for the next round).

Figure 7.3 shows the process.

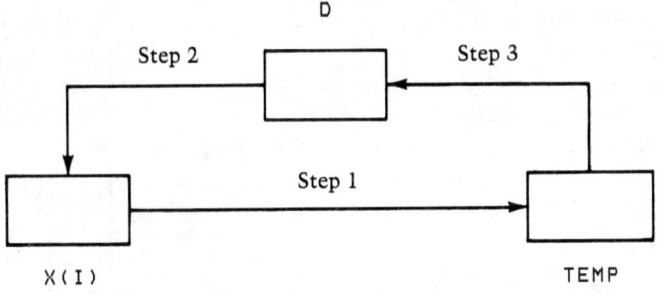

Figure 7.3 Interchanging the elements of an array

```
for I = 1    TEMP = X(1)    X(1) = D    D = TEMP
for I = 2    TEMP = X(2)    X(2) = D    D = TEMP
for I = 3    TEMP = X(3)    X(3) = D    D = TEMP
    :            :              :           :
```

Program Segment:

```
 90    REM D CONTAINS THE NEW VALUE
100    FOR I = 1 TO N
110        TEMP = X(I)
120        X(I) = D
130        D = TEMP
140    NEXT I
```

Note: Method 2 requires only two additional memory locations.

Method 3:

Shift the contents of array X up the list by one element, but start with the last one.

Program Segment:

```
100 FOR I = N TO 1 STEP -1
110     X(I + 1) = X(I)
120 NEXT I
130 X(1) = D
```

Note: Method 3 requires no additional memory.

Example 7.13 A Game—The Price Is Right

Problem: Write a program that stores the names and prices of ten items in arrays. Then let the user guess the price of the items. The program should help the player to arrive at the correct price by giving the clues "higher" or "lower."

Program:

```
10   DIM ANAME$(10), PRICE(10)
20   DATA "A SOFABED", 695.99, "A WOODEN DESK", 391.55
30   DATA "AN ANTIQUE CAR", 65900.99, "A MOVIE CAMERA"
40   DATA 279.79, "A FUR COAT", 3685.98, "A SUPPER MICRO"
50   DATA 9895.50, "A ROLLS ROYCE", 59695.50, "A V.C.R."
60   DATA 945.79, "A BOAT", 5345.85, "A MANSION", 2678935
70   FOR I = 1 TO 10
80     READ ANAME$(I), PRICE(I)
90   NEXT I
100  FOR K = 1 TO 10
110    PRINT "ARE YOU READY TO GUESS THE PRICE OF ITEM #";K
120    INPUT A$
130    IF A$ <> "YES" THEN GOTO 300
140    PRINT "WHAT IS THE PRICE OF "; ANAME$(K)
150      INPUT G
160      IF PRICE(K) = G THEN GOTO 190
170      IF G < PRICE(K) THEN PRINT "HIGHER" ELSE PRINT "LOWER"
180    GOTO 140
190    PRINT : PRINT"***THAT WAS RIGHT. . . VERY GOOD***"
200    PRINT
210  NEXT K
300  PRINT "********** BYE, CALL AGAIN *************"
999  END
```

Note: The program can be modified for a sophisticated interaction. For example, the player can be scored on the basis of the number of correct answers at the first guess, the number of correct answers after three guesses, and so on.

EXERCISES

7.1 Identify any errors in the following statements:

    a. `100 DIM XXX(N), I(100), B(5), K(N + 3)`

    b. `200 DIMENSION REAL A(100), B(2)`

    c. `150 INTEGER, I, J, K(100)`

    d. `10 DIM A(-20), B(100)`

    e. `50 DIM (300), P(20)`

    f. `100 DIM Q, R(100)`

    g. `150 DIM PAY(0), RATE(-300)`

h. `100 READ A(I), FOR I = 1 TO 100`
i. `100 PRINT N, Y(N), FOR N = 1 TO 300`

7.2 Identify any errors in the following statements or loops:

a.
```
10   DIM F(100), G(100)
       ⋮
110  G = F*F
```

b.
```
10   DIM X(100), B(100)
       ⋮
100  FOR I = 1 TO 100
110     X(I+1) = B(2*I)
120  NEXT I
```

c.
```
10   DIM H(30), Q(30), R(30)
       ⋮
100  FOR I = 1 TO 30
110     H = Q(I) + R(I)
120  NEXT I
```

d.
```
10   DIM Q(500), R(100)
       ⋮
110  FOR J = 1 TO 500
120     Q(J) = 2*R(J)
130  NEXT J
```

e.
```
10 DIM X(100), Y(100)
20 X = 0.0
30 Y = 0.0
```

f.
```
10 DIM EROR(500)
     ⋮
50 IF EROR = 0 THEN GOTO 100
```

g.
```
10 DIM PAY(30), GROSS(30)
     ⋮
100 FOR I = 1 TO 30
110    PAY(I+1) = GROSS(I)
120 NEXT I
```

7.3 What is the purpose and/or output of the following programs or program segments?

   a.
```
10 DIM K(100), L(100)
20 FOR J = 1 TO 50
30     K(J) = J*J
40     L(J) = J**3
50 NEXT J
60 FOR N = 1 TO 50
70     PRINT N, K(N), L(N)
80 NEXT N
```

   b.
```
10 DIM B(100), A(101)
20 FOR K = 1 TO 100
30     READ B(K)
40 NEXT K
50 FOR I = 1 TO 100
60     A(I+1) = B(I)
70 NEXT I
80 ...
    ⋮
```

   c.
```
10 DIM A(10)
20 FOR K = 1 TO 10
30     A(K) = K
40     PRINT A(K);
50 NEXT K
```

   d.
```
10   DIM B(100)
       ⋮
100 FOR I = 1 TO 100 STEP 2
110     TEMP = B(I)
120     B(I) = B(I+1)
130     B(I+1) = TEMP
140 NEXT I
```

   e.
```
10   DIM X(100)
       ⋮
100 FOR I = 1 TO N
110     M = N - I + 1
120     PRINT X(M)
130 NEXT I
```

f.
```
10 DIM N(10)
20 FOR I = 1 TO 10 : N(I) = 0 : NEXT I
30 REM READ THE DATA, EACH LESS THAN 9
40 FOR J = 1 TO 100
50    READ A
60    N(A) = N(A) + 1
70 NEXT J
```

g.
```
10 DIM N(10)
20 FOR I = 1 TO 10 : N(I) = 0 : NEXT I
30 REM READ THE DATA, EACH LESS THAN 99
40 FOR J = 1 TO 100
50    READ A
55    B = A/10
60    N(B) = N(B) + 1
70 NEXT J
```

h.
```
10  DIM GRADE$(5), COUNT(5)
20  GRADE$(1) = "F" : GRADE$(2) = "D" : GRADE$(3) = "C"
30  GRADE$(4) = "B" :   GRADE$(5) = "A"
40  FOR J = 1 TO 5  :    COUNT(J) = 0 :    NEXT I
80  REM ASSUME THAT THE TEST SCORES ARE BETWEEN 50 AND 100,
90  REM AND THE SYSTEM TRUNCATES A NONINTEGER SUBSCRIPT
100 FOR I = 1 TO N
110    READ ID, SCORE
120    KEY = (SCORE/10) - 4
130    AGRADE$ = GRADE$(KEY)
140    COUNT(KEY) = COUNT(KEY) + 1
150    PRINT "STUDENT NO.:"; ID, "GRADE:"; AGRADE$
160 NEXT I
        ⋮
```

7.4 Find logical errors in each of the following program segments:

a.
```
10 DIM XDATA(50), TOT(50)
20 FOR I = 1 TO 50 :SUM(I) = 0 : NEXT I
30 FOR J = 1 TO 50 :READ XDATA(J)  :   NEXT J
50 REM ACCUMULATE THE XDATA, CALCULATE THE SUM
60 FOR K = 1 TO 50
70    SUM(K) = SUM(K) + XDATA(K)
80 NEXT K
     ⋮
```

b.
```
10 DIM FACT(10)
20 FOR 1 = 1 TO 10 : FACT(I) = 1 : NEXT I
30 READ N
40 REM CALCULATE FACTORIAL OF N (N LESS THAN 10)
50 FOR K = 1 TO N
60    FACT(K) = FACT(K)*K
70 NEXT K
      ⋮
```

c.
```
100 REM MOVE THE ELEMENTS OF ARRAY A UP BY
        ONE ELEMENT
110 FOR I = 1 TO 99
120    A(I+1) = A(I)
130 NEXT I
      ⋮
```

Programming Exercises:

Write a complete BASIC program for each of the following problems, using appropriate arrays, headings, formats, and techniques. Use either a header or trailer value to terminate the loops.

7.5 Write a program that accepts 100 subscribers' names and their balances. Calculate and print the average of the balances. Print the names of subscribers with above-average balances. Also print their balances.

7.6 Write a program that accepts N value of arrays A and B, each with 100 elements. Calculate the elements of array C so that

$$C(I) = A(I) + B(I) + 2*A(I)*B(I)$$

Print all three arrays. N is to be read at the beginning of the program.

7.7 Write a program that accepts N elements of array EEE (N < 20), then prints the values of N elements in each of three ways:

  a. One element per line

  b. With all elements on the same line

  c. Ten elements per line

  N is to be read at the beginning of the program.

7.8 Write a program that accepts ten sales values into an array. The sales tax is 4 percent. Calculate the tax and totals for each sale. Print the sale, tax and total in each of two ways:

a. In three columns, as follows:

```
SALES            TAX            TOTAL
XXXXX            XXX            XXXXX
  ⋮               ⋮                ⋮
```

b. In three rows, as follows:

```
SALES   XXX   XXX   XXX ....
TAX     XXX   XXX   XXX ....
TOTAL   XXX   XXX   XXX ....
```

Print the totals of all sales at the end of the report.

7.9 Write a program that reads four characters, scrambles the order of the characters, and prints the scrambled characters in several ways. Can you develop an algorithm that prints all possible combinations of the scrambled characters?

7.10 Write a program that accepts a series of numbers and calculates (1) the sum of their squares and (2) the sum of the squares of the deviation of the numbers, that is

$$\text{SUM} = A_1^2 + A_2^2 + A_3^2 + A_4^2 + \ldots A_n^2$$

and

$$\text{SSS} = (A_1 - AVG)^2 + (A_2 - AVG)^2 + \ldots + (A_n - AVG)^2$$

7.11 Write a program that calculates and stores the square of the integers 1, 2, 3, ..., 20 in array SQUARE. Then have the program print the integers and their squares in each of these three ways:

a. In two columns, with the integers in the first column and their squares in the second column

b. In two rows, with the integers in the first line and their squares in the second line

c. In four columns, with the integers 1–10 in the first column, the squares of the numbers 1–10 in the second column, the integers 11–20 in the third column, and the squares of numbers 11–20 in the fourth column

7.12 Write a program that accepts N real numbers (N < 100) into an array and prints them in reverse order. N is to be read at the beginning of the program.

7.13 Assume you have received a message in a numeric code. You know that every two digits represent a character: digits 01 through 26 represent A through Z, respectively; and 27 through 40 represent a space, a period, a comma, a hyphen, and the numerals 0 through 9, respectively. Write a program that reads the codes and prints the decoded message. Each message has no more than 39 characters, and 00 indicates the end of the message. Test the program by decoding the following message:

25,15,22,27,01,18,05,27,14,15,28,27,15,14,05,00

7.14 Suppose data are stored in only N elements of array A with 200 elements (N < 200). Write a program that inserts value B in the Kth position of array A (K < N) while maintaining the existing data in the same order.

7.15 Variance of a series of numbers can be found by the formula

$$VAR = [(A_1 - X)^2 + (A_2 - X)^2 + (A_3 - X)^2 + \ldots (A_N - X)^2]/N$$

where X is the mean of the numbers. Write an interactive program that accepts a set of data and calculates the variance of the data. Print the data, the mean, and variance after all the data are accepted.

7.16 In Example 7.11 (Locating the Smallest Number in an Array) the smallest number was located by the algorithm that found the subscript of the smallest number. Write a similar program that finds the smallest and the largest number in a set of data by comparing the values of each element against the smallest or largest value. Print the data, the largest number, and smallest number.

7.17 Write a program that reads 200 test scores, then counts and prints the number of As (90–100), Bs (80–89), Cs (70–79), Ds (60–69), and Fs (below 60) with the technique shown in Exercise 7.3h.

7.18 The insurance premium for the employees of a company is as follows:

No. of dependents	Yearly premium
1	$101.00
2	$125.00
3	$140.00
4	$150.00
5	$158.00
6	$165.00
7	$171.00
8	$176.00
9 or more	$180.00

Write an interactive program that accepts the following information about N employees:

Name

Social Security number, 11 characters

Yearly salary

Number of dependents

Calculate the net pay after the premium deduction for the employees. Print (1) a report showing all information as well as the total pay, total deductions, and the total net at the end of the report and (2) the same report, but only for employees whose salary is over $50,000.00.

7.19 A class instructor has the following grade information:

Student's ID number

Student's name

Student's test score

Write a program that accepts the information and then prints the student's number, name, test score, letter grade, and the code AA if his or her score is above average. Use the techniques shown in Exercise 7.3h.

7.20 Write an interactive program that accepts a set of data. Find and print the average, the smallest number, the largest number, and the range and variance of the data (the range is the largest number minus the smallest number). Make sure to include statements that explain the purpose of the program and tell the user how the data should be input.

7.21 A personnel manager would like a report on the retirement situation of all employees in the organization. The following data are available:

Employee's number

Employee's name

Annual salary

Age

Number of years worked

The conditions for retirement are that the employee be older than 65 and have worked longer than 30 years. Write a program that reads the information, calculates the average salary, and prints the following information about each employee in report form:

a. Name, salary, age, number of years worked, code for retirement status (E for eligible and N for ineligible), code for salary status (A for above-average salary and B for average or lower-than-average salary)

b. The above information for all employees older than 65

7.22 Write a program that prints the number of students—categorized as freshmen (1), sophomores (2), juniors (3), and seniors (4)—who have successfully completed Engineering 101.

Input:

a. Student's class standing (1, 2, 3, or 4)

b. Grade for the course (A, B, C, D, or F)

Output:

a. Four reports, each indicating the names and grades of students in each class.

b. A report indicating the names, grades, and the number of students in each category who have passed the course (D or better), and the total number of students who have failed the course.

7.23 The following information is available about members of a book club:

Name

Account number

Address
  • Number, street
  • City, state, zip code

Date of last bill (3 fields, each 2 digits)

Balance due, such as 999.99

Write a program that reads the information and prints:

a. A report for the club manager showing, one client per line, the name, account number, address, date of last bill, and balance due

b. Bills for the members, each including name, account number, address, and balance due

Design the bill. An example of the bill follows:

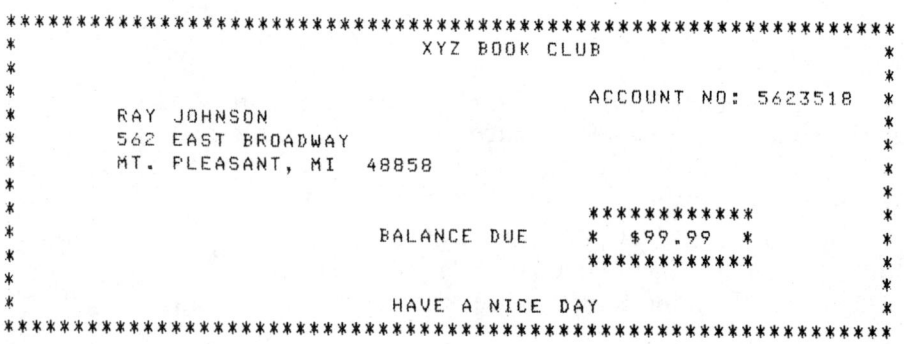

7.24 An instructor would like a final grade report for each student in a course. Design a program that will prepare the report as follows:

Input:
  a. Student's name
  b. Student's ID
  c. Class standing
  d. Student's sex (M or F)
  e. Three test scores (Tests 1, 2, and 3)

Output:
  a. The instructor's report, containing the student's name, ID, class standing, sex, three test scores, test average, and course grade (the average converted to a letter grade, where A is 90–100, B is 80–89, and so on). Print the grand average and number of As, Bs, Cs, Ds, and Fs at the end of the report.
  b. Report cards containing the above information for each student in a form that you design and that is ready to be cut and handed to students.

SUMMARY

You have learned:

1. An array is a group of variables having the same name, but each element is referred to by a different subscript. In most programming languages, including BASIC, the subscript must be placed in parentheses. Arrays give programmers flexibility and more programming power. Some algorithms are difficult to employ without using an array.

2. The array size must be defined by the DIM statement. The following are some examples:
```
10   DIM A(100), WAGE(450), I(300)
100  DIM NAMES$(100), SCORE(100), ID(100)
50   DIM ID%(300), A$(100), B(150)
```

3. An arithmetic expression can include only the individual elements of an array. A FOR-NEXT loop is an efficient tool for this purpose.

4. The subscript can be a constant, variable, or an arithmetic expression. The following is an example:
```
110    A(2*I+3) = 6.3
```

However, the value of the subscript cannot be negative or larger than the dimension size.

5. A FOR-NEXT loop can be used to input or print the elements of an array. The loop control variable controls the subscript of the array. The following is an example:

```
10 DIM B(100)
20 FOR K = 1 TO 100
30     READ B(K)
40 NEXT K
```

6. If it is necessary to print the elements on one line, a semicolon or a comma can be used at the end of the PRINT statement. The following is an example:

```
100 FOR I = 1 TO 10
110     PRINT A(I);
120 NEXT I
```

7. Mirror printing refers to using a PRINT statement immediately after the READ statement to check whether the input data are read correctly. The PRINT statement is normally removed after this check.

REVIEW QUESTIONS/SELF-TEST

7.1 Which of the following statements is not correct in BASIC?
   a. 10 DIM A(100), B$(50), C(10)
   b. 10 DIM Q(300%), B(100%)
   c. 10 DIM X(-20), B(100)
   d. 10 DIM P%(100), M(30)
   e. none of the above

7.2 Which of the following subscripts is not valid in BASIC?
   a. X(I+2)
   b. Y(R+1)
   c. YORK(3*M^2+1)
   d. K(-3)
   e. GROSS(100/3)

7.3 Which of the following loops is correct?

a.
```
10 DIM B(100)
20 FOR I = 1 TO 100
30    B = 0
40 NEXT I
```

b.
```
10 DIM X(500)
20 FOR K = 1 TO 500
30     X(K-2) = K
40 NEXT K
```

c.
```
10 DIM P(100), Q(100)
20 FOR M = 1 TO 100
30    P(M) = M
40    Q(M) = P(M)*P(M)
50 NEXT M
```

7.4 Suppose array A has 20 elements with stored values. Write a program segment that prints all 20 values on one line.

7.5 Suppose data are stored in 100 elements of array A. Write a program segment that interchanges the values of every 2 elements, that is, that interchanges the values of A(1) and A(2), A(3) and A(4), and so on.

7.6 Write a complete, interactive program for the inventory of a sport shop. Use arrays, headings, and formats. The program should ask for the following input for each item in the inventory:

  a. Item number
  b. Number of units available
  c. Minimum inventory level
  d. Ordering quantity
  e. Number of units sold

Processing:

The inventory level for each item is the number of items available minus the number of items sold. If the inventory level is below the minimum level, the item must be reordered.

Output:

  a. A report containing the item number, inventory level, minimum inventory level, and ordering quantity for each item

b. The same information shown in the first report for those items that must be ordered.

There are fewer than 100 items.

Answers:

7.1 c

7.2 d

7.3 c

7.4
```
100 FOR I = 1 TO 20
200     PRINT A(I);
300 NEXT I
```

7.5
```
100 FOR I = 1 TO 100 STEP 2
110     T = A(I)
120     B(I) = B(I + 1)
130     B(I + 1) = T
140 NEXT I
```

7.6
```
10  DIM ITEM(100), AVAIL(100), MLEVEL(100), ORDQ(100),
15  DIM SOLD(100), LEVEL(100)
20  PRINT "I WILL PRINT TWO REPORTS ABOUT THE INVENTORY LEVEL"
30  PRINT "TYPE THE NUMBER OF ITEMS"
40  INPUT N
50  PRINT"TYPE: THE ITEM NO, NUMBER OF ITEMS AVAILABLE, MINIMUM "
60  PRINT "LEVEL, ORDERING QUANTITY, AND NUMBER OF ITEMS SOLD, "
70  PRINT "SEPARATED BY COMMAS, ONE ITEM PER LINE"
100 FOR J = 1 TO N
110     INPUT ITEM(J), AVAIL(J), MLEVEL(J), ORDQ(J), SOLD(J)
120 NEXT J
200 FOR K=1 TO N
210     LEVEL(K) = AVAIL(K) - SOLD(K)
220 NEXT K
250 REM WRITING THE HEADING
260 H$="ITEM#   INVENTORY LEVEL MINIMUM LEVEL   ORDERING QUANTITY"
270 PRINT H$
280 PRINT
300 FOR K = 1 TO N
310     PRINT ITEM(K); TAB(14); LEVEL(K); TAB(30); MLEVEL(K);     &
            TAB(46); ORDQ(K)
320 NEXT K
330 PRINT
350 PRINT TAB(17); "ORDER THE FOLLOWING ITEMS"
360 PRINT
370 PRINT H$
400 FOR E = 1 TO N
410     IF LEVEL(E) <= MLEVEL(E) THEN                             &
            PRINT ITEM(K); TAB(14); LEVEL(K); TAB(30); MLEVEL(K) ; &
            TAB(46); ORDQ(K)
420 NEXT E
500 END
```

Two-Dimensional Arrays

In This Chapter:

Array Techniques
Dimension Statement
Arithmetic Expressions with Two-Dimensional Arrays
Two-Dimensional Array Input-Output
Summary of Important Points

Examples of Two-Dimensional Arrays and Programming Techniques

Matrix Operations
MAT Statement
Matrix Input-Output
Matrix Manipulation
Matrix Initialization

Exercises

Summary

Review Questions/Self-Test

8

Two-Dimensional Arrays

As discussed in the previous chapter, an array is a group of elements, all having the same name but each one referred to by a subscript. Multidimensional arrays have more than one subscript. BASIC can manipulate the elements of a two-dimensional array and the techniques of doing so are the main topics of this chapter. Matrix manipulation capabilities of some systems are discussed at the end of the chapter.

ARRAY TECHNIQUES

A two-dimensional array is composed of related data organized into rows and columns. For example, the following table of scores can be considered a two-dimensional array:

	Quarter 1	Quarter 2	Score Quarter 3	Quarter 4
Team 1	3	9	6	11
Term 2	2	7	13	0

Each element of a two-dimensional array is referred to by two subscripts. The first subscript shows the row number, and the second one shows the column number. For example, SCORE(2,3) is the element in the second row and the third column of array SCORE, which contains 13.

Figure 8.1 depicts the elements of two-dimensional array A, which has four rows and three columns.

328 Two-Dimensional Arrays

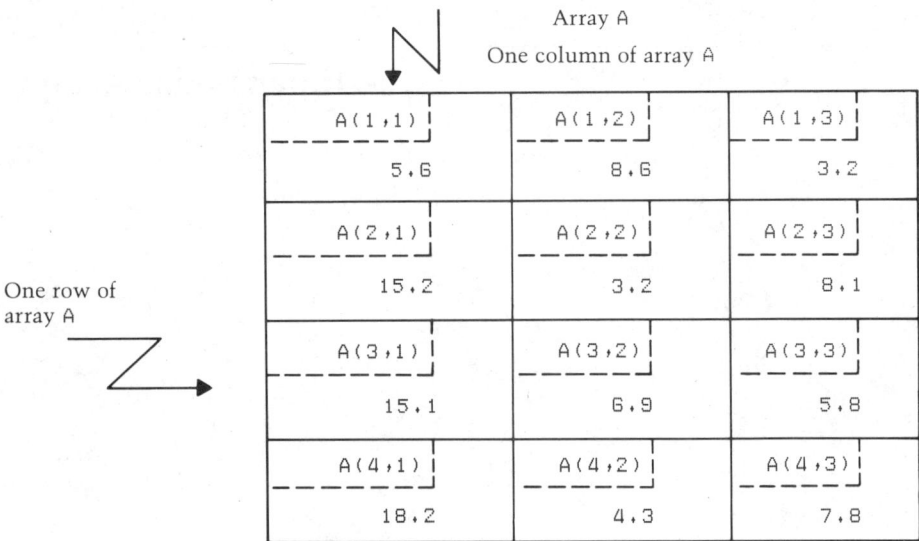

Figure 8.1 A two-dimensional array

Before an element in the array can be located, both the row number and the column number must be known. For example, A(3,2) represents the element of array A in the third row and second column. That element contains the real number 6.9 in Figure 8.1.

The elements of three-dimensional arrays have three subscripts; of four-dimensional arrays, four subscripts; and so on. A three-dimensional array can be imagined as several tables on different pages (or planes). For example, the names of students and their test scores in different courses, as shown in Figure 8.2, can be considered elements of a three-dimensional array. In a three-dimensional array, the first subscript shows the row number, the second subscript shows the column number, and the third subscript shows the page or the plane number. Thus, X(5,3,2) shows the element in the fifth row, third column, and second page of array X.

In mathematics, a two-dimensional array is called a *matrix*, whereas a one-dimensional array is called a *linear array* or a *vector*. All BASIC systems can manipulate two-dimensional arrays. The examples in this chapter are designed for two-dimensional arrays.

Dimension Statement

A two-dimensional array must be defined in a DIM statement before it is used in a program. The dimension statement defines an array, its dimensions, and each dimension's size. For example

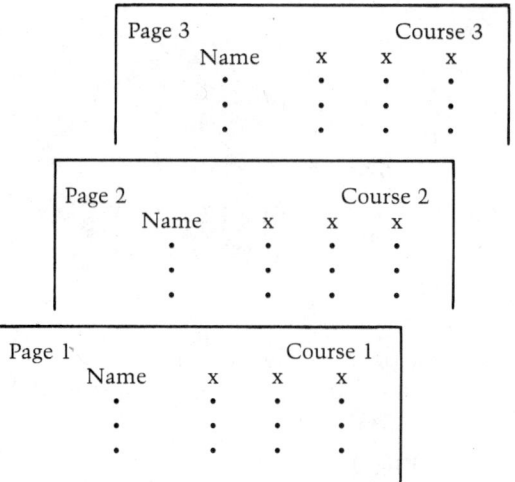

Figure 8.2 Data for a three-dimensional array

```
10 DIM TTT(4,6)
```

defines two-dimensional array TTT of four rows and six columns. When you define an array, the BASIC system reserves a certain number of memory locations for it. For example, a total of 24 elements (4 × 6) will be reserved for the array TTT. (Some systems create a zero row and zero column automatically; thus, array TTT will have 35 elements—5 × 7.)

Several arrays can be defined in a single DIM statement. Thus, the general form of array definition statement is

```
line no, DIM var1(i,j), var2(i,j),
```

where var1, var2, ... are BASIC symbolic names, and i, j are unsigned integer constants representing the array sizes. The following are examples:

```
DIM B(50), X(5,20), N(100,2)
DIM TABLE(5,30), COUNT(30), IN(50,13), D(100)
DIM A(100,21) B$(100,3), N%(100)
```

In some systems, the dimension size can be a variable as long as its value is defined.

Solved Problems

8.1 Find any errors in the following `DIM` statements:
   a. `DIM, A(10,5) INT(30,40)`
   b. `DIMENSION AMOUNT(M,N), LARGE(N,K)`
   c. `DIM AMT(5,500), NAME$(100), COUNT%(100)`
   d. `DIM A(5,0,8), B(5,-8,2), B(5), C(10,20)`

Answers:
   a. The comma after `DIM` must be omitted. However, a comma must separate the arrays in most systems (in others, a space is sufficient).
   b. The array size must be a constant in some systems.
   c. This is correct, assuming `$` indicates string variables and `%` indicates integer variables.
   d. The dimension size cannot be zero or a negative number.

Arithmetic Expressions with Two-Dimensional Arrays

As with one-dimensional arrays, the array name, used alone, indicates all the elements together, and the name followed by subscripts indicates an individual element. Only subscripted elements may be used in arithmetic expressions (except in MAT statements, explained at the end of this chapter).

The `FOR` loop is a convenient tool for manipulating arrays. Normally, a nested loop is necessary to control two subscripts. The following are two simple examples:

Example 8.1

Both of the following program segments add the elements of a row in array `A` and store them in one-dimensional array `TOT`. Array `A` has 4 columns and 50 rows. See Figure 8.3.

Program Segments:

```
100 FOR I = 1 TO 50
110     TOT(I) = A(I,1) + A(I,2) + A(I,3) + A(I,4)
120 NEXT I
```
or

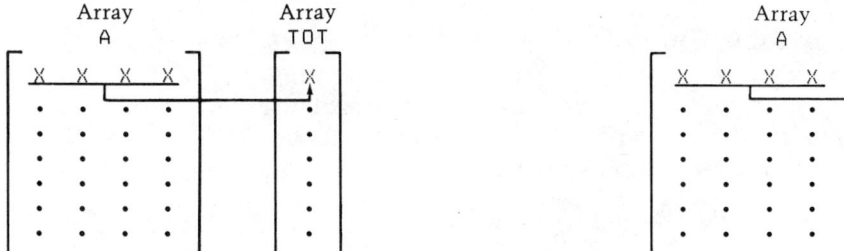

Figure 8.3 Adding the elements of a row in an array

```
100 FOR I = 1 TO 50
110     TOT(I) = 0
120     FOR J = 1 TO 4
130         TOT(I) = TOT(I) + A(I,J)
140     NEXT J
150 NEXT I
```

■ **Example 8.2**

Both of the following program segments store the sum of the first four elements of each row in the fifth element of the row (the fifth column). Array A has 5 columns and 50 rows. See Figure 8.3.

Program Segments:
```
100 FOR I = 1 TO 50
110     A(I,5) = A(I,1) + A(I,2) + A(I,3) + A(I,4)
120 NEXT I
```
or
```
100 FOR I = 1 TO 50
110     A(I,5) = 0
120     FOR J = 1 TO 4
130         A(I,5) = A(I,5) + A(I,J)
140     NEXT J
150 NEXT I
```

Each subscript in a multidimensional array can be a constant, a variable, or an arithmetic expression. As with a one-dimensional array, if the subscript is a noninteger value, the computer automatically converts the value to an integer before any manipulation.

Two-Dimensional Array Input-Output

As with a one-dimensional array, the elements of an array can be read individually, but a loop is more efficient. A nested loop is normally employed to input or output elements of a two-dimensional array. The following is an example:

```
10   DIM X(50,3)
100  FOR I = 1 TO 50
110    FOR J = 1 TO 3
120      PRINT X(I,J)
130    NEXT J
140  NEXT I
```

Note that control variable J, in the inner loop, changes more rapidly than I. This nested loop is equivalent to

```
PRINT X(1,1)
PRINT X(1,2)
PRINT X(1,3)
PRINT X(2,1)
PRINT X(2,2)
PRINT X(2,3)
PRINT X(1,1)
      ⋮
PRINT X(50,3)
```

The above example prints each element on one line. To print all the elements of an array on one line, use a comma or semicolon in the PRINT statement. For example, the segment

```
100  FOR I = 1 TO 50
110    FOR J = 1 TO 3
120      PRINT A(I,J);
130    NEXT J
140  NEXT I
```

would print 150 elements on one line if they would fit. Wrap around to the next line is automatic.

The following example demonstrates how a program can read, calculate, and print a two-dimensional array:

Example 8.3

Problem: Write a program that reads the scores at the end of each quarter of a football game and calculates the final score. Print the quarter scores and the final score. The scores for one occasion are:

	Scores at Quarters				Final Score
	1	2	3	4	
Team 1	3	9	6	11	?
Team 2	2	7	13	0	?

Program:

```
10   DIM SCORE(2,4), FINAL(2)
100  REM *************** READING MODULE *****************
110  FOR I = 1 TO 2
120      FOR J = 1 TO 4
130          READ SCORE(I,J)
140      NEXT J
150  NEXT I
200  REM *************** CALCULATION MODULE ****************
210  FOR K = 1 TO 2
220      FINAL(K) = SCORE(K,1) + SCORE(K,2) + SCORE(K,3) + SCORE(K,4)
230  NEXT K
300  REM *************** PRINTING MODULE   **************
310  FOR L = 1 TO 2
320      FOR M = 1 TO 4
330          PRINT SCORE(L,M);
340      NEXT M
350      PRINT
360  NEXT L
500  REM ****************** DATA   ******************
510  DATA 3, 9, 6, 11
520  DATA 2, 7, 13, 0
999  END
```

Notes:

1. The calculation module can also be written as

```
210 FOR K = 1 TO 2
220     FINAL(K) = 0
230     FOR L = 1 TO 4
240         FINAL(K) = FINAL(K) + SCORE(K,L)
250     NEXT L
260 NEXT K
```

2. The semicolon in the PRINT statement in line 330 causes the scores to be printed on one line. The PRINT statement in line 350 causes the printer to start on a new line the second time around the loop, so the second row of scores is printed on the second line.

Solved Problems

8.2 Find any errors in the following statements:

a.
```
10    DIM X(5,6)
20    FOR I = 1 TO 5
30      FOR J = 1 TO 6
40        X = 0
50      NEXT J
60    NEXT I
```

b.
```
100   FOR J = 1 TO 30
110     FOR K = 1 TO 300
120       XXX(J+5,K+3) = 1
130     NEXT K
140   NEXT J
```

c. `100 Y(1,J) = 0   FOR J = 1 TO 5`

d. `100 YORK (L**2,2*M + 1) = 5`

Answers:

a. Only individual elements may be used in an assignment statement. The assignment statement, then, must be corrected to X(I,J) = 0.

b. This is correct if array XXX has been defined to have more than 35 rows and 303 columns.

c. Only in BASIC-PLUS is this form valid. In other systems a FOR loop cannot be used in an assignment statement in this form.

d. This is correct if array YORK has been defined and the value of each subscript does not exceed its defined dimension size.

8.3 Identify any errors in the following loops:

```
a. 10   DIM M(50,5)
   100  FOR L = 1 TO 50
   110     FOR K = 1 TO 5
   120        READ M(K,L)
   130     NEXT K
   140  NEXT L
b. 10   DIM X(30,6)
   20   FOR I = 1 TO 30
   30      FOR J = 1 TO 6
   50         X(I+J, I+J) = I + J
   70      NEXT J
   80   NEXT I
c. 10   DIM A(100,30)
            ⋮
   40   FOR I = 1 TO 100
   50      FOR J = 1 TO 30 :   PRINT A :   NEXT J
   60   NEXT I
```

Answers:

    a. The subscript L is out of range, it cannot exceed 5.

    b. The subscripts are out of range.

    c. Subscripts must be used with A. The print statement on line 50 can be corrected to read PRINT A(I,J)

8.4 Suppose array TABLE has been defined as

```
10 DIM TABLE(9,5)
```

Write a program segment that prints the elements of the array row by row as follows: first the row number and then each value of a row at positions 8, 18, 28, 38, and 48 (intervals of 10), respectively.

Answers:

```
100 FOR I = 1 TO 9
105    PRINT I;
110    FOR J = 1 TO 5
120       TAB(10*(J - 1) + 8); TABLE(I,J);
130    NEXT J
140    PRINT
150 NEXT I
```

Summary of Important Points

The rules governing two-dimensional arrays are basically the same as those governing one-dimensional arrays. The most important rules are:

1. The array's name, its dimension, and its size must be defined by the DIM statement before it is used.
2. An array dimension cannot be negative.
3. The array name refers to all the elements in the whole array. Each element can be referred to by the array name followed by the subscript in parentheses. Only individual elements may be used in an arithmetic expression (except when you use the matrix capability of a system).
4. Subscripts may be constants, variables, or simple arithmetic expressions. However, after a subscript is converted to an integer, its value must not exceed the dimension size or be negative.
5. The array elements can be read or written in a FOR loop. Normally, two loops are necessary to input or output a two-dimensional array.

EXAMPLES OF TWO-DIMENSIONAL ARRAYS AND PROGRAMMING TECHNIQUES

As discussed before, arrays are challenging and flexible programming tools. Unfortunately most BASIC systems do not allow you to use an array with more than two dimensions. However, you can always convert a multidimensional array into a one-dimensional array. For example,

```
ATABLE(50,3)
```

can be converted to

```
TABLE1(50), TABLE2(50), TABLE3(50)
```

or converted to

```
TABLET(150)
```

Some simple examples of two-dimensional arrays are presented in the following section. Be sure to study each problem thoroughly and write an answer before you examine the solution to each problem.

Example 8.4 A Simple Example

Problem: Students of a BASIC course have taken three tests. There are fewer than 50 students. Write an interactive program that accepts and stores the name and the three test results. The program should then calculate each student's average and the class average, and print the information. The first value is a header indicating the number of students taking tests. The data will be similar to the data in the following sample:

Name	Test 1	Test 2	Test 3	Average
JOHN DOE	95.50	75.90	87.80	XXXX
PAT JOY	83.00	92.50	85.0	
.	.	.	.	.
.	.	.	.	.
JOYCE DOER	87.75	92.30	78.50	XXXX

Program:

```
10   DIM ANAME$(50), TEST(50,3), SUM(50), AVG(50)
20   PRINT 'THIS PROGRAM CALCULATES THE AVERAGE OF THREE TESTS'
30   PRINT 'FOR EACH STUDENT AND THE GRAND AVERAGE.'
35   PRINT 'HOW MANY STUDENTS ARE THERE'
40   INPUT N
50   GTOT = 0
100  REM ************** READING MODULE ******************
110  PRINT 'TYPE THE DATA: A NAME AND THREE TEST SCORES PER LINE'
110  FOR I = 1 TO N
120      INPUT ANAME$(I), TEST(I,1), TEST(I,2), TEST(I,3)
130  NEXT I
200  REM ************* CALCULATING AVERAGES ***************
210  FOR J = 1 TO N
220      SUM(J) = 0
230      FOR K = 1 TO 3
240          SUM(J) = SUM(J) + TEST(J,K)
250      NEXT K
260      AVG(J) = SUM(J)/3
270      XTOT = XTOT + AVG(J)
280  NEXT J
290  GAVG = XTOT/N
300  REM ********* WRITING THE HEADING AND THE DATA **********
310  PRINT 'NAME', 'TEST #1', 'TEST #2', 'TEST #3', 'AVERAGE'
320  FOR L = 1 TO N
330      PRINT ANAME$(L), TEST(L,1), TEST(L,2), TEST(L,3), AVG(L)
340  NEXT L
350  PRINT
360  PRINT 'THE GRAND AVERAGE:'; GAVG
999  END
```

Notes:

1. Test scores are stored in a two-dimensional array TEST. A row is reserved for each student's test scores.
2. The total of three test scores and the average of the scores are stored in one-dimensional arrays SUM and AVG, respectively.
3. The information is accepted and stored in a two-dimensional array and then manipulated.

Example 8.5   Table Look-Up

Problem: A store sells six products. Each product comes in two models, A or B. The unit price can be found from the following table:

Product No.	Model A	Model B
1	12.30	15.80
2	18.20	25.60
3	19.90	22.50
4	25.00	29.60
5	28.50	39.90
6	36.50	42.80

Write an interactive program that reads the values of the price table and then accepts a product number (a number from 1 to 6) and the model (A or B) of a product and prints its price. Entering a zero for the product number indicates end of data.

Program:

```
10    DIM PRICE(6,2)
20    REM READING THE PRICE TABLE
30    FOR I = 1 TO 6
40       READ PRICE(I,1), PRICE(I,2)
50    NEXT I
110   FOR J = 1 TO 1000
120      PRINT'ENTER THE PRODUCT NO. AND MODEL, TYPE 0 WHEN DONE'
130      INPUT PNO, MODEL
140      IF PNO = 0 THEN GOTO 990
150      IF MODEL = 'A' THEN K = 1
160      IF MODEL = 'B' THEN K = 2
180      PRINT 'PRICE:'; PRICE(PNO, K)
190   NEXT J
200   DATA 12.3, 15.8, 18.2, 25.6, 19.9, 22.5, 25, 29.6
210   DATA 28.5, 39.9, 36.5, 42.8
990   PRINT '*************** CALL BACK ********************'
999   END
```

Example 8.6 Table Manipulation

Problem: A school of engineering has seven departments, and each department has three secretarial positions. Write an interactive program that accepts the salaries of the secretaries and creates a salary table including:

1. The salaries by the department and position
2. The total and average salaries in each department
3. The total and average salaries in each position
4. The total and average of all salaries

The program should print the entire table after reading the data and also print those individual salaries that are below the average. The following is an example of the table:

Department	Positions 1	2	3	Total 4	Average 5
1	7890.00	9130.00	11500.00	?	?
2	.	.	.	?	?
3	.	.	.	?	?
4	.	.	.	?	?
5	.	.	.	?	?
6	.	.	.	?	?
7	.	.	.	?	?
8 (total)	?	?	?	?	?
9 (average)	?	?	?	?	?

Program:

```
10    DIM TABLE (9,5)
20 REM INITIALIZE THE ELEMENTS TO 0
30    FOR I = 1 TO 9
40       FOR J = 1 TO 5  :      TABLE (I,J) = 0  :         NEXT J
70    NEXT I
80 REM READ THE DATA
90    PRINT 'THIS PROGRAM PRINTS THE SALARY TABLE FOR THREE
95    PRINT '       POSITIONS AND SEVEN DEPARTMENTS.'
100 PRINT 'TYPE THE SALARIES, THREE ON EACH LINE'
110   FOR I = 1 TO 7
120      INPUT TABLE(I,1), TABLE(I,2), TABLE(I,3)
130   NEXT I
200 REM CALCULATE THE ROW TOTALS AND AVERAGES
```

```
210    FOR I = 1 TO 7
220        FOR J = 1 TO 3
230            TABLE(I,4) = TABLE(I,4) + TABLE(I,J)
240        NEXT J
250        TABLE(I,5) = TABLE(I,4)/3
260    NEXT I
300 REM CALCULATE THE COLUMN TOTALS AND AVERAGES
310    FOR I = 1 TO 3
320        FOR J = 1 TO 7
330            TABLE(8,I) = TABLE(8,I) + TABLE(J,I)
340        NEXT J
350        TABLE(9,I) = TABLE(8,I)/7
360    NEXT I
400 REM CALCULATE THE GRAND TOTAL AND AVERAGE
410    FOR I = 1 TO 7
420        TABLE(8,4) = TABLE(8,4) + TABLE(I,4)
430        TABLE(8,5) = TABLE(8,5) + TABLE(I,5)
440    NEXT I
450    TABLE(9,4) = TABLE(8,4)/7
460    TABLE(9,5) = TABLE(8,4)/21
500 REM WRITE THE HEADING AND DATA
510    PRINT 'DEPARTMENT'; TAB(21); 'POSITIONS'; TAB(41);'TOTAL';
515    PRINT TAB(51); 'AVERAGE'
520    X = 12
530    FOR I = 1 TO 5
535        PRINT TAB(X); I;
540        X = X + 10
545    NEXT I
550    FOR I = 1 TO 9
560        PRINT TAB(5); I;
565        FOR J = 1 TO 5
570            PRINT TAB(10*J); TABLE(I,J);
575        NEXT J
580        PRINT
590    NEXT I
600 REM WRITE BELOW-AVERAGE SALARIES
610    PRINT 'THE FOLLOWING SALARIES ARE BELOW THE AVERAGE:'
620    FOR K = 1 TO 7
630        FOR L = 1 TO 3
640            IF TABLE(K,L) < TABLE(9,5) THEN PRINT TABLE(K,L)
650        NEXT L
660    NEXT K
999 END
```

Notes:

1. Row totals are assigned to the fourth column and row averages to the fifth column of array TABLE.

2. Column totals are assigned to the eighth row and column averages to the ninth row of array TABLE.

3. The grand total is assigned to element TABLE(8,4). This can be calculated by adding either the column totals or the row totals.

4. The grand average is assigned to element TABLE(9,5). This can also be calculated by dividing the sum of the column averages by 7 or the sum of the row averages by 3.

5. The element TABLE(9,4) can also be calculated by

   ```
   445 FOR J = 1 TO 3
   450     TABLE(9,4) = TABLE(9,4) + TABLE(9,J)
   455 NEXT J
   ```

6. Line 535 prints 1, 2, 3, 4, and 5 as headings starting at column 12 (defined in line 520) with ten spaces between headings.
7. TAB(10*J) in line 570 causes the output to have 10 spaces between columns.

Example 8.7 Graphing a Histogram

Problem: Write a program that reads a set of about 100 integers between 1 to 9. Count the number of times each integer occurs in the set and print a histogram (an asterisk for each occurrence of each digit). For example, if the number of occurrences of each number is

Integer	Occurrences
1	3
2	4
3	8
4	13
5	20
6	12
7	10
8	6
9	4

then the program will print

```
1***
2****
3********
4*************
5********************
6************
7**********
8******
9****
```

Program:

```
10   DIM COUNT(9), CHART$(9,50)
20   REM   EACH COUNT REPRESENTS THE OCCURRENCES OF EACH DIGIT
30   REM   THE ARRAY CHART REPRESENTS THE WHOLE HISTOGRAM
40   REM   INITIALIZE COUNT AND CHART
50   FOR I = 1 TO 9
60      COUNT(I)=0
70      FOR J = 1 TO 50  :  CHART$(I,J) = ' '  :   NEXT J
80   NEXT I
90   REM ACCEPT THE DATA
100  PRINT'THIS PROGRAM PRINTS THE HISTOGRAM OF DATA BETWEEN 0 TO 9'
110  PRINT 'TYPE THE DATA, ONE PER LINE, WHEN FINISHED TYPE 0'
120     FOR I = 1 TO 100
130        INPUT A
140        IF A = 0 THEN GOTO 210
150        COUNT(A) = COUNT(A) + 1
160     NEXT I
200  REM FILLING THE ARRAY CHART WITH '*'
210     FOR I = 1 TO 9
220        K = COUNT(I)
230        FOR J = 1 TO K
240           CHART$(I,J) = '*'
250        NEXT J
260     NEXT I
300  REM PRINTING THE CHART
310     FOR I = 1 TO 9
320        PRINT I; ' ';
330        FOR J = 1 TO 50
340           PRINT CHART$(I,J); ' ';
350        NEXT J
360        PRINT
370     NEXT I
999  END
```

Notes:

1. A 9-by-50 two-dimensional character array is used to represent the whole graph.
2. The array is first filled with blanks, then the appropriate number of asterisks is stored in the appropriate positions.
3. A one-dimensional array also could have been used to print each line of the graph in this example. However, the advantage of the method used is that the graph can be turned 90 degrees and printed (see Example 8.10).

The matrix manipulation feature of BASIC is explained in the next section. Examples 8.8–8.10 are for general-purpose applications.

Example 8.8 Matrix Multiplication

Problem: Assume array A has M rows and N columns; array B (a linear array) has N rows and one column; and array C (also linear) has M rows and one column, as shown in Figure 8.4. Write a program segment that calculates array C so that

```
C(1) = A(1,1)*B(1) + A(1,2)*B(2) + . . . A(1,N)*B(N)
C(2) = A(2,1)*B(1) + A(2,2)*B(2) + . . . A(2,N)*B(N)
  .
  .
  .
C(M) = A(M,1)*B(1) + A(2,2)*B(2) + . . . A(M,N)*B(N)
```

Program Segment:

```
100 FOR I = 1 TO M
110     C(I) = 0.0
120     FOR J = 1 TO N
130         C(I) = C(I) + A(I,J)*B(J)
140     NEXT J
150 NEXT I
```

$$\begin{bmatrix} C(1) \\ C(2) \\ \vdots \\ C(M) \end{bmatrix} = \begin{bmatrix} A(1,1) & A(1,2) & \cdots & A(1,N) \\ A(2,1) & \cdot & & \cdot \\ \vdots & \vdots & & \vdots \\ A(M,1) & \cdot & \cdots & A(M,N) \end{bmatrix} \times \begin{bmatrix} B(1) \\ B(2) \\ \vdots \\ B(N) \end{bmatrix}$$

Figure 8.4. Matrix multiplication

Example 8.9 Transpose of an Array

Problem: Suppose array A has N rows and N columns. Write a program segment that interchanges the values of A(I,J) and A(J,I). For example, if array A is

$$A = \begin{bmatrix} 5 & 3 & 2 \\ 8 & 4 & 9 \\ 6 & 7 & 1 \end{bmatrix}$$

then the new array will be:

$$A = \begin{bmatrix} 5 & 8 & 6 \\ 3 & 4 & 7 \\ 2 & 9 & 1 \end{bmatrix}$$

Program Segment:

```
100 FOR I = 1 TO N
110     FOR J = I TO N
120         TEMP = A(I,J)
130         A(I,J) = A(J,I)
140         A(J,I) = TEMP
150     NEXT J
160 NEXT I
```

Note: The program segment

```
100 FOR I = 1 TO N
110     J = 1 TO N
120         A(I,J) = A(J,I)
130     NEXT J
140 NEXT I
```

will not work because the value of an element must be stored in a temporary location (TEMP) before a new value is assigned to it; otherwise, when a new value is stored in a memory location, the previous one is erased.

Example 8.10 Matrix Manipulation

Problem: Assume that array A has N rows and M columns and that array B has M rows and N columns. Write a program segment that inserts the values of array A into B so that the rows of array A turn 90 degrees and become the columns of array B, the first row of array A becomes the first column of array B, the second row of array A becomes the second column of array B, and so forth. An example of A and B follows:

Examples of Two-Dimensional Arrays and Programming Techniques 345

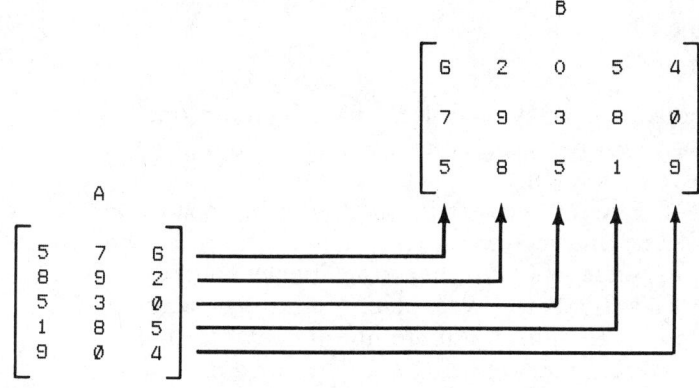

Program Segment:

```
100 FOR I = 1 TO N
110     FOR J = 1 TO M
120         B(J,I) = A(I, M-J+1)
130     NEXT J
140 NEXT I
```

An Application: This technique can be used to print the graph produced by the program in Example 8.7 on page 341, as Figure 8.5 shows.

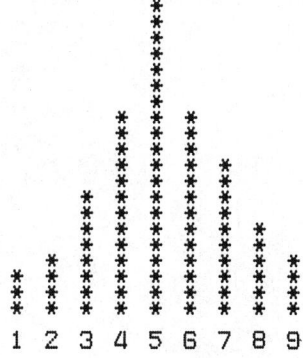

Figure 8.5. A histogram

MATRIX OPERATIONS

In mathematics, a two-dimensional array is called a matrix and a one-dimensional array is called a column vector. To create a row vector, you can define an array of one row with N columns, such as X(1,50). Some BASIC systems, such as BASIC-PLUS, have matrix-manipulating capabilities. This feature is explained in this section.

Matrix operations employ concepts of advanced matrix algebra. Furthermore, a small computer is less likely to have matrix operation features than a larger computer. Skip this section if you are not already familiar with matrix algebra or if the system you are using does not have matrix-manipulating capabilities.

MAT Statement

When the term MAT is used at the beginning of an input, output, or assignment statement the name of an array, without a subscript, refers to the entire array, the matrix. For example, if arrays Z, X, and Y are defined with appropriate sizes, then:

```
100 MAT Z = X + Y
```

adds up the elements of X and Y. (When you use matrix features, zero elements are not included in the operation.)

Matrix Input-Output

If an array is defined in a DIM statement, the name of the array in a MAT input-output list refers to the entire array. For example, the program

```
10 DIM A(2,4)
20 MAT READ A
30 MAT PRINT A
40 DATA 5, 6, 8, 3, 2, 9, 7, 1
99 END
```

will print

5	6	8	3
2	9	7	1

Notice that the statement MAT READ A reads the values of eight elements (2 × 4) from the DATA statement row by row in the order they appear, left to right and top to bottom.

If the name of the array is used with a subscript in a MAT statement, the array is redimensioned. For example,

```
10 DIM A(10,5)
20 DIM READ A(2,3)
30 MAT PRINT A
40 DATA 3, 9, 2, 5, 4, 8, 10, 20
50 END
```

will print

3	9	2
5	4	8

Note that (1) the elements are read and printed row by row and (2) the dimension size in MAT READ statement must be less than the one originally defined in the DIM statement.

Matrix Manipulation

You can use the name of an array in a MAT assignment statement to manipulate matrices. However, matrix addition, subtraction, and especially multiplication are different from ordinary operations. In all the matrix operations, the matrices must be defined and the dimensions and sizes must conform to the rules of matrix algebra. Only two matrices can be used on the right side of an assignment statement, for example:

```
100 MAT A = B + C
200 MAT Z = X - Y
```

Again, the matrices must be defined appropriately. In the examples above, the dimensions and sizes of matrices on the left must equal those of the matrices on the right.

Matrix Multiplication

The following statement is an example of matrix multiplication.

    100 MAT D = A*B

The number of columns of matrix A must be equal to the number of rows of matrix B in the above example. If the size of A is M by N and the size of B is N by K, the size of D must be M by K.

When a constant is multiplied by a matrix (*scalar multiplication*), the constant must be placed in parentheses, and the resulting matrix must have the same dimension and size as the original matrix. Example:

    200 MAT B = (3.5)*A

Transpose and Inverse Functions

The functions TRN and INV are of special interest in matrix manipulation. These two functions can be used to transpose and find the inverse of a matrix. Matrix A is transposed when the elements A(I,J) becomes A(J,I). (The columns become rows.) The inverse of A is B such that B*A is an *identity matrix*—a square matrix with 1s in its diagonal positions and 0s elsewhere. For example, when you use the statements

    150 MAT B = TRN(A)
    170 MAT C = INV(A)

the system computes B, the transpose of A; and C, the inverse of A. Again, the sizes of all the matrices must have been defined appropriately in a DIM statement.

Matrix Initialization

A matrix can be initialized to zero, one, or an identity with the reserved words ZER, CON, and IDN, respectively. The following are two examples:

Example 1:
    10   DIM P(10,5), Q(10,5)
    20   MAT P = ZER
    30   MAT Q = CON

Example 2:
    100 DIM X(30,2), Y(3,5)
    110 X = IDN

The dimensions and sizes of the matrices ZER, CON, and IDN are determined by the dimensions and sizes of the matrices P, Q, and X, respectively.

■ *Solved Problems*

8.5 Find the errors, if any, in each of the following MAT statements or program segments. (Assume the arrays have been defined.)

   a. `30  MAT READ E(M,N)`
   b. `100 MAT X = Y + Z + W`
   c. `200 MAT A = MAT B + MAT C`
   d. `150 MAT X = 3*Y`
   e. `110 MAT B = 0`
   f. `113 MAT A = ZER(5,6)`
   g. `120 MAT X = CON(8,9)`
   h. `100 MAT F = IDN(7,2)`
   i.
```
10  DIM G(10,3), H(5,15)
20  MAT READ H
30  MAT G = H
     :
```
   j.
```
10  DIM A(5,3), B(10,6)
20  MAT READ B
30  MAT A = INV(B)
     :
```
   k.
```
10  DIM X(7,3), Y(10,3), Z(8,4)
20  MAT READ X,Y
30  MAT Z = X*Y
     :
```
   l.
```
10  DIM P(5,3), Q(5,3)
20  MAT READ P
30  MAT Q = TRN(P)
     :
```
   m.
```
10  DIM A(5,3), B(10,2), C(8,4)
20  MAT READ A, B, C
     :
```

Answers:

   a. This is correct; remember that when you use a subscripted array in a MAT statement, the array will be redimensioned. Nevertheless, M and N must be less than the previously defined dimension sizes.

b. More than two matrices cannot be used on the right side of a MAT assignment statement. However, the statement can be written conveniently as

```
100 MAT X = Y + Z
110 MAT X = X + W
```

c. The assignment statement should have the term MAT only once, at the beginning.
d. The constant 3 must be in parentheses.
e. The reserved word ZER must be used.
f. This is correct; however, because the subscript is specified by ZER, matrix A will be redimensioned.
g. Same as f.
h. Same as f.
i. Both arrays G and H must have the same dimension sizes.
j. Both matrices A and B must be square and both must have the same dimension sizes (matrix algebra rules).
k. The number of columns of X must be equal to the number of rows of Y (matrix algebra rule).
l. Either the matrices should be square, or the number of rows in P must equal the number of columns in Q (matrix algebra rule).
m. This is correct; note that the matrices are read one after the other (the entire array A is read first, then B is read, and finally C is read).

EXERCISES

8.1 Find the errors in the following statements:

```
a. 100  DIMENSION A(10,2), B(30,5)
b. 100  DIM CHARACTER NAME (30,5)
c. 10   DIM X(5,-10), Y(0,10)
d. 10   DIM Q(5,3)
   20       Q = 0
e. 10   DIM P(10,30)
   20   READ P(I,J)
         ⋮
```

```
f. 100 FOR I = 1 TO 10
   110    X(I-2) = Y(I)
   120 NEXT I
g. 10  DIM E(5,30)
   20  READ E
h. 10  DIM A$(100,3)
   20  A$(1,1) = "JOHN"
   30  A$(1,2) = 95.5
          ⋮
```

8.2 Find the errors in the following loops:

```
a. 10   DIM KAY(100,3)
   20   FOR I = 1 TO 200
   30      FOR J = 1 TO 10
   40         READ KAY(I,J)
   50      NEXT J
   60   NEXT I
b. 10   DIM A(50,3)
   20   FOR I = 1 TO 50
   30      A = 0
   40   NEXT I
c. 10   DIM P(50,50)
   100  READ P
   200  FOR I = 1 TO 50
   210     SUM = SUM + P
   220  NEXT I
d. 10   DIM X(100,5), SUM(100)
             ⋮
   100 SUM = 0
   110 FOR I = 1 TO 100
   120    FOR J = 1 TO 5
   130       SUM(J) = SUM(I) + X(I,J)
   140    NEXT J
   150 NEXT I
```

Programming Exercises:

Write a complete BASIC program for each of the following problems. Use appropriate arrays, headings, formats, and techniques.

8.3 The following table shows the number of patients treated in four emergency rooms during three shifts.

Shift	Room Number			
	1	2	3	4
1	5	8	3	7
2	3	6	2	2
3	2	3	0	5

Write a program that reads the data into a two-dimensional array and prints the data, the total number of the patients treated during each shift, and the total number of the patients treated in each room.

8.4 The following table shows the number of products shipped to three warehouses during four weeks.

Warehouse Number	Week			
	1	2	3	4
1	529	628	580	320
2	6290	5890	6120	4190
3	1928	2018	1980	1620

Write an interactive program that accepts the data and then prints:
a. The data in a table form
b. The total number of products shipped to each warehouse
c. The total number of products shipped each week

8.5 Repeat the previous exercise, but this time assume there are N warehouses. N is to be read as a header record. Make up your own data.

8.6 Assume array Q has three rows and four columns. Write a program segment that prints the values of the elements in array Q:
a. Row by row; that is, the first row in the first line, the second row in the second line, and the third row in the third line
b. Column by column; that is, the first column in the first line, the second column in the second line, the third column in the third line, and the fourth column in the fourth line
c. With all values on one line
d. With all values in one column

8.7 The following table shows the number of votes, in thousands, cast in six states over three years.

State	Year 1	Year 2	Year 3
1	105.70	125.00	139.68
2	56.29	55.69	51.83
3	82.31	78.51	85.98
4	52.98	49.31	45.39
5	32.85	38.05	43.05
6	93.28	90.58	85.90

Write an interactive program that accepts the data and then:

a. Prints the data with a new row showing total votes in each year and a new column showing total votes in each state

b. Prints a new table that shows the percentages of votes in each state relative to the total number of votes cast in that year

8.8 Suppose a two-dimensional array is defined as

```
10 DIM X(100,5)
```

Write a program that reads the values of the elements, row by row, and finds the largest value in the array.

8.9 The variance of a set of data in a two-dimensional array can be calculated by the formula

$$\text{VAR} = [(X_{11} - X)^2 + (X_{12} - X)^2 + (X_{13} - X)^2 \ldots (X_{mn} - X)^2]/K$$

where $X_{11}, X_{12}, X_{13}, \ldots X_{mn}$ are the elements of the array, X is the mean (average), and K is the number of data (number of elements). Write an interactive program that accepts data in a table consisting of M rows and N columns. (Assume $M < 100$ and $N < 10$; M and N are also to be accepted as input.) Calculate the mean and the variance of the data. Print the data, mean, and variance.

8.10 Arrays A, B, C each have ten rows and ten columns. Write a program that reads the values of arrays A and B, and calculates array C so that

```
C(I,J) = A(I,J) + B(I,J)
```

that is, each element in array C is the sum of each pair of corresponding elements in A and B. Print all three arrays. If the system you are using allows matrix manipulation, repeat the exercise, using the MAT statement.

8.11 Assume when a ball is dropped from a height of H feet, it bounces 80 percent of its previous height and continues to bounce 80 percent each time until it comes to rest. Write an interactive program that accepts a height and prints a graph with asterisks to show the height of each bounce up to 13 bounces.

  a. Print the graph using Example 8.7 as a model.

  b. Write the program so that it prints a graph similar to the one in the following figure:

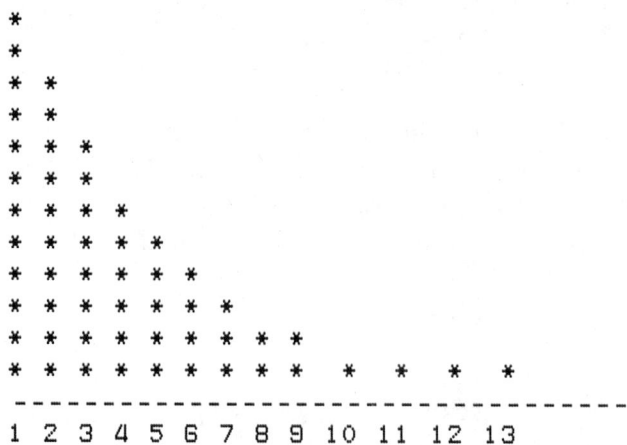

8.12 Write an interactive program that accepts students' test scores (on a scale of 1 to 100) and counts the number of As, Bs, Cs, Ds, and Fs.

  a. Print a histogram showing the number of As, Bs, Cs, Ds, and Fs on a graph such as the one shown in Example 8.7.

  b. Print a histogram similar to the one shown below.

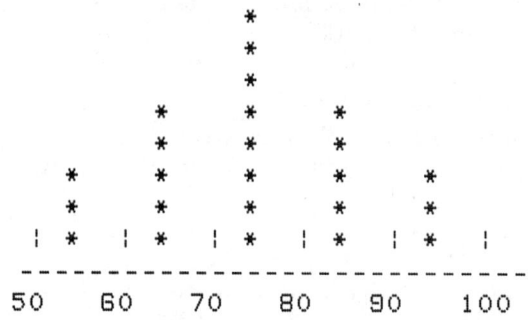

8.13 Write an interactive program that reads integer N and searches two-dimensional array TOT. If it finds a value in the array equal to N, it prints the location of the value and searches further until all the elements of array TOT are searched. If it finds no number equal to N, it prints a message. The program should also count and print the number of times that the number is found. Assume array TOT has ten columns and three rows.

8.14 A department store offers discounts to motivate customers to buy more. The discount on the amount purchased is calculated as follows:

Amount	Discount
0 to $ 100	0
$100 to $ 300	$ 2 + 2% over $ 100
$300 to $ 700	$ 6 + 5% over $ 300
$700 to $1500	$ 46 + 9% over $ 700
over $1500	$118 + 10% over $1500

Write an interactive program that accepts an amount and prints the discount. (Use the table look-up concept rather than several IF-THEN statements.)

8.15 The following table shows the product weight produced by five machines during three factory shifts:

	Shift		
Machine	1	2	3
1	22.5	22.7	22.9
2	23.5	23.0	23.8
3	21.4	22.0	20.5
4	24.0	23.8	24.2
5	25.1	24.8	24.9

Write an interactive program that accepts the data and then calculates:
a. The average weight of the porducts produced by each machine.
b. The average weight produced during each shift
c. The grand average weight

Print the data and averages.

8.16 A trucking company charges its customers a fixed amount per pound, as follows:

	Area Code		
Zone Code	1	2	3
1	.40	.55	.68
2	.60	.70	.85
3	.75	.78	.96
4	.90	1.05	1.10
5	.99	1.08	1.15

Write a program that accepts the names of the customers, zone codes, area codes, and weights of the items shipped. Assume there are fewer than 100 records per truck load. The last record is a trailer value. Print a report showing this information as well as the shipping charge to each customer. Print the total weights and the total charges at the end.

8.17 Suppose arrays A, B, and C each have two rows and two columns.

a. Write a program segment that calculates array C so that

$$\begin{bmatrix} C(11) & C(12) \\ C(21) & C(22) \end{bmatrix} = \begin{bmatrix} A(11) & A(12) \\ A(21) & A(22) \end{bmatrix} * \begin{bmatrix} B(11) & B(12) \\ B(21) & B(22) \end{bmatrix}$$

where:

```
C(11) = A(11)*B(11) + A(12)*B(21)
C(12) = A(11)*B(12) + A(12)*B(22)
C(21) = A(21)*B(11) + A(22)*B(21)
C(22) = A(21)*B(12) + A(22)*B(22)
```

b. Can you expand the idea for a general form of two arrays? (The number of columns of A must equal the number of rows of B. If A is M by N and B is N by K, then C is M by K.)

c. Use a MAT statement for this problem.

8.18 Write a program that reads two arrays, A and B, of equal sizes. The program then determines whether array A is equal to array B by comparing corresponding elements of each array one by one. The two arrays are equal if all the corresponding elements are equal. Print the arrays and a message saying whether or not the two arrays are equal.

8.19 Referring to the previous problem, calculate the ratio of one of the elements in array A to the corresponding element in array B. Call the ratio C. Then compare each element of array A with C multiplied by the corresponding elements of array B. If they are equal after multiplication, then arrays A and B are equivalent. If any one comparison reveals inequality, the arrays are not equivalent or related by a ratio. Print the arrays, the ratio, and a message saying whether or not the arrays are equivalent.

8.20 The hourly pay rate for the employees of the XYZ Company is based on the following table:

Job Code	Department				
	1	2	3	4	5
1	4.80	5.00	5.30	5.80	6.30
2	5.30	5.50	5.90	6.60	7.30
3	5.80	6.05	7.55	7.55	8.40
4	6.35	6.65	8.40	8.50	9.60
5	6.95	7.30	9.20	9.60	10.90
6	7.70	8.00	10.10	10.70	12.30
7	8.50	8.80	11.20	12.00	14.90

The federal tax deduction rate is:

Weekly Taxable Income	Tax
$100	0
More than $100 to $180	$ 3 + 3% over $100
More than $180 to $300	$ 27 + 7% over $180
More than $300 to $450	$111 + 12% over $300
More than $450 to $600	$291 + 18% over $450
More than $600	$531 + 25% over $600

Write a program that prints biweekly reports as follows:
Input:
a. Name, 15 characters
b. Social Security number, 11 characters
c. Sex, M or F
d. Marital status, S or M
e. Number of dependents
f. Pay code; consisting of
- A two-digit job code, such as 05
- A two-digit department code, such as 02

g. Hours worked in the first week

h. Hours worked in the second week

Processing:

a. Gross pay: the hours worked multiplied by the pay rate; over 40 hours per week are paid at 1.5 times the regular pay rate

b. Federal tax deduction; consisting of:
   - Taxable Income: the weekly gross pay, minus the number of dependents times 40
   - Tax based on the tax table

c. FICA deduction: the gross pay times .0665

d. State tax: gross pay times .045

e. Total deductions: the sum of all the deductions

f. Net pay: the gross pay minus total deductions

Output:

a. A biweekly report including all the input information, the gross pay, all the deductions, and the net pay for each employee.

b. A summary report consisting of:

   Total gross pay

   Total federal tax deductions

   Total FICA deductions

   Total state tax deduction

   Total of all deductions

   Total net pay

c. The checks and the check stubs for the employees. Design the checks and check stubs first.

SUMMARY

You have learned:

1. A multidimensional array has more than one subscript (dimension). For example, a table of data with several rows and columns can be represented as a two-dimensional array. The first subscript of a two-dimensional array shows the row number, and the second one shows the column number.

2. A two-dimensional array must be defined before it is used in a program. The DIM statement defines (a) the array, (b) the dimensions of the array, and (c) the size of each dimension. The following statements are some examples:

```
10   DIM TOTAL(200,50), NICE(300,50)
100  DIM GOOD(50), NONE(100,20)
10   DIM NAME$(100,3), ID%(30,5), K%(30,5)
```

3. Only the individual array elements—denoted by the array name followed by the subscript in parentheses—may be used in an arithmetic expression or in an assignment statement.

4. Array elements can be input or output in a FOR-NEXT loop. Example:

```
100 FOR I = 1 TO 100
110     FOR J = 1 TO 5
120         READ A(I,J)
130     NEXT J
140 NEXT I
```

5. In certain situations, two-dimensional arrays are useful tools for solving problems. Examples in this chapter are table manipulation, table look-up, histogram graphs, and matrix manipulation.

6. In some systems, the MAT statement can be used to read, process, or print the entire array—a matrix. Example:

```
10   DIM X(100,2), Y(100,2)
20   MAT READ X
30   MAT Y = (2)*Y
40   MAT PRINT X,Y
```

REVIEW QUESTIONS/SELF-TEST

8.1 Which of the following statements is not correct?
    a. `10   DIM AAA(100,200), BBB(M,N)`
    b. `50   DIM POOL(200,60), M(30)`
    c. `20   DIM NET(100,20), N$(50,2)`
    d. `100  DIM AROW(30,-20), P(100)`
    e. none of the above

8.2 Which of the following program segments is correct?
    a.
```
10   DIM A(100,10)
20   FOR I = 1 TO 100
30       READ A
40   NEXT I
```

360 Two-Dimensional Arrays

```
b. 10    DIM X(50,3)
         ⋮
   50    IF X = 0 GO TO 99
c. 10    DIM Y(5,20)
   20    FOR I = 1,20
   30       FOR J = 1,5
   40          READ Y(I,J)
   50       NEXT J
   60    NEXT I
         ⋮
d. 10    DIM X(30,2)
   20    READ X
         ⋮
```

e. none of the above

8.3 Explain what values will be printed when the following program is run and which positions they will occupy:

```
10    DIM A(5,2)
20    A(1,1) = 0
30    FOR I = 1 TO 5
40       FOR J = 1 TO 2
50          A(I,J)=A(I,J) + 1
60          PRINT A(I,J);
70       NEXT J
80    NEXT I
90    END
```

8.4 Assume data are stored in array A, which is defined as

```
10 DIM A(10,5)
```

Write a program segment that prints the last row first, the second-to-last row second, and so on.

Answers:

8.1 d (Also, some systems do not allow the variable sizes used in a.)

8.2 e

8.3 The sequence numbers from 1 to 10 will be printed on one line

8.4
```
100 FOR I = 10 TO 1 STEP -1
110    FOR J = 1 TO 5
120       PRINT A(I,J);
130    NEXT J
140    PRINT
150 NEXT I
```

Subprograms

9

In This Chapter:

Subroutines
Internal Subroutines
External Subroutines

Functions
Library Functions
User-Defined Functions
Summary of the Rules for Using Functions

Importance of Modular Programming
Exercises
Summary
Review Questions/Self-Test

9
Subprograms

A *subprogram* is a program unit that can be developed and executed independently. There are at least two advantages of using subprograms:

1. The process of writing a long and complicated program can become quite cumbersome. However, such programs become more manageable if they are broken down into smaller modules. Small modules make a program simple in its entirety and easier to work with. Subprograms offer a convenient modular approach: the subprogram is one of several modules of a larger unit.
2. Sometimes a series of instructions must be repeated several times at different places in a program. We can write those instructions once in a subprogram and use them whenever needed. Thus, by using a subprogram, we can avoid having to write the same sequence of instructions repeatedly throughout the program.

Subprograms are of two types: subroutines and functions. We will discuss these two important features of BASIC in this chapter.

SUBROUTINES

There are two types of subroutines:

1. Internal subroutines
2. External subroutines

Internal Subroutines

An *internal subroutine* is a series of instructions, program unit, that can be developed and placed separately. The subroutine then can be called when needed. Look at a simple example before we explain subroutines further.

Example 9.1

Problem: Write a program that calculates and prints the sum and the average of three variables. Use a subroutine.

Solution Plan:

1. Read the variables.
2. Calculate the sum and the average in a subroutine.
3. Print the data, the sum, and the average.
4. The subroutine.
   a. Compute the SUM by adding up the variables.
   b. Compute AVG = SUM/3.

Program:

```
10   READ X, Y, Z
20   REM *** CALL THE SUBROUTINE***
30   GOSUB 100
40   PRINT X, Y, Z, SUM, AVG
50   GOTO 199
100  REM *** THE SUBROUTINE ***
110  SUM = X + Y + Z
120  AVG = SUM/3
130  RETURN
140  REM **** END OF THE SUBROUTINE *****
150  DATA 56.9, 92.3, 38
199  END
```

Notes:

1. When the computer encounters GOSUB 100 in the program, control passes to the subroutine, and the instructions in the subroutine are executed. Control passes back to line 40 when the RETURN statement is encountered.
2. The subroutine is separated from the main program. It starts at line 100 and ends with the RETURN statement.

Generally, the control is transferred to a subroutine with a GOSUB statement:

```
Line no.      GOSUB n
```

or

```
Line no.      ON exp GOSUB n1, n2, . . .
```

Control returns automatically to the referencing program when the RETURN statement is encountered.

A main program may have several subroutines. A subroutine may in turn have one or several subroutines. The following is an example:

Example 9.2

Problem: There are 50 students in a course, and each student has taken three tests. Write a program that reads the test scores, drops the lowest score, and prints the average of the two highest test scores.

Program:

```
5     N = 50
10    FOR I = 1 TO N
20       READ T1, T2, T3
30          REM SUBROUTINE 100 CALCULATES THE AVERAGE
40          GOSUB 100
50       PRINT "THE AVERAGE OF THE TWO HIGHEST TESTS IS "; AVG
60    NEXT I
70    GOTO 999
80    REM ********** END OF THE MAIN ROUTINE **************
100   REM ********** THE SUBROUTINE SECTION **************
105   REM ***** THIS SUBROUTINE CALCULATES THE AVERAGE ****
110      SUM = T1 + T2 + T3
120         REM SUBROUTINE 200 FINDS THE LOWEST TEST SCORE
130         GOSUB 200
140      AVG = (SUM - LOWEST)/2
150   RETURN
160   REM ********* END OF AVERAGE SUBROUTINE *************
200   REM ** THIS SUBROUTINE FIGURES OUT THE LOWEST SCORE *
210      LOWEST = T1
220      IF T2 < LOWEST THEN LOWEST = T2
230      IF T3 < LOWEST THEN LOWEST = T3
240   RETURN
250   REM **************END OF LOWEST SCORE SUBROUTINE******
301   DATA 93.5, 82.1, 73.2
            :
350   DATA 81.3, 89.2, 97.5
999   END
```

Do This for my class

Note: The main program has a subroutine; the subroutine in turn has a subroutine. Control is transferred from the referencing program and back as shown below:

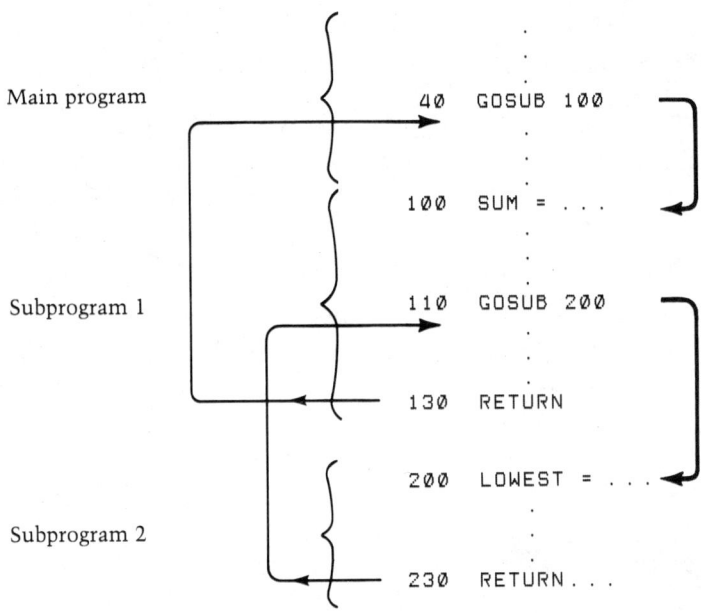

Any time that a GOSUB statement transfers control to a subroutine, the computer executes all the instructions until it encounters a RETURN statement. The RETURN statement transfers control back to the next statement after the GOSUB of the referencing program. Figure 9.1 shows the transferring of control from the referencing program to several nested subroutines and back.

The following example shows a subroutine in a program that uses an array:

Example 9.3

Problem: Write a program that reads 50 values into array A, finds the largest value in a subroutine, and prints the largest value.

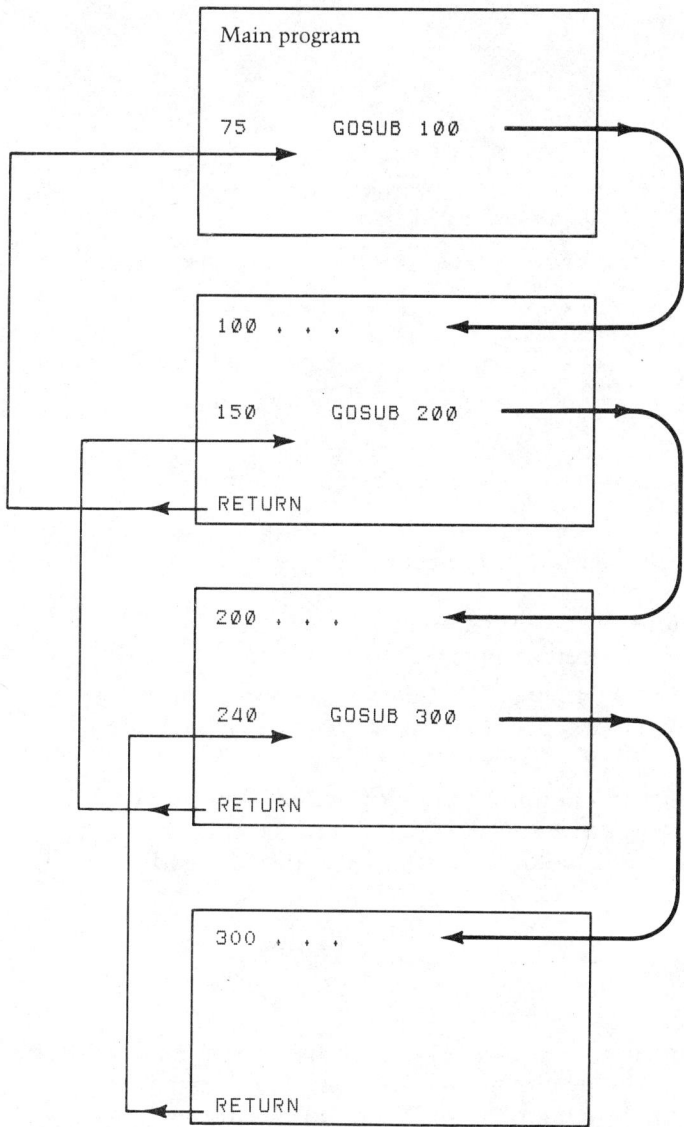

Figure 9.1 Transferring control to a subroutine

Program:

```
10   DIM A(50)
20   FOR I = 1 TO 50
30     READ A(I)
40   NEXT I
50   REM ** THE LARGEST NO. IS FOUND IN THE SUBROUTINE AT 100 **
60   GOSUB 100
70   PRINT "THE LARGEST NUMBER IS: "; LARGE
90   GOTO 999
100  REM *******THIS SUBROUTINE FINDS THE LARGEST NO.*****
110  LARGE = A(1)
120  FOR J = 2 TO 50
130    IF A(J) > LARGE THEN LARGE = A(J)
140  NEXT J
150  RETURN
160  REM ********* END OF THE SUBROUTINE *****************
200  DATA ...
       :
999  END
```

Pay attention to the following points when using subroutines:

1. Use a REM statement before any GOSUB statement to explain the purpose of the subroutine in the referencing program unit.
2. Separate each subroutine from the rest of the program with a line of asterisks or other characters, and then briefly explain the task of the subroutine.
3. Use only one entry and one exit point in a subroutine. The entry point is the beginning of the subroutine and the RETURN is the exit point. In other words, a subroutine should not contain GOTO or IF-GOTO statements that transfers control to another part of the program.

External Subroutines

An *external* subroutine is a complete BASIC program unit that can be called by its name from a referencing program. The CHAIN statement can be used to call another program into memory for execution. The following are examples of the CHAIN statement:

```
100 CHAIN A$
150 CHAIN "STAT"
50  CHAIN "MENU"
```

An external subroutine is a complete and independent program. It will be executed independently also. The variables, instructions, and line numbers are all local to the subprogram. The values of variables can be transferred from one program to another either by writing them on a file or by using a reserved "common core area." Some systems allow you to transfer the variables through an "option" in the chain statement. (MBASIC allows the ALL option in the CHAIN statement. This option transfers all variables to the called program. MBASIC also allows the MERGE option, which brings a subroutine into the called program.)

The following program chains and executes one of the several subprograms according to a menu:

Example 9.4

Problem: Suppose a decision support system consists of the following programs: (1) statistical analysis, saved under the name STAT; (2) forecasting, saved under the name FORECAST; (3) break-even analysis, saved under BREAK, and (4) market analysis, saved under MARKET. Write a menu program that loads a program according to the user's selection.

Program:

```
10   PRINT "HI, THIS IS AN ANALYSIS PROGRAM "
20   PRINT "WOULD YOU LIKE TO :"
30   PRINT "   1. DO STATISTICAL ANALYSIS"
35   PRINT "   2. DO FORECASTING"
40   PRINT "   3. DO BREAK-EVEN ANALYSIS"
45   PRINT "   4. DO MARKET ANALYSIS"
50   PRINT "   5. END THE ANALYSIS"
60   INPUT "PLEASE CHOOSE 1, 2, 3, 4, OR 5"; CHOICE
70      ON CHOICE GOTO 100, 200, 300, 400, 500
80      PRINT "THAT CHOICE IS NOT AVAILABLE"
90   GOTO 60
95                                                          REM
100     CHAIN "STAT"
105                                                         REM
200     CHAIN "FORECAST"
205                                                         REM
300     CHAIN "BREAK"
305                                                         REM
400     CHAIN "MARKET"
405                                                         REM
500  PRINT "********* BYE ~~~~~~~ CALL BACK **********"
999  END
```

Notes:

1. After one of the programs is loaded, control is not returned automatically.
2. It is assumed that the ON-GOTO statement is ignored if CHOICE is not 1, 2, 3, 4, or 5. (Thus, control passes back to line 60 for a new CHOICE.)

Generally, the simple form of the CHAIN command loads and executes another program, and control does not pass back to the referencing program. The new program, however, may chain back to the program that invoked it.

The chaining of programs is highly system dependent, and the subject is beyond the scope of this book. If you are interested in chaining your programs, your BASIC user's manual is a useful guide.

FUNCTIONS

A function is a subprogram invoked by appearance of its name in a statement. For example, if the function MIN is defined to return the smallest value among three variables, then the statement

```
10   LES = MIN(I, J, K)
```

invokes the function and assigns the smallest value among I, J, and K to LES.

There are two types of functions: Library functions, and user-defined functions.

Library Functions

Library functions are functions defined by the system and available to all users. To use any of these functions, you need only know its name, its purpose, and the arguments used in that function. For example, SQR is a library function that calculates the square root of a positive number. The following example demonstrates how SQR is used in a program.

Example 9.5

Problem: Write an interactive program that reads a number and prints its square root.

Program:

```
10  PRINT "THIS PROGRAM CALCULATES THE SQUARE
         ROOT OF A NUMBER"
15  PRINT "TYPE THE NUMBER"
20  INPUT A
30  B = SQR(A)
40  PRINT "SQUARE ROOT OF "; A; " IS: "; B
50  END
```

Library functions are also called *Compiler/interpreter-defined, intrinsic,* or *built-in* functions. Each system offers many useful library functions. Table 9.1 presents some of them. Look at the table and then review the examples that follow. However, make sure to check the list of the library functions for your system.

Table 9.1 Some Library Functions

Name and Form	Purpose	Examples
ABS(x)	Returns the absolute value of the argument x	10 X=ABS(-5.5)
INT(x)	Returns the greatest integer of an argument	10 X=INT(Y) 100 Z%=INT(S/Q)
FIX(x)	Returns the truncated value of an argument	100 X = FIX(X/Y)
LOG(x)	Returns the natural logarithm of an argument	10 A=LOG(B)
EXP(x)	Returns an exponential value of an argument (e**x)	10 X=EXP(5.3) 100 Y=EXP(A)
SGN(x)	Returns +1 or -1, depending on the sign of x, 0 if x=0	10 S=SGN(-5)
ATN(x)	Returns the angle in radians	10 X=ATN(Y)
COS(x)	Returns the cosine of x	100 Z=COS(P)
SIN(x)	Returns the sine of x	150 Q=SIN(A)
TAN(x)	Returns the tangent of x	100 B=TAN(R)
SQR(x)	Returns the square root of an argument	50 S=SQR(V)
RND(a)	Returns a random number, normally between 0 and 1	100 F=RND(9)

Argument x can be a constant or an expression.

Example 9.6

The standard deviation is equal to the square root of the variance of a set of data. If the variance is 395.5, the following program segment prints the standard deviation:

Program Segment:
```
100 STD = SQR(395.5)
110 PRINT STD
120 END
```

Example 9.7

The following program segment reads 100 values into an array and prints the absolute value of each:

Program:
```
10   DIM A(100)
20   FOR I=1 TO 100
30      READ A(I)
40      PRINT ABS(A(I))
50   NEXT I
60   DATA........................
```

Note: The arrays are not needed in this example but are used only to show the technique.

Example 9.8

The following program segment calculates the square root of the absolute value of A-B:

Program Segment:
```
100 X = SQR (ABS(A - B))
```

Example 9.9

Sometimes it is necessary to round off a number. Rounding off refers to reducing the number of decimal places. Normally all the digits after the desired digit are discarded. However, if the first discarded digit is 5 or greater, the last retained digit is increased by one. The following program segment rounds off a number to one decimal point:

Program Segment:

```
100 X1 = (INT(X*10 + .5))/10
```

Pay attention to the techniques used in this example. The number is multiplied by 10 (for one decimal point), .5 is added (to take care of the discarded digits), and then the integer of the result is divided by 10.

Solved Problems

9.1 What is the value of X in each of the following statements?

```
a. 100 Y = -2.5          e. 100 X = SQR(100)
   110 X = ABS(Y)        f. X = INT(-25.2)
b. 100 X = INT(25.9)     g. X = FIX(-25.2)
c. 100 X = EXP(1)        h. X = FIX(25.9)
d.  50 A = -56.2
    60 X = SGN(A)
```

Answers:

```
a. 2.5                   e. 10
b. 25                    f. -26
c. 2.71828               g. -25
d. -1                    h. 25
```

Note that FIX returns the truncated value. The difference between FIX and INT is that INT returns the next higher number for a negative value.

User-Defined Functions

A *user-defined function* is a program segment, normally a single statement, defined by the programmer in order to evaluate an expression. A function statement is similar to an arithmetic assignment statement and should be defined at the beginning of the program unit by the DEF statement. Once the function is defined, it can be used many times in a program.

A function statement is referenced in the same way a library function is. The following is an example:

Example 9.10

Problem: The optimal production quantity can be calculated by the formula

$$Q = \sqrt{2 \cdot d \cdot s / c}$$

where

d = the product demand for a specified time interval
c = the carrying costs
s = the set-up costs

Write an interactive program that accepts D, C, and S for a product. Calculate and print the optimal production quantity for the product. Assume that there are fewer than 50 products and that zeros indicate end of data.

Program:

```
10   DEF FNOPTQ(X,Y,Z) = SQR(2*X*Z/Y)
20   PRINT "THIS PROGRAM CALCULATES THE OPTIMAL
            PRODUCTION QUANTITY"
30   FOR I = 1 TO 50
40      PRINT "TYPE IN THE DEMAND, THE CARRYING COST,"
45      PRINT "AND SET-UP COSTS SEPARATED BY"
50      PRINT "A COMMA, TYPE ZEROS WHEN DONE"
60      INPUT D, C, S
70      Q = FNOPTQ(D,C,S)
80      PRINT "WHEN D = "; D; " C= "; C; " S="; S
85      PRINT "THE OPTIMAL PRODUCTION IS: "; Q
90   NEXT I
99   END
```

Notes:

1. The function FNOPTQ is defined at the beginning of the program (line 10) by the DEF statement.
2. The function is invoked when its name appears in the assignment statement (line 70).
3. When the function is invoked, the values of D, C, S are passed to X, Y, and Z in function definition; the instruction is executed; and the result is transferred back.

The general form of a user-defined function is as follows:

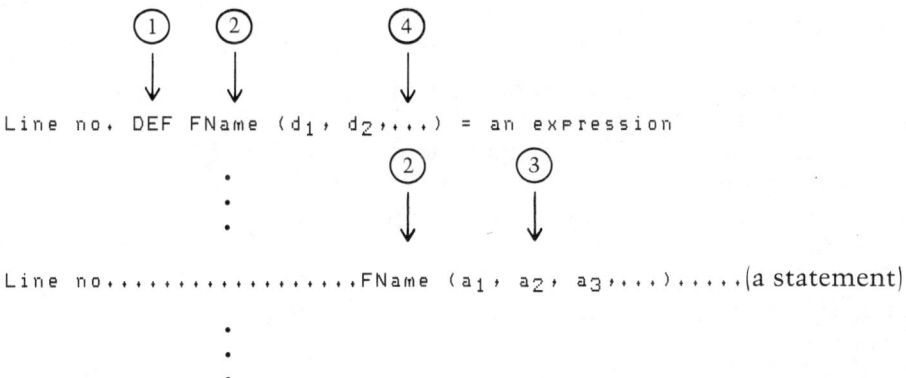

Its main components are:

1. The term DEF, followed by the definition of the function
2. The name of the function, which must be a BASIC symbolic name, preceded by FN
3. The list of the variables, constants, or other values in parentheses (The values in this list are called *actual arguments*.)
4. The list of variables (The variables in the list are called *dummy arguments*.)

Names of Functions

The name of a function must follow the BASIC rules for symbolic names. It is chosen by the programmer and must not be the same as any other name in the program. It is advisable to choose a descriptive name for the function if possible. The name must be preceded by FN in most systems.

Arguments of a Function

We referred to the variables list referencing a function as actual arguments and the variables in the function definition list as dummy arguments. The symbolic name of a dummy argument does not have to be the same as the name of an actual argument. Moreover, an actual argument can be a constant, a variable, an array element, or an expression. For example, all of the following statements are syntactically correct:

```
100 PRINT FNFUN1(A+B, M, 3)
100 Y = FNGAMA(X, Y*N, C, 3*Z)
150 ORDER = FNQUE(30, A(1), B(I), S-3)
```

When the name of a function appears in a statement, the values of actual arguments pass to the dummy arguments, the expression is evaluated, and the resulting value (assigned to the name of the function) is returned. If an actual argument is an expression, it is evaluated before association. The dummy arguments are matched with the actual arguments on a one-to-one basis. Therefore, the number, order, and type of the dummy arguments (real, integer, or character) must correspond to those of the actual arguments.

A variable in the function expression can be either a reference to a dummy argument or a reference to a variable in the program. For example, if a function is defined as

```
10   DEF FNFF(X, Y, Z) = A*X + B*Y + C*Z
```

the values of X, Y, and Z pass to the function through the actual arguments; and A, B, and C retain those values they have before the statement containing the name of the function is executed. In other words, the current values of variables A, B, and C are used to evaluate the function. The following is another example:

Example 9.11

Problem: Write an interactive program that calculates the area of a circle. Use a function for the calculation.

Program:

```
10   PI = 3.14159
20   DEF FNAREA(R) = PI*R^2
30   PRINT "THIS PROGRAM CALCULATES THE AREA OF A CIRCLE"
35   FOR TRY = 1 TO 100
40      PRINT "TYPE THE RADIUS, TYPE ZERO WHEN THROUGH"
50      INPUT RADIUS
60      IF RADIUS = 0 THEN GOTO 100
70      XAREA = FNAREA(RADIUS)
80      PRINT "THE AREA IS:"; XAREA
90   NEXT TRY
100  PRINT "************* CALL BACK *********"
```

If the program is run and the user inputs 5, the output will be

```
THE AREA IS: 78.53975
```

Summary of the Rules for Using Functions

1. The function name must be a valid BASIC name preceded by FN.
2. An actual argument can be a variable, array element, constant, or a simple arithmetic expression. A dummy argument, however, can be only a variable.
3. The symbolic names of the dummy arguments may be different from the symbolic names of the actual arguments. However, the number, order, and type of dummy arguments must match those of the actual arguments.
4. A function should not invoke itself (it creates an infinite loop).
5. The expression defining the function may include variables other than the dummy arguments. In this case, the current values of those variables are used when the function is executed.
6. There must be at least one argument in each argument list. (In some systems, however, only parentheses are required, and the argument list may be empty.)
7. The name of the function cannot be the same as any other name in the program unit.
8. A function must be defined before it is referenced.
9. A function is normally one statement, but a few systems allow multistatement function definitions.
10. A function cannot be defined in immediate mode.

Solved Problems

9.2 Identify the errors in the following statements:
   a. `10   DEF FNC1(A, B) = 2*A^3 + 5*B^4 + K`
   b. `100  DEF FNC2(X, 2) = 5*X + 2`
   c. `50   DEF FNQUE(E, F(1)) = E*F(1) + E + F(1)`
   d. `10   DEF(A, B) = A + B + 2*A*B`
   e. `10   FNEXPONE(NT, P) = D*NT^M + Q*P + 3.0`
   f. `     FNNET(M, N) = M - N`
   g. `10   DEF FNEXPO(P, Q) = P + Q + FNEXPO(A, B)`

h. `10 DEF FNQ(A$, P) = "X" + MID$(A$, P)`
i. `50 DEF FNF(A, B)=5.0 + SQRT(ABS(A*B + A + B))`

Answers:

a. This is correct.
b. A dummy argument cannot be a constant.
c. A dummy argument cannot be an array element.
d. The name of the function is missing.
e. The term `DEF` is missing.
f. The line number and the term `DEF` are missing.
g. A function should not invoke itself. This is an infinite loop.
h. This is a string function, thus its name must be `FNQ$`.
i. This is correct.

9.3 Identify any errors in the general form of the following function statements:

a.
```
10    DEF FNFACT(M, N) = 3*M + 5*N
        ⋮
100  V = FNFACT(X%, Y%)
```
b.
```
100 DEF FNPLOT(E, G) = X*G + 2*X*Y + E
        ⋮
500 D = FNPLOT(A, B, C)
        ⋮
```
c.
```
10    DEF FNPAY = A*B
        ⋮
100  WAGE = FNPAY
        ⋮
```
d.
```
10    DEF FNFUN1(X) = 2.0*X + A*B
20    DEF FNFUN2(Y) = 5.0*A + FNFUN1(B)*Y
        ⋮
100  Z = FNFUN2(D)
```

    e. `100 DEF FNPIE(C, D) = 2*C + D + FNRO(5)`
        `110 DEF FNRO(A) = A + A^2`

                ⋮

        `300 X = FNPIE(X, Y)`

    f. `10 DEF FNCT1(A, B) = A + B`

                ⋮

        `100 X = FNCT1(P, Q)`
        `110 PRINT FNCT1`

Answers:

    a. The types of the dummy arguments do not match the types of the actual arguments (assuming `X%` and `Y%` are integers).

    b. The number of dummy arguments must be the same as the number of actual arguments.

    c. A function must have an argument. (Some systems allow an "empty argument"—just the parentheses.)

    d. This is correct. Note that `FUN1` is defined before `FUN2`.

    e. The function `RO` must be defined before `PIE`.

    f. The name of the function cannot appear as a single variable. Line 110 could be corrected to read

        `110 PRINT FNCT1(P, Q)`.

9.4 What is the value of `V` in the following program segments?

    a. `10 DEF FNGAMMA(X, Y) = 2*X + X*Y`

                ⋮

        `100 A = 2`
        `110 B = 3`
        `120 V = FNGAMMA(A, B)`

    b. `100 DEF FNBETA(G, H) = G*H + A`

                ⋮

        `210 A = 5`
        `220 P = 3`
        `230 V = FNBETA(P, 2)`

c. 50   DEF FNFUN2(X) = X*X + 1
   60   DEF FNFUN1(E, F) = E + F + FNFUN2(F)
                ⋮
   500   V = FNFUN1(5, 1)
d. 10   DEF FNOVER(X) = 1.5*(X - 40)
                ⋮
   90   H = 42.0
   100   IF H > 40 THEN V = FNOVER(H) ELSE V = 0

Answers:

   a. V = 10
   b. V = 11
   c. V = 8
   d. V = 3

IMPORTANCE OF MODULAR PROGRAMMING

In Chapter 3, structured design was defined as top-down, modular program design. Furthermore, we have emphasized that breaking down a problem into small, manageable modules is the key to effective problem solving. Small manageable modules that perform well-defined subtasks facilitate the design and increase the readability of a program significantly. Some other advantages of the modular approach are:

1. Each module can be written once and used in many programs.
2. Debugging can be performed for each module rather than for the entire program. Thus, errors can be detected and corrected easily.
3. Teamwork is facilitated. That is, several people can write a large program, resulting in earlier completion.

    A module should not be chosen arbitrarily. It is not just "a chunk of a program." A module is a well-defined unit of the entire program. It should serve its own function. The combination of modules builds the organization of the entire program.

    Fortunately, BASIC facilitates modular programming through the subroutines. The following program shows the technique of using a subroutine as a module in BASIC. This program is in its simplest form to show the concept.

Example 9.12

Problem: Write an interactive program that accepts a series of numbers between 0 to 99.99 and prints (1) the data, (2) the mean and the variance, and (3) a histogram. The histogram should show the occurrence of each number in intervals of 0^+ to 10, 10^+ to 20, 20^+ to 30, 30^+ to 40, 40^+ to 50, 50^+ to 60, 60^+ to 70, 70^+ to 80, 80^+ to 90, and 90^+ to 99.99.

Solution Procedure: The problem is broken down into five modules, and each module is performed by a subroutine. The main module defines array A with 100 elements to hold the data and array COUNT with 10 elements to count the occurrences in each interval. The main module then transfers control to the modules consecutively. The modules are shown in the hierarchy chart in Figure 9.2. A brief description of the algorithms used in each module follows:

1. Housekeeping module
    Initialize the variables.
2. Data input module
    Accept the number of data N (should be less than 100).
    Accept the data.
3. Calculation module
    Compute the sum and sum of square of data by the formula
    SUM = accumulate the data
    SSS = accumulate the sum of the square of each number
    Compute the mean and then the variance by the formula
    MEAN = SUM/N
    VAR = SSS/N - MEAN*MEAN
4. Printing module
    Print the data.
    Print the mean and the variance.
    Pause until the user is ready.
5. Histogram module
    Find the occurrences in the Kth interval by
    K = integer of (each number/10) + 1
    Count the occurrences in one of the elements of array COUNT by
    COUNT(K) = COUNT(K) + 1
    Print the histogram.

Program:
```
5    REM ************ THE MAIN MODULE *************
10   DIM A(100), COUNT (10)
```

382 *Subprograms*

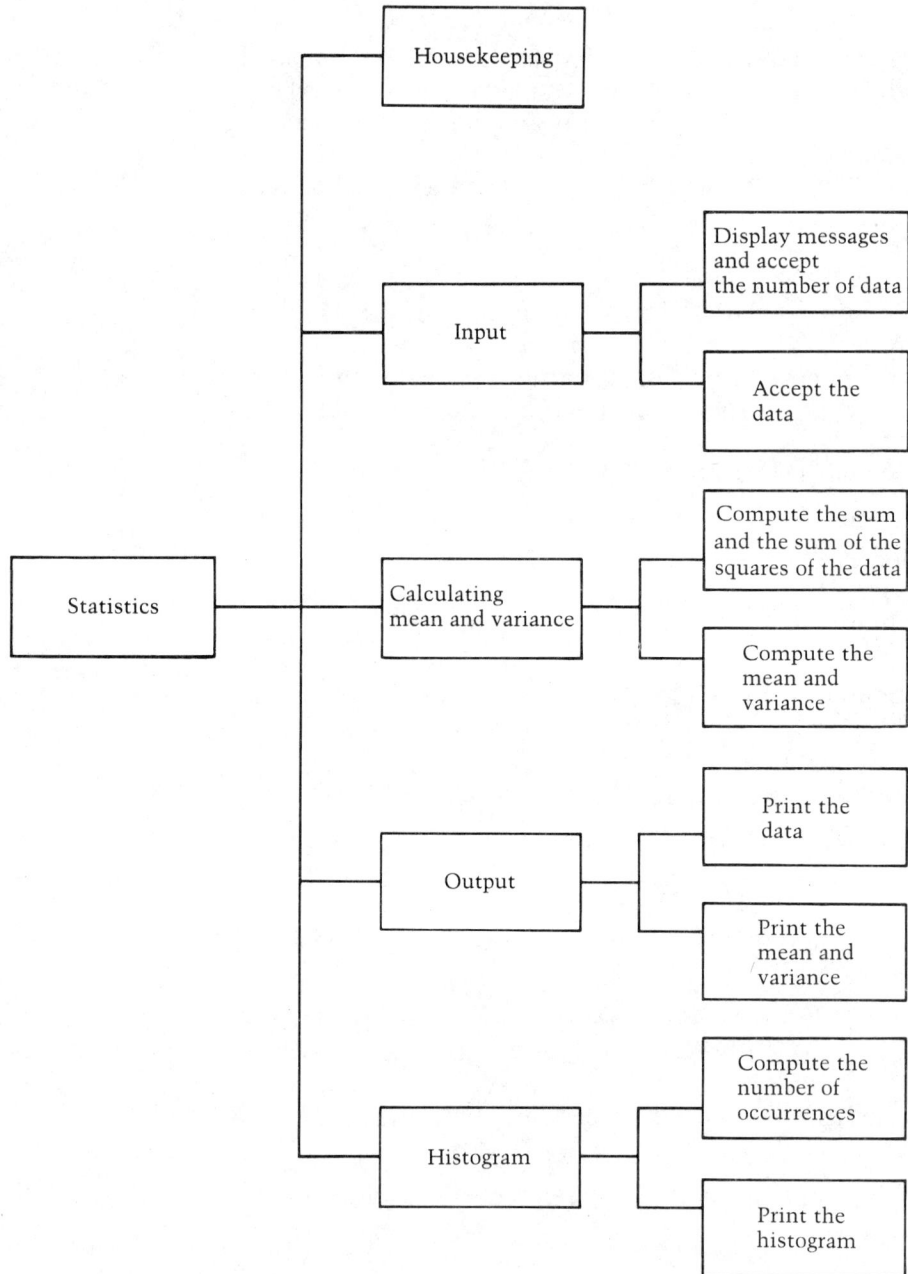

Figure 9.2 The hierarchy chart for Example 9.12

```
15   REM ***   HOUSEKEEPING MODULE ***
20      GOSUB 100
25   REM ****  DATA INPUT MODULE ****
30      GOSUB 200
35   REM *** CALCULATION MODULE (MEAN AND VARIANCE)   ***
40      GOSUB 300
45   REM *** PRINTING MODULE ***
50      GOSUB 400
55   REM *** HISTOGRAM MODULE ***
60      GOSUB 500
65   REM******   END OF THE MAIN MODULE   ***************
70   PRINT "***~~~~~~ BYE ~~~~~ SEE YOU SOON ~~~~~***"
80   GOTO 999
90   REM ************* THE SUBROUTINE SECTION *****************
100  REM ******** THIS SUBROUTINE IS A HOUSEKEEPING MODULE **
110  REM INITIALIZE ARRAY COUNT TO ZERO
120     FOR I = 1 TO 10
130        COUNT (I) = 0
140     NEXT I
150  RETURN
160  REM *** END OF HOUSEKEEPING SUBROUTINE ***
200  REM ************ THIS SUBROUTINE ACCEPTS THE DATA ******
205     PRINT "THIS PROGRAM CALCULATES THE MEAN AND VARIANCE OF A "
210     PRINT "SET OF NUMBERS BETWEEN 1 TO 99.9. IT ALSO PRINTS A "
215     PRINT "  HISTOGRAM OF OCCURRENCES IN INTERVALS OF 10"
220     PRINT "HOW MANY NUMBERS DO YOU HAVE"
225     INPUT N
230      IF N > 100 THEN PRINT "SORRY I CAN HANDLE ONLY 100 OF
235      IF N > 100 THEN N = 100
240     PRINT "TYPE THE NUMBERS, ONE PER LINE"
245     FOR I = 1 TO N
250        INPUT A (I)
255     NEXT I
260  RETURN
270  REM *** END OF INPUT SUBROUTINE ***
300  REM ***** THIS SUBROUTINE CALCULATES THE MEAN AND VARIANCE
310     SSS = 0           :           X = 0
320     FOR J = 1 TO N
330        X = X + A(J)
340        SSS = SSS + A(J)*A (J)
350     NEXT J
360     MEAN = X/N
370     VAR = SSS/N - MEAN*MEAN
380  RETURN
390  REM *** END OF CALCULATION SUBROUTINE ***
400  REM ********* THIS SUBROUTINE PRINTS THE INFORMATION ***
410     PRINT "THE DATA ARE:"
420     FOR I = 1 TO N    :      PRINT A(I);    :       NEXT I
430     PRINT "    THE MEAN IS : "; MEAN
440     PRINT "THE VARIANCE IS: "; VAR
450     PRINT "ARE YOU READY"       :       INPUT X$
460  RETURN
470  REM *** END OF PRINTING SUBROUTINE ***
500  REM ********* THIS SUBROUTINE PRINTS THE HISTOGRAM *****
505     REM COUNT THE OCCURRENCE OF EACH NUMBER:
510     FOR I = 1 TO N
515        K = INT(A(I)/10) + 1
520        COUNT(K) = COUNT(K) + 1
525     NEXT I
```

```
530      PRINT "     THIS IS THE HISTOGRAM OF YOUR DATA"
535      PRINT "AN * SHOWS AN OCCURRENCE IN THE SHOWN INTERVAL"
540 REM PRINT AN * FOR EACH OCCURRENCE OF A NUMBER
545      PRINT 0
550      FOR I = 1 TO 10
555         UP = COUNT(I)
560         PRINT TAB(7)
565         FOR J = 1 TO UP
570            PRINT "*";
575         NEXT J
580         PRINT
585         PRINT I*10
590      NEXT I
595      INPUT "ARE YOU THROUGH WITH THE HISTOGRAM"; X$
600 RETURN
605 REM *** END OF HISTOGRAM SUBROUTINE ***
999 END
```

Notes:

1. Explanations of some program lines are as follows:

Lines	Explanation
225–240	If the number of data is more than 100, the program accepts only 100 of them. This part should be modified to announce that only 100 numbers are accepted, or the DIM A(100) statement in line 10 should be changed accordingly.
450 and 595	These input statements interrupt execution temporarily and give the user a chance to read the entire screen. Note that the program continues no matter what key the user presses, as long as ENTER is pressed afterwards. The line can be modified so that pressing ENTER is not necessary (see Chapter 6).
515	This line calculates in which interval (K) the i th datum belongs. For example, if the i th datum is 64, then K = INT(6.4) + 1, or K = 7.
545	This line prints a zero as the lower boundary of the first interval.
585	This line prints the upper boundary of each interval.

2. The program can be modified to accept a new set of data if the user desires.

3. The program can be designed differently. One possible change is to make the program start with a menu, such as:

```
THIS PROGRAM DISPLAYS STATISTICS ABOUT A
SET OF DATA. WHAT DO YOU WANT ME TO DO?
1. ACCEPT THE DATA (A NEW SET OF DATA)
2. DISPLAY THE DATA
3. DISPLAY THE MEAN AND VARIANCE
4. DISPLAY THE HISTOGRAM
5. EXIT FROM THE PROGRAM
PLEASE TYPE 1, 2, 3, 4, OR 5
?
```

EXERCISES

Subroutines:

9.1 Identify any errors in the following statements or subprograms:

  a. `100  GOTO SUBROUTINE 500`
  b. `10   CALL SUBROUTINE`
  c. `50   GOTO SUB 300`
  d. `50   GOSUB 500`

```
        ⋮
500 X = 3*Y
510 IF X > 59 THEN Y = 3
520 STOP
530 END
```

  e.
```
        ⋮
40  GOSUB 310
        ⋮
310 Q = 3 * P
320 END
```

Library Functions:

9.2 Check the list of the library functions for your system and write a statement or program segment to:

  a. Calculate $A = \sqrt{(X + Y)}$.

b. Calculate $Y = e^x$.
c. Calculate x_1 and x_2 with the formula

$$x_1, x_2 = \frac{-b \pm \sqrt{b^2 - 4ac}}{2a}$$

d. Calculate log x.
e. Calculate $\log_e A$.
f. Calculate the integer of SCORE/10.
g. Calculate the absolute value of P - Q.
h. Find the sign of P = 3*Q^A.
i. Find the remainder of X divided by Y.
j. Print the integer part of real number X.
k. Round off a number to two decimal places.
l. Round off a number to three decimal places.
m. Find the length of ANAME$ = "JOHN".
n. Print the current date.
o. Print the time.
p. Generate and print 100 random numbers between 0 and 1.

Function Statement:

9.3 Identify the errors in the following function statements:
   a. `10   DEF FF(A, B(2)) = 5*A + 6*B(2)`
   b. `100  FORMULA(X, Y) = SQRT (X^2 - 4*Y*C)`
   c. `150  DEF GEE(P, 5) = 5*P + P^5`
   d. `50   DEF RO(K, G + A) = 2*K + 5*(G + A)`
   e. `100  DEF GAMA(A, B) = B^2 + A + X + GAMA (X, Y)`
   f. `DEF (X, Y) = E*X + Y`

9.4 Identify all the errors in the general form of the following function statements:
   a. `10   DEF FNFUN(A, B, I) = I*A + B`
       ⋮
       `50   X = F(X%, Y%, 2)`
       ⋮
       `100  END`

b.
```
20   DEF FNBETA(F, G, A, B) = F*G + A*B
       ⋮
50   Y = BETA(X, Y)
       ⋮
100  END
```
c.
```
10   DEF FNF(Z, B) = A*B + A + B + FNGE (A,B)
20   DEF FNGE(X, Y) = 3.0*X^2 + Y
       ⋮
50   P = FNF(X, Y)
       ⋮
100  END
```
d.
```
10   DEF FNPAGE(FIX, Z) = FIX^5 + FIX + Z
       ⋮
50   EX = FNPAGE(A$, B$)
       ⋮
100  END
```
e.
```
10   DEF FNPA(X, Y) = 2.0*X^3 + Y
       ⋮
50   X = FNPA(A, B)
100  PRINT FNPA
       ⋮
150  END
```

9.5 What is the value of X in each of the following program segments?

a.
```
10   DEF FNF(XX, YY) = XX + YY
       ⋮
50   X = FNF(5, 6)
       ⋮
100  END
```

b.
```
10    DEF  FNG(A, B)  =  A*B + C
       ⋮
110   Y = 2
120   C = 5
130   X = FNG(Y, 3)
       ⋮
500   END
```

c.
```
50    DEF  FNFUNCT(I, P, Q)  =  P^I + Q
       ⋮
90    J = 2
100   AKE = 3
110   B = 2
120   X = FNFUNCT(J, B, AKE)
       ⋮
999   END
```

d.
```
100   DEF  FNFUN1(A)  =  A + 3 + Y
110   DEF  FNFUN2(B)  =  B + FNFUN1(B)
       ⋮
250   Y = 2
260   C = 3
270   X = FNFUN2(C)
       ⋮
999   END
```

Programming Exercises:

Write a complete program for each of the following problems:

9.6 Write a program that reads the employee name, ID number, hourly rate, and number of hours worked during a week for 100 employees. Calculate the pay (hours over 40 are paid at 1.5 times the regular rate), deductions, and net pay for each employee. The deduction is 15 percent of the gross pay. Use a subroutine to calculate the pay. Print the information.

9.7 Write a subroutine that prints END OF THE REPORT and stops execution when invoked.

9.8 Write a program that reads N elements of array ZIP. Array ZIP can have up to 500 elements. Calculate the sum of N elements in a subroutine. Print the array and the sum.

9.9 One-dimensional arrays A, B, and C can each contain up to 100 elements. Write a program that uses a subroutine to read N values of array A. Use another subroutine to read M values of array B. M and N are to be read from two header values. Calculate array C so that $C_i = A_i - B_i$ in another subroutine. Assume N is larger than M; thus array C will have N values, where the remaining values of array B, up to N, are zeros. Write the values of the arrays with a fourth subroutine.

9.10 Write an interactive program that accepts a salesperson's ID number and three sales amounts in an array. The array should accommodate several salespeople. Prepare a sales report as follows:
   a. Calculate the total sales for each salesperson.
   b. Find the largest sale of each salesperson.
   c. Calculate the total sales of all salespeople and the average sales.
   d. Print the sales, the total sales, and the largest sale of each salesperson in report form.
   e. Print the total sales at the end of the report.
   f. Print the individual sales that are larger than the average of all sales.

   Use a subprogram for each module of the program.

9.11 Write a subroutine that finds the smallest value among a set of data stored in array AMT. Array AMT has 200 elements.

9.12 Write a subroutine that finds the largest value among a set of data stored in array BET. Assume array BET has a maximum of 100 elements but only N elements (N<100) are read and stored.

9.13 Write an interactive program that accepts a set of data between 1 and 15, counts the occurrence of each number, prints a histogram, and prints the mode (the mode is the number with the highest occurrence).

9.14 Assume array ART contains N values (N<100). Write a subroutine that inserts the value of D into the Kth element of array ART while maintaining the existing data in the same order.

9.15 Write a subroutine that interchanges the values of two variables, X and Y.

9.16 Write an interactive program that reads an integer M and prints all the divisors of M. (*Hint:* use a subroutine to find whether or not the remainder of M divided by 1, 2, 3, . . . , M is equal to zero.)

9.17 A prime number is a number that has no divisors except 1 and itself. For example, 3, 5, 7, 19, 39 are prime numbers, but 21 is not because it is divisible by 7 and 3. To find out if a number (N) is prime, we must check to see whether it is divisible by 2, 3, 4, ... up to $\sqrt{N}$. Develop a program that according to a menu (a) accepts a number and prints a message saying whether or not it is a prime number (use a subroutine for checking), and (b) accepts a number M and prints the prime numbers up to M.

9.18 Suppose x, y, z can be calculated by the following formulas:

$$x = \log_{10} a + \log_e a$$
$$y = 3a^2 + 4a - 3$$
$$z = ae^{3a + 2}$$

Write an interactive program that reads a and prints the values of X, Y, and Z. Use a function statement for any of the formulas.

9.19 Area of a triangle can be calculated by

$$\text{Area} = \sqrt{s(s-a)(s-b)(s-c)}$$

where

$$s = 1/2 \, (a + b + c)$$

and a, b, and c are the sides.

Write an interactive program that accepts the sides of a triangle and calculates the area. (Use two function statements.)

9.20 Write an interactive program to calculate kinetic energy t

$$t = 1/2mv^2$$

where m (mass) and v (velocity) are accepted as input. (Use a function statement.)

9.21 Write a subprogram that calculates the factorial of a given number (N). (Factorial N is N! = 1 × 2 × 3 × 4 × 5 × 6 ... x N.)

9.22 The number of combinations (C) of N items, when M of the items are taken at a time, can be calculated by

$$C = \frac{N!}{M!(N-M)!}$$

Write an interactive program that accepts M and N and calculates and prints C. Use a subroutine to calculate the factorial.

9.23 Write a program that reads a positive number (N) and calculates

$$X = \frac{1}{1^2} + \frac{3}{2^2} + \frac{5}{3^2} + \ldots \frac{2N-1}{N^2}$$

in a subroutine.

9.24 Write an interactive program that reads a real number (X) and an integer N, then calculates

$$\text{EXPOX} = 1 + X + \frac{X^2}{2!} + \frac{X^3}{3!} + \ldots + \frac{X^N}{N!}$$

in a subroutine. The program should print X, N, and EXPOX.

9.25 Write a program for printing a weekly salary report as follows:
Input
Name, ID number, hours worked during the week, department code (1 to 5), and wage code (1 to 3) for each employee.
Processing

a. Hours over 40 are paid at 1.5 times the regular rate, and the wage rate table is as follows:

Department Code	Wage Code 1	Wage Code 2	Wage Code 3
1	5.85	6.45	5.9
2	6.55	7.30	6.90
3	7.60	8.70	8.05
4	8.90	9.95	9.10
5	10.50	11.50	10.50

Calculate the pay in a subroutine. (Use the table look-up concept rather than several IF statements.)

b. The deduction is calculated as follows:

Pay	Deduction
0 to $100	2%
$100 to $200	5%
over $200	9%

Calculate the deductions in a function.
Output:

a. Write the input information as well as the gross pay, deduction, and the net pay for each employee in a report form. Use a subroutine. Also print the total pay, total deductions, and total net pay at the end of the report.

b. Prepare five reports similar to the report in a, above, for each department.

There are fewer than 100 employees, and the first value is a header value.

9.26 Consumer Electric Company would like a report about their customers' electricity consumption during a given period. The requirements and information are as follows:

Input:
a. Customer name
b. Customer account number
c. Date of the last bill (for example, 12/10/85)
d. Last month's balance
e. Payment
f. Last meter reading in KWH
g. Current meter reading in KWH
h. Code for industrial, residential, and farm usage: I, R, or F

Processing:
a. Use is calculated as

$$U = \text{Current meter reading} - \text{last meter reading}$$

b. Residential customers are charged a flat fee of $6.50 and a rate based on the following table:

Use	Rate
0 to 250 KWH	$.0589 per KWH
250 to 400 KWH	$.0659 per KWH
over 400 KWH	$.0789 per KWH

c. Industrial customers are charged a flat fee of $19.50 and a rate based on the following table:

Use	Rate
0 to 500 KWH	$.0618 per KWH
over 500 KWH	$.0700 per KWH

d. Farm use is calculated by the formula

$$\text{AMOUNT} = U \times .0685 + \frac{U + 55}{1000} + \frac{U + 25}{U}$$

where U is the electric use.

e. The amount due is calculated as current charges plus last month's balance minus the payment.

Output: Write a complete program that reads the input information and calculates:
a. Use by each customer. (Use a function.)
b. Charge to each residential user. (Use a subroutine.)

c. Charge to each industrial user. (Use a subroutine.)
   d. Total charge to each farm user. (Use a function.)
   e. Amount due for each user.
   f. Total use and the total use by each kind of user.

   Print the input information and the charges in a report form. There are fewer than 100 customers. The first data value is a header value showing the number of customers. Also print the date at the top of the report.

SUMMARY

You have learned:

1. Subprograms allow us to invoke one or more instructions whenever we wish to execute them. The use of subprograms facilitates the modular program writing and also avoids the necessity of repeating a sequence of instructions several times in a program. Subprograms in BASIC are of two types: subroutines and functions.
2. A subroutine is a program unit or program segment that can be invoked when necessary. There are two types of subroutines: internal subroutines and external subroutines.
   a. An internal subroutine is a program unit invoked by the GOSUB n statement. The RETURN statement ending a subroutine transfers control back to the referencing unit.
   b. An external subroutine is a complete and independent program executed when its name is invoked in a CHAIN statement. Communication between the variables in the referencing program and the external subroutine is through a separate file or through a "common core area."
3. A function is a subprogram invoked by the use of its name in a statement. There are two kinds of functions: library functions and function statements.
   a. Library functions are defined by the system. The following are examples of using library functions:

   ```
   50   IY% = INT(Y)
   100  Q = SQR(ABS(A - B))
   ```

   b. A function statement is a segment, normally a single statement, defined by a DEF statement at the beginning of a program unit in order to evaluate an expression.

REVIEW QUESTIONS/SELF-TEST

9.1 Which of the following statements is syntactically correct?
    a. `100 GOTO SUB 300`
    b. `100 GO SUBROUTINE 300`
    c. `20  GOSUB MEAN`
    d. `50  GOSUB 50`
    e. none of the above

9.2 Which of the following subroutines is logically correct?
    a.
```
100 GOSUB 200
     ⋮
200 P = 3*Q
210 END
```
    b.
```
50  GOSUB 100
     ⋮
100 IF A = 1 GOTO 120
110 GOTO 50
120 END
```
    c. none of the above

9.3 Write a statement using a library function to round off a number to four decimal places.

9.4 What is the value of X in the following program?
```
10   DEF FNF(A) = P*A + 1
20   P = 3
30   C = P
40   X = FNF(C + 2)
      ⋮
100  END
```

9.5 Write an interactive program that prints a simple customer invoice. Assume there are fewer than 20 items. The number of items ordered and the in-state customers code should initially be accepted. The information and requirements are as follows:

Input: The item number, the quantity ordered, the unit price, and a code for in-state customers.

Processing requirements
    a. The amount ordered equals price times quantity. Use a subroutine.

b. The tax is 4 percent of the amount for in-state customers only. Use a function.

c. The total amount ordered (the total charges).

Output: The input information and the amount for each item. Also print the totals at the end.

Answers:

9.1 e

9.2 c

9.3 X = (INT(A * 10000 + .5))/10000

9.4 16

9.5
```
10   DIM ID(20), ORD(20), PRICE(20), AMT(20)
20   DEF FNTAX (Y) = Y*.04
30   PRINT 'THIS PROGRAM PRINTS A SIMPLE INVOICE FOR A CUSTOMER.'
40   PRINT 'TYPE THE NAME OF THE CUSTOMER, AND THEN TYPE YES, '
45   PRINT 'IF THE CUSTOMER IS AN IN STATE CUSTOMER'
50   INPUT ANAME$, STATE$
60   PRINT 'TYPE IN THE NUMBER OF ITEMS ORDERED'
70   INPUT N
80   PRINT 'TYPE ITEM #, NO. OF UNITS, AND PRICE FOR '; N
90   PRINT 'ITEMS, EACH SEPARATED BY A COMMA.'
100  FOR J = 1 TO N
110     INPUT ID(J), ORD(J), PRICE(J)
120  NEXT J
130  REM TOTAL AMOUNT AND TAX IS CALCULATED BY A SUBROUTINE
140  GOSUB 300
150  REM PRINTING INFORMATION
160  PRINT TAB(20); 'XYZ STORE'
170  PRINT TAB(10); 'CUSTOMER'S NAME:'; ANAME$
180  PRINT
200  PRINT' ORDER#', 'UNITS', 'PRICE', 'AMOUNT'
210  FOR K = 1 TO N
220     PRINT ID(K), ORD(K), PRICE(K), AMT(K)
230  NEXT K
240  PRINT 'TOTAL AMOUNT:'; TAB(43); SUMAMT
250  PRINT 'TOTAL TAX:'; TAB(43); TOTTAX
260  PRINT 'TOTAL CHARGES:'; TAB(43); CHARGE
280  GOTO 990
290  REM*********** THE SUBROUTINE SECTION ***************
300  REM THIS SUBROUTINE CALCULATES THE CHARGES
310  SUMAMT = 0
320  FOR J = 1 TO N
330     AMT(J) = ORD(J)*PRICE(J)
340     SUMAMT = SUMAMT + AMT(J)
350  NEXT J
360     TOTTAX = 0
370     IF STATE$ = 'YES' THEN TOTTAX = FNTAX( SUMAMT )
380     CHARGE = SUMAMT + TOTTAX
390  RETURN
990  PRINT '************ CALL BACK *******************'
999  END
```

Problem Solving, Programming Techniques, and Some Applications

10

In This Chapter:

Data Processing
Sorting
Searching
Merging

Statistics
Median
Summation Notation
Regression Analysis

Graphing Techniques
Plotting a Function
Graphing a Histogram

Simulation
Random Numbers
Generating Random Numbers
Monte Carlo Simulation

Games

Management Information and Decision Support Systems

Exercises

Summary

Review Questions/Self-Test

10

Problem Solving, Programming Techniques, and Some Applications

As you read in Chapter 3, a computer program is merely a tool for solving problems. Before you begin to write any code, you need to make a thorough analysis of the problem and develop an appropriate solution procedure—an algorithm. In the previous chapters, most of the solution procedures have been straightforward. However, this is not always the case. Developing an algorithm is of itself an art. Throughout this chapter, you will see examples of algorithms that are not so simple.

In Chapter 3, algorithm was defined as a detailed, step-by-step set of solution procedures suitable for computer programming. Definitions of algorithm, however, can be more complex and theoretical. To avoid philosophical discussion about the theory of algorithms, we will continue to use the phrase *solution plan*, or simply *plan*, interchangeably with algorithm throughout this chapter.

Examples of algorithms and programs for specific applications in data processing, statistics, graphing, simulation, games, and management information systems are presented in the following sections. The examples are deliberately designed to be simple. Understanding these simplified examples will help you develop your own algorithms for more complicated problems.

Please note that knowledge of the subject matter of each application is necessary to understand the algorithm presented for that application. Explaining each subject in detail is beyond the scope of this text. Therefore, if you are not already familiar with the subject matter of one of the following applications, you may skip the section.

DATA PROCESSING

One difference between data processing and scientific computation is that several files are normally involved in data processing. For example, a payroll system may involve a master file (containing permanent information, such as names, Social Security numbers, and so on), a transaction file (containing temporary information, such as the number of hours worked by employees), and other files, (such as table files for wage tables and tax tables). Often, these files must be sorted, searched, merged, updated, and processed. In this section, simple examples of certain techniques for sorting, merging, and updating the files are presented. These examples use arrays. However, updating, merging, or searching can also be accomplished without arrays. File processing is discussed in detail in Chapter 11.

Sorting

Sorting is the process of arranging unordered items (or records) in a list in some predetermined order. The main advantage of a sorted list is that it allows rapid retrieval of a particular item. For example, finding the name of a person in a sorted telephone directory is much faster than finding it in an unsorted directory. If each record in a file contains several items, we can sort the file by only one of the items. In this section, we demonstrate the process of sorting with records consisting of only one item.

There are several sorting techniques. One common and straightforward method is the *bubble sort.* This is the basic idea behind the bubble sort procedure: during the first round of comparisons, two contiguous elements are compared, one pair at a time, and interchanged if the second element in the pair is smaller than the first (given, of course, that the elements are to be sorted in ascending order). Thus, during the first round of comparisons, the largest element goes to the bottom of the list. This can be accomplished by a loop such as

```
100 FOR K = 1 TO N-1
       IF A(K) > A(K+1); interchange A(K) and A(K+1)
200 NEXT K
```

(N-1 is used rather than N because A(K+1) will cause the last element to be taken into account.) Then, a second round of comparisons is made. However, there is no need to go to the last item in the list during the second round because the largest element is already last. This process is repeated during the third round, fourth round, and so on (see Figure 10.1). The following example illustrates the procedure and the program:

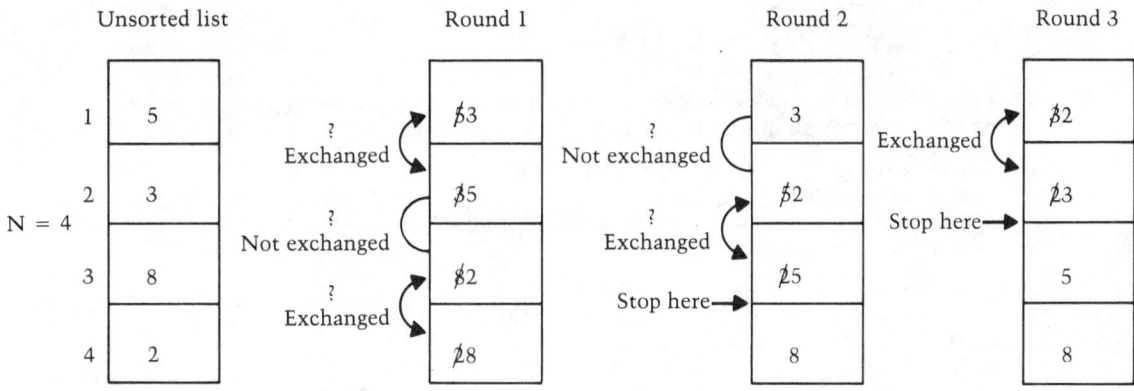

Figure 10.1 A bubble sort

Example 10.1

Problem: Develop a bubble sort plan and write an interactive program that accepts a set of data and sorts the data in ascending order.

Solution Plan:

1. Read the number of data, N.
2. Read the data into array A.
3. Begin the loop, FOR I = 1 TO N-1, repeat:
    3.1 Find the last item to be compared: LAST = N - I.
    3.2 FOR K=1 TO K=LAST, repeat:
         IF A(K) > A(K+1), then interchange the values of A(K) and A(K+1).
    3.3 Next K
4. End the loop, Next I
5. Print the sorted data.

Program:

```
10   DIM A(100)
20   PRINT "THIS PROGRAM SORTS A LIST CONTAINING UP TO 100 NUMBERS"
30   PRINT "TYPE HOW MANY DATA ITEMS DO YOU HAVE"
40   INPUT N
45   PRINT "TYPE YOUR DATA, ONE PER LINE"
50   FOR I = 1 TO N   :   INPUT A(I)   :   NEXT I
55   REM ----------   BEGIN THE SORT PROCEDURE   -----------
60   FOR I = 1 TO N - 1
65     LAST = N - I
70     FOR K = 1 TO LAST
80       IF A(K) > A(K+1) THEN GOSUB 200
90     NEXT K
100  NEXT I
105  REM --------------- END THE SORT -------------------
110  PRINT "SORTED LIST:"
120  FOR M = 1 TO N
130    PRINT A(M);
140  NEXT M
150  PRINT
160  PRINT "****** SEE YOU SOON ********"
170  GOTO 999
200  REM ------------------SUBROUTINE SECTION -------------
205  REM ----- THIS SUBROUTINE INTERCHANGES THE VALUE OF -
210  REM --------------- A PAIR OF ELEMENTS --------------
220    TEMP = A(K)
230    A(K) = A(K+1)
240    A(K+1) = TEMP
250  RETURN
260  REM --------- END OF INTERCHANGE SUBROUTINE ---------
999  END
```

The program in Example 10.1 sorts the list in ascending order. To sort a list in descending order, you must change the IF statement to

```
80 IF A(K) < A(K+1) GOSUB 200
```

It is obvious how numbers can be compared to determine their order. But how about character data? As you know, character data are represented in the computer by numeric codes, and the codes are assigned sequentially to the alphabet. Thus, to create an alphabetical list, you can use the same procedure you use to sort a numeric list.

The bubble sort is easy to understand but generally not very efficient. However, many improvements are possible. For example, one of the disadvantages of the program in Example 10.1 is that the computer must go through the list N-1 times, checking contiguous pairs each time even if the list is already sorted or partially sorted. The program can be improved by including a statement that terminates the loop when no interchange takes place during a particular round.

Many other sorting procedures have been proposed. The following are examples:

1. Start by sorting only two items. Then place the third item in its proper position, then the fourth item, and so on.
2. Start by sorting the first pair, then the second pair, then the third pair, and so on. After sorting the pairs, merge each of two pairs to form several properly sorted tetrads (groups of four). The pairs of tetrads are then merged to form several properly sorted octads (groups of eight). This process continues until the entire list is sorted. This method, called the *merge-sort method*, is especially efficient for large amounts of data.

The procedure for sorting a list that has more than one item per line (record) depends on the algorithm used. A simple approach is to use one of the previously mentioned methods but, when exchanging contiguous elements, also to exchange the other corresponding pairs in the list. This method can be applied easily to a list with two items per record but is cumbersome for sorting a list that has more than two fields per record.

Another method, called *pointer sort*, works as follows: Create a pointer array, P, whose contents indicate the order of the list. At the beginning, before sorting, P(1)=1, P(2)=2, P(3)=3, and so on. Then use a sorting algorithm to change the elements of the pointer array so that P(1) "points to" the first element of the sorted list, P(2) points to the second element of the sorted list, and so on. For example, assume you wish to sort the following list by ID number:

ID#	NAME	TEST SCORE
568	JOHN BROWN	94.5
562	PAT BLACK	83.2
565	JAY WHITE	72.5
564	KAY GRAY	89.3

The pointer array at the beginning, before sorting, is

    P(1)=1
    P(2)=2
    P(3)=3
    P(4)=4

After sorting by ID numbers, the contents of array P are

    P(1)=2
    P(2)=4
    P(3)=3
    P(4)=1

Thus, the following loop prints the sorted list:

```
100 FOR K = 1 TO 4
110    PRINT ID(P(K)); NAME$(P(K)); TEST(P(K))
120 NEXT K
```

Searching

Searching is a prerequisite of locating an item in order to retrieve, change, delete, or update it. Of course, if the address (location) of the desired item is known, searching is not necessary, and the information can be retrieved easily. There are several ways to search. Two techniques are explained below.

Sequential Search

In a *sequential search*, each item in the list is examined, one after the other, from the beginning of the list. The following example demonstrates the technique:

Example 10.2

Problem: Assume ID numbers and corresponding names are stored in N elements of arrays ID and ANAME$, respectively. Write a program segment that interactively reads an ID number, searches the array, and prints the corresponding name. If the ID number is not in the list, the program should print a message.

Program Segment:

```
           :
100 PRINT "WHAT IS THE ID#"
110 INPUT XID
200 FOR K = 1 TO N
300    IF ID(K) = XID THEN GOTO 500
400 NEXT K
450 PRINT "THE ID IS NOT IN THE LIST"
460 GOTO 600
500 PRINT "THE NAME IS:"; ANAME$(K)
600 ........................
```

Note: Each item in the array is compared, one by one, against `XID` (see Figure 10.2). This requires `N` comparisons if the item is in the last location, and only one comparison if the item is in the first location, an average of `N/2` comparisons. For example, if `N = 1000`, the average number of comparisons is 500.

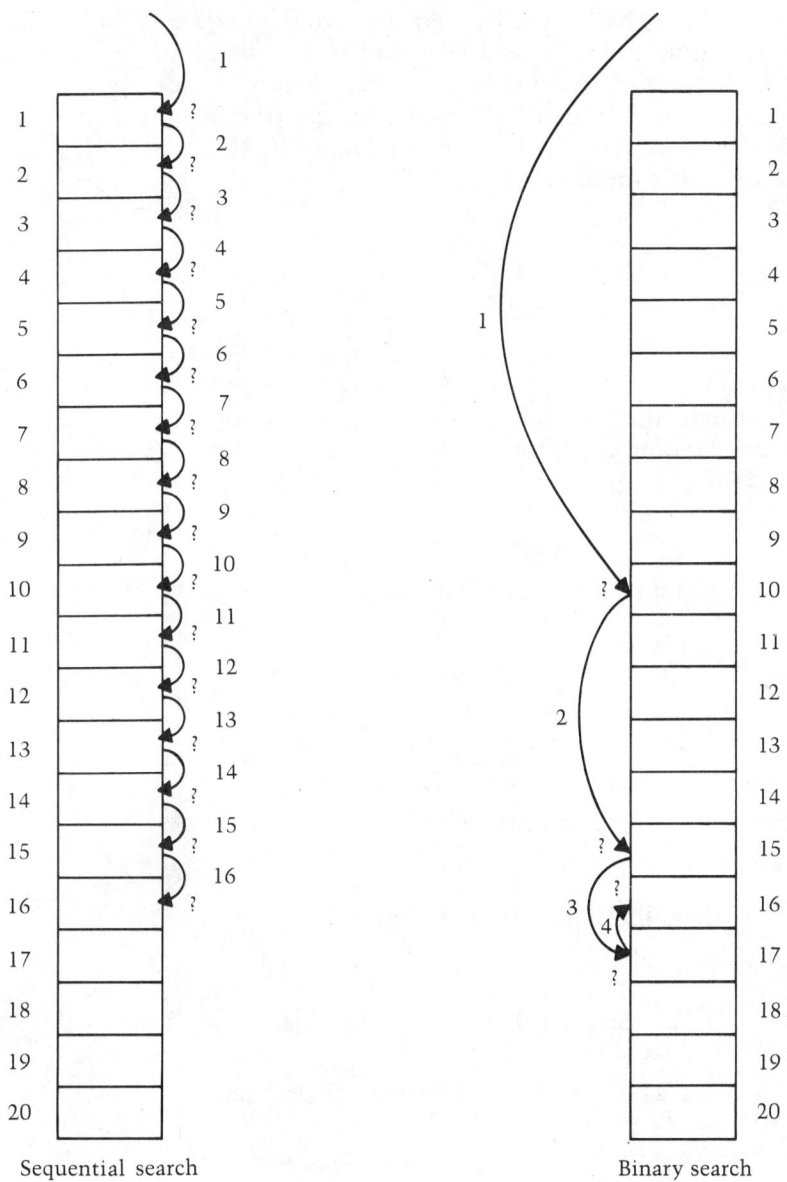

Figure 10.2 Searching for an item

Binary Search

A more efficient searching method, called *binary search*, is applicable to a list that is already sorted. Using this method, the computer starts by examining the item in the middle (or near the middle) of the list. If that item is not the one sought, then it determines whether the item is in the upper half of the list or in the lower half of the list. The item in the middle of the appropriate half is examined next. If that one is not the item sought, the computer determines whether the item is in the upper quarter or the lower quarter, and the search continues in the appropriate quarter. This process is repeated until the desired item is located (see Figure 10.2). The following example illustrates this method further:

Example 10.3

Problem: The same as in Example 10.2: write an interactive program segment that reads an ID number, searches the array, and prints the corresponding name. Assume the information is stored in N elements of arrays ID and ANAME$.

Solution Plan:

1. Make sure the array ID is sorted in ascending order.
2. Read an ID: XID.
3. Set the index of the first and last element to be searched as:
   FIRST = 1
   LAST = N
4. Begin the search and repeat until the item is found:
   4.1 Find K, the location of the item to be searched, with

   K = INT ((FIRST + LAST)/2)

   4.2 If ID(K) = XID then the location = K. Terminate the search.
   Otherwise:
       4.2.1 If ID(K) > XID, then LAST = K (K is the last item searched)
       4.2.2 Otherwise: FIRST = K (K is the first item searched)
5. End the search.

Program Segment:

```
    ⋮
100 INPUT XID
110 FIRST = 1
120 LAST = N
200 REM ----BEGIN THE SEARCH PROCEDURE-------
210 FOR I = 1 TO 500
220    K = INT((FIRST + LAST)/2)
230       IF ID(K) = XID THEN GOTO 500
240 REM    ELSE
250          IF ID(K) > XID THEN  LAST = K  ELSE  FIRST = K
260 REM    END-OF-IF
270 NEXT I
280 REM ----END THE SEARCH --------
500 PRINT "THE NAME IS"; ANAME$(K)
600 ..................
```

Notes: The program has several flaws and can be improved as follows:

1. The algorithm and program should be modified to print a message if XID is not in the list.
2. The program also should be modified for the cases N > 1 and ID(N) = XID (if X is the last item in the list).
3. The loop is repeated 500 times, or until the item is found.

Merging

Merging is the process of combining two lists to create a single list, normally sorted. One simple method of merging two lists is simply to combine the two and then sort them. This process, however, is not efficient. The following example demonstrates a more efficient method of merging two arrays:

Example 10.4

Problem: Develop a solution procedure and a program plan to merge arrays A and B, with N1 and N2 elements, into array C. Assume arrays A and B are already sorted in ascending order.

Solution Procedure:

Compare the first elements of arrays A and B and move the smaller of the two into array C. Continue the comparing and moving the remaining elements of arrays A and B until all the elements of one array are exhausted. Then move all elements remaining in the unexhausted array to C.

Solution Plan:

1. Set M = N1 + N2.
2. Set I1 = 1 (I1 represents a subscript of array A).
3. Set I2 = 1 (I2 represents a subscript of array B).
4. Set I3 = 1 (I3 represents a subscript of array C).
5. Begin the merge loop. Repeat:
    5.1 If A(I1) < B(I2) then do the following:
       5.1.1 C(I3) = A(I1)
       5.1.2 I3 = I3 + 1 (increase the subscript of array C).
       5.1.3 I1 = I1 + 1, (increase the subscript of array A).
       5.1.4 If I1 > N1, then:
            Terminate the merge loop.
            Move the remaining elements of B to C.
            Continue the program (go to Step 7).
       5.1.5 Else continue the merge loop (go to Step 5).
    5.2 Else do the following:
       5.2.1 C(I3) = B(I2)
       5.2.2 I3 = I3 + 1
       5.2.3 I2 = I2 + 1
       5.2.4 If I2 > N2 then:
            Terminate the merge loop.
            Move the remaining elements of A to C.
            Continue the program (go to Step 7).
       5.2.5 Else continue the merge loop (go to Step 5).
6. End the merge loop.
7. Continue the program.

Program Segment:

```
      :
100 M = N1 + N2
110 I1 = 1       :     I2 = 1      :      I3 = 1
200 REM *************** BEGIN THE MERGE LOOP ************
205 FOR TRY = 1 TO 1000
210        IF A(I1) < B(I2) THEN GOTO 250 ELSE GOTO 300
240     REM THEN
250            C(I3) = A(I1)
260            I1 = I1 + 1   :    I3 = I3 + 1
280            IF I1 > N1 THEN GOTO 400 ELSE GOTO 350
290     REM ELSE
300            C(I3) = B(I2)
310            I2 = I2 + 1   :    I3 = I3 + 1
330            IF I2 > N2 THEN GOTO 500 ELSE GOTO 350
340     REM END-OF-IF
350 NEXT TRY
360 REM *************** END THE MERGE LOOP ************
400     FOR J = I3 TO M
410        C(J) = B(I2)
420        I2 = I2 + 1
430     NEXT J
440 GOTO 700
500     FOR K = I3 TO M
510        C(K) = A(I1)
520        I1 = I1 + 1
530     NEXT K
700 . . .
```

STATISTICS

Statistics is concerned with collecting, summarizing, and analyzing data and then making inferences. Statistical analysis usually requires many data and is thus well-suited for computer applications. Programs that calculate the mean, variance, and standard deviation are examples of statistical applications. You have seen programs of this type in previous chapters. Programs that find the median and estimate the regression coefficients are presented in this section as further examples of the statistical applications.

Median

The *median* is a value that designates the middle point in a series of ordered values. The median refers to the middle value, where half of the data are greater than the median, and half are smaller. For example, if students' test scores are 99, 95, 92, 90, 85, 75, 70, the class median is 90.

The median can be found as follows:

1. The data must be sorted.
2. If N, the number of data, is odd, the median is the kth datum, where $k = (N + 1)/2$. If N is even, the median is the arithmetic average of the two data in the middle. That is, the median equals $(X_k + X_{k+1})/2$, where $k = N/2$. For example, if there are six test scores—95, 92, 90, 85, 80, 70—the median equals $(90 + 85)/2$.

The following example demonstrates how to write a program that finds the median:

Example 10.5

Problem: Write a subroutine that calculates the median of N observations stored in array A. Assume array A is sorted.

Subroutine:
```
100 REM*THIS SUBROUTINE CALCULATES THE MEDIAN *
110 R = (INT(N/2))*2 - N
120     IF R = 0 THEN GOTO 200 ELSE GOTO 300
200 REM THEN (THE NUMBER OF DATA IS EVEN)
210         K = N/2
220           MEDIAN = (A(K) + A(K+1))/2
230         GOTO 400
300 REM ELSE (THE NUMBER OF DATA IS ODD)
310         K=(N+1)/2
320           MEDIAN = A(K)
330 REM END-OF-IF
400 RETURN
```

Summation Notation

Before we discuss regression analysis, we will explain the summation symbol. The Greek letter sigma (Σ) is often used to denote the addition of a series of variables. For example, $\sum_{i=1}^{n} X_i$ is defined as

$$\sum_{i=1}^{n} X_i = X_1 + X_2 + X_3 + \ldots + X_n$$

where $i = 1$ shows the initial value of the subscript and n shows the final value. The following are further examples:

$$\sum_{i=1}^{n} X_i^2 = X_1^2 + X_2^2 + X_3^2 + X_4^2 + \ldots + X_n^2$$

$$\sum_{i=1}^{5} (Y_i - 3)^2 = (Y_1 - 3)^2 + (Y_2 - 3)^2 + (Y_3 - 3)^2 + (Y_4 - 3)^2 + (Y_5 - 3)^2$$

$$\sum_{i=1}^{5} X_i Y_i = X_1 Y_1 + X_2 Y_2 + X_3 Y_3 + X_4 Y_4 + X_5 Y_5$$

The summation notation can be translated into a BASIC program segment easily by a FOR loop. For example,

$$S = \sum_{i=1}^{n} A_i = A_1 + A_2 + A_3 + \ldots + A_n$$

can be performed by

```
100 S = 0
110 FOR I = 1 TO N
120     S = S + A(I)
130 NEXT I
```

Regression Analysis

Regression analysis is the methodology that investigates the relation between factors or variables. The purpose of regression analysis is to predict the value of a variable from known values of other variables. The prediction is made through a regression equation. The regression equation can be found by fitting a line to a set of data or observations (see Figure 10.3).

The general form of a regression equation with only one independent variable is

$$y = b + mx$$

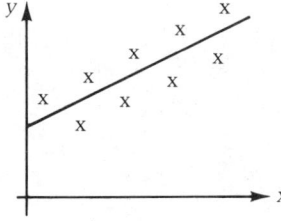

Figure 10.3 A regression line

A common technique for finding the values of b and m is the method of *least squares*. The method is based on the concept of minimizing the sum of the squares of the distances between the data points and the value of y in the equation. The two following formulas use the least squares method to estimate m and b:

$$m = \frac{\sum X_i Y_i - N \times XBAR \times YBAR}{\sum X_i^2 - N \times (XBAR)^2}$$

$$b = YBAR - m \times XBAR$$

XBAR is the mean (or average) of the X data, YBAR is the mean of the Y data, and N is number of data. We use these formulas to calculate the regression coefficients in the following example:

Example 10.6

Problem: Write an interactive program that accepts N pairs of observation for X and Y. Calculate the estimated regression coefficients B and M for the data, using the least squares method. There are fewer than 50 pairs of observations. The first value is a header value.

Program:

```
10   DIM X(50), Y(50)
20   A1SUMX = 0   :   A2SUMY = 0   :   A3SUMXY = 0   : .A4SUMXX = 0
30   PRINT 'THIS PROGRAM FINDS THE ESTIMATED SIMPLE '
35   PRINT '     REGRESSION COEFFICIENTS'
40   PRINT 'HOW MANY PAIRS OF DATA ARE AVAILABLE'
50   INPUT N
60   PRINT'TYPE THE DATA: X AND Y,RESPECTIVELY; ONE PAIR PER LINE'
70   FOR I = 1 TO N
80       INPUT X(I), Y(I)
90   NEXT I
100  FOR J = 1 TO N
110      A1SUMX = A1SUMX + X(J)
120      A2SUMY = A2SUMY + Y(J)
130      A3SUMXY = A3SUMXY + X(J)*Y(J)
140      A4SUMXX = A4SUMXX + X(J)*X(J)
150  NEXT J
160  XBAR = A1SUMX/N
170  YBAR = A2SUMY/N
180  M = (A3SUMXY - N*XBAR*YBAR)/(A4SUMXX - N*XBAR*XBAR)
190  B = YBAR - M*XBAR
200  PRINT 'FOR THE DATA:'
210  PRINT '   X',  'Y'
300  FOR K = 1 TO N
400     PRINT X(K), Y(K)
500  NEXT K
600  PRINT 'THE COEFFICIENTS ARE:'
700  PRINT 'B='; B,  'M='; M
800  PRINT 'THE EQUATION IS: Y= '; B ;' + '; M ;' X'
999  END
```

GRAPHING TECHNIQUES

Computers can be programmed to print graphs, charts, diagrams, or pictures. This is accomplished by printing a sufficient number of appropriate characters in the appropriate place. Two simple examples demonstrate some graphing techniques.

Plotting a Function

Suppose you wish to plot the graph of the function $Y = f(X)$. The simplest method is to (1) assign a value to X, (2) calculate the value of Y, (3) print a symbol at distance Y, and (4) repeat this process for different values of X. The printed symbol can be an asterisk, a plus sign, a period, and so on.

The following program demonstrates the method in its simplest form. For simplicity, we use the horizontal axis as the y axis and the vertical axis as the x axis.

Example 10.7

Problem: Write a program that plots the graph of the function
$$Y = 45/2^{\wedge}(X^{\wedge}2)$$
for values of X between -2 and 2 in increments of 0.1. Explain the plan before writing the program.

Solution Plan I:

1. Use the horizontal axis as the y-axis and the vertical axis as the x-axis.
2. Use character array ALINE$(45) to print a horizontal line of the graph.
3. Set ALINE$ equal to blanks.

4. FOR values of X from −2 TO 2 STEP 0.1, repeat:
   4.1 Calculate the value of Y for a given X, call the integer of Y K.
   4.2 Place an * in the Kth position of the array ALINE$.
   4.3 Print X with one decimal place, Y with two decimal places, and then ALINE$.
   4.4 Erase the * in ALINE$.
5. Print a line under the curve.
6. End the program.

Program I:

```
10   DIM ALINE$(45)
20   FOR I = 1 TO 45
30      ALINE$ (I) = " "
40   NEXT I
50   REM PRINT A HEADING FOR X AND Y
60   PRINT " X"; TAB(9); "Y"
70   FOR X = -2 TO 2 STEP .1
80      Y = 45/2^(X^2)
90      K = INT(Y)
100     ALINE$(K) = "*"
110     X1 = (INT(X*10 + .5)/10)
120     Y1 = (INT(Y*100 + .5)/100)
130        PRINT X1; TAB(6); Y1; TAB(13); "I";
140        FOR M = 1 TO K
150           PRINT ALINE$(M);
160        NEXT M
170        PRINT
180     ALINE$(K) = " "
190  NEXT X
200  PRINT "........................................."
999  END
```

Solution Plan II: We follow the same procedure as before except that TAB, rather than an array, causes the asterisks to be printed in the appropriate places.

Program II:

```
50   REM PRINT A HEADING FOR X AND Y
60   PRINT " X"; TAB(9); "Y"
70   FOR X = -2 TO 2 STEP .1
80      Y = 45/2^(X^2)
90      K = INT(Y)
110     X1 = (INT(X*10 + .5)/10)
120     Y1 = (INT(Y*100 + .5)/100)
130     PRINT X1; TAB(6); Y1; TAB(13); "I"; TAB(K); "*"
140  NEXT X
200  PRINT ".................................."
999  END
```

Notes:

1. The entire graph is printed on the right side of the y axis.
2. If the range (maximum/minimum values) of Y for a function is greater than the width of the paper (or the screen), then the range can be adjusted by dividing the function by a constant.
3. The statements

    `ALINE$(INT(45/2^(X^2))) = "*"`

    in Program I and

    `PRINT . . . TAB(INT(45/2^(X^2))); "*"`

    in Program II are also valid in most systems. The statements were broken down into several statements to make them more understandable.
4. The purpose of lines 110 and 120 is to print X with only one decimal place, and Y with two decimal places.
5. The graph printed by Program I is shown in Figure 10.4.

Graphing a Histogram

A histogram or bar chart is a graph illustrating the number of occurrences of given values. For example, Figure 10.5 shows a histogram of the number of As, Bs, Cs, Ds, and Fs given as grades in a course. There are several methods for plotting this type of graph. The simplest one is: (1) consider the entire graph as a two-dimensional array, (2) place asterisks or any other symbol in the appropriate places in the array, and (3) print the entire array.

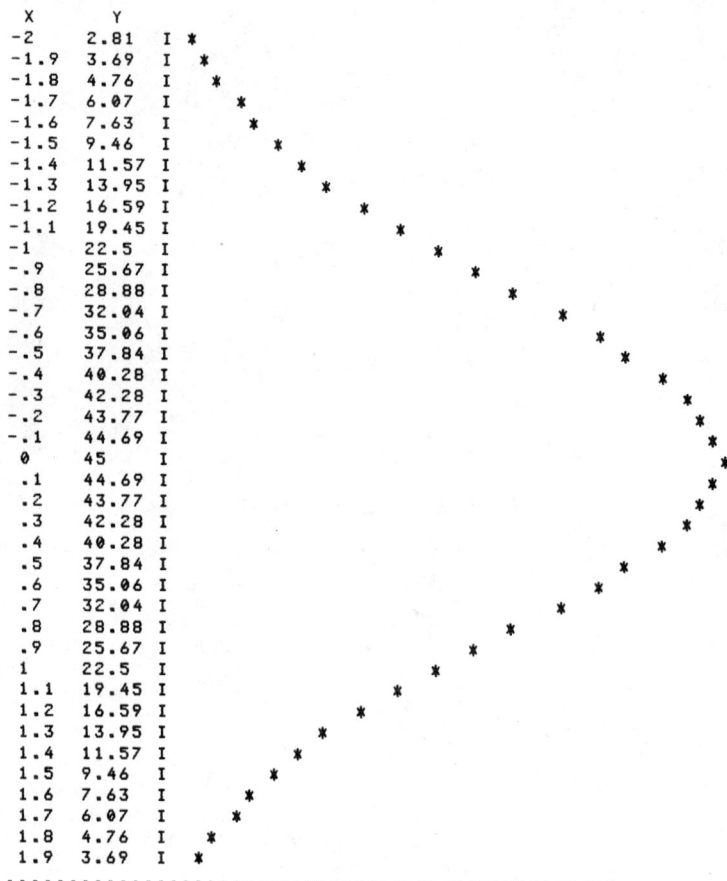

Figure 10.4 Graph of the function 45/2^(X^2)

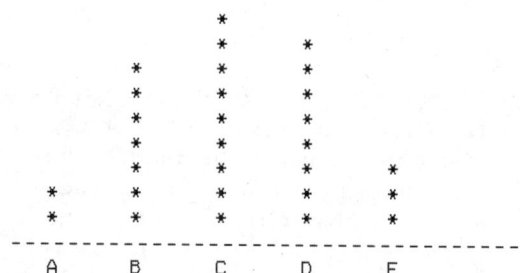

Figure 10.5 A histogram

The size of the array is determined by the maximum number of rows and columns necessary for the histogram. One example of this method was given in Chapter 8. Here is another:

Example 10.8

Problem: Write an interactive program that accepts the number of As, Bs, Cs, Ds, and Fs given as grades in a course and prints a histogram showing the grade distribution.

Program:

```
10   DIM GRAF$(20,5)
20   REM CLEARING THE GRAF$
30   FOR I = 1 TO 20
40     FOR J = 1 TO 5   :   GRAF$(I,J) = " "   :      NEXT J
60   NEXT I
80   REM FILLING THE GRAF$ WITH *, FROM TOP TO BOTTOM
90   PRINT "I WILL PLOT THE GRADE HISTOGRAM FOR YOU"
100  PRINT "TYPE NUMBER OF A'S, B'S, C'S, D'S, F'S; "
110  PRINT "EACH ON A SEPARATE LINE"
130  FOR I=1 TO 5   :   INPUT A(I)   :   NEXT I
140  FOR I=1 TO 5
150    FOR J=1 TO A(I)
160      GRAF$(J,I) = "*"
170    NEXT J
180  NEXT I
200  REM PRINT THE HISTOGRAM; GRAF$ IS TO BE PRINTED UPSIDE DOWN
210  FOR I = 20 TO 1 STEP -1
220    FOR J = 1 TO 5
230      PRINT GRAF$(I,J); "  ";
240    NEXT J
250    PRINT
260  NEXT I
270  PRINT
280  PRINT "A "; " B "; " C "; " D "; " F "
300  END
```

Notes:

1. First, array GRAF$ is filled with necessary numbers of asterisks in the appropriate places, from the top of the array to bottom, lines 140 to 180 (see Figure 10.6). Then this upside-down graph is printed from top to bottom; that is, the last row is printed first, the second-to-last row is printed second, and so on.
2. The maximum size of the histogram is 5 by 20. The program should be modified for a different size if necessary.

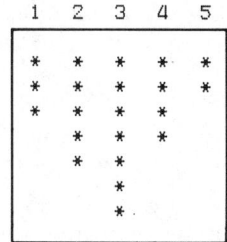

Figure 10.6 Filling an array with asterisks

SIMULATION

Simulation is the process of imitating a system by using a model. One can use simulation models to study both simple and complex systems. The basic principle behind computer simulation is to have a program imitate the behavior of a process as closely as possible. For example, a program can be developed to simulate traffic patterns (the number of automobiles arriving) at a specific intersection, or sales trends in a department store.

Real-life situations are usually too complicated to duplicate exactly by a computer program. However, if the model is somewhat representative of an actual situation, the simulation can give useful information about the real system. Of course, the more similar the model is to the real system, the more accurate the results will be.

Simulating a process has several advantages. One advantage is that we can predict the behavior of a system. Another advantage is that we can experiment with different strategies to find the best one to use in the real world.

Random Numbers

Random numbers are quantitative representations of chance. To be considered truly random, any number in a range of numbers must have an equal chance of occurring.

Normally, any real-world process involves some kind of randomness. Therefore, computer-generated random numbers are an important part of any simulation. For example, a random number generated by the computer can represent a single playing card drawn from a deck or the dots on thrown dice. Even if the process simulated is not a uniformly distributed system (for example, customers arriving in a department store), computer-generated random numbers can be used to produce a nonuniform distribution of random numbers from an appropriate distribution function.

Generating Random Numbers

Random numbers are generated by a library function in almost any computer system. Check your BASIC manual to find the name of the function in your system (see also appendix B). It is likely that the function will have the following name and form:

```
RND(a)
```

In this statement, a is an integer constant. It is also likely that this function generates random numbers between 0.0 and 1.0 whenever the function is invoked. For example, one run of the program

```
10 FOR I = 1 TO 10
20    X = RND(1)
30    PRINT X
40 NEXT I
50 END
```

generated the following numbers:

```
.950512
.297620
.006261
.305650
.382662
.831857
.098625
.620446
.990377
.693884
```

Notice that the numbers are between 0.0 and 1.0. If it is desirable to generate random numbers between A and B, then the following formula should be used:

```
X = (B - A)*RND(a) + A
```

For example, one run of the program

```
10 FOR J = 1 TO 10
20     Q = 100*RND(1)
30     PRINT Q
40 NEXT J
50 END
```

generated the following numbers between 0.0 and 100.0:

58.01136
95.05127
78.63714
29.76202
45.36999
00.62619
27.57364
30.56509
68.91007
38.26622

The following statement produces random integers between M and N:

```
L = INT((N - M + 1)*RND(a)) + M
```

For example,

```
L = INT(6*RND(1)) + 1
```

generates a random number between 1 and 6. The following program simulates ten rolls of one die:

```
10 FOR J = 1 TO 10
20     L = INT(6*RND(1)) + 1
30     PRINT L;
40 NEXT J
50 END
```

When this program was run, the results were

4 3 6 5 2 3 1 2 2 5

In a program, each random number generated by the computer has an equal chance of occurring. Nevertheless, the stream of numbers generated are predetermined by a mathematical formula. Therefore, whenever the random-number generator restarts, it produces the same sequence of numbers. That is, if you reexecute a program, you will see the same sequence of random numbers. To avoid this duplication, you may change the *seed* (the starting point) of the random-number generator. In most systems, the seed can be changed either by changing the parameter of the RND function or by placing a RANDOMIZE statement before the statement containing the RND function (see appendix B). If a system allows, the internal clock of the computer is the best way to get a seed. With the VAL function, you can change the seconds returned by the TIME$ function to a number, which can be used as the seed.

Monte Carlo Simulation

There are several forms of simulation; among them, the *Monte Carlo simulation* is especially suitable for programming. The Monte Carlo simulation technique uses random numbers and a known probability distribution of the variables. It incorporates rules, policies, and any other factors in the system to obtain simulated values. When simulation is repeated many times, the average of the simulated values will be similar to the results obtained in real situations. Of course, the degree of similarity depends on how closely the model resembles the real system. The following is an example of a simulation program:

Example 10.9

Problem: Assume the newest casino in Las Vegas has invented a die with ten sides. Any time the die is rolled, the probability that any number between 1 and 10 will occur is equal. If you bet $1, you win $6 if the number of your choice comes up. Suppose you have $500 and would like to play the game 500 times. Because 7 is your lucky number, you always bet on 7 and never on any other number. Write a program that simulates the game. The program should show how many times you might have won or lost and your net after 500 bets.

Program:

```
10   FIXED = 7    :    LOSS = 0    :    WIN = 0
20   FOR I = 1 TO 500
30     ROLL = INT(10*RND(1)) + 1
40     IF ROLL = FIXED THEN WINS   =   WINS + 1
50     LOSS = LOSS + 1
60   NEXT I
70   NET = 6*WINS - LOSS
80   PRINT "YOU WON "; WINS; " TIMES OUT OF "; LOSS
90   PRINT "THE NET WIN/LOSS IS = $"; NET
100  END
```

Notes:

1. LOSS = LOSS + 1 is always executed even when the player wins (the policy is that the house keeps the $1 wager).
2. Random numbers are assigned to ROLL as follows:

Random number	ROLL
0.0–0.099999	1
0.1–0.199999	2
0.2–0.299999	3
0.3–0.399999	4
0.4–0.499999	5
0.5–0.599999	6
0.6–0.699999	7
0.7–0.799999	8
0.8–0.899999	9
0.9–0.999999	10

   This is a uniformly distributed system (notice the equal intervals).
3. One run of this program yielded these results:

```
YOU WON 49 TIMES OUT OF 500
THE NET WIN/LOSS IS = $-206
```

4. The program can easily be changed to a game. The program should start by asking the player what number he or she chooses and the amount of the bet. The program then shows the roll, accumulates the win/loss, and continues if the player desires.

As mentioned before, random numbers generated by the computer can be used to generate nonuniformly distributed random numbers from any distribution function. To see how this method works, pay close attention to the subroutine of the following example:

Example 10.10

Problem: Suppose gambling is legal in your town and you would like to play the dice game in the local casino. The game is simple: a regular die is rolled, and players bet on numbers 1 through 6. If you bet $1 on a number, you win $4 if that number comes up. Write a program that simulates 500 rolls in the game. Pick 5 as your lucky number.

Program:

```
100  WIN = 0     :    LOSS = 0
110  FOR I = 1 TO 500
120    REM ROLLING THE DIE
130      GOSUB 200
140      IF ROLL = 5 THEN WIN = WIN + 4
150      LOSS = LOSS + 1
160  NEXT I
170  NET = WIN - LOSS
180  PRINT "LOST = $"; LOSS, "WON = $"; WIN, "NET = $"; NET
190  GOTO 999
200  REM _____ THIS SUBROUTINE ROLLS THE DIE _____
210    X = RND(1)
220    ROLL = 1
230    IF X > .166665 THEN ROLL = 2
240    IF X > .333332 THEN ROLL = 3
250    IF X > .499998 THEN ROLL = 4
260    IF X > .666665 THEN ROLL = 5
270    IF X > .833332 THEN ROLL = 6
280  RETURN
999  END
```

Notes:

1. The subroutine works as follows: The probability of each number between 1 to 6 occurring is equal (1/6 = .166666). The table below

shows what value ROLL assumes when the random number falls within a certain range.

Random Number	ROLL
0.000000–0.166665	1
0.166666–0.333332	2
0.333333–0.499998	3
0.499999–0.666665	4
0.666666–0.833332	5
0.833333–1.000000	6

2. Pay careful attention to the nice technique of the following subroutine, which performs the same function:

```
10    DIM PROB(6)
20    DATA 0.166666, 0.333333, 0.499999, 0.666666, 0.833333, 1.0
30    FOR I = 1 TO 6
40        READ PROB(I)
50    NEXT I
         ⋮
200   X = RND(1)
210   FOR J = 1 TO 6
220      IF X < PROB(J) THEN GOTO 140
230   NEXT J
240   ROLL = J
250   RETURN
```

3. Because the distribution is uniform (equal intervals), the following formula could also have been used:
   ROLL = INT(6*RNDF(1)) + 1

4. When this program was run, the output was

```
LOST = $500  WON = $356  NET = $-144
```

5. This program can easily be changed to a game. The program should ask for the number, bet, and then show the roll. The program then keeps track of the total win/loss and continues if the player desires.

The method in the subroutine of the previous example is often used to produce a random number for a nonuniformly distributed process, whereas the statement

```
L = INT((N - M + 1)*RND(1)) + M
```

can be used only for a uniformly distributed process. An example of nonuniform distribution is given next. This example demonstrates the Monte Carlo simulation technique for a business application.

Example 10.11

Problem: Farmer John's supermarket is known for its fresh milk. The store has the following sale policies:

1. The milk is purchased for $1.10/gallon and sold for $2.10/gallon.
2. Farmer John orders milk by telephone at the end of each day, basing the order on that day's demand. Milk is delivered early the following morning.
3. Any milk not sold during a day is discarded.
4. Past experience shows that the daily demand for milk varies between 50 and 350 gallons, with the following probabilities:

Demand (gallons/day)	Probability
Less than 50	.05
Less than 100	.15
Less than 150	.35
Less than 200	.65
Less than 250	.85
Less than 300	.95
Less than 350	1.0

Write a program that simulates the selling of milk at Farmer John's for 360 days. Assume the first day's order is for 200 gallons of milk. Print the first ten days' activities, and then the daily averages for demand, number of gallons sold, order, and profit at the end. Explain the plan before writing the program.

Solution Plan:

1. **Housekeeping**
   - **1.1** Set initial `ORDER = 200`.
   - **1.2** Set `PRICE = 2.10`.
   - **1.3** Set `COST = 1.10`.
   - **1.4** Set the accumulators for the total profit, total sales, total orders, and total demand equal to zero.
2. `FOR DAY = 1 TO 360`, repeat the following steps, up to Step 2.7:
   - **2.1** Determine the demand: X (from the demand function)
   - **2.2** If the demand is more than the order (stock out), then
         Set `SALE = ORDER`.
      Else
         Set `SALE = DEMAND`.
   - **2.3** Calculate the profit for the day.
   - **2.4** Print the first 10 days' activities.
   - **2.5** Calculate the totals.
   - **2.6** Set the next day's order equal to that day's demand.
   - **2.7** End the day's simulation.
3. Print the averages.

Program:

```
10    DIM GALLON(7), PROB(7)
20    REM BUILD THE PROBABILITY DISTRIBUTION
30    DATA 50,.05, 100,.15, 150,.35, 200,.65, 250,.85, 300,.95, 350,1
50    FOR I = 1 TO 7
60       READ GALLON(I), PROB(I)
70    NEXT I
80    REM INITIALIZE VARIABLES :
90       ORDER = 200 : EPRICE = 2.10 : COST = 1.10
100   TOTDEMAND = 0 : BTOTSALES = 0 : YTOTORD = 0 : ZTOTPROF = 0
105   REM A HEADING FOR 10 DAYS ACTIVITIES
110   PRINT "DAY","ORDER", "DEMAND"," SALES","PROFIT"
115   REM ..........SALES SIMULATION FOR 360 DAYS..........
120      FOR DAY = 1 TO 360
125   REM   FIND THE DAY'S DEMAND WITH SUBROUTINE 300
130         GOSUB 300
135   REM SET SALES = DEMAND ( BUT SALES = ORDER IF DEMAND > ORDER )
```

```
140         IF XDEMAND > ORDER THEN SALES = ORDER ELSE SALES = XDEMAND
150         APROFIT = SALES*EPRICE - ORDER*COST
160         IF DAY <= 10 THEN PRINT DAY, ORDER, XDEMAND, SALES, APROFIT
165 REM . . . . . . . ACCUMULATE TOTALS . . . . .
170         TOTDEMAND = TOTDEMAND + XDEMAND
180         BTOTSALES = BTOTSALES + SALES
190         YTOTORD = YTOTORD + ORDER
200         ZTOTPROF = ZTOTPROF + APROFIT
210 REM SET THE NEXT DAY'S ORDER EQUAL TO THAT DAY'S DEMAND
220         ORDER = XDEMAND
230      NEXT DAY
235 REM ........ END OF SIMULATION LOOP ............
240      PRINT 'THE DAILY AVERAGE DEMAND: '; TOTDEMAND/360
250      PRINT 'THE DAILY AVERAGE SALES : '; BTOTSALES/360
260      PRINT 'THE DAILY AVERAGE ORDERS: '; YTOTORD/360
270      PRINT 'THE DAILY AVERAGE PROFIT: '; ZTOTPROF/360
280      PRINT '*********** END OF SIMULATION ***********'
290      GOTO 999
295 REM -- THE FOLLOWING SUBROUTINE DETERMINES THE DEMAND --
300      R = RND(1)
310      FOR I = 1 TO 7
320         IF R < PROB(I) THEN GOTO 340
330      NEXT I
340      XDEMAND = GALLON(I)
350      RETURN
360      REM ------ END OF THE SUBROUTINE -------
999      END
```

Notes:

1. The following subroutine could also have been used:

```
300 XDEMAND = 50
310 R = RND(1)
320 IF R > .05 THEN XDEMAND = 100
330 IF R > .15 THEN XDEMAND = 150
340 IF R > .35 THEN XDEMAND = 200
350 IF R > .65 THEN XDEMAND = 250
360 IF R > .85 THEN XDEMAND = 300
370 IF R > .95 THEN XDEMAND = 350
380 RETURN
390 END
```

2. The following is a sample of the program output:

```
            THE FIRST   TEN DAYS ACTIVITIES
   DAY      ORDER       DEMAND      SALES       PROFIT
    1       200         150         150          95
    2       150         150         150         150
    3       150         150         150         150
    4       150         200         150         150
    5       200         100         100         -10
    6       100         250         100         100
    7       250         200         200         145
    8       200         200         200         200
    9       200         350         200         200
   10       350         300         300         245
   THE DAILY AVERAGE DEMAND:   195.694
   THE DAILY AVERAGE SALES :   152.361
   THE DAILY AVERAGE ORDERS:   195.694
   THE DAILY AVERAGE PROFIT:   104.694
   ********** END OF SIMULATION  **************
```

GAMES

An interactive program can simulate both imaginary and real games. Game programs usually incorporate some rules and an element of chance. The number of players, factors affecting the game, strategies, policies, rules, as well as the elements of chance can all be incorporated in the simulation process.

Developing a game program is a challenging job. It is much like creating a work of art. Developing the game can be even more challenging if you include pictures or graphs. The following game simulates a race:

Example 10.12

Problem: Write a program that simulates two horses racing across the screen. Assume both horses have the same chance of winning. Also assume the following ASCII control characters:

Code	Purpose
7	Sounding the beep
26	Clearing the screen
11	Moving the cursor up by one space

Solution Plan:

1. Housekeeping: Initialize the variables, clear the screen, and state the purpose of the program.
2. Let the player choose the horse, place the bet, and select the distance of the course (call this FEET).
3. Clear the screen, pause until the player is ready, announce the start of the race, ring the bell, and pause for a while.
4. Start the simulation:
    - **4.1** Set the distances (D1 for the first horse and D2 for the second horse) both equal to 1 (the first jump equals 1).
    - **4.2** Repeat the following steps FEET times:
      Print symbol D in line 1 at distance D1.
      Print symbol S in line 2 at distance D2.
      Move the cursor up two times.
      Add a random number between 1 and 2 to D1.
      Add a random number between 1 and 2 to D2.
    - **4.3** End the simulation.
5. Pause, ring the bell, and clear the screen.
6. If D1 > D2 then:
      Print "The winner is D."
      If the player has bet on D then:
         Announce the winnings, accumulate the total.
      Else
         Announce the losses, accumulate the total.
   Else if D1 = D2 then:
      Announce a tie.
      Else (D1 < D2)
      Print "The winner is S"
      If the player has bet on S then:
         Announce the winnings, accumulate the total.
      Else
         Announce the losses, accumulate the total.
   End-of-if
7. Announce the total winnings or losses.
8. If the player wants to continue, go to Step 2.
9. End the program.

Program:

```
10      CLEAN$ = CHR$(26)
20      BELL$ = CHR$(7)
30      UP$ = CHR$(11)
100     REM CLEAR THE SCREEN AND STATE THE PURPOSE
110     PRINT CLEAN$
120     PRINT "THERE ARE TWO UNKNOWN HORSES, D:DERBY, S:SUPER"
130     PRINT "BOTH HAVE THE SAME CHANCE OF WINNING"
140     PRINT "IF YOU WIN,  YOU DOUBLE YOUR MONEY"
150     REM THE PLAYER CHOOSES THE HORSE, BET, AND DISTANCE
200     PRINT "CHOOSE THE HORSE YOU WANT"
210        PRINT "TYPE D OR S"           :         INPUT A$
220        PRINT "PLACE YOUR BET"        :         INPUT BET
230        PRINT "CHOOSE THE DISTANCE, IN FEET"   :       INPUT FEET
300        REM CLEAR THE SCREEN AND PAUSE, WAIT UNTIL A KEY IS HIT
310     FOR I = 1 TO 24     :      PRINT  :    NEXT I
320     PRINT "THE MATCH STARTS IN A SECOND"   :    PRINT
330     PRINT :  PRINT "TYPE ANY KEY TO START"
340     X$ = INKEY$
350     IF X$ = "" THEN GOTO 340
360     PRINT "........ READY...SET...GO"
370     PRINT "YOU CHOSE ": A$
380       REM PAUSE FOR A WHILE, RING THE BELL, AND PAUSE AGAIN
385     FOR I = 1 TO 200    :   NEXT I   :   PRINT BELL$
390     FOR I = 1 TO 200    :    NEXT I
400     REM ************* START OF THE SIMULATION ************
410     D1 = 1    :    D2 = 1
420     FOR JUMP = 1 TO FEET
430        PRINT TAB(D1); "D"
440        PRINT TAB(D2); "S"
450        PRINT UP$; UP$;
460        D1 = D1 + RND(FEET) + 1   :   D2 = D2 + RND(FEET) + 1
470     NEXT JUMP
480     REM ****************** END OF SIMULATION  ************
500        REM PAUSE, RING THE BELL, AND CLEAR THE SCREEN
510     FOR I = 1 TO 200       :      NEXT I      :    PRINT BELL$
520     FOR I = 1 TO 24        :      PRINT       :    NEXT I
600        REM DETERMINE THE WINNINGS
605     IF D1 > D2 THEN GOTO 650 : IF D1 = D2 THEN GOTO 675
610     REM WHEN D1 < D2 THEN
620              PRINT "...THE WINNER...IS.........S U P ER"
630              IF A$ = "S" THEN GOSUB 900 ELSE GOSUB 950
640              GOTO 700
650     REM ELSE WHEN D1 > D2
655              PRINT "...THE WINNER...IS.......D E R BY"
660              IF A$ = "D" THEN GOSUB 900 ELSE GOSUB 950
670              GOTO 700
675     REM WHEN D1 = D2 THEN
680           PRINT "YOU WERE CLOSE, BUT THE RACE ENDED IN A DRAW"
690           PRINT "YOU GET YOUR $"; BET; "BACK"
```

```
700     REM ANNOUNCE THE TOTAL AND CONTINUE THE GAME IF DESIRED
710     PRINT "YOUR TOTAL WINNING/LOSING SITUATION IS : ";TOTBET
800     PRINT "WOULD YOU LIKE TO PLAY AGAIN"  :   INPUT Y$
810 IF Y$ <> "NO" THEN GOTO 200
820 PRINT "......*****... COME BACK TO THE RACE ...*****......"
890 GOTO 999
900  REM ******** THE SUBROUTINE SECTION ****************
910  REM **** WINNING SUBROUTINE ***
920     PRINT "CONGRATULATIONS, YOU JUST WON $"; 2*BET
930     TOTBET = TOTBET + 2*BET
940 RETURN
950 REM *** LOSING SUBROUTINE ***
960     TOTBET = TOTBET - BET
970     PRINT "SORRY, YOU JUST LOST $"; BET
980 RETURN
999 END
```

Notes:

1. It is assumed that both horses have the same chance of winning.
2. The purposes of some of the lines are listed below:

Line	Purpose
110	Clearing the screen
310 and 520	Moving the cursor to the bottom of the screen to print the message (also clears the screen)
340–350	Delaying the process until a character is typed in
385 and 510	Activating the buzz after a delay
390	Delaying the process
430	Printing a D at distance D1
440	Printing an S at distance D2 on the next line
450	Moving the cursor up two lines
460	Determining the next move based on random numbers
810	Transferring control to the beginning if the player would like to continue (The program accepts yes in any language. Try it!)

MANAGEMENT INFORMATION AND DECISION SUPPORT SYSTEMS

The objective of *management information systems* (MIS) is to give managers the information they need to perform their function effectively and efficiently. BASIC is a useful tool for processing data and providing information to support management functions. Typical applications include labor analysis, sales analysis, sales forecasting, production control, optimization of resources, scheduling, and reporting.

Decision support systems (DSS) go beyond transaction processing, reporting, and analysis. The main objective of DSS is to provide the information and feedback necessary to improve management's problem-solving abilities, rather than to eliminate managers' role in the decision-making process. A decision support system utilizes external and internal information, decision rules and models, and the decision maker's insight and judgment in an interactive decision-making process.

The flexibility and effectiveness of BASIC in model building and simulation, along with its interactive features, make it a powerful tool for DSS projects. For example, an interactive program can simulate the results of different decisions and strategies with a given set of factors. This kind of program allows the managers to ask "what-if" questions, for example: "What if costs rise by a given amount?" "What would happen if we institute a night shift paid at time-and-a-half?" Consequently, the manager can experiment with several alternative decisions before actually selecting a course of action. A DSS project is normally complicated because it should include factors and criteria important in business and decision making. A project may include forecasting, quantitative analysis, managerial decision making, psychological factors, and economic factors. The following example shows a simple and short interactive program.

Example 10.13

Problem: Write an interactive program that tells a manager how many items (N) must be sold in order to break even. Use the following formula:

$$N = \frac{\text{Fixed costs}}{\text{Price} - \text{Variable cost}}$$

Program:

```
10    PRINT "WOULD YOU LIKE TO KNOW THE BREAK-EVEN POINT (YES/NO)"
20    INPUT RESPONSE$
30    IF RESPONSE$ <> "YES" GOTO 999
40    PRINT "WHAT PRICE DO YOU HAVE IN MIND"
50      INPUT PRICE
60      PRINT "WHAT IS THE TOTAL FIXED COST"
70      INPUT FIXED
80      PRINT "WHAT IS THE VARIABLE COST PER ITEM"
90      INPUT VAR
100     N = FIXED/(PRICE - VAR)
110     PRINT "IN ORDER TO BREAK EVEN ";N;" UNITS MUST BE SOLD"
120     PRINT "WOULD YOU LIKE TO SEE THE EFFECT OF A PRICE CHANGE"
130     INPUT ANSWER$
140     IF ANSWER$ = "YES" THEN GOTO 40
999   PRINT "****** TAKE CARE ****"
1000  END
```

Notes:

1. The following is a sample output of this program:

```
WOULD YOU LIKE TO KNOW THE BREAK-EVEN POINT
(YES/NO)
?YES
WHAT PRICE DO YOU HAVE IN MIND
? 1200
WHAT IS THE TOTAL FIXED COST
? 2000000
WHAT IS THE VARIABLE COST PER ITEM
? 30
IN ORDER TO BREAK EVEN 1709 UNITS MUST BE
SOLD
WOULD YOU LIKE TO SEE THE EFFECT OF A PRICE
CHANGE
? NO
****** TAKE CARE ****
```

2. The information after each question prompt was typed in by the user.

3. To be of practical use, the program should be much more sophisticated.

EXERCISES

Write a complete BASIC program for each of the following problems:

10.1 Write an interactive program that prints the prime numbers from M to N, where M and N are given as input.

10.2 Develop an algorithm and write an interactive program that converts:

    Feet and inches *to* inches

    Inches *to* feet and inches

    Hours, minutes, and seconds *to* seconds

    Seconds *to* hours, minutes, and seconds

  a. Write a separate program for each of the above conversions.

  b. Write the program so that it starts with a menu and asks which conversion the user wishes to make. The program should then branch to the appropriate module.

10.3 Assume that the MID$ and LEFT$ functions are not available. Develop a mathematical procedure for the following problems:

  a. Write a program that reads a nine-digit Social Security number, such as 123456789, and prints it in the form 123-45-6789.

  b. Write a program that reads a date, such as 091885, and prints it in the form 09/18/85.

10.4 Develop a procedure and write an interactive program that accepts two values, M and N, and prints an appropriate message indicating whether or not M is a divisor of N.

10.5 Develop a game program that starts by showing two random integers and asks the user to guess whether the smaller is a divisor of the larger. The player should respond by typing yes or no. The program should then print the correct answer, keep track of the correct responses, and score the player. The game ends after N trials. (*Hint:* generate two random numbers—one between 1 and 10, for example, and the other between 10 and 20.)

10.6 Develop an algorithm that converts a base 10 number to its binary equivalent, or vice versa. Then, write an interactive game program that displays a number and asks the user to input its binary equivalent if the number is in base 10 or its base 10 equivalent if the number is in binary. The number of correct and wrong answers should be accumulated and the player scored. Give the player three chances to answer correctly. Generate the numbers randomly.

10.7 Write a subroutine that rearranges the elements of array A so that the last element becomes the first, the second-to-last becomes the second, and so on. Assume array A has 100 elements.

10.8 Design a calendar for next year and write a program that prints the calendar. Input could be (1) the day of the week on which January 1st falls and (2) a digit indicating whether the year is a leap year. Also consider the following information:

   a. Months 01, 03, 05, 07, 08, 10, and 12 have 31 days.

   b. Month 02 has 29 days in leap years and 28 days otherwise.

   c. Months 04, 06, 09, and 11 have 30 days.

Sorting:

10.9 Write an interactive program that accepts the names and telephone numbers of about 50 people and sorts the names in alphabetical order. Print the unsorted list first and then the sorted list.

10.10 Assume you would like to print a cross-referenced telephone directory. Develop and write an interactive program that accepts up to 100 names and telephone numbers, sorts the list in alphabetical order, and then prints the list. The list then should be sorted according to the telephone numbers and printed. Use a header value.

10.11 Write an interactive program that reads the names and Social Security numbers (nine digits, without the dashes) of students. Print the names and Social Security numbers:

   a. Sorted alphabetically by last names

   b. Sorted in ascending order by Social Security numbers

10.12 Suppose you have a list of information about your friends. Each record (line of information) includes: name, telephone number, address, hobbies (a limited number of predetermined hobbies), and spouse's name. Develop and write a program that reads all the records and then sorts the list (1) by last names and (2) by hobbies. (You may use the pointer sort explained in the text.)

Search:

10.13 Develop and write a program that first reads the names of your friends and their telephone numbers. The program then should print a name after accepting a phone number or print a telephone number after accepting a name. Repeat the process, this time use a binary search method.

10.14 Modify the binary search program in Example 10.13 so that the program prints a message if the desired number is not found after all the elements are searched.

10.15 A computer store has developed a coding system for its customers. Write a program that reads the names, telephone numbers, and the codes of the customers. Then the program should print a code when a name is typed in or a name when the code is typed in, according to a menu.

Merge:

10.16 Write a program segment that combines arrays A and B to create a single array C. Assume the size of array A is N and the size of array B is M. Accept the values of N, M, A, and B at the beginning of the program. Arrays A and B each have less than 100 elements and are not sorted.

10.17 Assume arrays A and B each have 100 elements. Write a program segment that creates array C so that entries are arranged in the following order: A(1), B(1), A(2), B(2), ..., A(100), B(100).

10.18 Write a program that reads arrays X and Y and merges them into array Z. Assume:

a. Arrays X and Y are sorted in descending order.

b. Arrays X and Y are not sorted.

Arrays X and Y each have 100 elements, and array Z must be sorted in ascending order.

Statistics:

10.19 In statistics, probability of M successes in N trials can be calculated by the *binomial probability distribution*. The formula is:

$$X = \frac{N!}{M! \times (N - M)!} \times p^M \times q^{M-N}$$

where X is probability of M successes in N trials, p is probability of success, and q is probability of failure ($q = 1 - p$). Write a program that generates a table of probabilities for N=10; M=1, 2, 3, 4, and 5; and P=.01, .02, .03, .04, .05, .06, .07, and .08. Use a subprogram to calculate the factorial of a number. The following table is an example of the output:

```
                            N = 10
   M / P   .01   .02   .03   .04   .05   .06   .07   .08
   1     | .0944  .     .     .     .     .     .     .
               .
   2           .
               .
   3           .
               .
   4           .
               .
   5           .
               .
```

10.20 The mean, median, variance, standard deviation, and range are some useful measures of a group of observations. Write an interactive program that accepts a series of N observations; calculates these measures; and prints the unsorted data, sorted data, or the measures according to a menu. Use the following formulas for calculations:

a. Mean $= \dfrac{\left(\sum_{i=1}^{N} X_i\right)}{N}$

b. Variance $= VAR = \dfrac{\sum_{i=1}^{N}(X_i - \text{Mean})^2}{N}$ or $VAR = \dfrac{\sum_{i=1}^{N} X_i^2}{N} - (\text{Mean})^2$

c. Median $= MED$ (the data must be sorted):
If N is odd:
$$MED = X_k \text{ where } k = \dfrac{(N+1)}{2}$$
If N is even:
$$MED = \dfrac{(X_k + X_{k+1})}{2} \text{ where } k = \dfrac{N}{2}$$

d. Standard deviation $= STD = \sqrt{VAR}$

e. Range $=$ (Largest number $-$ Smallest number)

10.21 Write an interactive program that asks for N pairs of observations and then prints the line estimated by the least squares method. Use the program to answer the following questions:

  a. What are the estimated sales during year 11 by XYZ Company? The following data show past performance:

Year	Sales (millions of dollars)
1	20
2	22
3	25
4	24
5	27
6	29
7	28
8	29
9	32
10	31

  b. What is the expected precipitate of a substance if the value of the chemical reagent is 7.5? The following data show the results of a chemical reagent (X) on the precipitate of a particular substance (Y) in a given solution:

X	Y
5.5	7.0
4.6	5.5
8.4	7.1
5.4	4.9
6.2	6.1
6.7	6.8
8.0	7.9
4.4	4.8
9.2	8.5
10.4	10.9
11.0	11.2

10.22 The *correlation coefficient* shows how two sets of observations are related. Write an interactive program that accepts N pairs of observations and stores them in arrays A and B. Calculate the correlation coefficient as follows:

a. Calculate the mean and standard deviation for each set of data; call them *ABAR*, *S1A*, *BBAR*, *S2B*. See Exercise 10.20 for the formulas.

b. Calculate the correlation coefficient by the following formula:

$$R = \frac{\sum_{i=1}^{N} (A_i - ABAR) \times (B_i - BBAR)}{N \times (S1A) \times (S2B)}$$

R must be between -1 and $+1$.

Print the information. Accept *N*, the number of observations, as a header value.

10.23 The formulas for calculating the coefficients of a linear equation

$$y = b + mx$$

were discussed earlier in the text. But in some situations the data may not fit a linear equation. Assume the price-to-earnings ratio of stocks follows the function

$$y = ax^b$$

Write a program that reads *N* pairs of data for *x* (earnings) and *y* (prices) and calculates the coefficients of *a* and *b*. (Hint: the formula can be changed to:

$\log y = (\log a) + b \times (\text{Log } x)$ or $Y = A + B*X$.

The program then should accept an earning and print an estimated price.

Graphing:

10.24 Write an interactive program that plots a graph. Use the program to plot the following functions:

a. $Y = 3x^2 + 6x + 5$ for $-2.5 < x < +2.5$ in intervals of 0.1

b. $Y = \dfrac{50}{(1 + x^2)}$ for $-5 < x < +5$ in intervals of 0.2

c. $Y = (x^2 - 1)(x^2 - 4)(x^2 - 9) + 25$

for $-2.5 < x < +2.5$ in intervals of 0.1

d. $Y = 1 + x^2$ for $-10 < x < 10$ in intervals of 0.3

10.25 Modify the program in Example 10.7 so that it prints a graph similar to the following one:

```
*
**
***
*****
********
************
****************
********************
**********************
************************
**********************
********************
*******************
****************
************
********
*****
***
**
*
```

10.26 Write an interactive program that accepts the results of a test taken by N students (N < 50). The scores are between 0 and 100. Calculate the number of As (90 to 100), Bs (80 to 89), Cs (70 to 79), Ds (60 to 69), and Fs (below 60). Plot a histogram showing the number of As, Bs, Cs, Ds, and Fs.

10.27 Write an interactive program that accepts a set of 100 real numbers between 1 to 100. Calculate the occurrences of numbers in intervals of ten; that is, how many numbers fall between 1 and 10, 10+ and 20, 20+ and 30, and so on. Print a histogram showing the distribution of numbers among intervals.

Simulation/Games:

10.28 Write an interactive program that simulates the rolling of two dice. The program should print the "roll" after the user presses a key.

10.29 Write a program that simulates the rolling of three dice 100 times. Print how many 7's and 11's occurred after 100 rolls of the dice.

10.30 Assume you would like to computerize the calls in a game of Bingo. The process is as follows:

Seventy-five tokens, numbered 1 to 75, are placed in a container. The caller draws out one token at a time and reads its number. If the number is between 1 and 15 the caller states that the number is under B; if between 16 and 30, under I; if between 31 and 45, under N; if between 46 and 60, under G; and if between 61 and 75, under O (see Figure 10.7).

Write an interactive program which simulates the drawing and calling. The program should print a number and a letter after a key is pressed.

10.31 Suppose you are planning a trip to Las Vegas. Simulate the crap game before you try it. The rules are as follows:

a. Two dice are rolled.

b. If the player rolls 7 or 11 (a natural), the player wins.

c. If the player rolls 2, 3, or 12, the player loses.

d. If the player rolls anything other than those mentioned above (i.e., 4, 5, 6, 8, 9, or 10), the result is not yet decided. The number rolled becomes the player's "point." In this case, the player must roll both dice again as often as necessary until he or she rolls either the point or a 7. The player wins if he or she rolls the point, but loses if he or she rolls a 7. All rolls other than the point or 7 are ignored.

Develop and write an interactive program that simulates the game.

B	I	N	G	O
3	23	33	50	63
7	25	44	51	67
11	16	FREE SPACE	55	68
13	29	39	56	72
2	17	31	60	61

Figure 10.7 A Bingo card

10.32 Some gamblers believe that doubling the bet after each loss works well. The system works like this: you start with a small bet, for instance, $1. If you lose, you bet $2 on the next game. If you lose again, you bet $4, then $8, and so on, until you win a game. Suppose that you have $100 and would like to play the dice game explained in Example 10.10. Write a program that simulates the game. Assume the payoff is one to four. Find the probability that you run out of money before you win anything.

Repeat the simulation for the crap game explained in Example 10.31 and find the probability of losing all your money.

10.33 The daily demand for cars at ABC Car Dealership is as follows:

Demand/day	Probability
fewer than 1	.05
fewer than 2	.15
fewer than 3	.35
fewer than 4	.55
fewer than 5	.75
fewer than 6	.85
fewer than 7	.95
fewer than 8	1.0

Write a program that simulates ABC's sales during 500 days. Assume the cars can be ordered now and delivered to the customers later. Calculate the average daily demand.

10.34 Cute Bakery Shop bakes fine birthday cakes every morning. The production costs are $1.75 per cake, and the cakes sell for $4.50 each. Leftover cakes are sold to a local supermarket at $1.30 per cake. Four cakes are baked every day. Historically, the daily demand for birthday cakes has been as follows:

Demand/day	Relative frequency
0	.05
fewer than 1	.15
fewer than 2	.30
fewer than 3	.45
fewer than 4	.65
fewer than 5	.75
fewer than 6	.9
fewer than 7	1.0

a. Write a program that simulates the Cute Bakery's sales during 360 days. Calculate the average daily demand, average number of cakes sold to customers, average number of cakes sold to the local supermarket, and the average profit per day.

b. Repeat the simulation several times, each time using trial production quantities of 1, 2, 3, 4, 5, 6, 7, and 8 cakes per day. Calculate and print the average profit per day for each trial quantity. Which production quantity do you recommend?

c. Develop the program into a decision support system for the manager of the bakery.

10.35 Write a program that simulates waiting in line for a service that takes exactly 10 minutes. Calculate the average waiting time for each customer if customers arrive irregularly on the average of six customers every 100 minutes. (The service time is not counted as part of the waiting time.)

10.36 A dog is lost in Manhattan. At each intersection, he chooses a direction at random and proceeds to the next intersection, where he again chooses another direction at random, and so on. Assume the blocks are all square and there are only nine intersections, as shown in Figure 10.8. Write a program to simulate many of these random walks. Find the probability that the dog will emerge on the north side in less than 1,000 walks. Assume that the walk starts at any corner and ends when the dog reaches any edge of the grid. (*Hint:* the process can be simulated several times. Each time, any intersection is chosen as the starting point. Random numbers 1, 2, 3,

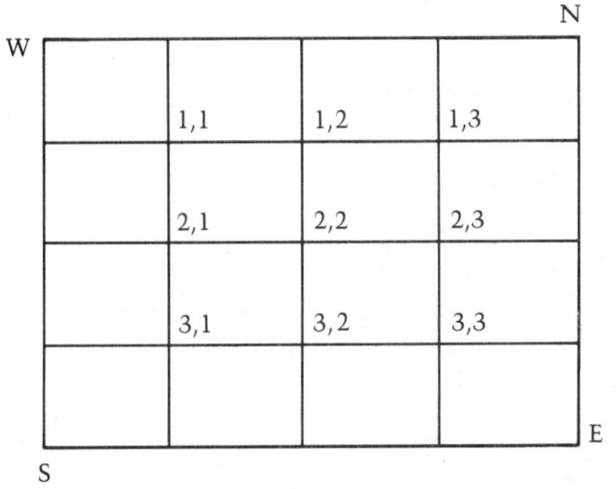

Figure 10.8 Street intersections

and 4—representing south, west, east, and north—determine which direction is taken. After a walk is over, it is counted as either a success or a failure, and another walk begins. After all trials, the ratio of successes to the total number of trials is an approximation of the probability.)

10.37 Write a program that simulates a race among three horses. Each horse should be given random odds. These odds should be posted before the player bets on a horse. Input for the program should be the name of the horse on which the player bets and the amount of the bet. At the end of the race, the results should be displayed. If the player wins, the bet times the odds should be added to the player's money. If the player loses, the bet should be subtracted from the money. Finally, the player should have the option of stopping or continuing to play. Considerations:

  a. The player should be given a fixed amount of money at the start of the race.
  b. The player should not be able to bet more money than he or she has.
  c. The amount of the bet cannot be negative.
  d. New odds should be posted for each race.
  e. Use graphics if your system has the capability.
  Extra credit: Adapt the program for more than one player.

Decision Support:

10.38 Design, develop, and write an interactive program that helps a manager find information about a product in order to determine one or several of the following factors:

  a. Price
  b. Variable cost (For example, can more expensive materials be used?)
  c. Fixed cost (For example, can a new piece of equipment be purchased?)
  d. Number of units that must be sold to break even
  e. Total revenue if a certain number of units is sold
  f. Total profit if a certain number of units is sold

  Use the following formulas in the model:

$$\text{Revenue} = U \times P$$
$$\begin{aligned}\text{Total profit} &= \text{Revenue} - \text{Costs}\\ &= U \times P - (F + V \times U)\end{aligned}$$
$$\text{NB} = \frac{F}{P - V}$$

where

U = Number of units sold

P = Price of the product

F = Total fixed costs

V = Variable costs per unit

NB = Break-even point

The program should ask questions and accept information from the user. For example, it can ask, "What factors—price, costs, number of units, and so on—do you wish to make decisions about?" After the computer receives enough information about a specific area, it prints the decision variables and the information, for instance:

```
IF THE FIXED COST IS $XX
THE VARIABLE COST IS $XX
THE ESTIMATED NUMBER OF UNITS THAT CAN BE SOLD
 IS XX

THEN THE PRICE SHOULD BE MORE THAN $XX IF YOU
 WANT TO MAKE A PROFIT
```

or

```
IF EQUIPMENT IS BOUGHT FOR $XX
THE VARIABLE COST IS $XX PER UNIT
PRICE IS $XX
OTHER INFORMATION THE SAME AS BEFORE

THEN THE BREAK-EVEN IS XX UNITS
```

Operations Research:

10.39 If you are familiar with the simplex method, develop an interactive program to solve a linear programming problem. Assume the problem is in the following form:
Maximize

$$Z = C_1 X_1 + C_2 X_2 + \ldots + C_k X_k$$

subject to

$$a_{11}X_1 + a_{12}X_2 + \ldots + a_{1k}X_k \leq b_1$$
$$a_{21}X_1 + a_{22}X_2 + \ldots + a_{2k}X_k \leq b_2$$
$$\vdots$$
$$a_{m1}X_1 + a_{m2}X_2 + \ldots + a_{mk}X_k \leq b_m$$
$$X_1, X_2, \ldots, X_k \geq 0$$

The program starts by accepting the input data as follows:

a. The number of variables, K
b. The number of constraints, M
c. Whether the problem is for maximization or minimization
d. The coefficients of the objective function
e. The coefficients of the constraints
f. The values of the right-hand side

The output is the final tableau, the value of each variable, and the value of the objective function. You may find the following eight steps helpful in solving the problem. The matrix manipulation feature of BASIC makes the programming much easier. This feature, however, is not used in the following eight steps. Answers to subroutines used in Steps 3, 4, and 6 are given at the end of the exercise.

Step 1:

Create the standard form of the linear programming problem. This is done by adding M slack variables to the model. Thus there are N = K + M variables in the system. Place all the coefficients in two-dimensional array A (Figure 10.9). Array A has N1 columns and M1 rows where

```
N  = M + K
N1 = N + 1
M1 = M + 1
```

The other elements of array A are:

a. Part I, the first row, is the negative of the coefficients of the objective function, including the coefficients for the slack variables. The coefficients of the slack variables in the objective function are zero for a maximization problem and a large num-

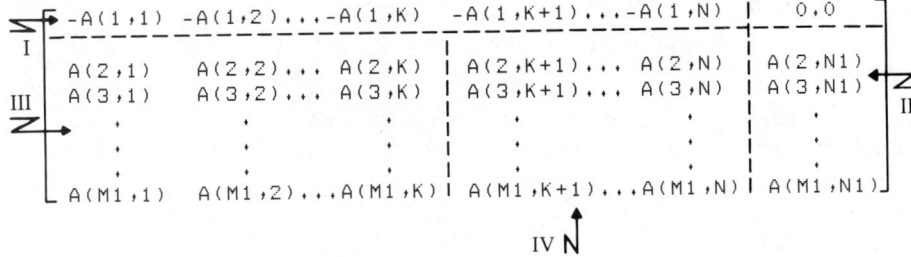

Figure 10.9 Array A for the simplex algorithm

ber (such as 99999.99, which becomes −99999.99 in the first row) for a minimization problem.

b. Part II, the last column, is the values of the right-hand side.
c. Part III is the coefficients of the constraints.
d. Part IV is the coefficients of the slack variables of the constraints. These coefficients are all equal to zero except the Ith one in the Ith constraint, which has a value of 1 (that is, 1's in its principal diagonal and 0s everywhere else). This can be accomplished by first setting all of the coefficients equal to zero in a loop

```
100 FOR I = 2 TO M1
110     L = K + 1
120     FOR J = L TO N
130         A(I,J) = 0
140     NEXT J
150 NEXT I
```

and then using another loop to set the principal diagonal equal to 1

```
160 FOR I = 2 TO M1
170     L = K + I - 1
180     A(I,L) = 1
190 NEXT I
```

Step 2:

a. Define array X with N elements to hold the values of the variables.
b. Keep track of the basic variables in array XB; define array XB as an integer array with M elements. There are always M basic variables. For example, the initial basic variables are

```
200 FOR I = 1 TO M
210     XB(I) = K + I
220 NEXT I
```

c. Find the initial basic feasible solution. All the variables in the basic feasible solution are equal to zero, except the variables in the basic solution. The statements

```
230 FOR I = 1 TO N
240     X(I) = 0
250 NEXT I
```

can be used to set all the variables equal to zero. Then the statements

```
260 FOR I = 1 TO M
270     J = XB(I)
280     L = I + 1
290     X(J) = A(L, N1)
295 NEXT I
```

determine the value of the basic variables.

Step 3:

Choose the variables to be introduced into the basic solution. This can be done by finding the *pivot column,* which is the column with the smallest negative value in the first row (the objective function). Call the column COL. If there is no negative value in the first row, the solution is optimal; then Go to Step 8. Use a subroutine for Step 3. Consider COL = 0 to indicate the optimal solution.

Step 4:

Choose the variable that must leave the basic solution by finding the pivot row. The pivot row can be found as follows:

a. For each element i in column COL (except the first row) compute the ratio of (b_i/a_{ij}) for every a_{ij} greater than zero in the pivot column. (Note that b_i is A(I+1, N1) and a_{ij} is A(I+1, COL) in array A).

b. The row with the minimum ratio is the *pivot row.* Call this row ROW. Use a subroutine for this purpose. Consider ROW = 0 to indicate no positive a_{ij} in column COL.

Step 5:

Find the variable that is entering the basic solution:

`XB(ROW - 1) = COL`

Step 6:

Perform the necessary row operations to convert column `COL` into a unit column. This can be accomplished as follows:

a. Find the pivot, which is `A(ROW,COL)`
b. Divide the pivot row by the pivot. This makes the value of the pivot equal to 1.
c. Make all the elements in the pivot column equal to zero, except the element in the pivot row, which must be equal to 1. This can be accomplished as follows:

 - For each row *i*, except the pivot row, find the multiplier `Y` as

   `Y = A(I,COL)`

 - Multiply each element in the pivot row by `Y` and subtract it from the corresponding element in row *i*.

Make sure to include all rows and columns of array `A` in the operations (including the first row and the last column). Use a subroutine for this purpose.

Step 7:

Go to Step 3.

Step 8:

If the optimal solution is reached, print the information in array `A`, the values for the variables (as shown in Step 2c), and the value of the objective function. Note that the value of the objective function is stored in element `A(1,N1)`.

450 Problem Solving, Programming Techniques, and Some Applications

Answers to Exercise 10.39:

Step 3 Subroutine:

```
500 REM ***** SUBROUTINE CEEJAY *****
510 N = N1 - 1
520 COL = 0     :      SMALL = 0
530 FOR I = 1 TO N
540     IF A(1,I) > =  0 THEN GOTO 580
550     IF A(1,I) > SMALL THEN GOTO 580
560         SMALL = A(1,I)
570         COL = I
580 NEXT I
590 RETURN
```

Step 4 Subroutine:

```
600 REM ***** SUBROUTINE BEES *******
610 ROW = 0
620 SMALL = 99999.99
630 FOR I = 2 TO M1
640     IF A(I,COL) < 0 THEN GOTO 680
645     Z = A(I,N1)/A(I,COL)
650     IF Z > SMALL THEN GOTO 680
660         SMALL = Z
670         ROW = I
680 NEXT I
690 RETURN
```

Step 6 Subroutine:

```
800 REM **** SUBROUTINE ROW-OPERATION ****
810 PIVOT = A(ROW,COL)
820 FOR J = 1 TO N1
830     A(ROW,J) = A(ROW,J)/PIVOT
840 NEXT J
850 FOR I = 1 TO M1
860         IF I = ROW GOTO 910
870         Y = A(I,COL)
880         FOR J = 1 TO N1
890             A(I,J) = A(I,J) - A(ROW,J)*Y
900         NEXT J
910 NEXT I
920 RETURN
```

SUMMARY

You have learned:

1. Developing an algorithm to solve a problem is an art. An algorithm is a detailed, step-by-step set of solution procedures suitable for computer programming.
2. Some techniques used in data processing are as follows:
   - *Sorting* is the process of rearranging the items of a list into a predetermined order. The bubble sort procedure starts by placing the largest (or the smallest) item at the bottom (or at the top) of the list. This is done by comparing pairs of contiguous items, one pair at a time, and interchanging them if necessary. The process is then repeated as many times as necessary until all the items are in the desired order. There are many other, more efficient, sorting techniques.
   - *Searching* is the process of finding an item in a list. Several searching techniques are available.
   - *Merging* is the process of combining two or more lists into one single sorted list.
3. Programs that find the median and coefficients of a regression line are examples of statistical applications.
4. Computers can be programmed to print graphs, charts, or pictures. The technique is to print a sufficient number of characters in the appropriate place. The techniques for plotting a function and a histogram were shown.
5. A computer simulation is a programmed imitation of a real-life process. One advantage of computer simulations is that they allow users to experiment with and thus predict the behavior of the real-life system. Generating random numbers is a necessary function of simulation programs.
6. A game program simulates a real or imaginary game. Game programs incorporate rules, policies, and the element of chance to simulate the play.
7. The interactive features of BASIC make it useful for MIS or DSS projects.

REVIEW QUESTIONS/SELF-TEST

10.1 Develop a solution procedure for a program that accepts an integer and determines whether the number is odd or even. Write the program.

10.2 Follow the logic of the program below and find out what it is supposed to do. Then rewrite the program. Use structured programming and any other technique that makes the program more efficient.

```
10  DIM DEMAND(1000), X(1000), PROF(1000)
20  TOPROF=0
30  Y=1
40  X(Y)=RND(1)
50  IF X(Y) < .5 THEN GOTO 70
60  IF X(Y) > .5 THEN GOTO 90
70  DEMAND(Y) = 5
80  GOTO 170
90  IF X(Y) < .8 THEN GOTO 110
100 IF X(Y) > .8 THEN GOTO 130
110 DEMAND(Y) = 14
120 GOTO 170
130 IF X(Y) < 1 THEN GOTO 150
140 IF X(Y) > 1 THEN GOTO 260
150 DEMAND(Y) = 14
160 GOTO 170
170 INVEST = 50
180 PRICE = 9
190 PROF(Y) = DEMAND(Y) * PRICE - INVEST
200 TOPROF = TOPROF + PROF(Y)
210 Y = Y+1
220 IF Y > 1000 THEN GOTO 240
230 GOTO 40
240 AVPROF = TOPROF/1000
250 PRINT 'AVG PROF =', PROF
260 STOP
270 END
```

Answers:

10.1 *Solution procedure* An even number is divisible by 2. Thus, if you divide the number by 2 and the remainder equals zero, the number is even; otherwise, the number is odd.

Program Plan:

   a. Accept the number, call it N.
   b. Find the integer of the number divided by 2.
   c. Find the remainder.
   d. If the remainder is zero, print "even."
   Otherwise, print "odd."

Program:

```
10  PRINT "I WILL TELL YOU IN A FLASH WHETHER A
           NUMBER IS ODD OR EVEN"
15  PRINT "TYPE THE NUMBER"
20    INPUT N
30    M = INT(N/2)
40    L = N - 2*M
50    IF L = 0 THEN PRINT "THE NUMBER IS EVEN"         &
          ELSE PRINT "THE NUMBER IS ODD"
80    END
```

10.2 Here is the rewritten program:

```
10   INVEST = 50   :   PRICE = 9   :   TOTPROF = 0
20   REM   THIS PROGRAM SIMULATES THE SALES DURING 1000 DAYS.
30   REM   THE INVESTMENT IS FIXED AT $50/DAY AND PRICE = $9
90   REM   THE NUMBER OF ITEMS DEMANDED (DEMAND) IS SIMULATED BY
95   REM   THE SUBROUTINE 200
100  FOR DAY = 1 TO 1000
110     GOSUB 200
120     PROFIT = DEMAND*PRICE - INVEST
130     TOTPROF = TOTPROF + PROFIT
140  NEXT DAY
150  REM CALCULATE THE AVERAGE PROFIT
160  AVGPROF = TOTPROF/1000
170  PRINT "AVERAGE PROFIT = "; AVGPROF
180  REM ************ END SIMULATION  ***************
190  GOTO 999
200  REM ******** THIS SUBROUTINE SIMULATES THE DEMAND *******
210  X = RND(1)
220     IF X < .5 THEN              &
230                 DEMAND = 5       &
240        ELSE IF X < .8 THEN      &
                    DEMAND = 9       &
                ELSE                 &
                    DEMAND = 14      &
250  REM END-OF-IF
260  RETURN
999  END
```

File Processing

11

In This Chapter:

File Processing—Section I
What is a File?
Storage Media
File Organization

Sequential File Processing
General Steps
Creating a File
Forms of the Statements
Accessing a File

File Processing—Section II
Control Break Reports
Sorting
Merging
File Maintenance

Random-File Processing
General Steps
Forms of the Statements
Multirecords
Random Accessing by an ID

Exercises

Summary

Review Questions/Self-Test

11

File Processing

FILE PROCESSING—SECTION I

A file is a collection of data or information stored under a name. Often information in files must be processed—retrieved, manipulated, or written. The processing of files is the subject of this chapter.

This chapter has two major sections. The first section defines important terms and reviews different storage media as well as methods of file organization. In the second section, sequential file processing and random file processing are examined in detail. The chapter is divided into two sections to make the presentation flexible. The introductory concepts are presented in the first section and can be reviewed after Chapter 2. In the second section, advanced topics are discussed.

Unfortunately, file storage and processing are the most machine-dependent areas of BASIC systems. Each system has different file processing statements. General concepts are presented in this chapter. Understanding the fundamentals will help you apply file concepts to a particular computer. Table 11.1, at the end of this chapter, illustrates the form of the file statements for several systems.

What Is a File?

A *file* is a collection of information or data considered as a unit. Normally, a file is a collection of several records, and a record is a collection of several fields. A *field* is the specific area assigned to a piece of information, that is, the number of consecutive columns or positions reserved for an item of data or information (see Figure 11.1). For example, several fields of data about an employee, such as his or her name, Social Security number,

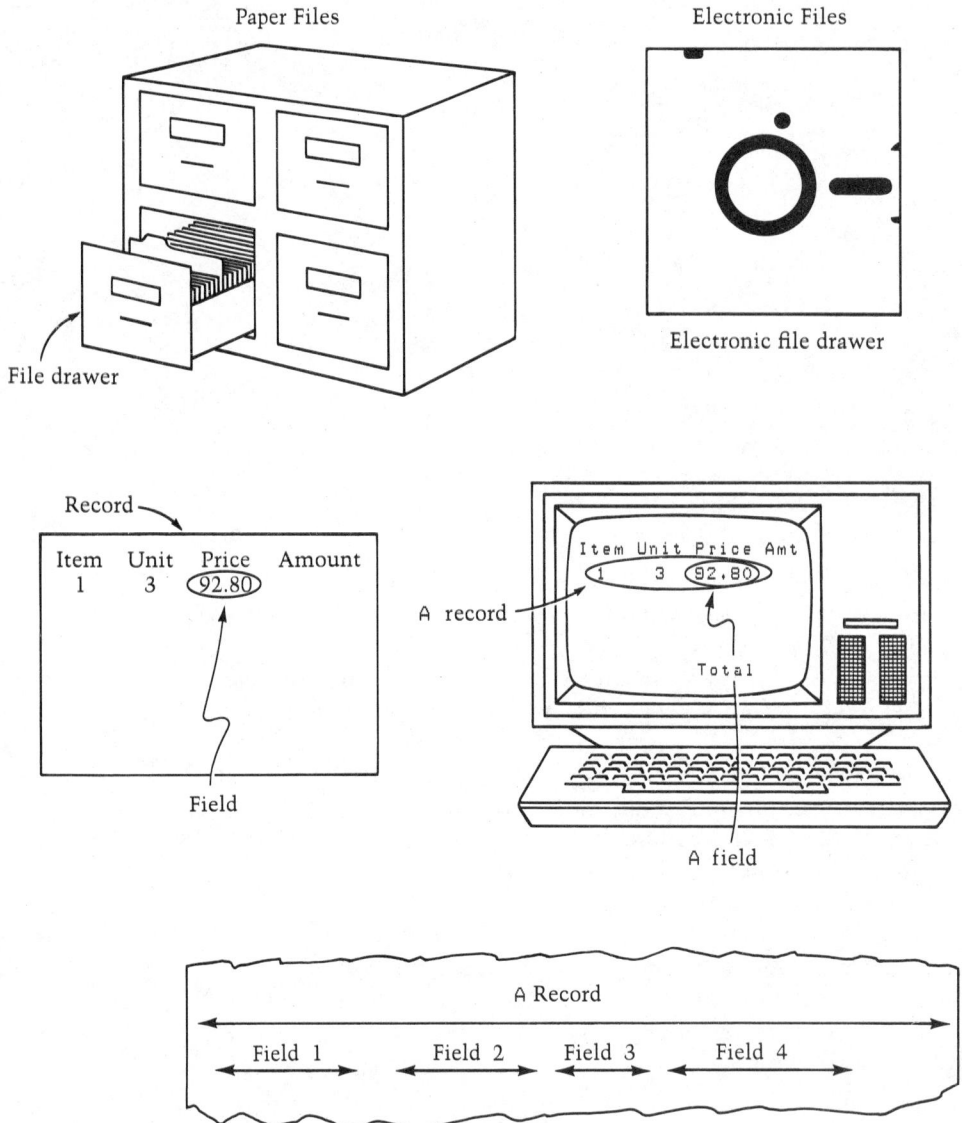

Figure 11.1 A file, a record, and a field

address, and so on, can constitute a record. Several employees' records placed together constitute the employees' file.

There is no standard size for a record. A record can be several related fields or simply a line of data. To picture a file, imagine that it is nothing but several lines of information. Remember, though, that a record need not be limited to one line. It is sometimes convenient, however, to consider one line of information as a record. If you choose to limit a record to one line, you should be aware of the number of allowable spaces on a line. For example, if you use one line of information on the video terminal as a record, the maximum number of spaces available is normally 80. The maximum number of spaces on a PRINT record is normally 80, 96, 120, 132, or 160.

There are several types of files. The following are some examples:

- *A program file* contains a program or several program units.
- *A master file* normally contains permanent data; for example, an employee master file (containing names, addresses, Social Security numbers, and so on), a customer master file, or an inventory master file.
- *A transaction file* contains temporary data. Normally, a transaction file is used to update a master file.
- *A table file* is a data file that contains tables, such as price tables, wage tables, and so on.
- *A temporary file* is temporarily created, used, and then saved or destroyed. For example, a file can be created to contain the information a program outputs. This file is then used as input to another program.
- *A backup file* is a copy of an original file, created as a safeguard in the event of damage to or loss of the original.

Storage Media

A file is not normally stored permanently in the main memory of a computer for two major reasons. First, it is not economical to do so. Second, the memory is volatile; that is, when you turn off the computer, the data stored in the memory are erased.

Files are stored in an external storage medium. The most common storage media are tapes, disks, and diskettes. Among these media, disks and diskettes are most widely used.

Several kinds of disks are available. Larger computers use disk packs, while smaller computers use diskettes. The data are stored on a track on the surface of the disk. A disk track is similar to a phonograph record track except that disk tracks are concentric circles (see Figure 11.2). A typical disk surface has more than 200 tracks.

A diskette (also called floppy disk) is a single disk made of flexible plastic. The popular sizes are $5\frac{1}{4}$ and 8 inches in diameter. The diskette is covered by a square black jacket, inside which it rotates. Diskettes are a common storage medium in microcomputers. As in disks, data are stored on diskette tracks. There are normally 40 tracks on the surface of a $5\frac{1}{4}$-inch floppy disk (see Figure 11.2).

460 *File Processing*

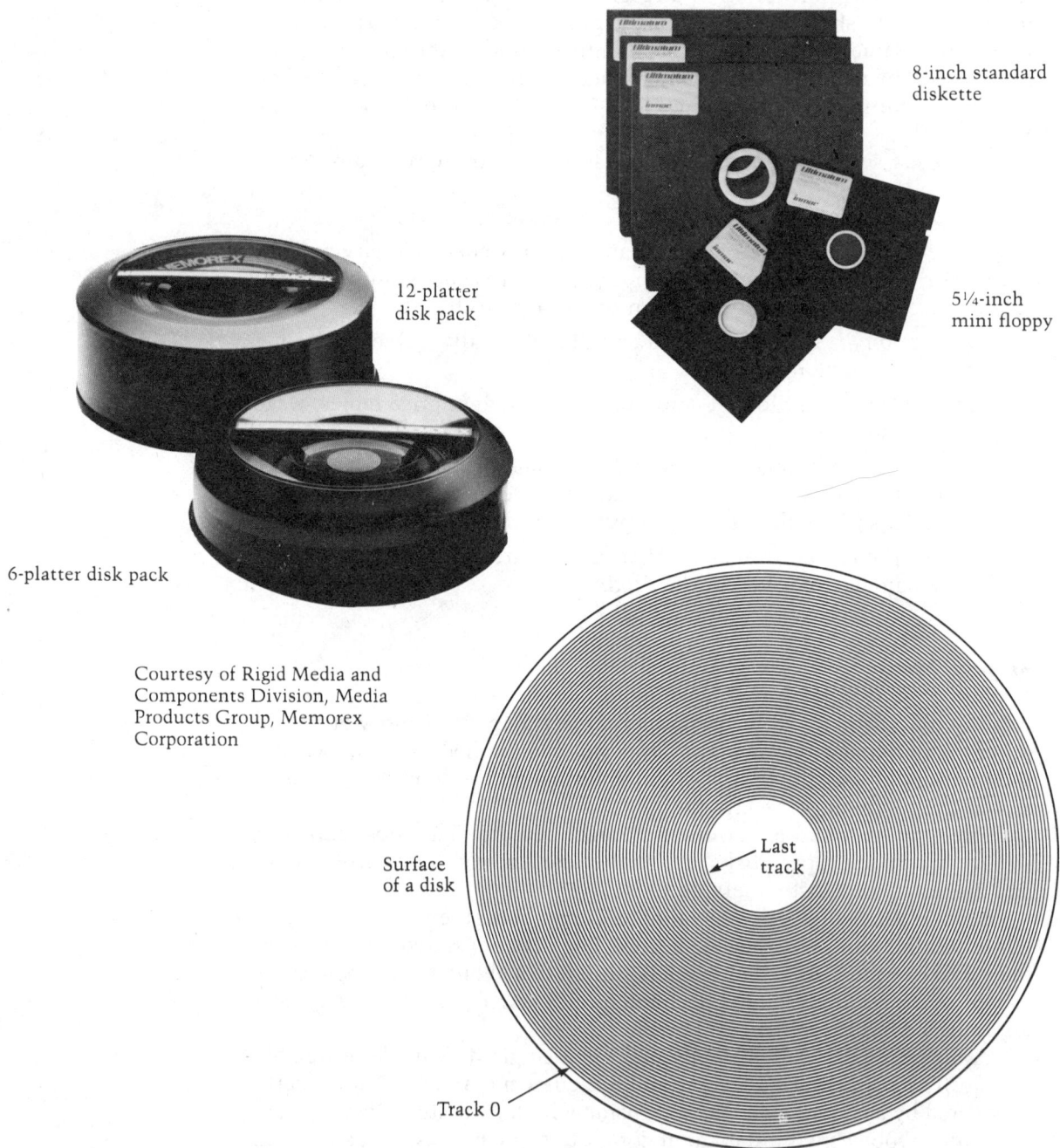

Figure 11.2 Disk pack and diskette

File Organization

File organization refers to the way records are arranged. File organization affects the methods of identifying and accessing a particular record. Basically, there are three methods of accessing a record in a file: (1) sequential, (2) random, and (3) index-sequential.

The records in *sequential files* must be written, read, or processed one after another. This means that before the desired record can be accessed, all previous records must be read and checked. Sequential organization is common in files whose records are generally read and processed at the same time.

Random-access organization, by contrast, permits the user to access any one record without the necessity of checking any other one. With this method, each record must have a key identifying its storage location. This key can be a name, an ID number, a code, or simply a sequence number. If the keys are sequence numbers (1, 2, 3, and so on), they are called *relative keys* because the location key of each successive record is one higher than the previous one. Random-access processing is also called *direct-access processing*.

In *index-sequential processing*, records are stored one after another with an address. The address indicates the location of the record and can be found from an index (a table) stored on the same disk. To find a record, the computer looks up the key (ID number, code, or so on) in the index and finds the address. Then the record is retrieved by its address. Of course, the process of looking up and retrieving is done by the program.

SEQUENTIAL FILE PROCESSING

File processing is the process of creating, using, and maintaining data files. *File maintenance*, in turn, is the activity of adding, changing, or deleting data to keep a file up to date. The processing of sequential files will be explained by several examples. The examples have been kept deliberately simple to show the general steps and procedures applicable to any system.

General Steps

When a file is processed, the following steps are generally necessary:

1. Opening the file
2. Reading

3. Processing-manipulating
4. Writing
5. Closing the file

Opening refers to associating the name of the file with a channel number where reading and writing take place. *Closing* refers to disassociating the file after reading or writing is completed. *Processing* can include searching, updating, calculating, summarizing, analyzing, or reporting. This step is common in any process, regardless of whether or not the data are stored in an external file.

Creating a File

To create a sequential file, you need to follow these basic steps:

1. Open a file for output.
2. Accept the data from the terminal or other medium.
3. Write the data to the file.
4. Close the file.

The following is an example:

Example 11.1

Problem: Suppose sample measurements are taken for a batch of a product. Each sample includes three measurements. Write an interactive program that accepts the data and saves them under the file name DATA1.

Solution Plan:

1. Open the file DATA1 as file #1 for output.
2. Repeat the following steps until there are no more data:
    2.1 Accept the three measurements.
    2.2 Write the data on file #1.
3. Close the file.
4. End.

Program:

```
10   OPEN "O", #1, "DATA1"
20   PRINT "TYPE IN 3 MEASUREMENTS. TYPE 3 ZEROS WHEN DONE"
30   INPUT A, B, C
40     PRINT #1, A; ","; B; ","; C
50     IF A = 0 THEN GOTO 70
60   GOTO 30
70   CLOSE #1
80   END
```

Notes:

1. The process plan is:
   a. Open the file DATA1 (line 10).
   b. Accept the data from the terminal (lines 20 and 30).
   c. Write the data on the file DATA1 (line 40).
   d. Close the file DATA1 (line 70).
2. Commas are written into the file to separate the data. The commas make it possible to read the data back when necessary.
3. The exact form of the statements depends on the system being used. See Table 11.1 at the end of this chapter for examples.

Forms of the Statements

The general form of the statements for using sequential files is explained in this section. The exact forms, however, are highly machine dependent. Check your BASIC reference manual before using the statements. Table 11.1 shows examples of statements used in different systems.

OPEN/CLOSE Statements

The first step in reading from a file or writing to a file is to associate the name of the file with a channel number from which the data are read or written. (A *channel* is the path that controls the input-output units.) This process is called opening the file. We use the following general form of an OPEN statement in this section:

```
                      "I"
  line no.    OPEN   "O",  #n,  "filename"
                      "R"
```

In this general statement, n is the channel number from which the data are read or to which they are written. This number is then used in the input or output statement that uses the file. The file mode—O, I, or R—indicates output, input, and random, respectively. Of course, a file must be opened before it is used.

READ#/INPUT# *Statements*

The READ or INPUT statement receives the data from a file. The general forms of these statements are:

```
line no,      INPUT #n, List
line no,      READ #n, List
```

Some systems allow both forms; others allow only one of the two statements.

PRINT#/WRITE# *Statements*

The form of the output statements for sequential files is:

```
line no,      PRINT #n, List or PRINT #n, USING List
line no,      WRITE #n, List or WRITE #n, USING List
```

The PRINT# statement writes data to a file exactly as it displays data on the screen. When a comma is used to separate the variables, each variable is written in one zone (approximately 15 columns). Naturally, extra blanks in the zone are not desirable because they waste space. Thus, a semicolon should be used as a separator.

After the data are written to a file, an INPUT (or READ) statement is used to read the data. To read the data, however, most systems require that a comma be used as a separator. Thus, you should insert a comma artificially between the items when writing so that the computer can read the data from an INPUT statement, for example:

```
100 PRINT #1, A; ","; B; ","; C
```

Some systems also allow a WRITE# statement. When a WRITE# statement is used, artificial comma insertion is not necessary. The WRITE# statement inserts the comma automatically when the data are written. In fact, this is the main difference between the PRINT# and WRITE# in some systems.

Error Trapping

An error may occur when a program is run even when the program is correct and works with the test data. This is especially true of a program that uses an external file. For example, FILE NOT FOUND, DISK FULL, or INPUT PAST END are typical error messages you may see during program execution. A good design should foresee these errors and "trap" them when they occur. *Error trapping* is the process of detecting the error, announcing it and a possible remedy to the user, and taking an action.

In most BASIC systems, an error statement and the value of two reserved variables can be used to trap the errors (see Appendix B). A typical error statement has the form:

```
ON ERROR GOTO   line no.
```

For example, the statement

```
100 ON ERROR GOTO 999
```

transfers control to statement 999, which is normally an error-trapping routine, if any error occurs during execution. The variables ERR and ERL will then have code values indicating the type of error and the line number in which the error occurred, respectively. Of course, specific values of codes vary among systems. These values can be used in an IF-THEN statement, such as:

```
999    IF ERR = code THEN . . . .
1009   IF ERL = line-no. THEN . . . .
```

The values of these variables can be tested only after the ERROR statement is executed.

End-of-File (EOF) Marker

As you have seen throughout the text, the end of a series of data can be marked with a trailer value (a value that is out of the range of the regular data). The BASIC system, however, can create an end-of-data indicator automatically for sequential files. There are two ways to detect the end of a file:

1. The end-of-data marker can be recognized with a function. The form of the function is

    ```
    line no.    v = EOF(n)
    ```

    where n is the file number. (See Table 11.1 for examples of this marker in different systems.) The value of v is normally 0 (for false) when the end-of-file marker has not yet been detected, and -1 (for true) when it has been detected. Examples:

```
100 IF EOF(1) THEN GOTO 999
500 IF EOF(4) THEN PRINT "END OF FILE #4"
```

2. Because an error occurs if an attempt is made to read past data, the ERROR statement can be used to detect the end of a file. For example, the statement 55 ON ERROR GOTO 200, used before an INPUT statement, transfers control to statement 200 if an error occurs. The program can then check value of the error code to make sure the error that occurred was indeed reading past data.

The end-of-file condition must be tested before an error occurs. That is, the EOF function or the ERROR statement must appear in the program before the statement that executes an INPUT.

LINE INPUT Statement

Some systems allow reading an entire record in a file through the LINE INPUT statement. The general form of the statement is

```
line no.   LINE INPUT #n, a$
```

where n is the file number and a$ is the variable name for the entire record (see Table 11.1). Normally, a line is regarded as a record, and the end of a line is marked by a carriage return.

LINE INPUT is very useful in certain cases, especially if the data are recorded in a fixed format, as in the following program. The program also includes examples of the statements discussed so far.

Example 11.2

Problem: The data about customer orders for a product are recorded in the file CUSDATA. Each record contains:

1. Customer's name in positions 1–12
2. Number of units ordered in positions 13–14

Write a program that reads the data and prints a report about the orders. Print the average order at the end of the report. Use the automatic EOF marker to terminate the reading loop.

Program:

```
10   OPEN "I", #1, "CUSDATA"
20   PRINT "CUSTOMER NAME", " NO. OF UNITS"
30   IF EOF(1) THEN GOTO 110
40   LINE INPUT #1, X$
50        N = N + 1
60        ORDER$ = MID$(X$, 13, 2)
70        UNIT = VAL(ORDER$)
80        PRINT LEFT$(X$, 12), UNIT
90        SUM = SUM + UNIT
100  GOTO 30
110  AVG = SUM/N
120  PRINT "THE AVERAGE NO. OF UNITS ORDERED WAS"; AVG
130  CLOSE #1
140  END
```

Notes:

1. The entire record (a line) is read into the string variable X$.
2. The fields in this record are segregated by the LEFT$ or MID$ function.
3. The numeric value of number of units ordered is assigned to variable UNIT (in line 70). This assignment is necessary for calculating SUM.

Accessing a File

The same general steps used to create a file are followed to access an existing file except that the file is opened as input. These general steps are:

1. Open the file as input.
2. Read the data from the file.
3. Manipulate and process the data as necessary.
4. Close the file.

Example 11.2 showed a sample program for accessing a file. The following is another example:

Example 11.3

Problem: Suppose data about a sample batch of a product are saved under the file name DATA1. Write a program that reads the data, calculates the average weight of each group of three items, and calculates the grand average. Assume 0 indicates end of data. Print the information in report form.

Solution Plan:

1. Open the file as input.
2. Print a heading.
3. Repeat the following steps until there are no more data:
   - **3.1** Read a record: X, Y, and Z.
   - **3.2** If X = 0, terminate the loop and go to Step 4.
   - **3.3** Calculate the average and accumulate the averages.
   - **3.4** Print the data.
4. Calculate the grand average.
5. Print the grand average.
6. Close the file.

Program:

```
10   OPEN "I", #1, "DATA1"
15   SUM = 0
20   PRINT "SAMPLE #1", "SAMPLE #2", "SAMPLE #3", "AVERAGE"
30   INPUT #1, X, Y, Z
40      IF X = 0 THEN GOTO 100
50      N = N + 1
60      AVG = (X + Y + Z)/3
70      SUM = SUM + AVG
80      PRINT X, Y, Z, AVG
90   GOTO 30
100  GAVG = SUM/N
110  PRINT "THE GRAND AVERAGE IS: "; GAVG
120  CLOSE #1
130  END
```

FILE PROCESSING—SECTION II

The following topics require more programming background than those in section I. This section first explores sequential file processing further and then presents random-file processing techniques.

Control Break Reports

Sometimes it is useful to prepare an itemized report categorized by a control field. For example, suppose different salespeople's weekly activities are stored in a file. A report showing the details of each transaction, the subtotal for each salesperson, and the grand total might be of interest to management. This kind of report contains detailed information, but a change in the value of a field causes a change in the sequence of information being printed. In this example, a control break occurs when the ID number just read is different from the previous ID number. A program that generates such a report is called a *control break program*. Writing a control break program for sequential processing is not difficult in BASIC if the data are sorted by the control field. The following example shows a simple control break program.

Example 11.4

Problem: The daily sales transactions in a department store are stored on the data file named SALES. Each record contains the following items:

1. Salesperson's ID number
2. Amount of the sale

Each salesperson can have one or more transaction records. The data are sorted by the salesperson's ID numbers. Develop a plan and write a program that prepares a sales report. The report should show each transaction, the total amount sold by each salesperson, and the total sales for the store.

Solution Plan:

1. Open the file.
2. Print the heading.
3. Initialize the variables:
   3.1 Set the first ID to 1; this signals the first record.
   3.2 Set the subtotal to zero (SUBTOT = 0).
   3.3 Set the grand total to zero (TOTAL = 0).
4. Repeat the following steps until there are no more data:
   4.1 If end of file, go to Step 5.
   4.2 Read an ID and a SALE.
   4.3 If first record, then set PREID to ID.
   4.4 If ID equals PREID then:

   >Print the ID and a SALE.
   >Accumulate the SALE into SUBTOT.

   Else:

   >Print the SUBTOT.
   >Accumulate the subtotal into the grand total.
   >Set PREID to ID.
   >Set SUBTOT to zero.
   >Print the ID and a SALE.
   >Accumulate the SALE into SUBTOT.

5. Print the subtotal for the last record.
6. Accumulate the subtotal into the grand total.
7. Print the grand total.
8. Close the file.
9. End.

Program:

```
10   OPEN 'I', #1, 'SALES'
20   PRINT TAB(15); 'XYZ CO. SALES REPORT'   :   PRINT
30   PRINT TAB(10); 'SALESPERSON ID'; TAB(30); 'SALES'   :   PRINT
40   PREID = 1         :         SUBTOT=0         :         TOTAL = 0
50   FOR I = 1 TO 500
60      IF EOF(1) THEN GOTO 110
70      INPUT #1, ID, ASALE
80      IF PREID = 1 THEN PREID = ID
90      IF ID = PREID THEN GOSUB 200 ELSE GOSUB 300
100  NEXT I
110  REM   END OF READING THE RECORDS
120  PRINT TAB(10); 'SUBTOTAL'; TAB(29); SUBTOT
130  TOTAL = TOTAL + SUBTOT
140  PRINT : PRINT : PRINT TAB(10); 'THE GRAND TOTAL'; TAB(29);TOTAL
150  CLOSE #1
160  GOTO 999
190  REM ************** SUBROUTINES SECTION ***************
200  REM *** THIS MODULE IS FOR THE CASE ID = PREID ***
210     PRINT TAB(12); ID; TAB(30); ASALE
220     SUBTOT = SUBTOT + ASALE
230  RETURN
240  REM *********** END OF MODULE *****************
300  REM *** ELSE SUBROUTINE FOR THE CASE ID <> PREID ***
310     PRINT TAB(10); 'SUBTOTAL'; TAB(29); SUBTOT
320     TOTAL = TOTAL + SUBTOT
330     PRINT
340     PREID = ID
350     SUBTOT = 0
360     PRINT TAB(12); ID ; TAB(30) ; ASALE
370     SUBTOT = SUBTOT + ASALE
380  RETURN
390  REM *********** END OF MODULE **********************
999  END
```

Notes:

1. This program works only if the data are sorted by ID numbers.
2. The program stores each ID in PREID for comparison with the next ID read. The value of the holding field is arbitrarily set to 1 to signal the first record.
3. If the ID just read equals the previous ID, then the program prints the information and accumulates the sales.
4. A control break occurs when the ID just read differs from the preceding ID. In this case, the program prints the subtotal, accumulates the subtotals, sets the PREID equal to the new ID, and sets the subtotal variable equal to zero. The program then proceeds to print and accumulate the data as before.

5. The following is a sample of the output generated by the program:

```
     XYZ CO. SALES REPORT
  SALESPERSON ID       SALES

       454958           757
       454958           378
       454958           678
    SUBTOTAL           1813

       564644          7888
       564644          2498
    SUBTOTAL          10386

       585767           788
       585767           677
    SUBTOTAL           1465

       615556           657
       615556           776
    SUBTOTAL           1433


    THE GRAND TOTAL   15097
```

6. To be of practical use, this program requires several modifications. For example, PRINT USING statements should be used to generate the output for financial reports.

Sorting

Sorting is the process of ordering records in a desired sequence. Sorting can become somewhat complex for files. The following example shows a simple procedure:

Example 11.5

Problem: Explain the main modules and write a program that sorts the records in the inventory file INVENT1. Each record in the file contains:

1. Item number in positions 1–5
2. Item description in positions 6–30

3. Number of units available in positions 31–35

Sort the file by item numbers, in ascending order. There are fewer than 100 records.

Modules:

1. Housekeeping
   a. Define array REC$(100) for the records, array AKEY(100) to hold the keys, and pointer array P(100).
   b. Initialize the pointer array.
   c. Open INVENT1 for input and INVENT2 for output.
2. Reading
   a. Read the records of the first file one by one.
   b. Assign the values of the item numbers to array AKEY.
3. Sorting

   Sort the array AKEY, rearranging the values of the pointer array at the same time.
4. Writing

   Write the data into INVENT2 in the order of the values of the pointer array.

Program:

```
10   REM HOUSEKEEPING MODULE
20   DIM REC$(100), AKEY(100), P(100)
30   FOR I = 1 TO 100    :    P(I) = I    :    NEXT I
40   OPEN 'I', #1, 'INVENT1'
50   OPEN 'O', #2, 'INVENT2'
60   REM *** READ THE VALUES ***
70      GOSUB 200
80   REM *** SORT THE ARRAY AKEY AND REARRANGE THE VALUES OF P ***
90      GOSUB 300
100  REM*** WRITE THE DATA ***
110     GOSUB 400
120  CLOSE #1, #2
130  GOTO 999
140  REM *************** SUBROUTINE SECTION **********************
200  REM * THIS SUBROUTINE READS THE DATA, A RECORD AT A TIME AND *
210  REM * ASSIGNS THE VALUE OF THE FIRST 5 POSITIONS OF EACH     *
220  REM * RECORD TO   ARRAY AKEY                                 *
230  FOR I = 1 TO 100
240     IF EOF(1) THEN GOTO 295
250     LINE INPUT #1, REC$(I)
260     N = N + 1
270     Y$ = LEFT$(REC$(I), 5)
280     AKEY(I) = VAL(Y$)
290  NEXT I
295  RETURN
```

```
300 REM**************************************************
310 REM*THIS SUBROUTINE SORTS ARRAY AKEY AND REARRANGES THE VALUES*
320 REM*OF THE ELEMENTS OF ARRAY P; BUBBLE SORT PROCEDURE IS USED *
330 FOR I = 1 TO N-1
340     FOR J = 1 TO N-I
350         IF AKEY(J+1) > AKEY(J) THEN GOTO 390
360             T1 = AKEY(J)              :    T2 = P(J)
370             AKEY(J) = AKEY(J+1)       :    P(J) = P(J+1)
380             AKEY(J+1) = T1            :    P(J+1) = T2
385 REM     END-OF-IF
390     NEXT J
395 NEXT I
399 RETURN
400 REM**************************************************
405 REM* THIS SUBROUTINE WRITES THE DATA ON FILE #2 IN THE ORDER *
410 REM* OF THE VALUES OF THE ARRAY P                            *
420 FOR K = 1 TO N
430     PRINT #2, REC$(P(K))
440 NEXT K
450 RETURN
999 END
```

Notes:

1. LINE INPUT is used to read the entire record into an element of array REC$. Then, values of the items numbers are assigned to array AKEY.

2. Array AKEY is sorted in ascending order with a bubble sort procedure. The values of the pointer array P, which at the beginning were 1, 2, 3, . . . , will change to reflect the order of sorted array AKEY.

3. The content of array REC$ is written in the order shown by array P.

Merging

Merging is the process of combining files. There are two ways to combine one or several files: (1) appending the files, one after another and (2) interspersing the files.

The process of appending the files is simple, and some systems even have a system command, such as APPEND A, B, for this purpose. If a system does not have such a command, then the following general procedure can be used:

1. Open all files as input.
2. Open a file as output (this file will contain the merged files).
3. Read the input files, one by one.

4. Print the files into the output file, one by one.
5. Close all the files.
6. Delete the unwanted files.
7. Give the final file any new name desired.

This procedure can be applied to merge existing files or newly created files, or to add new records to an existing file. The process becomes more complicated if a sorted file is desired. In this case, either the final file can be sorted after merging or the files can be interspersed by a procedure like the one explained in Chapter 10. The following example shows a program that uses a simple append procedure:

Example 11.6

Problem: Two files contain the inventory of a store: STORE1 and STORE2. Write a program that combines the files and saves the result under the name STORE.

Program:

```
10    OPEN "I", #1, "STORE1"
20    OPEN "I", #2, "STORE2"
30    OPEN "O", #3, "STORE"
50    FOR I = 1 TO 100
60        IF EOF(1) THEN GOTO 100
70        LINE INPUT #1, AREC$
80        PRINT #3, AREC$
90    NEXT I
100   FOR I = 1 TO 100
110       IF EOF(2) THEN GOTO 900
120       LINE INPUT #2, AREC$
130       PRINT #3, AREC$
140   NEXT I
900       CLOSE #1, #2, #3
999       END
```

Notes:

1. See Table 11.1 for the form of the file statements for different computer systems.
2. The statement
   INPUT #n, A, B, . . .
   could have been used instead of LINE INPUT statement.

File Maintenance

File maintenance can be defined as updating a file, that is, the process of changing or deleting a field in a record, adding a new record, or deleting an existing record. The process of updating sequential files can be as simple as merging two files, just explained. Updating, however, can become very complicated. For example, updating a master file with several temporary transaction files is a lengthy process. Generally, the records of the master file are read, changes are made, and then the records are written to a new file. The changes can be incorporated with a temporary transaction file. (The transaction file can be created on line with the terminal.) Several other files or reports may be created as by-products, such as a report for error messages that may occur during updating or an exception report for reporting extraordinary items. See Figure 11.3.

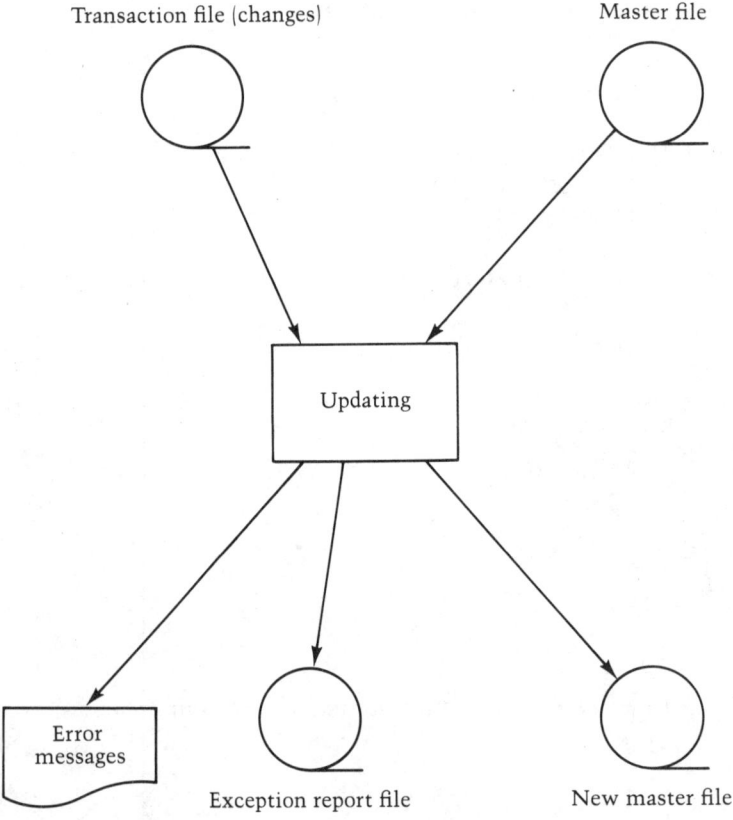

Figure 11.3 Sequential updating of a master file

Example 11.7 shows a simplified problem. Example 11.8, a more complex one, demonstrates the process of updating a master file by using a transaction file, thereby creating a new master file.

Example 11.7

Problem: Each record of the existing inventory file INVENT includes an item number, an item name, and the number of units available. Write an interactive program that incorporates changes (increased or reduced inventory) to each item in the file.

Solution Plan:

1. Open the file INVENT as #1 for input.
2. Open the file INVENT2 as #2 for output.
3. Repeat the following steps until the end of the file.
    - **3.1** Read a record of file 1; at the end, go to Step 4.
    - **3.2** Make the changes.
    - **3.3** Write the record to file 2.
4. Close both files.
5. Delete the file INVENT.
6. Change the name INVENT2 to INVENT.

Program:

```
10   PRINT "THIS PROGRAM UPDATES THE ENTIRE INVENTORY FILE"
20   OPEN "I", #1, "INVENT"
30   OPEN "O", #2, "INVENT2"
100  FOR I = 1 TO 100
110     IF EOF(1) THEN GOTO 900
120     INPUT #1, ID, ANAME$, UNITS
130     PRINT "TYPE THE INCREASE/DECREASE FOR ITEM # "; ID, ANAME$
140     PRINT "TYPE THE REDUCTION WITH A NEGATIVE SIGN."
150     INPUT CHANGE
160     UNITS = UNITS + CHANGE
170     PRINT #2, ID; "," ANAME$; ","; UNITS
180  NEXT I
900  PRINT "ALL DONE ... THANKS ..."
910  CLOSE #1, #2
999  END
```

Notes:

1. Check Table 11.1 for the forms of the file statement in different systems.
2. After updating, the file INVENT can be deleted, and then the file INVENT2 can be renamed INVENT. (Some systems have BASIC statements for this purpose.)

Example 11.8

Problem: Each record of the master inventory file INVENT includes:

1. The item number
2. The name of the item
3. The number of units available

The transaction file TRANS has been created for updating the master file. Each record of the transaction file includes:

1. The item number
2. The changes for each item (positive or negative)

Assume the last records of both files use zeros to indicate the end of data. Develop a procedure and write a program to update the master file.

Procedure: One possible method is to read each record in the transaction file, beginning with the first, and then to search the master file until the corresponding item is found. The process of changing and writing then continues. This process is performed for all the items in the transaction file. This method, however, is neither efficient nor practical. A more efficient method is used in the following plan and is explained in the flowchart in Figure 11.4. This method applies only if both files are sorted.

File Processing—Section II 479

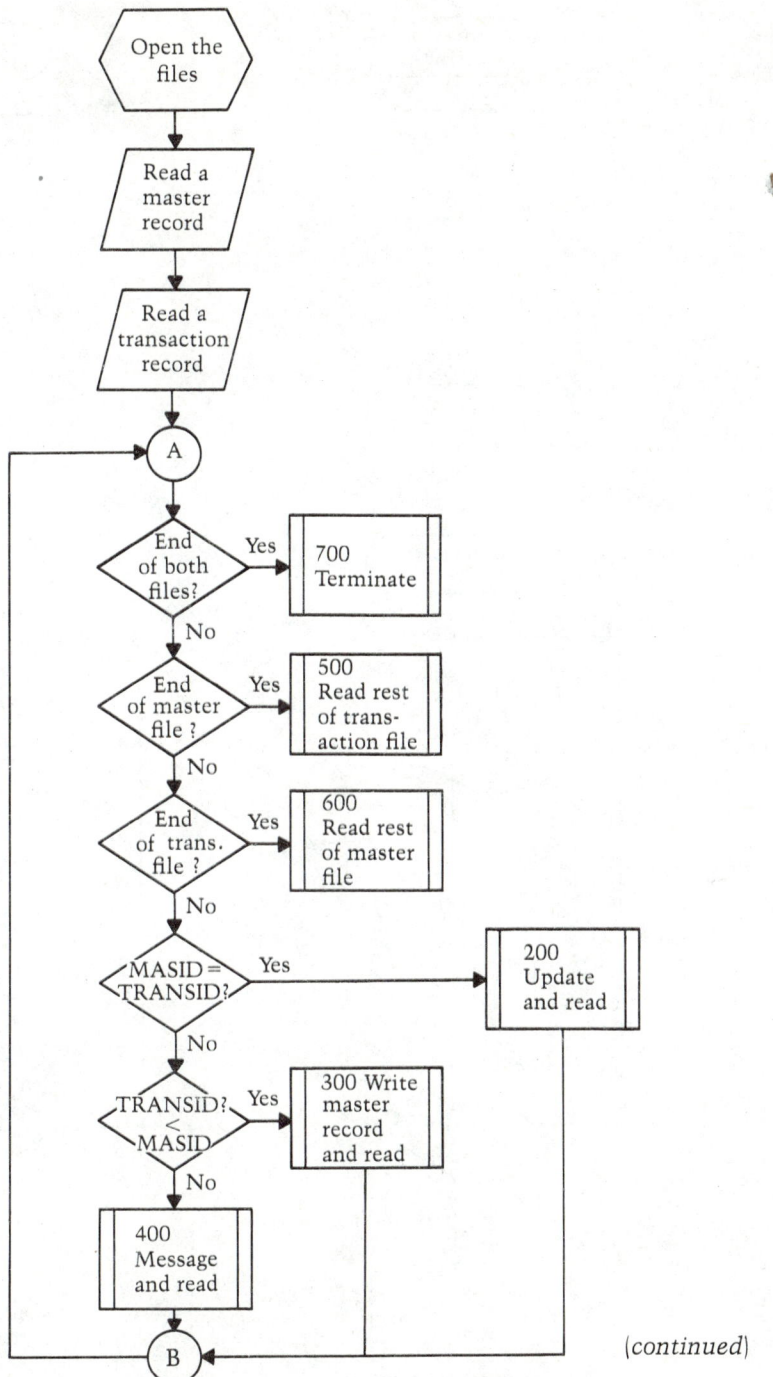

Figure 11.4 The flowchart for sequential updating of Example 11.8

480 *File Processing*

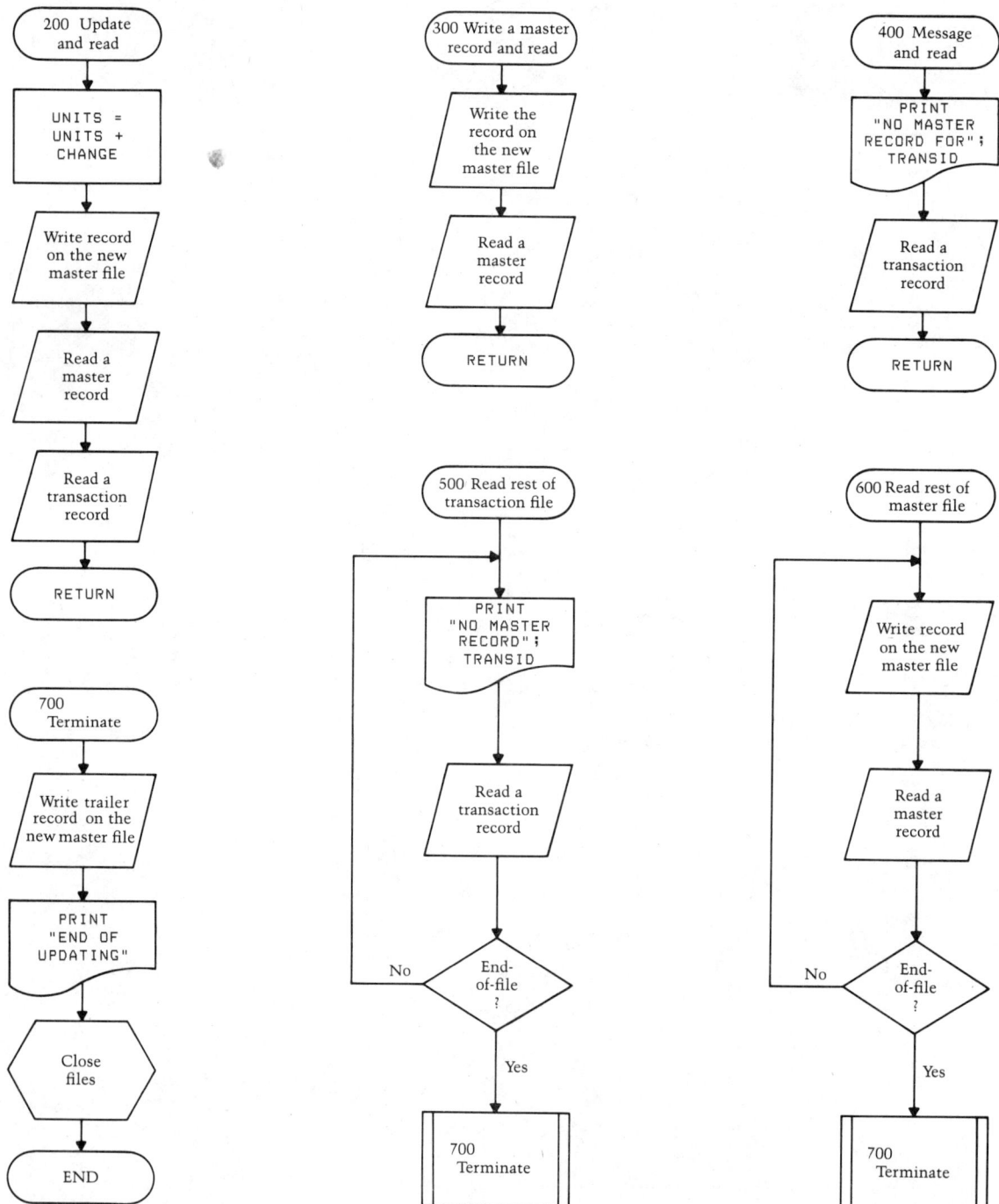

Figure 11.4 (continued)

Solution Plan:

1. Make sure both files are sorted.
2. Initializing
   - 2.1 Open the old master file, transaction file, and a new master file.
   - 2.2 Read the first record in the transaction file.
   - 2.3 Read the first record in the old master file.
3. Processing loop, repeat the following steps until the end of one of the files:
   - 3.1 If both MASTER-ID and TRANSACTION-ID are zero, go to step 7.
   - 3.2 If MASTER-ID = 0, go to Step 5.
   - 3.3 If TRANSACTION-ID = 0, go to Step 6.
   - 3.4 If MASTER-ID = TRANS-ID then:
       Update the inventory of the item.
       Write the master record to new master file.
       Read a record in the old master file.
       Read a record in the transaction file.

     Else If MASTER-ID < TRANSACTION-ID then (no activity for that master record):
       Write the master record to the new master file.
       Read a record from the old master file. If end, go to Step 5.
     Else (no master record for that transaction record):
       Write an error message for the item in the transaction file.
       Read a record from transaction file, if end, go to Step 6.

     End of if
4. End processing loop.
5. Write error messages for the remaining transaction records and go to Step 7.
6. Write the remaining master records to the new master file.
7. Write the trailer record to the new master file.
8. Close the files.

Program:

```
10  REM THIS PROGRAM UPDATES THE MASTER FILE USING A TRANSACTION
20  REM FILE SEQUENTIALLY, ASSUMING BOTH FILES ARE SORTED
30  OPEN 'I', #1, 'INVENT'
40  OPEN 'I', #2, 'TRANS'
50  OPEN 'O', #3, 'NUINVENT'
60  INPUT #1, MASID, ANAME$, UNITS
70  INPUT #2, TRANSID, CHANGE
100 REM BEGINNING OF PROCESSING, COMPARING, WRITING, READING
110 FOR I = 1 TO 500
120    IF MASID = 0 AND TRANSID = 0 THEN GOTO 700
130    IF MASID = 0 THEN GOTO 500
140    IF TRANSID = 0 THEN GOTO 600
150       IF MASID = TRANSID THEN                    &
                         GOSUB 200                   &
                ELSE IF MASID < TRANSID THEN         &
                         GOSUB 300                   &
                      ELSE                           &
                         GOSUB 400
160 REM    END-OF-IF
170 NEXT I
200 REM ** THIS MODULE IS FOR THE CASE   MASTID = TRANSID
210      UNITS = UNITS + CHANGE
220      PRINT #3, MASID; ','; ANAME$; ','; UNITS
230      INPUT #1, MASID, ANAME$, UNITS
240      INPUT #2, TRANSID, CHANGE
250 RETURN
300 REM *** THIS MODULE IS FOR THE CASE:  MASID < TRANSID
310    PRINT #3, MASID; ','; ANAME$; ','; UNITS
320    INPUT #1, MASID, ANAME$, UNITS
340 RETURN
400 REM *** THIS MODULE IS FOR THE CASE TRANSID < MASID *
410      PRINT 'NO MASTER RECORD FOR ITEM #';  TRANSID
420      INPUT #2, TRANSID, CHANGE
440 RETURN
500 REM    ** THIS MODULE WRITES ERROR MESSAGE FOR THE **
510 REM    ** REMAINDER OF THE TRANSACTION RECORDS    **
520 FOR I = 1 TO 500
530    PRINT 'NO MASTER RECORD FOR ITEM #';   TRANSID
540    INPUT #2, TRANSID, UNITS
550    IF TRANSID = 0 THEN GOTO 700
560 NEXT I
570 PRINT 'ERROR . . . . THERE ARE MORE THAN 500 ITEMS'
600 REM ** THIS MODULE WRITES THE REMAINING MASTER RECORDS **
610 REM ** ON THE NEW FILE                                 **
620 FOR I = 1 TO 500
630    PRINT #3, MASID; ','; ANAME$; ','; UNITS
640    INPUT #1, MASID, ANAME$, UNITS
650    IF MASID = 0 GOTO 700
660 NEXT I
700 PRINT #3, MASID; ','; ANAME$; ','; UNITS
900 PRINT 'END OF UPDATING'
910 CLOSE #1, #2, #3
999 END
```

Notes:

1. It is assumed that there are fewer than 500 records in each file.
2. This program shows only the fundamental steps in solving the problem. Many modifications and improvements are necessary. For example, the program could create a master record or print a message for the items that have no master record.

RANDOM-FILE PROCESSING

A *random* or *direct-access* file is organized so that any record in the file can be read from or written to directly with a key. A *key* is a field (or a combination of fields) that identifies a record. Usually, the records in a file are controlled and processed through key fields. For example, the Social Security number can be used as a key field in the processing of a personnel master file. A random-access file can be compared to the mail boxes in a post office. One can access any box if one knows its number without disturbing any of the other boxes.

Normally, a random file is stored on tracks of a disk or diskette. Each track has several sectors (see Figure 11.5). Any sector on the disk can be identified by its position relative to the first sector in the first track. If we assume that a whole record is stored in one sector, then each record can be written or retrieved by knowing its relative record number. In a later section, we will discuss how to store more than one record in a sector.

General Steps

When the computer reads data from or writes it to a file, the data actually go through a buffer. A *buffer* is a temporary storage area where data await processing. Fortunately, the programmer does not have to worry about this for sequential files because the INPUT# (or READ or PRINT) statement takes care of the buffer automatically. When using direct-access files, however, the programmer must manage the buffer area in many systems. For example, to write a record to a file, the programmer needs to create the record, move it to the buffer area, and then write it to the file from the buffer (see Figure 11.6). Therefore, processing random files requires the additional steps of defining the records and fields, and moving the data from the buffer to the disk, or vice versa.

484 *File Processing*

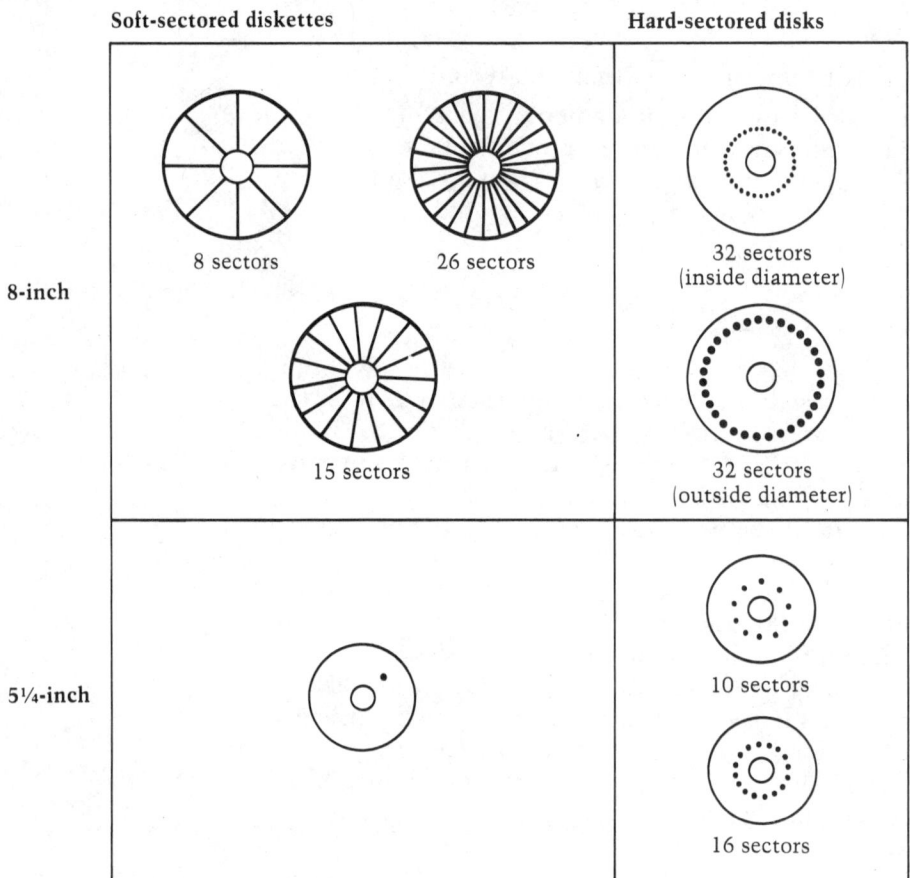

Figure 11.5 Sectors of a disk

The general steps for processing a random file are as follows:

1. Open the file as a random-access file.
2. Define a record by defining the fields and their lengths in the record.
3. Move the data from the disk to buffer or from the buffer to the disk.
4. Process the data.
5. Close the file.

Of course, the precise order of tasks depends on whether a file is being accessed for inquiry or for updating. For example, Step 4 above would be performed before Step 3 if the data were being output.

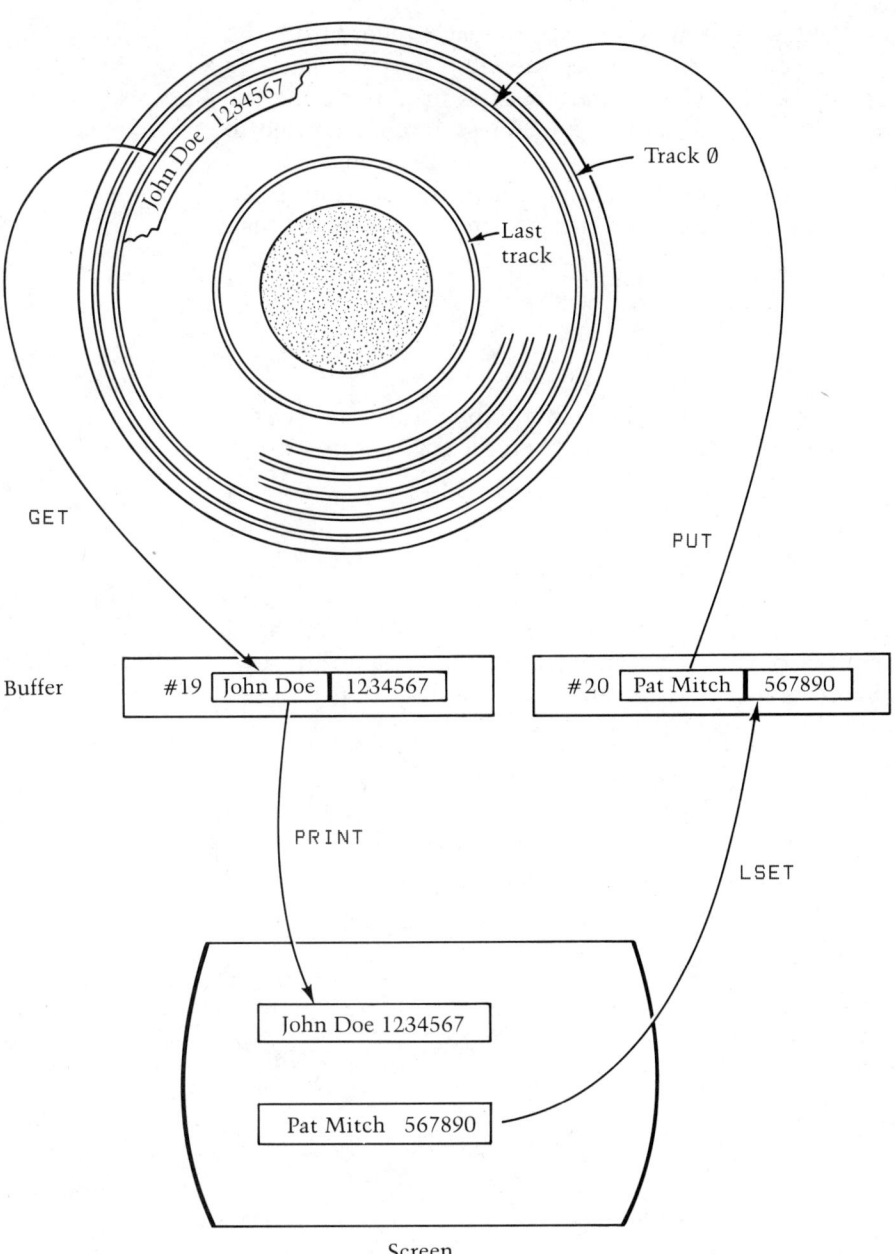

Figure 11.6 Reading from and writing to a disk

In many systems, the `GET` statement is used to read a record from the disk into the buffer. The `PUT` statement does the job of writing the data from the buffer to the disk. The `FIELD` statement is used to define the fields and their sizes in a record. Finally, the `LSET` statement is used to move the data into the buffer.

All the above statements are explained further in this section. First, however, look at a simple example of how the information in the file can be retrieved.

Example 11.9

Problem: Suppose certain information about inventory items is stored in the random-access file `INVENT`. Each record contains the following fields:

1. The name of the item, 25 characters
2. The number of units available, 2 characters

Furthermore, each record's key is the *part number*, which is the item's position relative to the first item in the file. Write an interactive program that asks for a part number and displays that part's name and the number of units available.

Solution Plan:

1. Open the file `INVENT` as #1 for random access.
2. Define the fields and their sizes in a record.
3. Repeat the following steps until the key code (`AKEY`) is zero:
    3.1 Accept a key code.
    3.2 Get the item directly.
    3.3 Display the information.
4. Close the file.

Program:

```
10   OPEN "R", #1, "INVENT"
20   FIELD #1, 25 AS ANAME$, 2 AS UNITS$
30   FOR I = 1 TO 100
40      PRINT "TYPE THE PART NUMBER--2 DIGITS,
             TYPE 0 WHEN THROUGH"
50      INPUT AKEY
60      IF AKEY = 0 THEN GOTO 900
70      GET #1, AKEY
80      PRINT "PART: "; ANAME$
90      PRINT "NUMBER OF UNITS AVAILABLE "; UNITS$
100  NEXT I
900  PRINT "*** CALL BACK ***"
910  CLOSE #1
999  END
```

Notes:

1. The FIELD statement in line 20 defines the length of each field in the record. Each field is defined as a string variable.
2. The GET statement retrieves the item that is stored in the relative position identified by AKEY (see Figure 11.6).
3. For the exact form of the file statements, see Table 11.1.

The process of creating a file is slightly more complicated, as the following example demonstrates:

Example 11.10

Problem: Create a file that contains the names (20 characters each), and telephone numbers of the customers of a store. Each customer is identified by a unique sequential code number—1001, 1002, 1003, and so on.

Solution Plan:

1. Open file PHONES as a random access file.
2. Define the fields of each record.
3. Begin the loop; repeat until no more data:
   3.1 Accept a name and a phone number; at end go to Step 5.
   3.2 Move the name and the phone number to the buffer.
   3.3 Write the buffer to the file.

4. End of loop.
5. Close the file.
6. End.

Program:

```
10   OPEN 'R', #1, 'PHONES'
20   FIELD #1, 20 AS CUS$, 7 AS FONE$
30   PRINT 'THIS PROGRAM CREATES A FILE OF THE NAMES AND PHONE '
40   PRINT 'NUMBERS OF THE CUSTOMERS'
50   FOR AKEY = 1 TO 100
60       CODE = 1000 + AKEY
70       PRINT'TYPE THE NAME AND PHONE NUMBER OF THE CUSTOMER'
80       PRINT 'NUMBER: '; CODE; ' TYPE NO-MORE WHEN DONE'
90       INPUT ANAME$, NUMBER$
100          IF ANAME$ = 'NO-MORE' THEN GOTO 900
110          LSET CUS$ = ANAME$
120          LSET FONE$ = NUMBER$
130          PUT #1, AKEY
140  NEXT AKEY
900  PRINT 'ALL DONE *** SEE YOU ***'
910  CLOSE #1
999  END
```

Notes:

1. The FIELD statement defines a record and its fields in the buffer.
2. After ANAME$ and NUMBER$ are accepted, they are moved to buffer with the LSET statement (lines 110 and 120). They are then written to the file by the PUT statement (line 130) (see Figure 11.6).
3. See Table 11.1 for some examples of the form of the statements in different systems.

Forms of the Statements

Again, be aware that forms of statements vary among systems. Check your BASIC manual. See Table 11.1 for examples of variations.

OPEN/CLOSE Statements

The general form of the OPEN/CLOSE statements is explained in the Section I of this chapter. The same form is used for random-access files, except that the file mode is always R for "random." Thus, the form of the OPEN statement is

```
line no. OPEN "R", #n, "filename"
```

Some systems allow you to define the record length in the OPEN statement. For example, in Microsoft BASIC, the statement

```
10 OPEN "R", #1, FILE1, 64
```

opens FILE1 as a random file with a maximum record length of 64.

FIELD Statement

The FIELD statement is an executable statement that defines the record, its fields, and their lengths in the buffer. The general form of this statement used in this section is

```
line no. FIELD #n, w¹ AS var¹$, w2 AS var2$, ...
```

where n is the file number under which the file is opened, $var^i\$$ is the field name for the variable i, and w^i is the length of each field (in bytes). The field buffer name is always a BASIC string name. The following are some examples:

```
100 FIELD #1, 225 AS AREC$
50  FIELD #5, 20 AS CUS$, 25 AS ADRES1$, 25 AS ADRES2$, 5 AS ZIP$
90  FIELD #4, (N*62) AS DUMY$, 50 AS ADRES$, 12 AS NUM$
```

The total number of bytes (characters) specified in the FIELD statement must not exceed the input-output buffer capacity and must be smaller than the record length defined when the file was opened; otherwise, a FIELD OVERFLOW error occurs.

PUT/GET Statements

The general form of the GET/PUT used in this section is

```
line no.  PUT #n, k
line no.  GET #n, k
```

where n is the file number and k is the relative record number in the file. PUT writes a record to disk, and GET reads a record from the disk. Of course, the file n must be opened before reading or writing. These are two examples:

```
100 GET #1, 3
500 PUT #1, N
```

LSET/RSET Statements

The LSET or RSET statement places a string into a buffer field.
The general form of the LSET and RSET statements is

```
line no. LSET var₁$ = var₂$ (or an expression)
line no. RSET var₁$ = var₂$ (or an expression)
```

Both of these statements assign $var_2\$$ to $var_1\$$. Of course, $var_1\$$ should have been defined, in the FIELD statement, as the field name for the random-file buffer. When you use LSET, the blank spaces, if any, are placed to the right of the field; when you use RSET, the blank spaces are placed to the left of the field. For example, if ANAME$ equals "JOHN" and LNAME$ equals "DOREY", then

```
100 LSET Y$ = ANAME$ + " " + LANAME$
```

places "JOHN DOREY" in the buffer field Y$.

Multirecords

As mentioned before, a record in a buffer can be placed in a sector of the disk. A sector can contain a certain number of bytes (256 is very common). A *byte* is a memory unit that can contain one character, such as "A", "-", or "X". (Numeric data, however, are stored as numeric values and take less than one byte per digit. For example, in most systems a simple numeric value written as a decimal (single-precision, real number), such as 1234.56, occupies only four bytes. Integer values need even less—two bytes per value. You can convert numeric values to string data with a function.)

As an example, let's see how many bytes are needed to store a name and address. The required bytes for a hypothetical situation are as follows:

Item	Length (characters)	Bytes
First name, middle initial	15	15
Last name	15	15
Number and street	25	25
City, state, zip	25	25
	80	80

Thus, we can store about three sets of names and addresses in a 256-byte sector; in this example, (3 × 80 = 240) if we can divide a record into three *sub-records*. In data processing terminology, a record is called a *physical record*, and each subrecord is called a *logical record*.

Nevertheless, writing and accessing a subrecord is not as simple as writing and reading a record. One method of accessing a subrecord is to read the entire record and then ignore the subrecords that are not needed. To do that, we need to know the relationship between the records and subrecords in a file. Table 11.2 shows the relationship between the relative keys (the subrecord numbers) and the records in the sector containing three sets of names and addresses.

Table 11.2 The relationship between records and subrecords in a sample sector

Record Number	Relative Key or Sub-Record Number
1	1
	2
	3
2	4
	5
	6
3	7
	8
	9

Remember that we would like to search for the item number, which is the subrecord number. Thus, for example, if we are looking for item #8, the second subrecord of the third record should be searched. This relationship can be found by the formulas

```
Record# = REC = INT((KEY - 1)/N) + 1
Subrecord # = SUBREC = KEY - N*(REC - 1)
```

where N is the number of subrecords in the record and KEY is the item number. (Basically, these formulas find the quotient, Q, and the remainder of KEY-1 divided by N.)

For example, if there are five subrecords per record, the location of item 29 is as follows:

```
REC = INT ((29 - 1)/5) + 1 = 6
SUBREC = 29 - 5*5 = 4
```

Thus, item 29 should be searched for (or recorded in) in the fourth subrecord of the sixth record. This procedure is used in the following example:

Example 11.11

Problem: Write a program that creates a random file for the names and addresses of the customers of a store. The length of each record is as follows:

First name	10 characters
Last name	10 characters
Number and street	20 characters
City, state, zip	20 characters
	60 characters

Each customer has been assigned one of the sequence numbers as a code. Assume up to 256 bytes can be held in a record and in the I/O buffer. Use four subrecords per record.

Program:

```
10   OPEN "R", #1, "ADRES"
20   PRINT "THIS PROGRAM RECORDS THE CUSTOMERS' ADDRESSES"
30   FOR I = 1 TO 1000
40      PRINT "TYPE THE CUSTOMER'S NUMBER, TYPE ZERO IF DONE"
50      INPUT CNUM
60      IF CNUM = 0 THEN GOTO 900
70      REC = INT((CNUM - 1)/4) + 1
80      SUBREC = CNUM - 4*(REC - 1)
90      FIELD #1, ((SUBREC - 1)*60) AS DUMMY$, 10 AS ANAME$,
                  10 AS LNAME$, 20 AS STREET$, 20 AS CITY$
100     PRINT "TYPE THE FIRST NAME" :    INPUT N1$
110     PRINT "TYPE THE LAST NAME" :     INPUT N2$
120     PRINT "TYPE NUMBER AND STREET" :    INPUT A1$
130     PRINT "TYPE THE CITY, STATE, AND ZIP":   INPUT A2$
140     LSET ANAME$ = N1$  :  LSET LNAME$ = N2$
150     LSET STREET$ = A1$ :  LSET CITY$ = A2$
160     PUT #1, REC
170  NEXT I
900  PRINT " *************** SEE YOU SOON *************** "
910  CLOSE #1
999  END
```

Notes:

1. The length of the first field in the FIELD statement (DUMMY$) varies from one subrecord to another. This method allows you to define as a "dummy" those subrecords that are not needed. For example, if the customer's number is 19, then

```
REC = 5
SUBREC = 3
FIELD #1, 2*60 AS DUMMY$, 10 AS ANAME$, ....
```
In this case, the FIELD statement causes the first 120 characters in sector 5 to be ignored, and the 10 characters starting from the 121st character to be assigned to ANAME$.

2. The number of bytes the I/O buffer can hold varies among systems. See Table 11.1 for examples.
3. This program is designed to show the concept of accessing a subrecord. In practice, the program needs some modifications. For example, if the purpose is to create a file, then keys can be generated in the loop.

Random Accessing by an ID

The sequence numbers 1, 2, 3, ... were used in the previous examples as keys for recording or finding an item. But how can we find the item if we do not know the record number? Furthermore, in some applications we would like to find the item by its name, a known ID number, or some other *key field*. If the key fields follow a pattern, it is easy to change them into a relative key. For example, if we know that the ID numbers are in sequence and start with a constant,—10000, for instance—we simply subtract the constant from each ID to find the relative record number. If the key fields are not in sequence, one simple method is to search a table for the record number after entering the key field. A more sophisticated index, however, must be developed for the large files.

Another method for finding a relative record number when an ID number is known is to convert the ID number to the relative key by certain procedures (see Figure 11.7). Transforming a key field into a new key is often called *hashing*. A frequently used hashing algorithm is an arithmetic procedure known as the division-remainder method. This procedure converts numeric key fields into a uniformly distributed set of record numbers. The technique is simple; it starts by dividing the key field by a prime number. The remainder of the division represents the relative record number. The prime number is usually slightly larger than the size of the file. For example, if there are about 85 records in a file, the prime number 101 would be chosen. Assume a customer's ID number is 946856. The ID 946856 divided by 101 equals 9374 with a remainder of 82. The remainder 82 represents the record or item number. The prime number must be greater than the number of records in the file (about 30% greater), but less than the number of storage locations available.

Figure 11.7 A procedure converting a key field into a relative key

In this example, the division-remainder method ensures a key number between 0 and 101 (that is, the remainder is always between 0 and 101). However, it does not guarantee that all the spaces for records 1 to 101 will be used because the generated addresses may have gaps between them. For instance, the generated addresses for a file might be 2, 5, 6, and 11. This implies that the spaces for records 1, 3, 4, 7, 8, 9, and 10 stay empty. Furthermore, the procedure does not guarantee that each address for an ID number will be unique. Any hashing algorithm may generate the same address for two or more keys. In the example, for instance, this will happen if the value of an ID is 101 more than the value of the previous one.

If two keys have the same address, they are called *synonyms*; generating the same address for a second key is called *collision*. To overcome these problems, the programmer should create a special "overflow" area and place the synonyms, after the first one, in the overflow area. It is common to choose a divisor 130% to 140% greater than the size of the file in order to reduce the number of synonyms. (The divisor, by the way, does not have to be a prime number. Any odd number will perform as well as a prime number.)

Designing a numeric sequential code for the records and organizing the file by relative keys is very common in business applications. In these cases, if searching by a key field is necessary, then an index table can be created. The following example shows a very simple program that converts a code to a relative address for retrieving information randomly:

Example 11.12

Problem: Write a program that displays a customer's name and telephone number from file PHONES (created in the Example 11.10) when the customer's code number is entered. Each customer has a unique sequential code number starting from 1000. The customer's name contains up to 20 characters, and the telephone number contains 7 characters.

Program:

```
10   OPEN "R", #1, "PHONES"
20   FIELD #1, 20 AS CUS$, 7 AS FONE$
30   FOR AKEY = 1 TO 100
40   PRINT "WHAT IS THE CUSTOMERS CODE, TYPE 0 IF DONE"
50   INPUT CODE
60   IF CODE = 0 THEN GOTO 900
70      AKEY = CODE - 1000
80      GET #1, AKEY
90      PRINT CUS$, FONE$
100 NEXT AKEY
900 PRINT "ALL DONE *** SEE YOU ***"
910 CLOSE #1
999 END
```

EXERCISES

Creating a File:

11.1 Create a sequential data file for the inventory items of a sporting goods shop. The information to be recorded about each item is as follows:

   a. Item number
   b. Name of the item
   c. Number of units in stock
   d. Minimum inventory level
   e. Ordering quantity

   The data file should be created on line.

11.2 Write a program that creates a sequential master file for the employees of a shop. The information about each employee is as follows:

   a. Social Security number
   b. Name
   c. Address 1—number and street
   d. Address 2—city, state, and zip code
   e. Marital status code (M or S)
   f. Yearly salary

Reporting:

11.3 Prepare an inventory report for a furniture store. The product information is stored under the name `ITEMDATA`, and each record contains:

   a. Code of the item
   b. Name of the item
   c. Number of units in stock
   d. Average weekly sales of the item
   e. Cost of the item

   The last record contains zeros in each field, indicating the end of the data. The output is a report containing all the input information and the value of each item (the number of units times the cost). Also print the total values of all the items at the end of the report.

11.4 Information about customer orders is stored in file `ORDER`. Customer information includes account number, name, and previous balance, followed by the several order records for that customer. Each record contains:

   a. Name of the product ordered
   b. Number of units ordered
   c. Unit price of the product

   Zeros are recorded as the last item ordered. Then information about the next customer is recorded. Design and write a program that reads the file and prepares a report about customer orders. The output includes all the input information, the total value of orders for each product, and the total amount ordered by each customer. Print the total amount of orders at the end.

Control Break Report:

11.5 The information about the employees of a factory is stored in file `EMPLOYEE`. Each record contains:

   a. Name of the employee
   b. ID number
   c. Department
   d. Salary

   Write a program that generates a report showing all the input information, the total salary in each department, and the grand total salary. List the department number only once. Assume the data are sorted by department number. Use output editing features to make the report readable.

11.6 A sales analysis report by store is to be prepared. Write a program to prepare the report.

Input:

Store number in columns 1–2

Salesperson ID in columns 3–7

Salesperson name in columns 8–27

Current sales (9999.99) in columns 28–33

Output:

A sales analysis report consisting of:

a. The name of the company, date, page number, and an appropriate heading

b. Detailed records about each store and the total sales for the store

c. Total sales for all stores

Control Break, Sorting:

11.7 Each record of the sales file of a company contains:

Branch code (numeric)	2 digits
State	2 characters
Date of sale	8 characters
Product code	7 characters
Product description	20 characters
Quantity sold	Less than 99.99
Unit price	Less than 99.99
Tax code: I or O (in or out of state)	1 character

The tax is 4.5 percent for in-state sales only. Write a program that reads the input information and generates a report containing:

a. Detailed input information, the sales (gross, before taxes), tax, and the total after tax for each record

b. Subtotals for each branch

c. Grand total at the end

When you design the output, make sure to include:

d. The company logo at the top (design some kind of logo)

e. The name of the report (the purpose)

f. Detailed data headings

g. Subheadings for each total

Assume the data are not sorted.

Merging:

11.8 A newly established computer club acquires new members each week. The membership file is stored in sequential file MEMBERS. Each record contains:

Telephone number	7 digits
Name (last name, first name)	20 characters
Address 1: number and street	25 characters
Address 2: city, state, and zip	25 characters
Active/nonactive code (A or N)	1 character
Balance on membership dues	Less than 999.99

Write a program that adds the new members each week.
Assume:
a. The file is not sorted and need not be.
b. The file is sorted by member names and must stay sorted.
The merging should take place on line.

Updating:

11.9 An instructor has stored information about students in file STUDENTS. Each record already contains:

Social Security number	9 digits
Name	20 characters
Test 1 score	5 digits
Test 2 score	5 digits
Homework 1	2 digits
Homework 2	2 digits
Homework 3	2 digits

For the items listed below, write a program module that:
a. Inserts the next test score (test 3)
b. Inserts the next homework grade (homework 4)

c. Calculates the average for each student by the following formula:

$$AVG = \left(\frac{Test\,1 + Test\,2 + \ldots + Test\,n}{N}\right) \times .75$$
$$+ \left(\frac{HW\,1 + HW\,2 + \ldots + HW\,m}{M}\right) \times .25$$

Record each student's average as the last item of the record.

d. Generates a report showing detailed information about each student.

Next, write a program that combines the above modules and starts with a menu. The program should proceed to a module depending on which menu selection the user makes.

11.10 A wholesale distributor furnishes products to certain customers weekly. Customers' master records are stored under the filename `CUSMAS`. Each record contains:

Customer's code (numeric)	5 digits
Customer's name	20 characters
Year-to-date purchases	Less the 99999.99
Discount code 1, 2, or 3	1 digit

    1 indicates a wholesaler
    2 indicates a retailer
    3 indicates an end user

The discount schedule is based on the following table:

Year-to-Date Amount	Discount Code 1	Discount Code 2	Discount Code 3
Up to $1000	3%	2%	1%
Up to $10,000	4%	5%	6%
Up to $100,000	6%	8%	10%

The weekly order is placed on a transaction file named `TRAN1`. Each record in the transaction file contains:

Customer's code
Name of the product ordered
Quantity ordered
Unit price

Develop and write a program that reads the master file and the transaction file and creates (1) a new updated master file and (2) a report of customers' orders. The discount on newly ordered items is based on the previous year-to-date amount (before the new order) and the above table. The total amount ordered after the discount should be added to the accumulated order. (*Hint:* Store the information about the report on a newly created file. After updating is complete, read and generate the report.)

Data File Processing:

11.11 One forecasting method is the *moving average method*. By this method, the averages of data obtained during the most recent time period are used to estimate data for the next period. For example, if the moving average is to be calculated over three time periods, the following are a few moving averages:

$$XBAR2 = (X1 + X2 + X3)/3$$
$$XBAR3 = (X2 + X3 + X4)/3$$
$$\vdots$$

The number of periods used to calculate a moving average depends on the situation and affects the accuracy of the prediction directly. Assume the following data represent the average monthly sales of a certain product.

782.96	756.21	777.62	771.65	691.96	699.30
712.80	731.97	759.38	763.72	769.27	821.51
849.04	879.69	901.29	932.54	925.49	900.43
887.81	875.40	901.22	872.15	822.11	869.90
904.65	914.37	939.23	958.16	948.22	943.43
925.92	958.34	950.58	944.10	1001.19	1020.32
1026.82	974.04	957.35	944.10	922.41	893.90
903.61	883.73	909.98	967.62	878.98	824.08
857.24	831.34	874.00	847.79	830.25	831.43
783.00	729.30	651.28	637.76	642.10	596.50
659.09	724.89	765.06	790.93	836.56	845.70
856.28	815.51	818.28	831.26	845.51	840.80
929.34	971.70	988.55	992.51	988.82	985.59
993.20	981.63	994.37	951.95	944.58	976.86
970.62	941.77	946.11	929.10	926.31	916.56

908.20	872.26	853.30	823.96	828.51	818.80
781.09	763.57	756.37	794.66	838.56	840.26
831.71	887.93	878.64	857.69	804.29	807.94
837.39	825.18	847.84	864.96	837.41	838.65
836.95	873.55	878.50	840.39	815.78	836.14
860.74	878.22	803.56	786.33	828.19	869.86
909.79	947.33	946.67	949.17	971.08	945.96

Read the monthly sales across the columns: 782.96 is first, 756.21 is second, ... 699.30 is sixth, 712.80 is seventh, and so on.

Develop an algorithm and write a program that accepts M, the number of periods to be included in the moving average, reads M data items from the file, and processes M items. Processing includes calculating the moving average, comparing the moving average of M periods with the actual data for that period, and printing the data as well as the difference. The program should then continuously read one more data item and process the latest M items until the end of the file. The program should also compute and print the sum of the squares of the differences. Try to arrive at an optimal M by minimizing the sum of the squares of the differences.

Creating a Random File:

11.12 Create a random master file for the members of a computer club. Each record contains the following information:

Member's code	5 digits
Last name	25 characters
Middle initial and first name	25 characters
Address 1: number and street	30 characters
Address 2: city, state, and zip	30 characters
Type of computer the member owns	30 characters
Telephone number	10 digits
Specialty	15 characters

The first and second digits of the member's five-digit code show the region where the member resides, and the last three digits are a sequential number between 100 and 999. The sequential number of each member is unique. Dump the entire file after creating it; that is, print a listing of each record in the file in order to verify the contents.

11.13 Create a random-access file for the customers of a mail-order store. Information about each customer is stored as follows:

Customer's code	5 digits
Name	25 characters
Telephone number	7 digits
Balance due	Less than 999.99

Each customer has a unique code, as follows:
a. The first three digits are a sequential number from 100 to 999.
b. The fourth digit shows the city where the customer lives.
c. The fifth digit shows the number of people in the customer's family.

Dump the entire file to verify the contents after creating it.

Updating a Random File:

11.14 Inventory programs are an interesting application of random-access file processing. The following problems refer to inventory file processing in a system with fewer than 900 items. Write a program for each of the following cases:

a. A program that creates a random-access file. Each record contains the following information:

Part number, a sequential number between 100 and 999	3 digits	positions 1–3
Part code	7 characters	positions 4–10
Part description	20 characters	positions 11–30
Quantity on hand	Less than 999	positions 31–33
Quantity on order	Less than 999	positions 34–36
Reorder level	Less than 999	positions 37–39
Unit cost	Less than 999.99	positions 40–45
Unit weight	Less than 99.99	positions 46–49

b. A program that adds new items to the file.
c. A program that updates the file when there is a change, such as the arrival of a new order. The input information should include the part number. The program should display a menu that lets the user select which information to change.
d. A program that prints an inventory report. The report should include all the information in the file.

e. A program that prints a report about all items sorted by part description. (*Hint:* one simple method for sorting is to load the part descriptions, sort them with the pointer sort, and then print the items by the value of the pointer array.)

f. A program that prints the item description if the item code is typed in and prints the item code if the item description is typed in.

g. A program combining the programs in b through f. The new program should start with a menu and proceed according to the user's choice. The menu should include:
- Adding a new item
- Changing an item
- Printing the information about all items:

    —Sorted

    —Unsorted

- Inquiring about an item

11.15 A mail-order store uses the last four digits of customers' telephone numbers as the customer code. Create a customer file that includes the following information about each customer (assume there are fewer than 100 customers):

Name	15 characters
Telephone number	7 digits
Address 1	15 characters
Address 2	15 characters
Last order number	5 digits
Unpaid balance	Less than 999.99

Write a program that starts with a menu and accomplishes the following:

a. Adds a new customer to the file

b. Displays all information about a customer when the last four digits of the customer's telephone number are typed in

c. Changes or updates one or several fields of a customer's record

d. Generates a report giving complete customer information, according to a menu:
- For all customers
- For customers whose balance is above a certain limit

SUMMARY

You have learned:

1. A file is a combination of several records. Files can be saved in an auxiliary storage medium under a name.
2. In sequential file processing, records are processed one after another. The basic steps for sequential file processing are:
   a. Opening the file
   b. Reading, if necessary
   c. Processing-manipulation
   d. Writing, if needed
   e. Closing the file
3. The forms of statements for opening, reading, writing, and closing files are system specific. It is important to learn the correct forms. Table 11.1 presents some examples.
4. Often files need to be manipulated, merged, sorted, and updated with appropriate techniques. Files can be used to generate reports.
5. In random-file processing, any record can be accessed directly by its key without the need to access any other record. The key is, or can be converted to, the address of the record in the file.
6. The basic steps necessary for random-file processing are:
   a. Opening the file for random access
   b. Defining the fields in each record and the lengths
   c. Moving the data between the disk and the buffer
   d. Processing-manipulation
   e. Closing the file
7. The specific forms of the statements for random file processing depend on the system used. Table 11.1 presents some examples.

REVIEW QUESTIONS/SELF-TEST

11.1 A doctor's office has two patient files: FILE1 and FILE2. In both files, each record contains the name of the patient and the balance due. Write a program that displays all the names and the amounts due in a report form. Print the total amount due at the end of the report.

11.2 Write a program that creates a random file for the names and telephone numbers of the clients of a firm. Each record contains:

a. Client's name   25 characters
b. Client's telephone number   10 characters

Assign a sequential number to each customer. Have the program display the client's key and then ask for the information. NO-MORE indicates end of data. Put seven subrecords in each sector.

Answers

11.1
```
10   OPEN 'I', #1, 'FILE1'
20   OPEN 'I' , #2 , 'FILE2'
30   PRINT ' NAME'; TAB(30); 'BALANCE'
40   TOTBAL = 0
50   FOR I = 1 TO 200
60      IF EOF(1) THEN GOTO 110
70      INPUT #1, ANAME$, BAL
80      PRINT ANAME$; TAB(31); BAL
90      TOTBAL = TOTBAL + BAL
100  NEXT I
110  FOR I = 1 TO 200
120     IF EOF(2) THEN GOTO 200
130     INPUT #2, ANAME$, BAL
140     PRINT   ANAME$; TAB(31); BAL
150     TOTBAL = TOTBAL + BAL
160  NEXT I
200  PRINT
210  PRINT 'TOTAL'; TAB(30); TOTBAL
220  CLOSE #1, #2
999  END
```

11.2
```
10   OPEN 'R', #1, 'CLIENT'
20   PRINT 'THIS PROGRAM RECORDS THE NAMES AND PHONE NUMBERS'
30   PRINT 'OF THE CLIENTS.'
100  FOR K = 1 TO 1000
110     PRINT 'TYPE NAME AND PHONE NUMBER FOR CLIENT NO. #:'; K
115     PRINT 'TYPE NO-MORE IF DONE'
120     INPUT A$, N$
130     IF A$ = 'NO-MORE' THEN GOTO 900
140     REC = INT((K - 1)/7) + 1
150     SUBREC = K - 7*(REC - 1)
160     FIELD #1, ((SUBREC-1)*35) AS XXX$, 25 AS ANAME$, 10 AS PHONE$
170     LSET ANAME$ = A$
180     LSET PHONE$ = N$
190     PUT #1, REC
200  NEXT K
900  PRINT '*** ALL SET, SEE YOU SOON ***'
910  CLOSE #1
999  END
```

Table 11.1 Example of the Forms of Different File Statements

Function or Description	Radio Shack, TRS-80 (DOS) Syntax	MBASIC, IBM-PC Syntax	CDC BASIC Version 3 Syntax
Opening a file	`OPEN "O",n,"filename"`[a] `I` `R`	`OPEN "O",#n,"filename" [,record length]`[k] `I` `R` or `OPEN "filename" [FOR OUTPUT]`[e] `AS #n [,LEN= record length]`[e] `INPUT` `APPEND`	`FILE #n="file name"`
Closing a file	`CLOSE n`	`CLOSE #n`	`CLOSE #n`
Reading a sequential file	`INPUT #n,varlist`	`INPUT #n,varlist`	`INPUT #n,varlist` `READ #n,varlist`
Reading a line of a file	`LINE INPUT #n,Var$`	`LINE INPUT #n,var$`	—
Printing a sequential file	`PRINT #n,varlist`[b]	`WRITE #n,varlist` `PRINT #n,varlist`	`PRINT #n,varlist` `WRITE #n,varlist`
Defining a field length	`FIELD n,w1 AS var1$,,`[c]	`FIELD#n,w1 AS var1$,,`	See below[g]
Reading a random record	`GET n,Recno`	`Get n,Recno`	`SET #n,wordno.`[g] `READ #n,varlist`
Writing to a random file	`PUT n,Recno`	`PUT n,Recno`	`SET #n,wordno.` `WRITE #n,varlist`[g]
Placing data into a buffer	`LSET X$ = Y$` `RSET X$ = Y$`	`LSET X$ = Y$` `RSET X$ = Y$`	—
End-of-file marker	`EOF(n)`[d]	`EOF(n)`	`NODATA line no.` or `IF END #n THEN line no.`
Maximum I/O for random access	256 bytes	256 bytes[f]	

[a] I for input; O for output; R for random; n for the channel number.
[b] A blank separates numeric data; a blank or a comma separates string data.
[c] wi is the length of the variable.
[d] Returns 0 for false; −1 for true (end of file).
[e] If dropped, random is assumed; the record length is only for random mode.
[f] The default for the record length is 128.
[g] In CDC, a real number occupies one word, and m characters occupy M words, where $M = INT((m+9)/10) + 1$.
[h] K = record length.
[i] K = record number.
[j] f = file name.
[k] Brackets indicate optional part of statement.

Applesoft BASIC (Apple II) (DOS 3.3) Syntax	BASIC PLUS (PDP-11) (RSTS/E) Syntax	Examples
PRINT CHR$(4);"OPEN filename"	OPEN "f"[j] FOR [OUTPUT][k] AS FILE n [INPUT]	OPEN "XDATA" AS FILE1
PRINT CHR$(4);"CLOSE filename"	CLOSE #n	CLOSE #1
PRINT CHR$(4);"READ filename" INPUT varlist	INPUT #n,varlist	INPUT #1,S,X1,A$
—	INPUT LINE #n,var$	INPUT LINE #1,S$
PRINT CHR$(4);"WRITE filename" PRINT varlist	PRINT #n,varlist	PRINT #3,S,X1,A$
PRINT CHR$(4);"OPEN filename,Lk"[h]	FIELD #n,w1 AS var1$,...	FIELD #3,215 AS N$
PRINT CHR$(4);"READ filename,R",K[i] INPUT varlist PRINT CHR$(4)	Define: DIM #n,var$(N) Then: INPUT var$(m)	DIM #3,A$(500),N(5) INPUT A$(3)
PRINT CHR$(4);"WRITE filename,R",K[i] PRINT varlist PRINT CHR$(4)	Define: DIM #n,var$(N) Then: PRINT var$(m)	DIM #3,N$(500),A(5) PRINT N$(3)
	LSET X$ = Y$ RSET X$ = Y$	LSET X$ = "ABCDEF" RSET P$ = A$
EOF(n)	ON ERR GOTO line no. or EOF(n)	ON ERR GOTO 99 IF EOF(3)... THEN 99
256 bytes	512 bytes	

Program Efficiency 12

In This Chapter:

Efficiency Factors
Interpreter Optimization
Sparing Use of Arrays
Efficient Algorithms
Human Resources

Structured Approach
Structured Design
Readability
Documentation and Reliability

12

Program Efficiency

A problem can be solved with various algorithms, each with a different quality. Obviously, an efficient algorithm will result in an efficient program if the algorithm is implemented correctly. But the efficiency of a program in turn depends on:

1. The amount of computer time required to compile and execute the program
2. The amount of memory the program requires
3. The human effort required to write, document, and maintain the program
4. The degree of accuracy desired in the solution
5. The generality required in the algorithm (for instance, must negative numbers be ignored?)

Unfortunately, there is always a trade-off among these factors. For example, there is a trade-off between time and memory requirements. One program may require relatively less running time but more memory space than another. Alternatively, a program that requires relatively less storage area and less running time may require greater human effort to develop, test, and maintain than another.

EFFICIENCY FACTORS

It is sometimes possible to use algorithm techniques that result in more efficient, faster, and more accurate programs. For example, incorporating certain mathematical techniques in algorithms may lead to more efficient programs. For instance, consider the function

$$y = 3x^2 + 2x + 5$$

If this function is written as

```
Y = 3*X*X + 2*X +5
```

it requires three multiplications and two additions. However, if the same function is written as

```
Y = (3*X + 2)*X + 5
```

it requires only two multiplications and two additions. (This reduction of mathematical steps is called *Horner's method*.) This change not only makes operation more efficient and faster (multiplications are done faster than exponentiations) but may also increase accuracy.

Good programming style directly affects the efficiency of a program. The following are some recommendations.

Interpreter Optimization

Consider the features and limitations of the language you use. For example, in BASIC it is more efficient to use integer values than real or character values because integer values take less space in memory. Arithmetic operations are also performed faster on integers than on real numbers. Thus, use integer values if possible. Control variables of FOR-NEXT loops and subscripts of arrays, especially, should be defined as integers. The following is a list of further hints for optimizing execution of a program.

1. Avoid mixed modes of operations; that is, do not use both integers and real numbers in an arithmetic expression.
2. Avoid repeating instructions unnecessarily. For example, the expression X = A*B/C in the loop

    ```
    100 FOR I = 1 TO 1000
    110     X = A*B/C
    120     Y = X*I
    130 NEXT I
    ```

    should be removed from inside the loop, so that it is executed once rather than 1000 times.
3. Use the IF-THEN-ELSE structure rather than the IF-GOTO structure.
4. Use FOR-NEXT loops rather than IF-GOTO loops.
5. Test the most probable condition in an IF statement first. For example, assume most of the CODEs in a program are equal to 3, and a few are equal to 1 or 2. Thus

```
IF CODE = 1 THEN GOTO 100
IF CODE = 2 THEN GOTO 200
IF CODE = 3 THEN GOTO 300
```

should be changed so that the condition IF CODE = 3 is checked first.

6. Use built-in functions because they take less execution time than user-defined functions.
7. The relative speed of arithmetic operations is as follows:

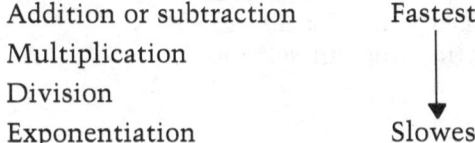

Addition or subtraction — Fastest
Multiplication
Division
Exponentiation — Slowest

Thus, use expressions that increase speed. For example:

```
Y = A+A    is faster than Y = 2*A
P = X*X*X  is faster than P = X^3
Q = Z*.25  is faster than Q = Z/4
```

Sparing Use of Arrays

Unless you find it necessary, do not use arrays in a program. Arrays require a large amount of memory and computer time. For example, if the objective is only to calculate the sum of 1000 data, the program segment

```
100 FOR I = 1 TO 1000
110    READ X
120    SUM = SUM + X
130 NEXT I
```

is more efficient than

```
10  DIM A(1000)
100 FOR I = 1 TO 100
110    READ A(I)
120    SUM = SUM + A(I)
130 NEXT I
```

Furthermore, if you need to use an array, pay attention to its size. Avoid using unreasonably large arrays.

Program Efficiency

Efficient Algorithms

Choose algorithms that will result in efficient programs. For example, suppose you want to interchange the values of memory locations A and B. Of course, the program segment

```
100 A = B
110 B = A
```

will not work because when you place the value of B into A, the original content of A is erased. One possible method is to copy A and B into temporary memory locations C and D and then transfer them back into the original locations A and B in reverse order. Thus the program segment would be

```
100 C = A
110 D = B
120 A = D
130 B = C
```

This method, however, requires two additional memory locations and four assignment statements. Another method is simply to save the contents of A in a temporary memory location—TEMP, for example—before assigning B to A and then to assign the value of TEMP to B (see Figure 12.1). The program segment is

```
100 TEMP = A
110 A = B
120 B = TEMP
```

This method requires only one additional memory location and three assignment statements. The value of this method becomes apparent when we try to do the same kind of interchange in an array with 1000 elements,

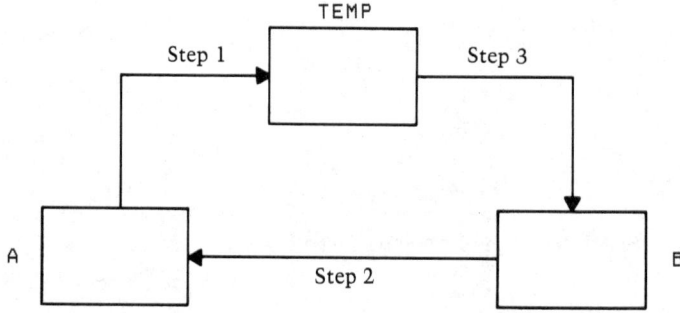

Figure 12.1 Interchanging the values of two variables

as the next example shows. The first method requires 1000 additional memory locations, but the second method requires only one additional memory location.

Example 12.1

Problem: Assume arrays A and B each have 1000 elements that contain data. Develop a procedure for a program segment that interchanges the values of the elements of the two arrays. Write the segment.

Solution Plan:

1. Begin the loop, FOR I = 1 TO 1000 repeat:
   - **1.1** Store the Ith element of A into TEMP.
   - **1.2** Assign the Ith element of B into the Ith element of A.
   - **1.3** Assign TEMP into the Ith element of B.
2. End the loop.

Program Segment:

```
100 FOR I = 1 TO 1000
110     TEMP = A(I)
120     A(I) = B(I)
130     B(I) = TEMP
140 NEXT I
```

Techniques of searching for an element in an array provide another example of how an algorithm affects the efficiency of a program. In a sequential search, the elements of the list are searched from beginning to end, one by one, until the desired value is found. In a binary search, the computer checks the item in the middle of a sorted list. If that item is not the one sought, the computer finds out whether the item lies in the first or second half of the list and searches the middle of the appropriate half. Repeating this process until the item is found results in a shorter search time. Of course, the binary search works only if the list is already ordered. To compare the efficiency of these two methods, apply them to finding someone's telephone number in a long directory. Obviously, finding a telephone number in a directory by searching sequentially is cumbersome.

As mentioned before, incorporating certain mathematical techniques in algorithms increases their efficiency, for example, techniques that reduce mathematical steps, such as Horner's rule. The following example shows another mathematical procedure that makes an algorithm more efficient.

Example 12.2

Problem: Develop a solution procedure and write a program segment that determines whether or not an integer greater than 1 is a prime number.

Solution Procedure:

A prime number is a number that has no positive integer divisor except 1 and itself. For example, 17 is a prime number because none of the numbers 2, 3, 4, ..., 15, 16 are divisors of 17. Although a program that tests all divisors between 2 and N-1 will work, there is a more efficient method. It can be proved mathematically that N is prime if no number between 2 and the integer closest to $\sqrt{N}$ divides N exactly. Thus, if any remainder of N divided by 2, 3, 4, ... $\sqrt{N}$ is zero, the number is not prime.

Solution Plan:

1. Read the number N.
2. Compute M = the integer of the square root of N.
3. Begin the loop, FOR I = 2 TO M, repeat:
   3.1 Divide N by I.
   3.2 Find the remainder R.
   3.3 If R = 0 then:
      3.3.1 Terminate the test loop.
      3.3.2 Print "The number is not prime."
      3.3.3 Go to the next procedure.
4. End the loop, NEXT I.
5. Print "The number is prime."
6. Next procedure.
   ⋮

Program Segment:

```
100    READ N%
120    M% = INT(SQR(N%))
130    FOR I% = 2% TO M%
140       K% = N%/I%
150       R% = N% - K%*I%
160       IF R% = 0% THEN GOTO 200
170    NEXT I%
180    PRINT "THE NUMBER IS PRIME"
190     GOTO 210
200    PRINT "THE NUMBER IS NOT PRIME"
210    ............
```

Notes:

1. It is assumed that `%` defines integer values.
2. This program will not work for `N = 1`.
3. The efficiency of the program also depends on the method used to compute the square roots.
4. The efficiency of the algorithm could be improved substantially if divisibility by 2 were checked separately. Then, only odd numbers would be tested in the loop with the statement

   `FOR I% = 2% TO M% STEP 2%`

Human Resources

Consider human resources in the program development process. The human factor is an extremely important consideration in program efficiency because the computer time has become less expensive than the time of programmers and others who work with programs. The cost of human resources for developing, debugging, testing, documenting, and maintaining a program is far greater than the cost of running a program. The underlying concept of structured programming emphasizes this point. Structured programming techniques make programs easier to understand, debug, maintain, and update. Therefore, structured programming techniques increase overall efficiency. Structured programming has been discussed throughout the text. The following section presents a summary of techniques and recommendations.

STRUCTURED APPROACH

In Chapter 3 structured programming was defined as a method of designing and writing organized programs so that they are easier to code, easier to understand, and less prone to errors. A structured approach exhibits the following characteristics:

1. Structured design
   a. Top-down design
   b. Modularity
2. Readability
3. Reliability
4. Full documentation

Structured Design

Structured design is a systematic approach to analyzing, designing, and developing a program. In particular, the design should have a well-organized structure that is top-down and modular.

Each module can contain one or several BASIC structures: sequence, decision, and iteration structures. Each structure should be distinct, and have only one point of entry and exit.

To design a structured program, you need a clear understanding of the requirements of the program. Communication with the people who will use the program is essential. This communication should take place before, during, and after the program design.

The guidelines for structured design are as follows:

1. Plan and design first; do not write any code until the plan is completed.
2. Start at the top—take an overall look at the entire program. Determine what the program will do before you develop the details of how the functions will be performed.
3. Refine the problem by working down to modules and submodules.
4. Refine and further develop each module or submodule in greater detail through successive levels.
5. Both the design and the coding should be done from top to bottom.

A module is a collection of related instructions that can be grouped together logically. Limiting the size of a program unit and ensuring that each unit performs a well-defined function:

1. Simplifies the design
2. Increases readability
3. Makes debugging easier
4. Makes maintenance and modification easier

Some other advantages of the modular approach are:

1. One module, once written, can be used in many programs.
2. Each module can be debugged separately. This is more efficient than debugging the entire program because errors can be detected and corrected more easily.
3. Teamwork is facilitated; that is, several people can write a large program, resulting in earlier completion.
4. Companies that hire individual programmers who excel in certain areas of programming can assign parts of the program to those individuals most qualified to write them.
5. A library of commonly used routines can be created.
6. Checkpoints for measuring progress can be provided.

A module should not be chosen arbitrarily. A module is a well-defined unit of the entire program. It should serve its own function. The combination of modules builds the organization of the entire program. A hierarchy diagram is a good tool for showing how the modules fit together.

Some desiderata for modules are:

1. A module should perform a well-defined function.
2. A module must return to the unit it was called from rather than to other parts of the program.
3. A module should have a single entry and a single exit point.
4. A module should be small, typically shorter than a page.

Sometimes modularity has to be weighed against computer resource costs. Subprograms are more expensive to run than regular branches. Typically, however, the costs of program development, debugging, and maintenance outweigh the costs of computer resources.

Readability

By now you have noticed that programs exhibit different styles, methods, and algorithms. At one time, clever and tricky codes that required relatively little storage and run time were considered to make the best use of computer resources. As a result, many inefficient programs were written. These programs were not only difficult to understand, debug, and maintain but also troublesome to modify. Almost every program written is subsequently modified to meet changing specifications or to eliminate bugs. If a program is intricate to begin with, future changes only make it more difficult to read.

Today, it is generally accepted that the efficiency of a program is increased by reducing the human effort required to develop, debug, or modify it. This can be accomplished by writing a readable program, avoiding tricks, and providing useful documents.

A recurring theme of this book is that good programming starts with good planning. Devote ample time to planning before you begin coding. The following steps, outlined in Chapter 3, should be adhered to carefully:

1. Understand the problem fully; define it precisely in writing.
2. Design the output and the input.
3. Design the solution procedure; use top-down design and a modular approach. An appropriate, efficient algorithm should be devised for each module.
4. Write the entire program in easy-to-understand pseudo-BASIC (pseudocode) or a flowchart.
5. Code and test each module.

The value of modular programming cannot be overemphasized. Fortunately, BASIC provides a simple way to create a module or submodule by means of subprograms. Consequently, subroutines and functions are extremely helpful in modular programming. In addition, a subprogram containing a repeatedly used function is especially valuable, because it ultimately enhances the program's efficiency.

Do not attempt to accomplish more than one task in a module. A good test of whether or not a module serves a well-defined objective is: "Can you assign a precise name to the module?" Be certain that the connection between modules is clear. Run and test each module sequentially and separately, if possible.

Write the codes clearly, even if doing so makes the program less efficient to run. Remember that the computer's time is cheaper than yours. As mentioned earlier, the best way to minimize computer running time is to choose an efficient algorithm. A good way to test a program's readability is to read it aloud to a friend (or even to yourself). If he or she understands the program's logic, the program is likely to be right. Do not hesitate to rewrite any part that is not clear. Never use a GOTO statement to fix a coding error; rewrite the entire part.

The important points discussed so far can be summarized as follows:

1. Plan ahead (that is, plan and design the details before you begin coding).
2. Use top-down design and a modular approach.
3. Use subprograms for repetitive tasks.
4. Run and test modules one by one.
5. Make sure the input data are read correctly before anything else is done.
6. Never use a GOTO to patch an error; rewrite the entire module instead.

Also, remember that the physical appearance of a program plays an important role in the readability of its logical structure. Readability considerations discussed throughout the text are summarized below:

1. Each variable's symbolic name should suggest its meaning. For example, A, S, L, D may be obscure: AREA, SPEED, LENGTH, and DISTANCE are more meaningful. Of course, this is possible only when the system allows symbolic names with more than one character. If not, make sure that the program has a good variable dictionary.
2. Always initialize variables and define arrays even if an array has fewer than ten elements.
3. Do not use GOTO or IF-GOTO statements unless they are absolutely necessary.
4. Indent lines appropriately to make your programs more readable. Indented IF-THEN-ELSE and FOR-NEXT loops are a must.
5. Most BASIC systems allow several statements per line. However, it is best to group statements on one line only if the readability of the program is not reduced.
6. Always use structured IFs for comparisons or decisions. Furthermore:
   a. Avoid THEN-IF, THEN-GOTO, and ELSE-GOTO.
   b. Do not use mixed modes when checking equality (3% is seldom equal to 3.0).
   c. Indent statements appropriately under THEN or ELSE.
7. Use structured FOR-NEXT or WHILE loops. Furthermore:
   a. Indent the statements in any loop by at least 3 spaces.
   b. If loops are nested, indent inner loops relative to outer loops.
   c. Do not use more than one exit from a loop.
8. DATA statements should be grouped together and placed at the end of the program unit.
9. If you need to continue a statement on the next line, always break the statement after a comma.

10. Use extra pairs of parentheses in arithmetic expressions to group the variables and avoid ambiguity. Also use parentheses inside a compound logical expression to help make the order of logical operations clear.
11. Use blanks to separate the components of a statement. Use a blank between a key word and the rest of the statement. Use also blanks:
    a. After a comma
    b. Before and after an equals sign (=), plus signs, and minus signs
    c. Before and after relational and logical operators

    Do not use blanks:
    a. Before or inside the parentheses of an array subscript
    b. Before or after the multiplication, division, and exponentiation operators
       Example:
       RESULT(I) = (A + B - C*D)/E^2
12. Use blank lines or a line of asterisks with REM to separate a module from the rest of the program.
13. Follow the program format developed and adopted by your organization. For example, most organizations use a remark block at the beginning of a program. The block gives the purpose and a brief description of the program, the algorithms used, and the variable dictionary.

The following is an example of a program before and after readability considerations are implemented:

Before:

```
10DIMX(100)
20FORI=1TO100
30READX(I)
40IFX(I)<0GOTO70
50N=N+1
60NEXT
70FORI=1TON:S=S+X(I):NEXT
100A=S/N
110FORI=1TON
120PRINTX(I)
130PRINTA
140END
```

After:

```
10   REM  AUTHOR:   TAMMY LORD
20   REM
30   REM  THIS PROGRAM CALCULATES THE AVERAGE OF A GROUP OF DATA
40   REM
50   REM  ************************************************
60   REM  VARIABLE DICTIONARY:
70   REM    X     THE ARRAY CONTAINING THE DATA
80   REM    SUM   THE SUM OF THE DATA
90   REM    N     THE NUMBER OF DATA
100  REM    AVG   THE AVERAGE OF THE DATA
110  REM  ************************************************
120  REM    DEFINE ARRAY X WITH A MAXIMUM OF 100 ELEMENTS
130  REM    AND INITIALIZE VARIABLES
140                                                          REM
150      DIM X(100)
160      SUM = 0   :   N = 0
170      FOR I = 1 TO 100   :   X(I) = 0   :     NEXT I
180  REM    READ THE DATA, ONE PER LINE, A NEGATIVE NUMBER
190  REM    TERMINATES THE LOOP
200                                                          REM
210      FOR I = 1 TO 100
220          READ    X(I)
230          IF X(I) < 0 THEN GOTO 300
240          N = N + 1
250      NEXT I
260                                                          REM
270  REM   ACCUMULATE THE DATA AFTER THEY ARE ALL READ
280  REM
300      FOR I = 1 TO N
310          SUM = SUM + X(I)
320      NEXT I
330                                                          REM
340  REM   CALCULATE THE AVERAGE:   DIVIDE THE SUM BY THE
350  REM   NUMBER OF DATA
360                                                          REM
370     AVG = SUM/N
380                                                          REM
400  REM   WRITE THE SCORES AND THE AVERAGE, SCORES ARE TO BE
410  REM   PRINTED ON ONE LINE
420  PRINT 'DATA:'
430      FOR I = 1 TO N
440          PRINT X(I);
450      NEXT I
460                                                          REM
470      PRINT 'AVERAGE = '; AVG
480                                                          REM
500  REM ************* DATA STATEMENTS   *********************
510                                                          REM
520  DATA 79, 69, 87, 98, 67, 59, 89, 79, 89, 86, 68, 76
530  DATA 83, 76, 82, 71, 97, 65, -99
999  END
```

Documentation and Reliability

Documentation and reliability were discussed in detail in Chapter 3. Documentation is the process of reporting how the program was developed, designed, coded, and tested. Reliability refers to minimizing the chance of errors in all aspects of program development, design, and coding. Any program should work correctly under a wide range of conditions and must go through extensive testing before it can be considered reliable and ready for use.

APPENDIX A

Reserved Words for Selected Systems

The lists do not include graphics commands.

MicroSoft BASIC Reserved Words (IBM-PC, DEC Rainbow, and Others)

ABS	DATA	GOSUB	LSET
AND	DATE$	GOTO	MERGE
ASC	DEF	HEX$	MID$
ATN	DEFDBL	IF	MKD$
AUTO	DEFINT	IMP	MKI$
BEEP	DEFSNG	INKEY$	MKS$
BLOAD	DEFSTR	INP	MOD
BSAVE	DELETE	INPUT	MOTOR
CALL	DIM	INPUT#	NAME
CDBL	DRAW	INPUT$	NEW
CHAIN	EDIT	INSTR	NEXT
CHR$	ELSE	INT	NOT
CINT	END	KEY	OCT$
CIRCLE	EOF	KILL	OFF
CLEAR	EQV	LEFT$	ON
CLOSE	ERASE	LEN	OPEN
CLS	ERL	LET	OPTION
COLOR	ERR	LINE	OR
COM	ERROR	LIST	OUT
COMMON	EXP	LLIST	PAINT
CONT	FIELD	LOAD	PEEK
COS	FILES	LOC	PEN
CSNG	FIX	LOCATE	PLAY
CSRLIN	FNxxxxxxxx	LOF	POINT
CVD	FOR	LOG	POKE
CVI	FRE	LPOS	POS
CVS	GET	LPRINT	PRESET

(continued)

PRINT	RUN	SWAP	WEND
PRINT#	SAVE	SYSTEM	WHILE
PSET	SCREEN	TAB(	WIDTH
PUT	SGN	TAN	WRITE
RANDOMIZE	SIN	THEN	WRITE#
READ	SOUND	TIME$	XOR
REM	SPACE$	TO	
RENUM	SPC(	TROFF	
RESET	SQR	TRON	
RESTORE	STEP	USING	
RESUME	STICK	USR	
RETURN	STOP	VAL	
RIGHT$	STR$	VARPTR	
RND	STRIG	VARPTR$	
RSET	STRING$	WAIT	

BASIC-PLUS Reserved Words

In EXTEND mode, keywords, including predefined function names, cannot be used as variable names.

ABS	COS	FILE SIZE	LENGTH
AND	COUNT	FIX	LET
APPEND	CVTF$	FNEND	LINE
AS	CFT$F	FOR	LIST
ASCII	CVT$%	FOR INPUT AS FILE	LISTNH
AS FILE	CVT$$	FOR OUTPUT AS FILE	LOG
ASSIGN	CVT%$	GET	LOG10
ATN	DATA	GOSUB	LSET
BLOCK	DATE$	GOTO	MAGTAPE
BUFSIZ	DEASSIGN	HELLO	MAT
BYE	DEF	IDN	MID
CAT	DELETE	IF	MODE
CATALOG	DET	IFOR	MOUNT
CCONT	DIF$	IMP	NAME
CHAIN	DIM	INPUT	NEW
CHANGE	ELSE	INPUT LINE	NEXT
CHR$	END	INSTR	NO EXTEND
CLOSE	EQV	INT	NOT
CLUSTER SIZE	ERL	INV	NUM
COMPILE	ERR	KEY	NUM$
COMP%	EXP	KILL	NUM1$
CON	EXTEND	LEFT	NUM2
CONT	FIELD	LEN	OLD

ON	RETURN	TIME$
ON ERROR GOTO	RIGHT	TO
OPEN	RND	TRN
OR	RSET	UNLESS
PEEK	RUN	UNLOCK
PI	RUNNH	UNSAVE
PIF	SAVE	UNTIL
PIFOR	SCALE	USING
PLACE$	SGN	VAL
POS	SIN	WAIT
PRINT	SLEEP	WHILE
PROD$	SPACE$	XLATE
PUT	SPEC%	XOR
QUO$	SQR	ZER
RAD$	STATUS	
RANDOM	STEP	
RANDOMIZE	STOP	
READ	STRING$	
REASSIGN	SUM$	
RECORD	SWAP%	
RECORD SIZE	SYS	
RECOUNT	TAB	
REM	TAN	
RENAME	TAND	
REPLACE	TAPE	
RESTORE	THEN	
RESUME	TIME	

Radio Shack TRS-80 Level II Reserved Words

Many of these words have no function in LEVEL II BASIC; they are reserved for use in LEVEL II DISK BASIC. None of these words can be used inside a variable name.

@	CLS	DEFFN	EOF
ABS	CMD	DEFINT	ERL
AND	CONT	DEFSNG	ERR
ASC	COS	DEFSTR	ERROR
ATN	CSNG	DEFUSR	EXP
CDBL	CVD	DELETE	FIELD
CHR$	CVI	DIM	FIX
CINT	CVS	EDIT	FOR
CLEAR	DATA	ELSE	FRE
CLOSE	DEFDBL	END	GET

(continued)

GOSUB	LINE	POKE	SQR
GOTO	LIST	POS	STEP
IF	LOAD	PRINT	STOP
INKEY$	LOC	PUT	STR$
INP	LOF	RANDOM	STRING$
INPUT	MKD$	READ	TAB
INSTR	MKI$	REM	TAN
INT	MKS$	RESET	THEN
KILL	NAME	RESTORE	TIME$
LOG	NEW	RESUME	TROFF
MEM	NEXT	RETURN	TRON
MERGE	NOT	RIGHT$	USING
MID$	ON	RND	USR
LEFT$	OPEN	SAVE	VAL
LEN	OUT	SET	VARPTR
LET	PEEK	SGN	
LSET	POINT	SIN	

APPLESOFT Reserved Words

&	GOTO	NORMAL	SCALE=
ABS	GR	NOT	SCRN(
AND	HCOLOR=	NOTRACE	SGN
ASC	HGR	ON	SHLOAD
AT	HGR2	ONERR	SIN
ATN	HIMEM:	OR	SPC(
CALL	HLIN	PDL	SPEED=
CHR$	HOME	PEEK	SQR
CLEAR	HPLOT	PLOT	STEP
COLOR=	HTAB	POKE	STOP
CONT	IF	POP	STORE
COS	IN#	POS	STR$
DATA	INPUT	PRINT	TAB(
DEF	INT	PR#	TAN
DEL	INVERSE	READ	TEXT
DIM	LEFT$	RECALL	THEN
DRAW	LEN	REM	TO
END	LET	RESTORE	TRACE
EXP	LIST	RESUME	USR
FLASH	LOAD	RETURN	VAL
FN	LOG	RIGHT$	VLIN
FOR	LOMEM:	RND	VTAB
FRE	MID$	ROT=	WAIT
GET	NEW	RUN	XDRAW
GOSUB	NEXT	SAVE	XPLOT

APPENDIX B

Some BASIC Syntaxes for Selected Systems

System Commands/Statements	Microsoft Basic[b] (IBM-PC,[c] DEC Rainbow, and others)	Apple II (Applesoft)	Commodore Pet (BASIC 4.0)
Program Line Editing	DELETE key or cursor control keys and FUNCTION keys when the editor is used (hardware dependent)	BACKSPACE or ESC key/ A,B,C or D	DELETE key or cursor controls
Break	CTRL/BREAK key (hardware dependent)	CTROL/C	RUN/STOP key
Screen Width	80	40	40
Load Program	LOAD "device:filename"	LOAD filename in system mode; use quotes for the file name in BASIC mode	LOAD "filename",device#
Save Program	SAVE "device:filename"[,A][d] (A for saving in ASCII format)	SAVE filename in system mode; use quotes for the file name in BASIC mode	SAVE "filename",device #
List Files	FILES "device:filespec", or DIR drive:filespec in the operating system	CATALOG in the system mode; NAME in the BASIC mode	DIRECTORY
Delete Files	KILL "device:filename" or ERASE device:filespec in the operating system	DELETE filename in the system mode; use quotes for the file in BASIC mode	SCRATCH "filename"
Enable Printer	CTRL-PRTSC key in IBM-PC (not in cassette) and LLIST, or LPRINT	PR#1 transfers the output to a specific slot	OPEN "file#,device" [,secondary address]:CMD file#
Auto Line Number	AUTO number, increment	No	No
Line Resequence	RENUM new number, old number, increment	No	No
Program Listing	LIST line1-line2, LIST line1- LIST -line2	LIST line1-line2, LIST line1- LIST -line2	LIST line1-line2, LIST line1- LIST -line2
Trace	TRON and TROFF	No	No
Clear Screen	CLS in IBM-PC (system dependent)	HOME	CLR key
Remarks in Listing	REM or apostrophe (') at the end of a line (may be branched to)	REM or !	REM
Spaces for numerics [a]	Before (for the sign) and after	None	Before (for the sign) and after
Tab	TAB(i)[;] expression	TAB(i); expression	TAB(i)[;] expression
PRINT USING	Yes; for example, PRINT USING "\ \ $#,###.##"; A$; X	No	No
Variable Name Length	Any length (Only the first 40 characters are significant; in the 8K version only the first two characters are significant. Can include embedded reserved words. A variable beginning with FN is assumed to be a user-defined function.)	Up to 238 characters, but only the first two characters are significant	More than two characters, but only the first two characters are significant
Zone Width	14 columns	16 columns	10 columns
Matrix Operations	No	No	No
Exponentiation Symbol	^	^	^
Indention	Yes	No	Yes, if first character in the line is a colon
Random Function	RND[(i)] (Use RANDOMIZE or i<0 to reseed; range is 0 to 1.)	RND(i) (i>0 generates a new random number; i<0 generates the same number; range is 0 to 1.)	RND(i) (i=0 seeds random function from internal clock; i>0 repeats pseudo-random series; i<0 continually reseeds; range is 0 to 1.)
Quotes in String Data	Yes, if string includes comma	No, unless string includes comma	No, unless string includes comma
STOP & CONT	Yes	Yes	Yes
IF-THEN Statement	IF expression THEN statements (in one line separated by colons) or IF expression GOTO line	Yes; IF condition THEN line or statement(s) or IF condition GOTO line	Yes; IF condition THEN line or statements (on one line separated by colons)
IF-THEN-ELSE Statement	Yes, with ELSE statements (in one line separated by colons); nesting allowed but limited to the length of one line	No	No
WHILE Loop	Yes; WHILE expression	No	No
WHILE Loop END	WEND	N/A	N/A
String Concatenation	Use + between strings	Use + between strings	Use + between strings
Multiple Assignment	No	No	No
Multi-Statements/Line	Yes, with colon as separator	Yes, with colon as separator	Yes, with colon as separator
Multi-Lines/Statement	No	No	No
Logical Operators	AND, OR, and NOT	AND, OR, and NOT	AND, OR, and NOT
Error Trapping	ON ERROR GOTO line; error variables: ERR and ERL	ONERR GOTO line; use PRINT PEEK(222) to see which error was encountered	No

[a] Spaces for numeric values when a semicolon is used in the PRINT statement.
[b] MBASIC is the most extensive implementation of BASIC. MBASIC is used in many systems with different operating environments. IBM-PC and DEC Rainbow are among them.

CDC Cyber 172	Radio Shack TRS-80 II (DOS)	PDP-11 (BASIC PLUS)
BACKSPACE	Cursor controls	RUBOUT key or DELETE key or ESCAPE + A, B, C or D
CONTROL/T	BREAK key	CTRL/C
Terminal dependent	64	Terminal dependent
OLD, filename	LOAD "filespec"	OLD filename
NEW, filename (at the beginning) SAVE after typing the program	SAVE "filespec"	NEW filename at beginning SAVE after typing the program
CATLIST	DIR :drive#	CAT
PURGE, filename	KILL "filespec"	KILL "filename", or UNSAVE filename
Submit job control or route statements	LPRINT	Job control language submission
No	AUTO line number, increment	No
RESEQ, new number, increment	No	No
LIST (lists the lines of a primary file) or LIST F=filename (lists the lines of a local file)	LIST line1-line2, LIST line1-, or LIST -line2	LIST line1-line2
REM TRACE, ALL; must be activated by control command	TRON and TROFF	No
CONTROL/L	CLEAR key or CLS	CLR key
REM and apostrophe (') for comments at the end of a line	REM or '	REM or !
Before (for the sign) and after TAB(i); expression	Before (for the sign) and after TAB(I); variable or expression	Before (for the sign) and after Tab(i); expression
Yes; 100 PRINT USING 110, variable 110 : "$###,##" or 100 PRINT USING "$###,##", variable	Yes, for example 100 A$="$###,##" 110 PRINT USING A$; variable	Yes, for example, PRINT USING "$#,###,##", X
Two characters, second may be a digit	Two characters, second may be a digit	One letter plus one digit or, in EXTEND version, up to 30 characters, including periods
15 columns	16 columns	15 columns
Yes	No	Yes
^ or **	^	^ or **
Yes, if first character in the line is a colon	Yes	Yes
RND(i) i>0 generates the same number each time, i=0 generates the same sequence each run, i<0 initiates a seed based on the time of day; range is 0 to 1.)	RND(0) gives range 0 to 1 or RND(i) with : 1 to 32767 gives range 1 to 32767	RND (Can use RANDOMIZE; range is 0 to 1.)
Yes if string begins with +, -, period, comma, digit or blank	No, unless string includes comma	Yes
No	Yes	Yes
IF condition THEN line or statement	IF condition THEN line or statements (on one line separated by colons)	IF condition THEN line or statement or IF condition GOTO line
Yes; ELSE statement or line	Yes; ELSE line or statements (on one line separated by colons)	Yes; with ELSE line or statement
No	WHILE condition on newer versions WEND	Use WHILE condition or UNTIL condition at the end of FOR statement NEXT
N/A		
Use + between strings	Use + between strings	Use + between strings
Yes, for example, 100 X=Y=Z=130	No	Yes, for example, LET B,C,D=0
No	Yes, with colon separator	Yes, with backslash separator
No	No	Yes, with & connector
AND, OR, and NOT	AND, OR, and NOT	
ON ERROR GOTO line; error variables: ESM and ESL	ON ERROR GOTO line; error variables: ERR and ERL	ON ERROR GOTO line; error variables: ERR and ERL

[c] IBM-PC offers three different versions of the BASIC interpreter: (1) cassette, (2) disk, and (3) advanced compiler. The three versions are upwardly compatible.
[d] Brackets [ ] indicate options.

APPENDIX C

True BASIC

True BASIC is a new version of BASIC developed in 1984 by the creators of the original BASIC language, John Kemeny and Thomas Kurtz. This version is designed for educational purposes and is built around the Standard BASIC (proposed by American National Standard for BASIC in 1981). Some of the features and characteristics of True BASIC are:

1. It is built around a flexible screen editor.
2. It includes structured programming features: SELECT-CASE, DO-WHILE and LOOP-UNTIL, multistatement functions, and subroutines.
3. It includes the proposed ANSI BASIC graphics, which makes it easy to plot graphs or draw pictures.
4. It allows recursive functions (a function can call itself).
5. It is based on a compiler/interpreter combination.

Some of the syntax is as follows:

1. Line numbers are not required; they are necessary only if referred to by a GOTO statement.
2. The program can be typed in either uppercase or lowercase letters.
3. Either REM or ! can be used for remarks. Remarks can appear on separate lines or be added at the end of lines of code.

4. Several statements can appear between THEN and ELSE in the IF-THEN-ELSE structure. For example:
```
IF SCORE > 90 THEN
     PRINT "PASSED WITH A HIGH SCORE"
     GRADE$ = "A"
     NA = NA + 1
ELSE
     PRINT "PASSED"
     GRADE$ = "B"
     NB = NB + 1
ENDIF
```

APPENDIX D

BASIC Keywords Summary

Keyword (page)	Action	Example
AND (174)	Used to test the truth of more than one boolean test	X > 3 AND X < 6
BYE (34)	Logs off	BYE
CHAIN (368)	Instructs to execute another program	CHAIN "Progname"
CLOSE (463)	Closes a file	CLOSE 1
CONT (105)	Resumes the execution of a program halted with a STOP command.	CONT
DATA (57)	Provides data to be read in by READ statements	DATA 45, "JONES"
DEF (373)	Defines a function	DEFY(X)= X + 3
DIM (291)	Defines arrays and number of elements	DIM X(12)
END (14)	Ends execution of the program	END
FOR-TO-[STEP] (207)	Starts a loop	FOR I=1 TO 9 STEP 2
GET (489)	Reads data directly from a device	GET#1, N
GOSUB (365)	Passes control to a subroutine	GOSUB 900
GOTO (66)	Passes control to a specified line	GOTO 320
IF-THEN (147)	Tests a specified condition	IF X = 2 THEN Z = X
INPUT (56)	Prompts and accepts values from a terminal	INPUT X$
INPUT# (464)	Reads data from a file	INPUT#2, X$

(continued)

Keyword (page)	Action	Example
LET (30)	Assigns values to variables	LET X = 5
LIST (34)	When used in direct mode, prints the listing of the program	LIST
LOAD (34)	Loads in a program from an auxilliary storage device	LOAD "B:PROGRAM"
MAT (346)	Causes reading, writing, and manipulation of arrays (matrices)	MAT B = A + B
NEW (33)	Creates a new file	NEW ABC
NEXT (209)	Marks the end of a FOR-NEXT loop	NEXT I
OLD (34)	Recalls a saved program	OLD, file-name
ON-GOTO (176)	Passes control to the Nth line	ON X GOTO 10,90
OPEN (463)	Opens a file	OPEN "O",1,"FILE"
OPTION BASE (242)	Defines the lower boundary of an array	OPTION BASE 1
OR (174)	Tests for the truth of more than one condition	IF X>G OR X<10 THEN Z=X
PRINT (47)	Displays the values	PRINT "BASIC"
PRINT# (464)	Writes the values to a file	PRINT#1, "BASIC"
PRINT USING (246)	Prints formatted data	PRINT USING C$, X, Y
READ (56)	Reads values from DATA statement	READ X,Y
REM (31)	Sets up a line for comments	REM THIS IS ..
RESTORE (63)	Sets the pointer to the beginning of the data pool	RESTORE
RETURN (366)	Returns control from a subroutine	RETURN
RUN (34)	Begins execution of a program	RUN
SAVE (34)	Saves the current program	SAVE "B:FILE"
STOP (105)	Halts the execution of a program	STOP
TAB (83)	Used with PRINT, tabs the printed values	PRINT TAB(24); A
USING (246)	Used in conjunction with PRINT, formats the output	PRINT USING A$; 25
WHILE (231)	Starts a while loop	WHILE X < 12
WEND (231)	Marks the end of a while loop	WEND

Index

ABS(x) 371
Accessing, see File
Addition symbol 16
Algebra, matrix 346
Algorithm 107, 108, 399
    efficiency of 511–514
    speed of 513
Alphanumeric data, (see also String data) 69–71
American Standard Code for Information Interchange, see ASCII codes
Ampersand (&) 84, 164–165
AND operator 174
APPEND statement 474
Apple II, AppleSoft 530
Application programs 11
Arguments of functions
    actual 375
    dummy 375–376, 492
Arithmetic-logic unit (ALU) 9
Arithmetic operators 16
    priorities of 20
Arrays 287–311, 366
    arithmetic expression 296, 330
    elements of 290
    input/output 299, 322, 346
    merging 407
    one-dimensional 290
    searching 306, 404–406, 513
    subscript 290, 327–328, 512
    two-dimensional 290, 327–346, 348, 415
ASCII codes 264–266
Assignment statement 24, 263
Asterisks, use of 368
ATN(x) 370
Auxiliary storage devices 9

Bad data 129
Bar chart, see Histogram
BASIC 12–13
Beep 267
Bell character 265
Blank spaces 126, 152, 263
Blocks, program 163–167, 179
Branching 151, 153, 163
    conditional 176
Break key 530
Bubble sort, see Sort
Buffer 483, 489
Bugs in programs, see Debugging
Built-in functions, see Library functions
BYE 34
Bytes 489, 490

Card reader 6–7
Carriage return 33
Cathode Ray Tube (CRT) 7, 459
Central processing unit (CPU) 5, 8
Chain statement 368–370
Character codes 264
Character data, see Strings
CHR$ 264, 266
CLOSE statement 462, 463, 484, 488–489
Coding 107, 118
Comma as a separator 49
Comma in edited fields 252
Comment lines 31, 127–128
Common core area 369
Comparing values 147, 153, 176
    computational 152
Compilation 98
Compiler 98
Compiler-defined function, see Library functions

537

Computer 5, 39
CON 348
Concatenation operator, *see* Operators
Conditional statements 147
CONT 105
Continuation of line 84, 164–165
Control break program 469, 472
Control characters 266–267
Control design 274
Control program 11
Control Program Monitor 11
Control, system 9
Control variable, (*see also* Looping) 214, 226, 232
Constants 24, 46, 91, 151
    character 71
    numeric 46, 91
    string 46, 91, 247, 263
COS(x) 370
Counter block 74
CPM 11

DATA 57–60, 151
    double precision 261
    precision of 260
    processing of 399–432
    types 257
Debugging 101–107
Decimal point in E-notation, *see* Exponential
Decision structure 167, 176
Decision Support Systems (DSS) 432
DEC Rainbow 530
DEF statement 373
Detecting errors, (*see also* Debugging) 104
Descriptive names 26, 126
Descriptor, field 251, 253, 255
DIMension statement 289, 291, 329
Direct access, to tables, (*see also* Random access) 307
Direct access method, *see* Random access
Disks 9, 459–460
Disk drive 6–9
Diskettes (floppy disks) 9, 459–460
Division symbol 16
Documentation 120–121, 129–130, 137, 524
Dollar sign editing 252, 255
Double precision 261
DO-WHILE 123, 232
Dynamic allocation of an array 291

Echo-printing, *see* Mirror printing
Editing 245–256
    character data 247, 263
    format line 255
    numeric data 251–257
    symbols 251–256

Efficiency factors 511
Elements, *see* Arrays
ELSE 164–167
END 14, 20, 40
End of File (EOF) 465–466
E-notation, *see* Exponential
Enter, (*see also* Carriage return) 33
Equal sign 24
ERL variable 465
ERR variable 465
ERROR statement, for end of file 466
Error trapping 465
Exclamation mark for REM 31, 531
Executable statements 101
Execution errors 103
EXP(x) 370
Exponential
    form 259–260
    input/output 261–262
    notation 259
Exponentiation symbols 16
Expression
    logical 173, 231
    character 268

Factorial 161, 223–225
FEED key 167
Field 109, 251, 457
Field descriptor 251, 253, 255
FIELD statement 486, 489
File
    accessing 461, 467, 493
    closing 462
    creation 462
    maintenance 461, 476
    merging 474
    opening 462–464
    processing 457–483
    types 459–460
File organization
    indexed-sequential 461, 494
    random 461, 483
    sequential 461
FIX(x) 370
Floating point values, *see* Real numbers
Floppy disks 9
Flowcharts 111–113
    structured 114
    symbols 112
FN 375
FOR-NEXT, *see* Looping
Fraud, prevention of 274
Functions 370–376
    plotting 414–415
    user-defined 373–376

Game program 80, 180, 428–431
GET statement 486, 489
GO SUB 364–368
    REM for 368

GOTO 66, 92, 151, 157, 162–165, 169, 176–179, 180, 207, 220, 369, 465, 520
GOTO style 162
GOTO-less style 163
Graphing techniques 412

Hard copy terminal 7–8
Hardware 5, 39
Hashing 493–494
Header value, record 158–159, 300
Hierarchy charts 118, 119, 125
Histogram 415
HOME key 267
Horner's Method 512
Human resources, cost of 517

IBM-PC 530
Identity matrix 348
IF 68, 147–176
    block 161, 165, 167, 176
    compound 173
    ELSE 164–167
    GOTO 180, 232, 512
    logical 147, 153, 162, 176, 231
    nested 167
    syntax for a specific machine 530–531
    THEN 68, 151, 153, 263, 512
Immediate mode 35
Indentation, (see also Readability) 67, 127, 163, 232, 512
Indentity function 348
Indentity matrix 348
Index-sequential, see File organization
Infinite loop 157, 219, 231
Initializing 76
INKEY$ 270
I/O (Input/Output) 11
INPUT 56, 92, 464
    LINE 273, 466
Input devices 5, 7
Input/output design 119
INT(x) 370
Integer, see Numeric data
Interactive programming 63, 78, 156, 181, 225, 226, 294, 338, 406, 428
Interpreters 12, 100
Invalid numeric constants 46
Inverse function 348
Iteration (loop) 121
    structure 123, 232

Joining, see Strings

Key fields 461, 483, 493

Language, computer 12
Large scale computer systems 11
LEFT$ 269

LEN(A$) 270
LET statement 30
Library functions 370–373, 513
Limit check, see Testing
LINE input statement 273, 466, 475
Line number 14, 40
Linear array, see Array, one-dimensional
LIST 34
LLIST 35
LOAD 34
LOG in 32
LOG(x) 370
Logical errors 103
Logical expression, see Expression
Logical operators, see Operators
Logical record, see Record
Logic charts 117
Looping 65, 92, 207–240, 287
    FOR NEXT 123, 207–224, 232, 299, 330, 411
    GOTO 66
    infinite 157, 219, 231
    nested 225–230, 330, 332
    STEP 210
    terminating 159–160, 218–219
    transferring, within and from 219
    WHILE 231–232
LPRINT 35
LSET 486, 489

Machine independent 98
Machine language 98
Main frame 6
Main memory 9
Magnetic character readers 8
Management Information System (MIS) 432
Management the 11
MAT statement 346
Matrix, (see also Array, two-dimensional)
    input/output 346
    functions 348
    manipulation 344, 347
    statement 346
MBASIC, see MicroSoft BASIC
Median 409
Memory cell 23, 260, 261, 290, 291, 329
Memory space 40, 369
Memory word, see Memory cell
Menu in programs 178, 181
Merge-sort, see SORT
Merging, (see also File) 407
Microcomputer system 11
Micro processor 9
MicroSoft BASIC 254, 530
MID$ 269
Minicomputers 11
Mirror printing 302
Mixed mode of operation 258, 512

Modularity 123–126, 380, 518
Modules, (see also Programming) 116, 118, 125–126, 182
Monte Carlo, see Simulation
Multiplication symbol 16
Multirecords 490
Multistatements per line 85

Nassi-Schneiderman chart 117–118
NEW 33
Nonexecutable 101
NOT operator 174
Null string 265, 270
Numeric code 152
Numeric data
    integers 257–258, 292, 512
    real numbers 257–258

Object program 98
OLD command 34
ON ERROR 465
ON GOTO 176–180, 369
On line 32
OPEN statement, form of 462, 463, 484, 488–489
Operating systems 11
Operations 40
Operations research 445
Operators
    concatenation 268
    logical 173–174
    relational 150–151, 173
Optical Character Readers (OCR) 7
OPTION BASE statement 292
OR operator 174
Out of data 67
Output 45
Output design 132
Output devices 5, 8
Overflow 251
    in buffer 489

Parentheses, the use of 40, 175
Physical record, (see also Record) 490
Plotting, see Graphing techniques
Point of sale (POS) terminals 8
Programs 5, 11, 12, 14, 30
Prime number 516
PRINT 14, 40, 47–55
PRINT# 464
Print charts 109
Print position 53
PRINT USING 246–248
Process design 120
Programming
    definition 12
    cycle 118
    modular 380

    structured 121, 123, 167–172, 232, 380, 518
    style 161–165
Pseudocode 30, 115
PUT statement 486, 489

Quotation marks 263

Radio Shack 529
Random access, see File organization
Random numbers 418–421
    generating 419, 530–531
    seed of 421
RANDOMIZE statement 421
Range check, see Testing
READ 56–61, 159, 464
Readability 126–129, 232, 519–520
Real numbers, see Numeric data
Reasonableness check, see Testing
Record 458
    logical 490–492
    relative 493
    separation of 273
Regression analysis 411–412
    least squares 412
Relational operators, see Operators
Relative keys, (see also Direct access) 461
Reliability in programs 129, 424
REM 31, 40
REPLACE 34
RESAVE 34
Reserved words 27, 525
RESTORE 63
RETURN statement, 364–368
RIGHT$ 269
RND(A) 370, 419
Rounding 251, 261, 262, 372
RSET 489
RUN 34, 134
Run-time error 103

SAVE 34
Scalar multiplication 348
Screen design 110
Screen width 110, 529
Searching 306, 404–406, 513
Sector, see Disks
Selection structure 122
Semicolon 52
Sentinel value 68, 159–160, 218, 228, 232, 300
Separator 47
    comma 49
    semicolon 52
Sequence structure 121
Sequential, see File organization
SGN(x) 370

Index

Sign check 274
Significant digits 260–262
Simulation 418–426
    Monte Carlo 421–426
SIN(x) 370
Size, *see* Testing
Software 5, 11, 39
Solution plan, example 13–14
SORT
    bubble 400
    merge 403
    methods 400–404, 472–475
    pointer 403
Source program 98
Spacing 16, 82–84
SQR(x) 370
Standard deviation 372, 437
Statistics 409
STEP, *see* Looping
STOP 105
Storage media 459–460
Strings
    assignment 71, 263
    comparison 152, 263
    constant 46, 91, 247, 263
    descriptors 253, 255
    functions 269–271
    input/output 70, 263
    printing 70, 247
    size check 274
    variables 69, 254, 263, 273
Structure chart, *see* Hierarchy charts
Structured design 123–124, 518–522
Structured flowcharts 114–115
Structured programming 161, 121–130, 167, 232, 380, 518–523
STR$(x) 270
Substring reference 269
Subscripted variables 290
Subscripts, *see* Arrays
Subprograms 363–370
Subroutine
    external 368–370
    internal 364–368

Subrecord, *see* Record, logical
Syntax errors 101, 104
System commands 33

TAB function 82–83, 92
Table look up 306, 338, 461
Table manipulation 339
TAN(x) 370
Tape drive 6–9
Terminating, (*see also* Looping) 153, 157, 159
Testing, editing 274–275
    data type check 274
    limit check 274
    presence check 274
    range test 274
TIME$ 421
Top-down design 124, 518
Trailing blank 52–53
Trailing values 105
    facilities 106–107
Trailer record, *see* Sentinel value
Transferring, *see* IF, Looping, *and* GOTO
Transpose, an array 343
    function 348
TRUE BASIC 533
Truncation 255, 261, 297

Unconditional jump, *see* GOTO

Variables 23, 39, 46, 151
Variance 198, 409, 437
Video terminal 6–8
VAL(a$) 270

WHILE, *see* Looping
WRITE statement 464
Writing better programs 30, 121–130, 167, 232, 380, 518

ZERO function 348
Zone 49–50, 464

A few minutes of your time, please . . .

Your comments and suggestions play a vital role in our textbook revision process.

1. What do you like about this book?

2. What suggestions do you have for improvement?

Optional:

Name _____

School _____

Department _____

Address _____

City _____ State _____ Zip _____

_____ I am a student.

_____ I am an instructor.

Please return this form to: Marketing Manager, Computer Science
Mayfield Publishing Co.
285 Hamilton Avenue
Palo Alto, CA 94301